FR. STEFANO M. MANELLI, F.I.

ALL GENERATIONS SHALL CALL ME BLESSED

Biblical Mariology

Revised and Enlarged Second Edition

Translated by

FR. PETER DAMIAN FEHLNER, F.I.

ACADEMY OF THE IMMACULATE
NEW BEDFORD, MA
2005

Title of Italian original:
Mariologia Biblica
1989 Casa Mariana – Frigento

1st English edition – New Bedford 1994
2nd revised and enlarged Italian edition – Frigento 2004
2nd revised and enlarged English edition – 2005
- - - - - - - - - - - - - - - - - - -
Reprint of 2nd revised and enlarged English edition – 2012

Imprimatur: ✠ Most Rev. Salvatore Nunnari
Archbishop of Sant'Angelo dei Lombardi
September 15, 2004

The *Imprimatur* is the Church's declaration that a work is free from error in matters of faith and morals, but does not imply that the Church endorses the contents of the work.

About the Cover

The cover is an inspiring reproduction of the famous icon *Salus Populi Romani* which is enshrined at the Basilica of Saint Mary Major in Rome. Placed in the backdrop of grafitti from the walls of the ancient Catacombs of Rome, the artwork expresses the apostolic and scriptural origin of Marian doctrines expounded in this book.

ISBN: 978-1-60114-000-5

PRINTED IN THE UNITED STATES OF AMERICA

Table of Contents

Translator's Note

Since the publication of the original Italian edition in 1989, the Congregation for the Doctrine of the Faith has issued a directive entitled *Interpretation of the Bible in the Church.*[1] On the presentation of this document to the Holy Father, Pope John Paul II, on April 23, he remarked that a balanced, adequate exposition of the sacred text must always avoid two extremes.[2]

The first extreme would expound the meaning of the Bible solely in view of its natural aspect as human literature, without consideration of that divine inspiration which makes it unique or of that Faith guided by a divinely instituted Magisterium indeed often enough on premises quite contrary to that Faith.

This is the error of rationalism, consisting not in having employed philology or history or semiotics to study the word of God, but in having used such tools as though they supplied the primary criterion for determining the literal and spiritual sense intended by the Holy Spirit.

The second extreme would interpret the Sacred Page quite apart from any relation to its form as a human word. This is the error of pietism and fideism in an overreaction to the excesses of rationalism, to see in even the use of a dictionary the source of error. Evidently, one cannot read Chaucer or Shakespeare without the aid of a dictionary and without knowledge of the times and the linguistic usage characteristic of particular ages and the writers under study.

1 Eng. ed. in *Origins*, Jan. 6, 1994.

2 Text in *L'Osservatore Romano*, April 25, 1993, pp. 8–9.

But neither does mere ability to use a dictionary give one access to the mind of Chaucer.

Biblical-theological exegesis, keeping before it the guidance of the Magisterium and the spiritual purpose of scriptural inspiration, and at the same time utilizing the best fruits of philological, historical, and structural analysis, may be considered as a contemporary form of that traditional method of reading the Scriptures as the Church reads them.

The Holy Father, in the course of his remarks on April 23, 1993, underscored the mystery of the Incarnation as the central truth of the Bible, the mystery providing the objective point of reference for differentiating a theological from a merely "philological" exposition of the sacred text. And since there is no access to this mystery apart from the great sign of the virginal maternity of Mary, we can expect that a sound and balanced exegesis will be profoundly Marian.

This is exactly what is so evident in the study of Fr. Stefano Manelli, precisely because his use of the biblical-theological method is organized around the prophetic-historical character of divine revelation, viz., first the prophetic announcement of the divine counsels of salvation in the Old Testament and then their historic fulfillment in the New. In such a context, the way in which the figure of Mary Immaculate pervades every great biblical theme can easily be discerned. Today, it is the prophetic character of the Old Testament Marian texts and their historical fulfillment in the New that are most violently attacked. Hence, Fr. Stefano has taken great pains to defend both in the course of expounding the theological sense of the inspired text.

While his exposition does not pretend to be exhaustive, it is sufficiently detailed, with multiple references to the best Catholic expositors, of the past and of the present, to enable the student to appreciate just how central a role the Virgin Mary occupies in the Bible (and so in the divine counsels of salvation) and how her singular person figures in all its major themes. Her role is that of maternal Mediatrix in Christ and in the Church, and her person is that of the Immaculate, for the sake of Christ and of the Church, preserved free of all taint of original sin by the foreseen merits of her Son: the perfect fruit of a perfect Redemption by a perfect Redeemer (Bl. John Duns Scotus).

Rightly all generations call her blessed, for He who is mighty has done great things in her; and with her and through her, we rejoice in God our Savior, Jesus, blessed fruit of her womb.

Note: *to the revised and enlarged second edition, 2005*

This second edition contains considerable new materials and updated bibliography in relation to the first English edition published just 10 years ago. Teachers and students will find the new materials, especially those in the Old Testament section, most helpful in understanding the presence of Our Lady in the inspired Word of God from its beginning.

FOREWORD

It gives me great pleasure to introduce Fr. Stefano Manelli's *All Generations Shall Call Me Blessed: Biblical Mariology* with its extensive treatment of the entire Old and New Testaments. This author's wide ranging coverage of so many Marian themes is well-balanced, tactful, and devout. His is a sober analysis, unaffected by bias or the desire to promote novelty or unproven hypotheses.

This is because Fr. Manelli is faithful to ecclesiastical tradition. He does not permit himself to disagree with the Magisterium of the Church, and he is unaffected by the "itch for novelty." He does not ignore the value of historical and literary criticism, nor does he fail to ponder the fruits of scholarly research. But neither does he base his conclusions solely or primarily on such approaches. Instead, he examines the Bible in the light of the whole of revelation, because he is eager to find that true wisdom which enables one to ponder God's word without adulterating or diluting it.

He is not concerned with being original. He does not try to pander to the curiosity of those who favor the latest fashionable theory, whatever the cost. For he is bent on seeking the truth, the sense intended by God and by the sacred writers, as he expounds these themes in complete fidelity to the Church and to her Magisterium, the only voice authorized to give authentic interpretations of Sacred Writ.

Fr. Manelli does not develop the Marian texts of the Old Testament—Genesis 3:15, Isaiah 7:10–14, Micah 5:1–2—as fully as he does those of the New Testament, even though these and many other Old Testament texts are considered by the holy Fathers as exceptionally meaningful for our understanding of the mystery of Mary. In part, this is because his is an introductory presentation and so must per-force deal with the question of Mary in the Bible as formulated by many contemporary exegetes, who—sad to say—assign little or no Marian significance to these texts, focusing, instead, all their attention on the New Testament. Unlike the holy Fathers, these exegetes, instead of finding in the infancy narratives of Matthew and Luke the fulfillment of so many Marian prophecies and types of the Old Testament, ascribe to those chapters legendary or mythical sources, both written and oral.

The result of such speculation, at odds with tradition, is of course a plethora of mutually contradictory hypotheses. No wonder, for their premise is false. Fr. Manelli rightly observes that the source of these inspired narratives, at the center of biblical Mariology today, must have been the Blessed Virgin—either her direct or indirect testimony. Not without reason does St. Luke, with his customary care, alert us to the truth of the matter, when in the prologue of his Gospel he indicates his sources: witnesses who had seen and heard the facts. Fr. Manelli, then, very correctly warns us about reducing the gospel to a species of midrash. Whatever positive values can be ascribed to this literary form by the sympathetic scholar via distinctions and plausible euphemisms, it retains the questionable, ambivalent savor of a romanticized, historically untrustworthy record.

It is possible in this introduction to indicate briefly only a few highlights in the author's careful and detailed New Testament exegesis. Clearly, the most important episode from the infancy narrative is the account of the Annunciation, wherein is recorded the most perfect response ever given by a creature to the Creator, one motivated by a total faith and humility. The commentary on the Annunciation is sober and balanced, rich in its scriptural references and thoroughly updated bibliography. Fr. Manelli puts the maternity of Mary in its correct perspective—portraying her as willingly and knowingly accepting Jesus as the Messiah and Son of God and as willingly and knowingly accepting the divine invitation to become His Mother in pure and simple faith.

The Magnificat is the hymn of Yahweh's poor and comes straight from our Lady's heart. She is the composer of this hymn, even if, as Fr. Manelli notes, the Evangelist when translating it into Greek may have colored it with his own style.

In explaining the worry of St. Joseph, Fr. Manelli adheres to the traditional interpretation in which St. Joseph finds the maternity of his bride beyond his understanding, yet does not lose confidence in her proven virtue. He planned to send her away secretly, but God intervened to clarify the problem.

The miracle worked by Jesus at the wedding feast of Cana in response to the maternal solicitude of Mary is taken in the literal sense. But the spiritual sense is not overlooked. The author indicates that the wedding symbolizes the marriage between the Word and mankind: within Mary and through Mary. The symbolism is suggested particularly by the changing of water into wine through the intercession of Mary, who thus offers Christ a motive for the miracle.

Fr. Manelli is at pains throughout his study to accent Mary's intercessory role, her maternal qualities, and her concern for men. In this, he is simply underscoring what Pope John Paul II affirms so strongly in *Redemptoris Mater*, number 21.

The figure of the Blessed Virgin and her place in the gospel are stressed not only during Jesus' public ministry, but also at Pentecost and in Revelation, particularly in regard to the "woman clothed with the sun," the conqueror of the infernal dragon.

These few references are enough to show how thorough a biblical–theological synthesis of Mariology is presented by Fr. Stefano. His approach has recently been reaffirmed by no less an authority than the well-known exegete Lucien Cerfaux. He writes: "After two centuries of scientific exegesis, demythologization and the historical-critical method, we are on the verge of returning to our point of departure, discovering unexpectedly that the simplest and most spontaneous reading of the Gospels, that of tradition, that of all Christians for so many centuries, was perhaps in reality also the most scientific."

— Fr. Paolo Pietrafesa
Biblicist 1989

Preface

Our Lady figures in all the great events comprising the history of salvation. Her presence in each has been as constant as her appearance and activity have been discrete, but regular. Across the span of divine revelation, the person of Mary stands at the crucial points, fulfilling the role assigned her by God at the side of her Son, from the first pages of Genesis to the last in the Book of Revelation, from Isaiah to St. Luke, at the Incarnation and during the Redemption, at Pentecost and at the end of time.

In these pages we seek to define Mary's active presence in God's saving plan as it is disclosed in His written word. It is the person, the mission, and the mystery of Mary that interests us as we "search the Scriptures" (Jn 5:39) in accord with our Lord's command.

But to discern the ineffable reality of Mary all holy in the Sacred Page, working within the parameters of personal research and a merely literal evaluation of the inspired Word is quite insufficient. Rather, one must seek to portray her in accord with the mind and thought of God as expressed in the written Word and authenticated by the Church. In short, such a portrait must be drawn in terms of the full view afforded by a biblical-theological exegesis, and not merely of that attainable from the analytic canons of a purely biblical philological exegesis.

In fact, the methodology of those engaged in the work of semantic research and textual criticism, both diachronic and synchronic, cannot go beyond the letter, and so stops, as it were, at the grammar of the revealed message, employing a variety of methods such as the "historical-critical," "narrative analysis," "redaction history," "structuralism," "rhetorical criticism," "narrative analysis," "stories of findings," "sociological analysis," and "critique of the canon."[1] By contrast, biblical-theological exegesis, guided by theology including its multiple aspects, such as patrology and tradition, the Magisterium and the Liturgy, the analogy of faith and *sensus fidelium*, is directed to the study of God's mind as discovered in His words so as to grasp the full sense of revelation. One might call it, then, an exegesis dealing not with the grammar, but with the structure and syntax of God's plan of salvation.

In this study, therefore, we limit considerations drawn from biblical-philological exegesis to the minimum, and concentrate instead primarily on the cultivation of biblical-theological exegesis. For it is in this way, and only in this way, that we come to understand the truth contained in holy Scripture, authenticated and infallibly guaranteed by the Church. This, precisely, is the approach recommended by Vatican II, which teaches that biblical texts are to be read "as they are read by the Church."[2]

Hence, as Fr. Roschini rightly observes:

> A scriptural text cannot be interpreted independently of other texts, of the interpretation given it by Tradition, and of the meaning it has assumed in the life and in the thought of the Church. Since it is to the Magisterium of the Church that Holy Scripture has been entrusted, it is necessary that

1 Cf. H.G. REVENTLOW, *Storia dell'interpretazione biblica*, Casale Montferrato 1999, 3 vols. For a rapid overview and synthesis, cf. G. ODASSO, *Percorsi dell'esegesi e della teologia biblica*, in *Prospettive attuali di Mariologia* (supplement to *Theotokos* 1/2001), pp. 18–22.

2 *Lumen Gentium*, no. 55. Pope Pius XII in the encyclical *Humani Generis* had already taught that exegetes must not explain holy Scripture "solely on the basis of human reason," but "in accord with the mind of the Church, which has been appointed by Christ the Lord guardian and interpreter of the entire deposit of divinely revealed truth" (*Acta Apostolicae Sedis* [*AAS* hereinafter] 42 [1950]: 569).

Holy Scripture be read in the Church, with the Church. But above all, it must be read as the Church reads.[3]

Only the teaching Church can give to us and guarantee for us the genuine meaning and truth of every biblical text, for "the office of authentically interpreting the written or transmitted word of God is entrusted only to the living Magisterium of the Church whose authority is exercised in the name of Christ."[4]

In the "final report" of the extraordinary synod of bishops held in Rome from November 25 to December 8, 1985, we find this clear and precise statement, an evident reference to the dogmatic constitution *Dei Verbum*: "The exegesis of Holy Scripture's original sense, so highly recommended by the Council, cannot be separated from the living tradition of the Church, nor from the authentic interpretation of the Church's Magisterium."[5]

A letter from the Congregation for Catholic Education on the subject "the Virgin Mary's role in intellectual and spiritual formation" reaffirms that "research work on Scripture and tradition, conducted according to the most

---

3 G. Roschini, O.S.M., *Maria nella storia della salvezza*, vol. i ([sola del Liri, 1969), p. 59. Cf. also J. A. de Aldama, "De valore Magisterii Ecclesiae in interpretatione Sacrae Scripturae," in *Maria in Sacra Scriptura*, vol. 3 (Rome, 1967), pp. 199–208. See also the entire issue of *Communio* (May-June, 1986) no. 87, "Leggere la Sacra Scrittura," with contributions by Sicari, Lacoste, de La Potterie, Jean Nesmy, Alves, Bertoldi, von Balthasar, Barbolin, Ratzinger. [Some of the studies published in the Italian edition of *Communio* appeared as well in the English edition of the same periodical, 13 (1986): 280ff.] The editorial (Ital. ed.) states that holy Scripture is "a word and letter addressed to the Church, to the Spouse, to the Mother. And it is She who imparts it to her children" (ibid., p. 7); and M. I. Alves writes that "the interpretation of the word of God is entrusted only to the living Magisterium of the Church" (ibid., p. 56).

4 Dogmatic constitution *Dei Verbum*, no. 10.

5 The final report of the synod, in *Presenza Pastorale* 55 (1985): 45. The same criteria also apply to the more recent type of interpretation conducted according to the canons of the so-called "structuralist biblical analysis" or "semiotics." See the essay of G. Savoca, "L'analisi biblica strutturalista," in *Ecclesiae Sacramentum*, ed. G. Lorizio and V. Scippa (Naples, 1986), pp. 227–243.

productive methodologies and with the best critical tools, must be guided by the Magisterium, because the deposit of the word of God has been entrusted to that Magisterium for its safekeeping and authentic interpretation."[6]

It is enlightening, in this regard, to ponder the position taken by the scholars who recently edited *The Navarre Bible.*

> Only the Church, speaking through her Magisterium, is the authentic interpreter of Sacred Scripture. This is to be understood both in the positive and in the negative sense. Positively, we are obliged to accept as the biblical sense the one which has been proposed by the Church (directly or indirectly). Negatively, we must reject as false any interpretation at odds with the meaning proposed by the Magisterium.[7]

To these documents and authoritative reminders are to be added two no less important and more recent documents of the Pontifical Biblical Commission: *Interpretation of the Bible in the Church* (1993) and *The Hebrew People and its Scared Scriptures in the Christian Bible* (2001).

In the document, *Interpretation of the Bible in the Church*,[8] we read that according to *Dei Verbum* exegesis must always be conscious of "the content and unity of Scripture," seeking not only a philological reading, but one in accord with "the living Tradition of the entire Church" and "the analogy of faith" (DV 12).

There is in fact a point of departure to consider: "Exegetes necessarily bring to their study of the biblical

---

6 Letter of the Congregation for Catholic Education, *The Virgin Mary in Intellectual and Spiritual Formation*, no. 26, printed in *Marian Studies* 39 (1988): 203–221.

7 The Navarre Bible. *St. Mark's Gospel* (Dublin, 1985), p. 22.

8 See the organic synthesis of M. Tabet, *Introduzione generale alla Bibbia*, Cinisello Balsamo 1998, pp. 256–296.

text certain presuppositions concerning their meaning. In the case of Catholic exegetes those presuppositions are based on certainties of faith. The bible is a text inspired by God and entrusted to the Church to arouse faith and guide Christian life. These certainties of faith do not reach the exegete immediately, but only on elaboration by the ecclesial community upon theological reflection. Hence, the research of exegetes is guided by dogmatic theology on the inspiration of Sacred Scripture and its scope in the life of the Church."[9]

Among many other affirmations in the second document, *The Hebrew People and Its Sacred Scripture in the Christian Bible*, we also read that "Christian faith is grounded not only on events, but on the conformity of these events with the Revelation contained in the Jewish Scriptures" (n. 7). This means that in the texts of the Old Testament one can find the root of all genuine content of each revealed fact found clearly and expressly in the New Testament. The genuine content of each point of Revelation in fact "finds its realization in Jesus" (n. 21, 6). Consequently, "only the Christian, in the light of Christ and of the Church finds in the texts that surplus of meaning hidden in them" (ibid.). Without this *surplus of meaning* given only to him who reads the Scriptures "in the light of Christ and the Church," every other interpretation cannot help but be reductive, and indeed deviate from the genuine and real content of revealed truth.

In view of this, in relation to Jewish hermeneutics, more precisely rabbinic hermeneutics of the Old Testament, this document indicates the criteria for discovering the profound bond between Old and New Testaments, in order to set in relief how the Christian interpretation of

9 *Enchiridion Biblicum* (Bologna 1993) no. 1489, p. 1323.

the Old Testament, "much different certainly than that of Judaism, nonetheless corresponds to a potential meaning really present in the Old Testament texts" (n. 64). *Potential meaning really present in the texts*: therefore, this is a meaning *truly* there and not merely an *accommodation* of the text or something read into it by the exegete, much less legendary or fictional embellishments of the pious. But this *hidden* meaning can only be discerned by one reading the Scriptures "in the light of Christ and of the Church." Only such a reader can grasp that *surplus of meaning* enabling the reader to pass from *potential* to *active* or effective understanding in harmony and in line with that *surplus meaning* without recourse to reinterpretations so often torturous and downright contradictory.

Christians alone, then, can read and understand these Scriptures of the Old Testament in the sole correct manner. That manner, surely, is not the reductive method of the Jews who do not believe in Christ and by that fact of disbelief are incapable of "reading in the light of Christ" (n. 19: viz., so long as they continue not to believe in Christ), and of grasping that *surplus of meaning* fully expressive of and in harmony with the real and historical sense of every revealed truth. Only Christians (i.e., Jewish and Gentile believers alike), reading the Old Testament texts "in the light of Christ and of the Church," can discover the "*potential* meaning really present in them," and so come to understand their hidden *surplus of meaning*. In such wise one discovers the harmonious "realization in Jesus" of that Old Testament *potential* ordered precisely to such "realization in Jesus." St. Matthew, for instance, does just this when he unveils and displays the only real meaning of the prophecy of Is. 7:14 (not understood, indeed incomprehensible to the non-believing Jew) as realized harmoniously and concretely in

Jesus' virginal conception and from Mary of Nazareth. So, too, do the Holy Fathers of the Church proceed in their biblical-sapiential interpretation of the Sacred Scripture.

In conclusion "to understand the Scriptures fully, not only the necessarily *reductive* interpretation of the non believing Hebrews: reductive because excluding the *potential* meaning objectively present in them, but also their integral historical-theological content, Christians must read these texts not as those blind to the New Covenant do (2 Cor 3:14), but as those 'enlightened by Christ.' In a word, Christians must read them 'in the light of Christ and of the Church' in order to grasp their full and true content, *hidden*, but for all that no less *real and historical.* That content is naught else than the divine Revelation contained in them and made plain to us. This is exactly what is meant by biblical-theological exegesis, which this document also calls 'theological interpretation, but at the same time fully historical' (n. 21).[10]"

10 S.M. Manelli, *La Mariologia nella storia della salvezza. Sintesi storico-teologica*, in *Immaculata Mediatrix* 2 (2002) 51–52.

Part One

The Old Testament

- *The Woman of the Protoevangelium*
- *The Virgin Mother*
- *The Woman in Travail*
- *Marian Figures and Symbols*
- *Marian Passages in the Liturgy*
- *Mary in the Old Testament: A Portrait Sketched*

1
The Woman of the Protoevangelium

Genesis 3:15

I will put enmity between you and the woman, between your seed and her seed: he shall crush your head.[1]

The historical datum of this fundamental text of Genesis opens our eyes to that stupendous drama whose conclusion is the promised salvation. At the dawn of human history, our first parents, Adam and Eve, were living happily in the earthly paradise. The woman, Eve, unfortunately was seduced by the cunning of the serpent. She fell into sin and induced the man, Adam, to fall with her.

It was a tragic moment in that history. Its entire future had been compromised. In its first ancestors, the human race was forever lost, unless a Redeemer capable of restoring man to friendship with God was found. But precisely then, at the onset of the gloomy darkness of sin, there shone a ray of future hope. God intervened to tell how a "woman," with her "seed," would do battle against the serpent and crush its head. This text of Genesis has rightly been called the "Protoevangelium," i.e., the first and most important

1 Translation of this text for the new Italian edition is from the Latin Vulgate by St. Jerome. In this translation the feminine pronoun (*ipsa*) refers directly to the *mulier* (woman), recalling the declaration of the Council of Trent that on questions of faith the text of the Vulgate enjoys infallibility (Trent, Sess. IV, DH1506).

prophetic announcement heralding the good news of salvation for mankind.

> Philologically, the 'woman' of this text poses a critical problem for exegesis. Fr. Testa writes in this regard: 'Is it the woman (= *hi'–she*), or her offspring (= *hû'–he*) who treads upon the serpent?...' The feminine reading of some manuscripts of the old Latin (*ipsa*) later passed into the Vulgate, as attested by the better manuscripts of the Vulgate: G (Turonensis), A (Amiatinus).
>
> ... Nonetheless, so ancient and respectable a tradition must give way to the masculine reading found in the Masoretic text, in the Samaritan, and also in the Syriac version. In fact, even if the present consonant reading *hw'* can be pointed either as *hû'* (he) or as *hi'* (she), whose archaic written form was *hûw',* it now appears that the masculine form must prevail either because of the verbal form of 'will crush' (*yesafeka*; the feminine would have required *tesûfeka*) or because of the masculine pronominal suffix (*–ennû,* and not *–ennâh*) added to the verb 'you shall try to wound' (*him, not her*; *or you shall try to wound his–not her–heel*).[2]
>
> This notwithstanding, according to more recent philological studies, it is now admitted to be certain that the translation of the pronoun *ipsa*, chosen by St. Jerome, must be regarded as quite legitimate because as Donatella Scaiola affirms 'from the philological standpoint the reading in the feminine is possible in so far as in the Pentateuch we find many masculine pronouns (*q're*) to be understood in the feminine sense.'[3] In respect to the three versions of the pronoun of Gen 3:15: in Hebrew (neuter), in Greek (masculine: the *Septuagint*) and in Latin (feminine: the *Vulgate*), the masculine reading (*ipse*) entails 'a violent grammatical passage from the neuter to the masculine' as Vanni writes, noting that 'the variant *ipse,* witnessed by codices O, S, T is obviously an addition

2 E. Testa, OFM, *La Sacra Bibbia. Genesi*, Roma–Torino 1977, 1, p. 310

3 D. Scaiola, *Testi tradizionale rivisitati (Gn 3,15; Is. 7,14)*, in *Theotokos* 8 (2002) 563; in a note Scaiola cites in fact P. Jouon, *Grammaire de l'hébreu biblique*, Roma 1947, § 16f. 39c.

> to the LXX and therefore is rather a confirmation of the authenticity of *ipsa*.'
>
> For this reason one cannot 'qualify as arbitrary a directly Mariological interpretation of Gen 3:15.'[4]
>
> On the other hand the competence and carefulness of St. Jerome cannot but guarantee the value of his translation in the feminine (*ipsa*). It acknowledged on all sides that in order to achieve as exact a translation as possible, as P.L. Ferrari writes, 'St. Jerome underscored the importance of knowing Greek and Aramaic to understand the Scriptures and stressed the superiority of the original text over the Greek LXX translation.' In confirmation of this well-nigh scrupulous scholarship, St. Jerome himself 'purchased from the Jews the best Hebrew manuscripts, and on the basis of a comparative analysis, what is called today textual criticism, chose those readings which to him seemed closest to the original.'[5]

In the dogmatic bull *Ineffabilis Deus* on the Immaculate Conception of Mary, Pope Pius IX explained the content of the *Protoevangelium* in this way:

> The Fathers and ecclesiastical writers, enlightened by instruction from on high, taught that the divine prophecy: I will put enmity between you and the woman, between your seed and her seed, clearly and plainly foretold how there was to be a merciful Redeemer for mankind, namely, the only-begotten Son of God, Jesus Christ. They also taught how the prophecy pointed to His Blessed Mother, the Virgin Mary, and how it clearly expressed at the same time their common enmity toward the devil. Just as Christ, the Mediator between God and men, by taking our nature, cancelled the decree of condemnation against us, triumphantly nailing

---

4 U. Vanni, "La Donna della Genesi (3,15) e la Donna dell'Aposcalisse (12,1) nella 'Redemptoris Mater,'" *Marianum* 50 (1988) 428–429, note 14.

5 P. L. Ferrari, "Due millenni di lettura cristiana della Bibbia," in Aa. Vv., Guida alla lettura della Bibbia. Approccio interdisciplinare all'Antico e la Nuovo Testamento, Cinisello Balsamo 1995, p. 150. Cf. also Fr. Settimio M. Manelli, "The Immaculate Conception in Genesis 3:15," in *Mary at the Foot of the Cross V* (New Bedford, MA 2004).

> it to the Cross, so too the most holy Virgin, intimately and indissolubly united to Christ, became with Him the everlasting enemy of the venomous serpent, and thus shared with her Son His victory over the serpent, crushing as she did the serpent's head with her virginal foot.[6]

Hence, as Pope Pius IX summarizes it, both according to tradition (the Fathers and ecclesiastical writers)[7] and according to the express declarations of the papal Magisterium,[8] the *Protoevangelium* "clearly and plainly" foretold the Redeemer, indicated the Virgin Mary as the Mother of the Redeemer, and described the common enmity of Mother and Son against the devil and their

---

6 A. Tondidi, *Le encicliche mariane* (Rome, 1950), p. 43.

7 Cf. D. Unger, O.F.M.CAP., "Patristic Interpretation of the Protoevangelium," *Marian Studies* 12 (1961): III-64; T. Gallus, S.J., *Interpretatio mariologica Protoevangelio*, vol. 1, *Tempore post-patristico ad Concilium Tridentinum* (Rome, 1949); vol. 2, *A Concilio Tridentino usque ad annum 1660* (Rome, 1953); Vol. 3, *Ab anno 1661 usque ad definitionem dogmaticum Immaculatae Conceptionis (1854)* (Rome, 1954). The precision and thoroughness of Fr. Gallus' studies have strikingly confirmed the Mariological interpretation the Church has always given to Gen 3:15. It is enough to note, for example, that out of 385 authors examined by Fr. Gallus, at least 321 of these (i.e., 83%) affirm the Marian sense of Genesis, "and that many," Cardinal Bea comments, "in spite of opposition from non-Catholics, the influence of rationalism, and the ever-increasing pressure to understand the Hebrew text as contrary to the Vulgate reading *ipsa*" (A. Bea, S.J., "Il Protoevangelio [Gen. 3:15] nella tradizione esegetica," *L'Osservatore Romano* [October 30, 1954]: I). Subsequently, Fr. Gallus extended his studies to the field of Protestant exegesis and published two further volumes, the first on the leaders of the Reform (Luther, Zwingli, Calvin), the second on Protestant scholars from those contemporary with Luther to the end of the 18th century: *Der Nachkomme der Frau in der Aitlutheran ischen Schriftauslegung*, vol. 1 (Klagenfurt, 1964); *Der Nachkomme der Frau in der Alt lutheranischen Schriftauslegung. Ein Beitrag zur Geschichte der Exegese von Gen 3, 15*, vol. 2 (Kiagenfurt, 1973). In this second volume, "Fr. Gallus gives an account of the exegesis of seventy Protestant professors, showing that all of them fully accept the messianic and Mariological significance of Gen. 3:15. The followers of Luther do nothing more than deepen and clarify the exegesis of the German Reformer. The seed of the woman is Christ and only Christ. In the phrase 'the seed of the woman' is indicated the virginal birth of Christ from Mary, a promise confirmed by Isaiah 7:14" (S. Virgulin, "*Ricerche su Genesi 3,15* dal 1970 al 1977," Marianum 40 [1978]: 28–29).

8 After *Ineffabilis Deus*, cf. Leo XIII, *Augustissimae Virginis, Actae Sanctae Sedis* [*ASS* hereinafter] 30 (1897): 129; St. Pius X, *Ad diem ilium ASS* 36 (1904): 462; Pius XI, *Divini Redemptoris, AAS* 29 (1937): 96; Pius XII, *Munificentissimus Deus, AAS* 42 (1950): 768; *Fulgens Corona, AAS* 45 (1953): 579.

complete triumph over the poisonous serpent. One can, therefore, without hesitation affirm that the content of the *Protoevangelium* is "Marian" as well as messianic. Not only this, but the Mariological dimension in reference to the "woman" must be also understood literally to be exclusive to that "woman," to Mary, that is, to the Mother of the Redeemer, and not to Eve.[9]

When Pope Pius IX interrogated the commission preparing for the definition of the Immaculate Conception on the import of Genesis 3:15, the consultors unanimously replied that this text, as may be inferred from its very wording, is the basis of the doctrine of the Immaculate Conception. For "if the seed of the woman is the Redeemer who, according to Catholic doctrine, was first promised to mankind in this passage of Genesis, for this reason customarily known as the *Protoevangelium*, then the woman is His Most Holy Mother."[10]

9 For extensive and authoritative commentary in depth, although with considerably differing nuances of meaning, cf. A. Bea, S.J., "Maria SS. nel Protovangelo (Gen 3, 15)," *Marianum* 15 (1953): 1–21; M. Peinador, "El sentido mariológico del Protoevangelio y su valor doctrinal," *Estudios Marianos* 7 (1948): 15–50; *idem*, *Los temas de la mariologia bíblica...* (Madrid, 1963); *idem*, *Historia de la salvación (Ensayo de teologla bIblica sobre Gen 3,15; Apoc 12, 1–5)* (Madrid, 1966); D. Unger, O.F.M. CAP., *The First Gospel, Gen 3, 15* (New York, 1954); *idem*, "Mary Is the Woman of the First Gospel (Gen 3, 15)," *Marianum* 18 (1956): 62–79; B. Rigaux, O.F.M., "La femme et son lignage dans Genèse 3:14, 15," *Revue Biblique* 61 (1954): 321–348; C. L. Feindberg, "The Virgin Birth in the Old Testament," *Bibliotheca Sacra* 117 (1960): 313–324; V. M. Buffon, "La donna del Protovangelo," *Tabor* 40 (1966): 443–451; F. Spedalieri, S.J., *Maria nella Scrittura e nella tradizione della Chiesa primitiva* (Messina, 1961), pp. 35–59; S. Rowe, "An Exegetical Approach to Gen. 3:15," *Marian Studies* 12 (1965): 49–79; D. Squillaci, "Maria santissima nella Donna del Protovangelo," *Miles Immaculatae* 4 (1968): 412–416; G. Roschini, O.S.M., *La Madonna secondo la fede e la teologia*, vol. 2 (Rome, 1953), pp. 53–67; *idem*, *Maria Santissima neila storia della salvezza*, vol. I (Isola del Liri, 1969), pp. 66–71. In particular, see M. Varón Varón, *Maria en la Sagrada Escritura* (Monachil, 1978), pp. 7–17. T. M. Sennott, *Woman of Genesis* (Cambridge MA, 1984); M. O'Carroll, C.S.Sp., *Theotokos* (Wilmington, Del., 1984), pp. 370–373; Fr. Settimio M. Manelli, "The Immaculate Conception in Genesis 3:15," in *Mary at the Foot of the Cross V* (New Bedford, MA 2004) pp. 263–322.

10 V. Sardi, *La solenne definizione dell'Immacolato Concepimento di Maria SS., Atti e Documenti*, vol. I, p. 706.

The bull *Ineffabilis Deus* also affirms that "the most glorious Virgin... was foretold by God when He said to the serpent: 'I will put enmity between you and the woman.' Without doubt it is that same woman who crushed the poisonous head of that serpent."[11] It is perfectly evident, then, according to the exegesis of the solemn papal Magisterium, that the woman of Genesis 3:15, at enmity with the serpent and victorious over him, is Mary, not Eve.[12]

On the other hand, one may quite naturally ask why it is not possible to envision Eve as somehow included in the "woman" of Genesis. Superficially, the position of those who argue for an interpretation of Genesis 3:15 in reference to Eve alone, since at that moment she was the only existing woman, would seem plausible. How could "woman" not be taken in reference to her, or if not to her alone, at least as also connoting her? On reflection, however, this exegesis seems rather naïve, for its strength rests solely on exclusive attention to a single word, rather than on the text and context of that word. It involves a methodology that in practice may be described as arbitrary vivisection of

---

11 Tondini, *Le encicliche mariane*, p. 47. The same bull also specifies a detail of the "woman's" victory over the serpent: she will crush the serpent's head with her "immaculate foot." Obviously, the "immaculate foot" of Mary is meant, not the foot of Eve.

12 This interpretation of the passage of Genesis has been and continues to be consistently present up to our day in the ordinary papal Magisterium as well. Pope John Paul II, in fact, in a homily for the Feast of the Nativity of Mary, spoke as follows: "This very child, still so tiny and fragile, is the 'woman' referred to in the first announcement of a future redemption, and placed by God in opposition to the cunning serpent: 'I will put enmity between you and the woman!'" (the citation is taken from *Maria nel Magistero di Giovanni Paolo II*, ed. by D. Bertetto, S.D.B. [Rome, 1981], p. 86). The foregoing renders the position of those who contend that Mary is not present in the "woman," but only in the "seed" of the woman (Eve), where the term "seed" is taken in the collective sense, clearly indefensible. On this point cf. Roschini, *La Madonna*, vol. 2, pp. 68–72; *idem*, *Maria Santissima*, vol. I, pp. 67–69.

a biblical passage, without reference to real differences of content or to its general meaning.[13]

For this a reflection as simple as it is basic suffices: if Genesis 3:15 contains a prophecy projected into the future, it follows that the real content of this text and its overall meaning are likewise projected into the future. Therefore, it follows that the text's content and overall meaning cannot be determined from that present moment in which it is first spoken. Rolla writes that "the *Protoevangelium* before all else has a prophetic character setting it apart from the rest of the narrative. Moreover, its orientation is messianic and universal, because it is projected toward the future."[14] The *Protoevangelium*, then, is a prophetic text. Indeed, it is the "queen of prophecies,"[15] announcing the promise, messianic and universal, of future victory linked to a "woman" and her "seed," who will crush the serpent's head.

Moreover, the woman of the promise, victorious over the serpent and bearer of the Savior, finds no echo in poor, sinful Eve, who will live and die in the obscurity of her days. In fact, immediately after that divine oracle of Genesis 3:15, Eve heard God speak to her those bitter words: "I will multiply your sorrows and your conceptions; in sorrow you shall bear children. You will be drawn to your husband, but he shall have dominion over you" (Gen 3:16).[16]

---

13 "The context," Fr. Bonnefoy wryly observes, "is not measured with centimeters. A certain delicacy of touch rather than the spirit of geometry must be brought to its study. More than 'words' and their repetitions or grammatical combinations, the realities and their interplay in the unfolding drama must be pondered." The citation, here taken from *La Madonna* by Roschini, vol. 2, p. 57, is from J. F. Bonnefoy, O.F.M., *La mystère de Marie selon le Protoévangile et I'Apocalypse* (Paris, 1949), p. 35.

14 A. Rolla, *Il messaggio della salvezza*, vol. 2 (Turin, 1967), p. 126. Cf. also M. Cimosa, *Genesi 1-11 Alle orgini dell'uomo* (Brescia, 1984), pp. 92–93.

15 G. Nolli, "Maria nella Bibbia," *Rivista di vita spirituale* 28 (1974): 388.

16 However as Muncunill had already noted in his day, even in the hypothesis that Eve repented and was thus freed from her bondage to the serpent, this was possible precisely because of the merits of the Messiah and of His

The two verses of Genesis 3:15 and 16, so sharply contrasting one another, make it psychologically impossible for them to refer to one and the same person. Immediately after having spoken so solemnly of how the "woman" with her "seed" is to triumph over the serpent, God speaks of how Eve must endure suffering and humiliation for the rest of her life. On what grounds is it possible to understand in each the same "woman"? Nor, similarly, can one, with any kind of consistency, suppose in the same person, Eve, a plan of life to unfold simultaneously under the sign of victory (Gen 3:15) and the sign of subjection to suffering and man (Gen 3:16).

Rather, the point of departure for the logical development of this powerful and fruitful antithesis between Eve and Mary, noted by the earliest Fathers, such as St. Justin and St. Irenaeus, and commented upon down the centuries since, is the reality of that contrast between Eve and the "woman" of Genesis 3:15. It is a contrast that makes it impossible for both verses to refer to the same "woman." The antithesis between the "woman" and Eve is clearly evident both in God's manner of speaking of the "woman" (Gen 3:15) and to the woman Eve (Gen 3:16), as well as in the diametrical opposition between Eve and the "woman," considering the fundamental role each exercised historically. The formula of St. Jerome has become classical: "Per Evam mors, vita per Mariam [through Eve death, life through Mary]."[17]

Mother, the sole subjects of the divine oracle. Cf. J. Muncunill, *Tractatus de Verbi Dei Incarnatione* (Madrid, 1905), p. 529.

[17] St. Jerome, *Epistula 22 ad Eustochium*, no. 21. On the antithesis Eve–Mary, cf. L. Cignelli, O.F.M., *Maria nuova Eva nella Patristica greta* (Assisi, 1966); *idem*, "Maria, Vergine volontaria nell'esegesi patristica," *Studii biblici francescani Liber annuus* 22 (1972): 169–203 (with copious bibliography). The entire account ought to be read, Fr. Bonnefoy observes—in particular the first sentence passed by God: *Since you have done this* ... —with this perspective in mind, because without it the narrative is unintelligible. And, then, no one will be in the least surprised to see appear in the divine plan a woman other than Eve, so different to be her antithesis: namely, the woman Mary" (as cited by Roschini, *La Madonna*, vol. 2, p. 57).

Essentially, a salvific prophecy so solemn as that of Genesis 3:15 cannot but refer to an exceptional woman of the future, the bearer and Mother of the Messiah–Savior, with whom she is intimately united in enmity to the serpent, who will be crushed by her "immaculate foot."

Now, if God had also intended Eve, or only Eve, to be victorious over the serpent as our avenger,

> one could hardly understand why in the verses immediately following (Gen. 3:16–21) God addresses Eve only in terms of reproach and chastisement; nor why throughout the history of redemption 'the victory of Eve' is never even alluded to. Rather, every time mention is made of Eve, she is indicated as the cause of our ruin, never as the beginning of our restoration (Sir 25:24; 2 Cor 11:3; 1 Tim 2:14).[18]

Hence, only by way of arbitrary and contradictory interpretation can one find Eve as well as Mary in the "woman" of Genesis 3:15. There is simply nothing in her entire life in any way related to the great salvific mission of the two protagonists described by the Protoevangelium: the Messiah and His Mother.

In fact, in the New Testament, we see how the divine oracle concerning the "woman" who is to battle victoriously against the serpent of hell clearly finds its fulfillment in the Virgin Mary, that exceptional woman, the Mother of the Messiah, the invincible enemy of Satan, victorious

18 P. L. Da Fonseca, S.J., "L'Assunzione di Maria nella S. Scrittura," *Biblica* 28 (1947): 348. The Magisterium of the Church, however, has never taught that one ought to or even can see Eve in the woman of Gen 3:15. Rather, the Church makes use of the Protoevangelium in the liturgy of Marian feasts, and in particular for the liturgy in honor of the Immaculate Conception. In regard to the papal Magisterium, see Unger, "Mary Is the Woman," pp. 62–79.

over him in her Immaculate Conception[19] and glorious Assumption.[20]

Thus, those other exegetical opinions identifying the "woman" of Genesis 3:15 with Eve in the literal sense and with Mary only in the typical, or with Eve and Mary together with Eve—that is, in a literal sense and with Mary in the full or eminent sense, as, well as other possible interpretations[21]—not only do not shed light on our understanding of the *Protoevangelium*, but also artificially becloud the clarity of the portrait revealed by God and explained by the Church. So doing, they impede or complicate that limpid understanding of it which is beneficial to salvation.[22] The exegetical research and conclusions, particularly the more recent, on which these opinions rest, so often cited in support of mutually exclusive views and almost always minimizing the Mariological import of the *Protoevangelium*, for the most part do no more than provide a demonstration of philological and semantic erudition.

19 Cf. B. Mariani, O.F.M., "L'Immacolata nel Protovangelo: Gen 3, 15," *Virgo Immaculata*, vol. 3 (Rome, 1955), pp. 29–99, with copious bibliography.

20 In the dogmatic bull *Munificentissimus Deus*, Pope Pius XII affirms that the truth of the corporal Assumption of Mary Most Holy into heaven finds in the *Protoevangelium* its "radical basis" (AAS 42 [1950]: 768). Cf. A. Bea, S.J., "La S. Scrittura 'ultimo fondamento' del domma dell'Assunzione," La Civiltà Cattolica 101 (1950): IV, 554–558; M. Peinador, "De argumento scripturistico in Bulla dogmatica," *Ephemerides Mariologicae* 1 (1951): 27–43, 395–404; F. Spedalieri, S.J., "L'Assunzione di Maria nella Sacra Scrittura," *Renovatio* 7 (1972): 39–50.

21 For a fuller critical and analytical overview of the various interpretations, Cf. V. G. Bertelli, "L'interpretazione mariologica del Protovangelo negli esegeti e teologi dopo la Bolla *Ineffabilis Deus* di Pio IX (1854–1948)," *Marianum* 13 (1951): 257–291; *idem*, "Il senso mariologico pieno ed il senso letterale del Protovangelo (Gen 3:15) dalla Ineffabilis Deus al 1948," *Marianum* 13 (1951): 369–396. These studies show that of 166 authors examined, a good 93 defend the literal, Mariological sense of Genesis; cf. also Spedalieri, "L'Assunzione di Maria," pp. 35–59.

22 At times, a certain type of scholarly exegesis, including that of some Catholics, almost entirely empties the Protoevangelium of Mariological significance, or plainly distorts and deforms its salvific content. Such views not only are not compatible with the Magisterium, but are contrary as well to those of all other exegetical currents. See the positions of C. Westermann, O. H. Steck, E. Lipinski, D. Loretz, R. Davidson, A. Gunneweg, F. Haag, W. Wifall, N. Fueglister. Cf. Virgulin, "Ricerche su Genesi 3, 15," pp. 15–27.

This is a matrix not only for the most sharply divergent, but also for the most contradictory hypotheses and suppositions, in no wise illuminating, but rather detracting from the one objective truth of the *Protoevangelium*. This *Protoevangelium*, according to *Ineffabilis Deus*, "clearly and plainly" informs us that the "seed" is the Messiah–Savior and that the "woman" is the Mother of the Messiah. An exegesis currently widespread both in Catholic and non-Catholic circles that would see in Gen 3:15 only a generic struggle between good and evil is one, it is necessary to note, that is gratuitous and unfounded.[23] Such views depend on a "maximizing" of *philological* exegesis, while illogically "minimizing" the *theological*. In fact, in Genesis 3:15 God speaks specifically of the struggle, not between good and evil, but between the woman and the serpent, between the woman's seed and that of the serpent. The question is: Who might the "woman" and her "seed" be, who victoriously battle against the serpent? Who might the "serpent" and its "seed" be, they who are doomed to defeat? *Theological* exegesis replies to just such questions, making use of all the texts and scriptural references, including those of the New Testament, reading them *"as they are read in the Church"* (*Lumen Gentium*, no. 55),[24] or "*in the light of Christ and of the Church*."[25]

A clear and accurate synthesis of biblical–theological exegesis in accord with the constant tradition of the Church, reading

23 Cf., e.g., Schökel, *La Bibbia*, vol. I, p. 11, n. 15. See also the preceding note 23.

24 See, e.g., the references of Gen 3:15 to the woman and the dragon of the Revelation: L. Cerfaux, "La vision de la femme et du dragon de l'Apocalypse en relation avec le Protoévangile," *Virgo Immaculata*, vol. 3, pp. 116–131. With Settimio Cipriani, therefore we conclude that "exegetically speaking the Mariological interpretation of the passage traditional in Christian exegesis is to be held as well founded": Aa.Vv., *Come leggere nella Bibbia il mistero di Maria*, Roma 1989, p. 155; in note 2, l.c., Cipriani refers to the studies of J. Coppens, B. Rigaux, H. Cazelles, Ortensio da Spinetoli, A. Bea.

25 Pontifical Biblical Commission, *The Hebrew People and Its Sacred Scriptures in the Christian Bible*, n. 21.

Genesis 3:15 in a Christological–Mariological sense, more simply set forth in its essential terminology with reference to *Dei Verbum, Lumen Gentium* and to the texts of the Fathers, is found in the recent *Navarre Bible.*

The chastisement inflicted on the serpent by God entails an unceasing conflict between the Woman and the devil, between mankind and evil, with the promise of victory for man, symbolized in the crushing of the head of the serpent. This passage is called the *Protoevangelium,* because it is the first announcement of the good news received of the promised Redeemer Messiah by mankind. Vatican II teaches: 'God who creates and conserves all things through his *Word* (cf. Jn 1:3) offers men in created things a perennial testimony of himself (cf. Rom 1, 19–20). Further, in accord with his intention of opening a way to heavenly salvation, from the beginning revealed himself to our first parents. After their fall, with the promise of redemption, he supported them with the hope of salvation (cf. Gen 3:15) and took constant care of the human race, so as to give eternal life to all who seek salvation by persevering in doing good (cf. Rom 2:6–7)' (*Dei Verbum*, 3).

The victory over the devil would be won by a descendant of the woman, the Messiah. The Church has always understood these verses in the Messianic sense, referring them to Jesus Christ: and in the Woman has always understood the Mother of the promised Savior, the Virgin Mary or the new Eve. These early documents, as read in the Church, are understood in the light of the subsequent and complete Revelation, step by step setting more clearly in relief the figure of the Woman, Mother of the Redeemer. In this light she is already prophetically foreshadowed in the promise to our first parents after the fall into sin (cf. Gen 3:15)... Not a few ancient Fathers positively affirm in their preaching that 'the knot of disobedience tied by Eve was untied in the obedience of Mary: and what the virgin Eve had bound by infidelity, the Virgin Mary had released by her faith' (St. Irenaeus, *Adversus Haereses* 3, 22, 4), and in contrast with Eve Mary is called 'Mother of the living' (St. Epiphanius, *Adversus Haereses Panarium* 78, 18). They often assert that

> 'death came through Eve, life through Mary' (St. Jerome, *Epistula* 2, 21, etc.) (*Lumen Gentium*, nos. 55–56).

> The Woman, in fact, would have an important role in this victory over the devil. In this regard St. Jerome in his Latin version of the Bible, the Vulgate, translated: 'She (the Woman) will crush your head.' This Woman is the Most Holy Virgin, the new Eve and Mother of the Redeemer, who participates in anticipation and eminently in the victory of her Son. In her is no stain of sin. Hence, the Church proclaims her Immaculate from her conception.[26]

Mariology in a Nutshell

Instead, in terms of a broader context, the prophetic portrait of the *Protoevangelium* is better interpreted in its essential lines and in its ramifications when it is considered, even if briefly, in the light of both prophecy fulfilled and the teaching of the Church. The latter discovers in the *Protoevangelium*, as Vatican II states, the reality of the ineffable mystery of Mary to be already "prophetically foreshadowed."[27]

Thus, if the "seed" of the woman in fact is Jesus, the Son of God, consubstantial with the Father, then the text implies that the "woman" is the Mother of God. And so, in the *Protoevangelium*, one can discover the reality of the Divine Maternity of Mary. It is surely a fascinating as well

---

26 *La Bibbia di Navarra*, Antico Testamento [1] Pentateuco, Milano 2002, pp. 81–83.

27 *Lumen Gentium* no, 55. While the truth of the Immaculate Conception, according to *Ineffabilis Deus*, is based upon Gen which "clearly and plainly" speaks of the "woman" as the invincible enemy and conqueror of the demon and sin, one may observe that the total transcendent reality of Mary, according to Lumen Gentium, is found instead in Gen 3:15 to be only "prophetically foreshadowed." For the rest, it seems certain that the adjective foreshadowed best expresses and corresponds to the genre of the oracle: cf. P. Franquesa, "Uso del A. T. en el cap. VIII de la Lumen Gentium," *Estudios Marianos* 28 (1966): 239. See also S. M. Meo, O.S.M., *Maria nel capitolo VIII della Lumen Gentium* (Rome, 1975), p. 55.

as instructive fact that God would present His Mother to humanity at the very beginning of the history of salvation.

Moreover, that "seed" is the seed of the woman only. And her offspring, therefore, will be the fruit of a virgin. This is the very reality of the Virgin Mother. So, too, the divine and virginal Motherhood of Mary is "prophetically foreshadowed" in the Protoevangelium.

Another persuasive consideration, well grounded objectively, concerns the word "woman." There exists, as has been rightly observed, a clear parallel between God's use of the term "woman" in the *Protoevangelium* and Jesus' use of the same term in addressing His Mother at Cana and Calvary.[28]

Further, the enmity between the "woman" and the serpent cannot be reconciled with sin in the woman: not only with original sin, but with any sin whatsoever, mortal or venial. Any sin at all would constitute a victory for the enemy. This is the basis for ascribing to Mary Most Holy a real immunity from every kind of moral failure and from concupiscence. "Here is already clear the heavenly figure of the Immaculate," says Fr. Vaccari.[29]

Even more, the "woman" associated with her "seed" (according to *Ineffabilis Deus*), in common enmity against the serpent, is she who collaborated with her Son in ransoming and redeeming mankind, crushing the head of the enemy. "In Genesis 3:15," writes Cimosa, "the hostility

---

[28] Cf. P. Gaechter, *Maria im Erdenleben. Neutesiamentliche Marien Studien* (Inns bruck, pp. 205–212, 224–226; F. M. Braun, O.P., *La Mère des fidèles* (Tournai and Paris, 1953), pp. 80–96 (Eng. ed.: *Mother of God's People* [New York, 1967], pp. 82–93); A. Feuillet, "La Vierge Marie dans le Nouveau Testament," *Maria. Etudes sur la Sainte Vierge*, vol. 6 (Paris, 1961), pp. 63–64; Ortensio Da Spinetoli, O.F.M. Cap., *Maria nella Bibbia* (Genoa, 1964), pp. 23–27, 33, 61, 173, 203, 222–226.

[29] *La Sacra Bibbia. Il Pentateuco*, Roma 1942, Vol. I, p. 70, note 15.

of the woman does not differ from that of her offspring."[30] In such wise, the soteriological Marian dimension, or the salvific mission endured by Mary as Mediatrix and Coredemptrix of the human race is also "foreshadowed" in Genesis 3:15. This is underscored and confirmed by wide-ranging studies on the part of biblicists, patrologists and theologians of the past, and even more today.[31]

Finally, she who is victorious over the enemy from hell could not possibly have a body subject to the corruption of the tomb, a punishment for sin. And she who shared her Son's struggle for the Redemption of mankind must also reign with her Son in the Kingdom of heaven. Hence, the reality of Mary's corporal Assumption and of her Queenship are also foreshadowed in the text of Genesis 3:15.[32]

J. Gamberoni has correctly noted how

> in the course of history, certain texts, one of which is Genesis 3:15 have served as the point of departure for developments leading to and culminating in propositions far surpassing in sophistication those which initiated the process. This unique relation can be likened to that between seed and adult plant:

30 M. Cimosa, *Genesi 1–11*, p. 93.

31 The bibliography on the theme of Coredemption in the bible, in the Fathers, in theology is vast. We cite here only a few titles: Stef. M. Manelli, *Mary Coredemptrix in Sacred Scripture*, in *Mary Coredemptrix, Mediatrix, Advocate. Theological Foundations II* (Santa Barbara, CA 1997, pp. 59–104); on the text of Gen 3:15, pp. 71–80. In the updated Italian version of this study, *Maria Corredentrice nella Sacra Scritura*, in *Maria Corredentrice. Storia e Teologia I* (Frigento 1998) pp. 53–65, the following biblicists are cited R. Rabanos, T. Gallus, G. M. Allegra, M. Peinador, R. Laurentine, L. Cignelli, G. Most, J. Nicolas; Thomas M. Sennott, *Mary Coredemptrix*, in *Mary at the Foot of the Cross II*, New Bedford, MA 2002, pp. 49–63; Th. Spidlik, "Eva-Maria nella Tradizione dei Padri," in Aa. Vv., *Maria Corredentrice. Storia e Teologia*, pp. 159–172. Of great value are the studies of numerous authors on Marian soteriology found in the series: Bibliotheca Coredemptionis B. V. Mariae, *Maria Corredentrice. Storia e Teologia*, vols. I-IV, Frigento 1998–2003, and in the series: *Acts of the International Symposiums on Marian Coredemption, Mary at the Foot of the Cross*, Academy of the Immaculate, New Bedford, MA 2000–2004, 4 vols.

32 On these points contained in Gen 3:15, cf. Peinador, *Los temas de la mariologia biblica*; *idem*, *Historia de la salvación*. See also T. Gallus, S.J., "Beata Virgo Maria Protoevangelio praesignata," in *Alma Socia Christi*, vol. II (Rome, 1953), pp. 58–67; Roschini, *La Madonna*, vol. 2, pp. 72–74.

only someone acquainted with the latter is able to discern concretely what is contained and prepared in the former.[33]

The Church's ongoing, in-depth reflection in faith, which has seen the little acorn grow into a majestic oak, assures us that this indeed is true of the case at hand: the text of Genesis is the original sprout containing in itself, i.e., as in a seed, the entire, ineffable mystery of Mary.

Quite different, and of little practical import, are the conclusions of the so-called 'revisitation' of this celebrated text of Genesis. The process of reinterpretation, it seems, is one of filtering via contrast. First, as D. Scaiola observes, by reason of this method it is claimed that the 'interpretation of this verse cannot be separated from its context as the Fathers so often do' (p. 562) and 'the Messianic–Mariological interpretation is not tenable' (p. 563); next it is claimed, to the contrary, that 'it is possible to reestablish the patristic reading by situating the verse within the overall symbolic meaning of the entire Bible' (p. 563).[34]

Obviously the commentary here passes from the impossibility of the patristic Messianic–Marian interpretation of Gen. 3:15 on the basis of a philological–literary analysis of chapters 2–3 of Genesis to the possibility of that very interpretation on the basis of the 'symbolic meaning of the entire Bible,' with direct references to Genesis 1–11; 12:2–3; Galatians 3:16; Isaiah 11; and Apocalypse 12 and 21:9 (pp. 563–564).

In substance, therefore, the whole can be summarized stating that while biblical-philological exegesis will not support the Messianic–Marian interpretation of the Fathers, the Liturgy and the Magisterium, biblical-theological exegesis will support this. But this is, precisely, the true, constant exegesis of the Church.

In conclusion, the *Protoevangelium* has been described as a complete synthesis of Mariology, wherein the whole

---

33 J. Gamberoni, "Il Protovangelo testimone della fede nella salvezza," in *La parola per l'assemblea festiva* (Brescia, 1972), no. 63, p. 34.

34 Scaiola, *op. cit.*, pp. 562–563

of Mariology is found "in a nutshell."[35] This is indeed so. We might also compare the *Protoevangelium* to a "sketch" for a painting by the Supreme Artist. While contemplating today the finished portrait, one realizes how the luminous figure of Mary is "sketched" in the *Protoevangelium* as the Mother of God, the Virgin Mother, the Immaculate: free of every stain of actual sin, the associate of the Savior in the work of Redemption, the Mother and Mediatrix of men, the one assumed body and soul into heaven, the victorious Queen united to her Son, the King of the universe. The painting is truly on a grandiose and stupendous scale![36]

A final, brief reflection upon woman from an anthropological point of view is appropriate. The mystery of Eve–Mary is also the mystery of every woman. In life, every woman is capable of being Eve or Mary, can conduct herself and fulfill herself either like Eve or like Mary. The first is the woman who degrades herself, the second is the woman who ennobles herself. The first capitulates to temptation; the second resists and defeats the tempter. The first brings ruin upon herself and others; the second saves herself and others. The first also involves Adam in her disgrace; the second collaborates with the new Adam in the work of Redemption.

---

35 Cf. Roschini, *La Madonna*, vol. 2, pp. 50, 72.

36 The importance and value that the solemn Magisterium and tradition, together with the liturgy and sacred art, have attributed to the Mariological content of Gen 3:15 is clearly indicative of the superficiality with which some Catholic scholars, even some of note, treat the Mariological content of the Protoevangelium, going so far as to empty it almost completely of any such significance, thereby compromising their *sentire cum Ecclesia* (thinking with the Church) as well. Fr. T. Gallus, in his last work, rightfully and strongly complains that in spite of the fact that tradition, scholarship (including Protestant exegesis from Luther to the Enlightenment), and the Magisterium have been in favor of ascribing to Gen 3:15 a messianic and Mariological sense, today not only Protestant exegetes, but some Catholics as well lightly and rashly refuse to acknowledge Gen 3:15 as the Protoevangelium (cf. T. Gallus, S.J., *Die "Frau" in Gen. 3:15* [Klagenfurt, 1979], p. 167).

The woman of Genesis 3:15 invites every woman to fulfill herself by keeping herself ever in God's friendship, ever resolved to fight and radically to resist sin, i.e., to live the life of grace, and at the heart of the family, of the Church, and of society to assume responsibility for the good to be won for herself and for others. The "woman" of Genesis is the woman–salvation.[37]

[37] Cf. P. Evdokimov, *La donna e la salvezza del mondo* (Milan, 1980).

2
The Virgin Mother

Isaiah 7:10–14

Again the Lord spoke to Ahaz: "Ask a sign from the Lord your God, either unto the depth of hell or unto the height above." But Ahaz said: "I will not ask; I will not tempt the Lord. "And Isaiah said: "Hear then, O house of David! Is it too little for you to weary men, that you weary my God also? Therefore the Lord himself will give you a sign. Behold, a virgin shall conceive and bear a son, and shall call his name Emmanuel."

The historic setting of this prophecy is linked to the dramatic situation of King Ahaz, about to be dethroned by the king of Syria and the king of Israel for having refused to join them against the Assyrians. Ahaz, instead, contemplates calling upon the Assyrians for help. The prophet Isaiah, however, encourages him to trust in God and to ask God for a sign guaranteeing that the royal house of Judah would not be destroyed by the kings of Syria and Israel. But Ahaz refuses to entrust himself to God, because he thinks the Assyrian army will suffice for his defense.

At this point, the prophet Isaiah, angered by Ahaz' lack of trust in God, foretells that the house of Judah will be ruined by the very Assyrians on whom Ahaz prefers to rely. Further, he indicates that a pregnant virgin will bear the Emmanuel, the royal son with divine attributes of

"Wonderful Counselor, Mighty God, Father everlasting, Prince of Peace" (Is 9:6).

Biblical–theological exegesis correctly insists on one literal, messianic, and Marian interpretation of this well-known prophecy: the Emmanuel of whom the prophet speaks is exclusively the future Messiah, Jesus Christ, and the childbearing virgin is exclusively Mary, the Virgin Mother of Jesus.

> Critical problems with regard to the meaning of the term 'virgin' involving philological exegesis of the text have now been definitively resolved. Rolla writes: '*The Virgin* (in Hebrew *ha 'almah*)*:* the presence of the article indicates that the person in question is someone definite, if not from the context, at least in the prophet's mind. The person in question is *'almah,* that is, a young girl, a girl of marriageable age, maiden, virgin. In fact, the Hebrew term, in the eight places where it does appear in the Hebrew Bible apart from the present text (Esther 2:8; Gen 24:43; 1 Chron 15:20; Song 1:3, 6:8; Ps 45:1, 67:26; Prov 30:19), always indicates a woman both sexually and chronologically mature, not named, and, therefore, ordinarily still a virgin. The Hebrew term, however, directly connoting sexual integrity is *betûllāh.*'[1]

> Earlier Fr. Alberto Vaccari clearly wrote: 'in the Hebrew text the specific term denoting virginity (*Betulah*) is absent, instead there is found the generic term maiden (*'almah*), normally indicating an intact virgin (cf. Gen 24:16, 43); nevertheless the Jews before Christ understood this word in the technical sense of virgin as the Greek translator (of the LXX) witnesses. He employed for his translation of *'almah* the specific term *parthenos*, and so did the primitive Christian Church (Mt. 1:20–25).'[2]

Apart from the great number of Catholic scholars who, on strictly exegetical grounds, support such an

1 ROLLA, *Il messaggio della salvezza*, pp. 393–394.
2 VACCARI, *La Sacra Bibbia*, Roma 1955, vol. VI, p. 41, notes 13–14.

interpretation of the oracle of Isaiah, one must also consider the well-nigh unanimous agreement with this interpretation on the part of the Fathers and ecclesiastical writers, both in the East and in the West, from St. Justin on. So, too, the uninterrupted teaching of the Magisterium of the Church, the witness of the liturgy and of sacred art (as early as that of the Catacombs of Priscilla in Rome) have favored this interpretation. All this unquestionably lends weight to the Church's belief that the announcement made by the prophet Isaiah to King Ahaz is an unequivocal proclamation heralding the Messiah, Jesus, and Mary, His Mother.[3]

Notwithstanding the impressive Faith of the Church, however, there are some scholars, Catholics included, especially in recent years, that propose interpretations of Isaiah's prophecy denying that in the literal sense its content is to be understood as exclusively messianic and Marian. They allow such content only in an indirect, oblique, and typical sense and deny in particular that the prophecy has any relation to the virginal conception and parturition of Mary Most Holy as affirmed in the Gospels. For them, the so-called virgin in Isaiah would, in fact, be an already married woman: either the wife of Ahaz and mother of Hezekiah; the wife of the prophet himself, Isaiah; or an unidentified spouse.[4] As Mattioli states, these are the interpretations

---

3 Cf. F. C. Ceuppens, *De Mariologia Biblica* (Turin, 1951), pp. 18–38; J. Coppens, "La prophetic de la *'Almah,"* *Ephemerides Theologicae Lovanienses* 28 (1952): 648–678; Peinador, C.M.F., *Los temas de mariologia bíblica*; P. Pietrafesa, C.SS.R., *La Madonna nella Rivelazione* (Naples, 1970), pp. 3749; Varón Varón, *Sagrada Escritura*, pp. 19–28. See in particular the recent study of F. Spadafora, "Il vaticinio della Vergine e dell'Emanuele," *Marianum* 41 (1979): 67–75, with an extensive, up-to-date bibliography. This author claims that at the present stage reached by research on the prophecy of Isaiah "there seems to be nothing more to be written on the subject." In effect, the author reaffirms the correctness of the "directly messianic exegesis which has always prevailed in the Catholic Church" (p. 68).

4 All these questions and opinions, cf. D. Bertetto, *Maria nel domma cattolico* (Turin, 1955), pp. 52–70; J. Coppens, "Le messianisme royal: VI. Jesus

favored by "a modern, rationalistic exegesis," and they run counter to the practically unanimous view of the exegetical tradition and of the Faith of the Church.[5] Yet modern, rationalistic exegetes cannot avoid facing the fact that if there are any prophecies of the Old Testament expressly cited in the New as fully verified, one is this precise passage from Isaiah, cited verbatim by St. Matthew and clearly referred to by St. Luke.

St. Matthew, after describing how an angel appeared to St. Joseph to reassure him with regard to the virginal conception of Mary by the Holy Spirit, expressly states that this virginal conception fulfills this very prophecy of Isaiah: "All this was done in order to fulfill that which the Lord had spoken by the prophet: Behold, a virgin shall be with child and bring forth a son who will be called Emmanuel, which means God with us" (Mt 1:22–23).

St. Luke, recording in his Gospel the dialogue between the angel and Mary at the Annunciation, quotes the angel as follows: "Behold you shall conceive in your womb and bear a son, and you shall call him Jesus. He will be great,

---

et l'accomplissement de l'attente royale messianique," *Nouvelle Revue Theologique* 100 (1962): 483–90. As for more recent authors who deny the literal messianic and Mariological sense, cf. M Rehm, *Der Koenigliche Messiad im Licht des Immanuel Weissagungen des Buches Jesaja* (Kevelaer, 1968), p. 84, no. 194.

The odd interpretation according to which Emmanuel is to be identified with Hezekiah (son of King Ahaz: cf. Is 36–39) was defended in early times only by Jews against the Christians. It was quickly subjected to sharp criticism by St. Justin (Dialogue with Trypho the Jew, nos. 66, 68, 71, 77) and was refuted and ridiculed by St. Jerome (*Commentary on Isaiah*, PL 24, 111ff.). Recently, however, this strange view has been adopted by a number of Catholic scholars (cf. *La Bibbia di Gerusalemme* [Bologna, 1771, p. 1566, nn. 7, 14; Eng. ed.: *The Old Testament of the Jerusalem Bible* [New York, 1966], pp. 1153–1154]; for still worse examples, see *La Bibbia, Parola di Dio scritta per noi* [Turin, 1980], II, p. 635, nn. 14–15), who in reproposing it indulge in ambiguous verbal subtleties so as not to appear to contradict the Faith of the Church, which from St. Matthew onward—that is, always—has professed this oracle of Isaiah to be a prophecy referring exclusively to the Messiah and His ever-virgin Mother.

5 Mattioli, *Dio e l'uomo nella Bibbia d'Israele* (Turin, 1980), p. 393.

and will be called the Son of the Most High; the Lord God will give to him the throne of his father David, and he will reign over the house of Jacob forever, and of his kingdom there will be no end" (Lk. 1:31–33).

Obviously, direct reference is being made here to two Isaiah texts: "Behold, a virgin shall conceive and bear a son, and shall call his name Emmanuel" (Is. 7:14); and "The government is upon his shoulder, and his name is called Wonderful Counselor, Mighty God, Father everlasting, Prince of Peace. Great will be his dominion and of peace there will be no end. He will sit upon the throne of David, and over his kingdom: to establish it and to strengthen it with judgment and with justice, from now on and for ever" (Is 9:6–7).[6]

With precisely these two explicit references of the two Evangelists to the prophecy of Isaiah interpreted directly in the messianic and Marian sense begins a unanimous and uninterrupted tradition of the Church. This tradition attributes this prophecy of Isaiah exclusively to Mary, the virgin who virginally conceives and virginally bears the Emmanuel, the Son of God and Messiah, Jesus Christ.[7]

---

[6] To learn what untenable exegetical hypotheses to which one must have recourse in order to deny the evident connection between the prophecy of Isaiah and the thought of St. Matthew who cites it, cf. A. Serra, *Maria nel mistero di Cristo secondo l'Antico Testamento*, lecture notes (Rome, 1977), pp. 39–43. Equally dubious, as well as distorted, are the so called reinterpretations of G. Odasso, *Il segno dell'Emanule nella tradizione dell'Antico Testamento*, in *Theotokos* 4 (1996) 151–188. Summarily, the author via analysis and allusion clearly seems to conclude by making the prophet Isaiah say *everything exactly the opposite* of revealed facts, whereas the Evangelist St. Matthew writes with a limpid simplicity when, without sophisticated analysis based on hypotheses and counter-hypotheses, he identifies *sic et Simpliciter*, the virgin of Isaiah with the Virgin Mary in the miraculous sign of the virginal Motherhood and birth of the Davidic Messiah, God and King. This has been the constant interpretation of the Fathers, of the Liturgy, and so of the Church and of the most reliable Catholic exegesis. Unfortunately, this author ascribes to traditional exegesis the inability "to situate itself in the salvific perspective of Scripture" (p. 155).

[7] A. Rolla, *Il messaggio della salvezza*, p. 596.

Rolla also writes: "Catholic exegetes agree that the passage is to be interpreted as a prophecy of the virginal parturition of Mary Most Holy. They are led to this conclusion in view of St. Matthew 1:22–23 and of the unanimous agreement of the Fathers. The greater number of these exegetes support the exclusively literal, Messianic sense." Fr. Ceuppens, referring to St. Matthew and St. Luke, writes: "The entire Christian tradition unanimously taught that Isaiah 7:14 foretold the virginal conception and parturition of Mary."[8]

Theological–biblical exegesis also enables us to discover factors defining the specifics of this well-known prophecy. Such, for instance, is the link between the prophecy of Isaiah and that which Nathan made to David, promising him an eternal kingdom (2 Sam 7:8–17). The eternity of that Davidic kingdom will be assured by Jesse's offspring, who is to rule and to guarantee a peace that "shall have no end upon the throne of David and over his kingdom" (Is 9:7). In virtue of the divine attributes ascribed to the Emmanuel, it appears clear that He alone is the "God with us," a Messiah, that is, human and divine, "Mighty God and Prince of Peace," who has such dominion over time as to reign forever upon the throne of David.[9] St. Luke confirms all this in even more precise terms, calling the Messiah "the Son of the 'Most High," "the Son of God,"

---

8 F.C. Ceuppens, *De Mariologia Biblica*, p. 31. Cf. also Boschi, "Maria nell'Antico Testamento," p. 21.

9 Pietrafesa writes that "Emmanuel is a name that is used only by Isaiah. In itself, the name could simply be a divine epithet. However, in the text and context of Isaiah's book (cf. Is 8:8–10; 9:5–6; 11:1–5) Emmanuel is said to have certain qualities such as to denote a person endowed with divine attributes. The witness of the holy Fathers, the liturgy, and the Doctors of the Church in interpreting this passage dissipate all doubt on this point" (Pietrafesa, *La Madonna nella Rivelazione*, p. 41).

who "will reign forever over the house of Jacob" and whose kingdom "will have no end" (cf. Lk 1:31–35).[10]

One of the fundamental points, however, of Isaiah's prophecy surely concerns the virginal conception and parturition of the Mother of the Emmanuel. This is the object of the Church's belief in the perpetual, virginal integrity of Mary, before, during, and after, childbirth.[11] The special sign that Isaiah offers the King on behalf of God is in fact this: a pregnant virgin, that is to say, a virgin who conceives a child while remaining a virgin; and a virgin giving birth, that is to say, a pregnant virgin who bears a son while still remaining a virgin: hence, a virginal conception and virginal parturition, the one and the other miraculous. For this is Isaiah's affirmation: in conception and in the act of giving birth the Mother of the Emmanuel remains always "the virgin."[12]

---

10 One understands, then, why the Emmanuel cannot be—as a group of scholars currently opines—the son of Ahaz, Hezekiah, to whom no divine marks can be ascribed and who accomplished very little during his reign. "The destiny of Hezekiah," Laurentin writes, "was under certain aspects disappointing. He was unsuccessful in his reform. And soon after came the exile" (R. LAURENTIN, *La Vergine Maria* [Rome, 1983], p. 266). Rolla also points out that Hezekiah was accused by Isaiah himself of being "thoughtless and imprudent"; for the rest it seems almost certain that at the time of the prophecy Hezekiah had already been born. Still less can the Emmanuel be identified with the son of Isaiah, since Isaiah's son was never king; or with anyone else in an indeterminate or in a collective sense. (Cf. ROLLA, *Il messaggio della salvezza*, pp. 597–598). See also M. de TUYA, "La Virgen Maria en la Biblia," in *Enciclopedia Mariana Posconciliar* (Madrid, 1975), pp. 295–296; A. Feuillet, "De fundamento mariologiae in prophetiis messianicis Veteris Testamenti," in *De Mariologia et Oecumenismo* (Rome, 1962), pp. 40–41; BOSCHI, "Maria nell'Antico Testamento," p. 21.

11 Rolla rightly calls two facts to the attention of those who claim that the Emmanuel of whom Isaiah speaks is a son of Ahaz or of the prophet himself, the "type" of the future Messiah (Christ): first the absence of "any biblical evidence supporting an interpretation of either of these historical figures as a type of the Savior," and second, even more importantly, the absence of the extraordinary "sign," to consist in the parthenogenesis. "Above all, it does not appear that the essential element of the sign, consisting in the supernatural, virginal conception of the Messiah, can in any way be linked with the type, since Hezekiah and the son of the prophet were conceived in a simply natural manner" (ROLLA, *Il messaggio della salvezza*, p. 596).

12 Of important significance is the absence of the "father" of the Emmanuel. Cf. J. COPPENS, "La prophetic de la *'Almah*," p. 565. For this reason Vaccari can affirm that the prophet Isaiah in speaking of the Emmanuel "also

The authoritative Fr. Albeto Vaccari states that "The miraculous character of the birth of the Messiah more than from the word [*'almah*], is made clear by the context. In fact, the *sign* which God gives (v. 14) is not different in nature from that offered by him (v. 11), namely miraculous. And there can be no miraculous element in a conception and birth, except that it be a conception and birth without loss of virginity by the mother."[13]

On this the observations of Fr. Bertetto are correct and opportune.

> Adjectives employed to modify nouns define the latter more exactly, but do not in general change the original meaning of the nouns. Thus, for example, in the phrase tall, thin virgin, the adjectives do not negate the idea of virginity conveyed by the subject modified.
>
> Hence, the prophet sees and announces a pregnant and child bearing virgin *sensu composito* [in the joint sense, or simultaneously]: that is, pregnant and childbearing and still a virgin; and not *sensu diviso* [in the separate sense, or successively]: that is, a virgin who remained such until she conceived and who at the moment of conceiving lost her virginity. In the latter hypothesis, there would be no reason for the prophet to call that woman a virgin in so solemn a tone, and to present her as something extraordinary.[14]

---

insinuates the divinity of the Messiah" (in *La Sacra Bibbia, I Profeti 1*, vol. VI p. 41 notes 13–14.

13 *La Sacra Bibbia*, vol. VI, p. 41, notes 13–14. To the simple and well grounded affirmation of Fr. Vaccari, G. Odasso, *Il segno dell'Emmanuele nella Tradizione dell'Antico Testamento*, in *Theotokos* 4 (1996) 151–188, seems to be opposed, in a manner however hardly clear or simple.

14 Bertetto, *Maria nel domma cattolica*, pp. 57–58. Just beyond this, the same author resolves the ingenious objection, proposed among others by Serra, *Maria nel mistero di Cristo*, p. 26, n. 21, which is based on the gospel phrase "the blind see" (Mt. 11:5). Bertetto states: "It is useless to attempt to weaken our conclusions with an appeal to the *sensus divisus*, as if the prophet had said: 'She who is now a virgin shall conceive (after having lost her virginity) and bring forth as son...,' thus paralleling the sense of Jesus' statement: the blind see, the lame walk ..., meaning *sensu diviso* that the blind having been healed of their blindness see... and the lame having regained their health walk.

St. Ambrose expressed this magnificently when he wrote: "This is the Virgin who conceived in her womb, the Virgin who bore a son. For thus it is written: Behold, a virgin shall conceive and bear a son (Is. 7:14). Not only is it said that the virgin would conceive, but that the virgin would bear a child."[15]

For the consistent and luminous thought of a St. Ambrose with his biblical–sapiential exegesis of the Old and New Testaments (Is. 7:10–14; Mt. 1:20–21) some today, however sincerely committed to scholarly research, would substitute a new exegesis, in no wise convincing in its conclusion, and too sure of itself, not only in discovering and transmitting novel interpretations of biblical Revelation, but also of knowing how to do better what the Holy Fathers themselves: e.g., St. Justin, St. Irenaeus, St. Ambrose, St. Jerome, St. Augustine..., did, forgetting—it is to be feared—that the Holy Fathers, together with Sacred Scripture, are a source of divine Revelation. Nor is it to be forgotten that surely the Fathers were acquainted with codices and documents existing in their day, but no longer accessible to us.[16]

"If Isaiah, in fact, had spoken *sensu diviso*, he would not have used expressions indicative of an extraordinary fact, a divine prodigy. If the prophet had wanted to say that the conception and parturition were to be quite ordinary and natural, the solemn exordium adopted to foretell this would have been ridiculous and meaningless" (ibid., p. 62). Cf. also D. Bertetto, *Maria Madre Universale* (Florence, 1969), p. 66.

15 St. Ambrose, *Epistle* 42, PL 16, 1125. Ceuppens incisively concludes his exhaustive textual exegesis thus: "Hence, after her conception (i.e., during pregnancy) and in the very act of giving birth (or during childbirth) the prophet always calls her with the same solemnity—*'almãh* (with the article)—and never by the term *ha 'iššâh*, or by any other name. This cannot be explained except by saying the prophet thus shows us a woman who both in conception and in childbirth preserves her virginity intact" (Ceuppens, *De Mariologia Biblica*, p. 23).

16 On this point cf. the articles of G. Odasso, *Il segno dell'Emmanule nella tradizione dell'Antico Testamento*, in *Theotokos* 4 (1996) 151–188; *Percorsi dell'esegesi e della teologia biblica; prospettive la Mariologia* in the supplement to *Theotokos* 9 (2001) 14–15; D. Scaiolo, *Testi tradizionali rivisitati (Gen 3,15; Is. 7,14)*, in *Theotokos* 8 (2000) 551–568. It is difficult to avoid the impression that with this type of "procedure" reality is turned

In regard to Isaiah 7:10–14 and to St. Matthew 1:22–23, in fact the biblical–sapiential and theological exegesis of the Holy Fathers, and therefore of the Church, teaches the unity of thought and content of the two texts, by virtue of which the virgin and child prophesied by Isaiah are precisely the Virgin Mary and the Child Jesus of whom the Evangelist St. Matthew speaks. According to some recent scholars, instead, among whom the above-cited Odasso, the two texts in question must be subjected to a battery of analytic tests, undergoing correction and Old Testament reinterpretations. According to him, during an initial phase of development there did not exist in the text of Isaiah 7:10–14 any mention of the celebrated prophecy cited by St. Matthew 1:22–13. Hence, that text must not be so read as including such mention. Indeed, one should read exactly the *contrary* of what Matthew affirms, since the woman spoken of by Isaiah is not a virgin, but a married woman, wife of King Achaz, already pregnant by him. The child, Hezekiah, son of Achaz, has no special attribute to justify the name *Emmanuel,* or to be considered 'God with us,' since he is an ordinary child and will be a mediocre king held rather in 'contempt,' indeed a 'tragic disappointment' (according to A. Rolla and R. Laurentin). Prophecy and miraculous sign of the *virgin birth* of the *God with us*, therefore, are not present in the text of the prophet Isaiah 7:10–14, and consequently are pointlessly cited by St. Matthew 1:22–23.

In second phase of development, however, involving the text of Isaiah 9:1–6 as well, the text listing the divine attributes

upside down, in the sense that the Old Testament is more important than All this is undertaken to guarantee the new approach as fruit of negation and affirmations in chain like sequence, at times without any support except references to "a wider context," to "broadening the meaning," to situating the passage "in the today" of God's word, to "it proper perspective," to the "paschal experience," to "compliments," to expressions of "final fidelity of God" (see, e.g., D. Scaiola, *art. cit.*, pp. 567–568). For the rest, with reference to E. Zenger, *Der Neue Bund in Alten. Zur Bundestheologie der beiden Testamente*, Freiburg 1993, Odasso effectively seems to invert the relation, expressly stating that the New Testament, in the light of the Risen Savior "was written beginning with the Old Testament, and consequently only by starting with the Old Testament can the New be understood correctly." One should note, however, as Augustine writes, that exactly the contrary is true: only in the New Testament can the Old be understood correctly, since only in the New does the "Old become clear." (St. Augustine, *Quaestiones in Heptateuchum*, II, 73).

of the Messiah which the poor King Hezekiah is obviously lacking, the surprising fact is discovered that Isaiah himself has transfigured as it were Hezekiah, projecting into him and personifying in him the future divine and kingly Messiah, the 'God with us.' Hence, according to this 'reinterpretation,' whereas initially no mention could be found in the text of Isaiah 7:10–14 of a divine Messiah, little by little the exact *contrary* came to be understood. By reason of this a simple man like Hezekiah, conceived and born normally came to be considered something quite different and totally contrary: the divine King and Messiah, 'God with us' with all those divine attributes which in fact we know Hezekiah did not possess. Here one passes, contradictorily, from the non-existent to the existent, and vice versa, in the same subject: a transition altogether too facile and superficial, indeed inadmissible, a transition that is sheer myth.

In the third and final phase the *contrary* (of the initial, non-messianic meaning) is understood still more clearly by reading the text of Isaiah 11:1–5, in the light of Isaiah, ch. 62. Reading and interpreting the later chapter, not without a certain sense of doing violence to the text, one is supposed to perceive how the wife of Achaz, already pregnant with Hezekiah, is now transformed into nothing less than a *virgin*: the biblical and davidic *Zion*, at first 'unfaithful,' 'abandoned,' and 'desolate,' but afterwards espoused by God himself. That fact makes her a *virgin* so as to give us the Messiah. This 'reinterpretation,' as is obvious, seems to have all the qualities characteristic of and consistent with what is commonly called a metamorphasis, or better a mythologization. A more precise definition would be a creation out of nothing.

According to such a 'reinterpretation' of Isaiah 7:10–14, then, via a sophisticated selection of numerous other biblical texts, related and linked in some way among themselves (e.g.: Ez 34:23–25; Zach 6; 1 Sam 10; 11; 16; 19; 20; 2 Sam 7; Jer 23:1–6; Gen 3:17–18; Dt 28:18, 23–24; Ps 72:9–17; Ps 89:3. 15. 25; Ps 103:11–13; Ps 132:11. 13. 15. 17; Is 54:1. 4. 5–8; 61:10–11; 55:3–5; Hs 1; 3; Jer 3:1–2; Ez 16; 23), an Old Testament tradition is produced, whereby a married woman, the wife of Achaz already pregnant with a son, Hezekiah, a future mediocre king, is transformed into the *Virgin–Mother* of Emmanuel, the '*God with us*.' I'm sorry to say it, but in fact for the poor reader seeking the truth, Tradition and contradiction of Tradition, serious research and uncontrolled hypothesizing have been hopelessly confused here beyond measure.

And for this reason one comes to realize why two Holy Fathers of the stature of St. Justin and St. Jerome were correct in opposing any exegesis of Isaiah 7:10–14 excluding all reference to the virgin birth and to the reality of the Emmanuel. In their day, they firmly refuted any such exegesis characteristic of those Jews who opposed Christians.[17]

It is also noteworthy that this kind of research and construction of so-called 'reinterpretations' in order to create, on the basis of Isaiah 7:10–14, an Old Testament tradition so non-homogeneous and contradictory, is grounded, even stylistically, in a whirl of approximations and insinuations, virtualities and symbols, sayings and recollections, perspectives and profiles, chances and probabilities, allusions and contexts, syntagmas and connotations, comparisons and metaphors, implications and delineations, hypotheses and correlatives, etc., etc.[18]

At this point, one must ask what concrete consistency can so sophisticated an Old and New Testament exegetical study have, which *directly* seems to eliminate the literal and real content of the prophecy of Isaiah 7:10–14 on the Virgin–Mother of the Emmanuel, a prophecy instead presented by the Evangelist St. Matthew with the very words of Isaiah as historically realized concretely in Mary, the Mother of Jesus, with the miraculous *sign* of the virgin *birth of Emmanuel*, the Word Incarnate, true *'God with us,'* King and Messiah. In St. Matthew, we find all the clarity and simplicity of revealed truth, expressed in terms of the full correspondence content-wise between the text of Isaiah 7:14 and the text of the Evangelist, illumined by the Spirit. Gila, therefore, has

---

17 See above, note 4.

18 Cf. *passim* in the above-cited articles.

correctly written that 'the understanding of the Scriptures is not the fruit of human effort, but a gift of the grace of Christ. He alone who has the Spirit of Jesus can understand them.'[19]

The prophecy of Isaiah, therefore, affirms the virginity of the Mother of the Emmanuel, before and during childbirth. But with the virginal maternity is foreshadowed the royal and divine maternity, given that the Emmanuel is the Messiah, the Son of God,[20] and that, He is a royal descendant of David because, being born of Mary, He is also of David's lineage.[21]

Still another detail, particularly significant, is this: the prophet Isaiah states that the Mother of the Messiah will herself name her son, the fruit of her virginal womb ("She shall call his name Emmanuel" [Is 7:14]), even though this was contrary to traditional usage, whereby the father named the child. St. Luke underscores this same detail in recounting how the angel informed Mary she was to name the child she bore: "You shall call his name Jesus" (Lk 1:31). The correspondence between prophecy and fulfillment on this point is perfect.

---

19 A. Gila, *La Vergine Madre e l'Antico Testamento secondo i primi Padri della Chiesa*, in *Theotokos* 9 (2001) 91. In the second article of Odasso cited above great insistence is placed on recognizing the reliability of the dynamics fueling the new "exegetical procedures." He affirms that "the knowledge of this dynamic is shown to be fundamental today in order to grasp adequately the witness of the New Testament and in order to be able to develop a theology animated by Sacred Scripture" (ibid., p. 15) grounded effectively, as also de Fiores expressly asserts, on the "rabbinic method of interpreting Scripture with Scripture" (S. de Fiores, *Teologia biblica e Mariologia*, in the supplement to *Theotokos* 9 [2001] 43). Thus one comes to rely on rabbinic interpretations, declared opponents of Christian Tradition and hence of the Word of God. On these same contorted "procedures" of the new exegesis, see also D. Scaiola, *Testi tradizionali rivisitati (Gen 3, 15; Is 7, 14)*, in *Theotokos* 8 (2000) 551–568. But could not the tortuous character of these new types of exegetical research in reality, confirm the truth of Wisdom: "Perverse counsels separate a man from God" (Wis 1:3)?

20 Cf. Feuillet, "De fundamento mariologiae," p. 44.

21 Cf. D. Judant, "Maria figlia di Levi o figlia di Davide?," *Renovatio* 10 (1975): 303–329, 451–471; J. Masson, *Jésus fils de David dans les généalogies de saint Mathieu et de saint Luc* (Paris, 1982).

Finally, the relation between the prophecy of Isaiah and that of Genesis is not to be overlooked. Mattioli writes: "The reference of the Isaiah text to the *Protoevangelium* (Gen 3:15) seems clearly evident. The mother and son, the Almah and the Emmanuel, announced by Isaiah, appear neither more nor less than further delineations of the 'woman' and of the 'seed,' the *Iššāh* and the *Zera*, promised in Genesis."[22]

In regard to Isaiah's prophecy, however, there remains one difficulty that no scholar can avoid. How can Ahaz verify the "sign" the prophet offers, if the "sign" will come to pass only eight centuries later? The difficulty can be resolved in this way. Isaiah in prophesying does not address himself to Ahaz, but to the "house of David" (7:13), because the prophecy was intended to serve a far broader and weightier end, namely, that the Lord would keep his promise to preserve the line of David and to make David's throne "for ever" stable through the Emmanuel.

It can be objected further that in this case the prophet's word ill accords with his other assertion foretelling that the Assyrians would devastate the kingdom of Judah, an event in fact transpiring shortly after.

This objection can be met by taking account of the so-called "prophetic perspective," not uncommon in prophecies,[23] according to which the prophet foretells the future, juxtaposing events of the near and distant future without giving any specification of time differentials,

---

22 Mattioli, *Dio e l'uomo*, p. 393; cf. also *idem*, "La dottrina di Isaia nella prima sezione del suo libro (1–12)," *Rivista Biblica* 12 (1964): 387–388.

23 Cf. E. Tobac and J. Coppens, *Les prophètes d'Israel* (Malines, 1932), pp. 64–70; Rolla, *Il messaggio della salvezza*, p. 513. "The chronological difficulty can be explained by the prophet's lack of perspective," writes A. Penna in *A New Catholic Commentary on Holy Scripture* (New York, 1984), p. 576.

stressing rather the content and meaning of the prophetic message.

At this juncture, and by way of conclusion, we might also raise a basic point of speculation in theological exegesis, namely, whether it be possible to defend the messianic and Marian content of Isaiah's prophecy by applying it in the exclusively literal sense to the Messiah and His Mother, this solely on grounds strictly exegetical, prescinding from the interpretation above all of St. Matthew and St. Luke, as well as from that of the holy Fathers and of the Magisterium, of the liturgy and of sacred art.

The authoritative biblicist, F. Ceuppens, claims such is possible.

> Prescinding from the texts of St. Matthew and St. Luke and the patristic tradition, we can conclude after critical examination that the text of the prophecy of Isaiah 7:14, taken as such, designates the Messiah and His Mother in the literal sense: Mary shall conceive and bear her Son without loss of her virginity. She is a virgin in conceiving, and she is a virgin in bearing her Son. Therefore, the assertion that the Church's belief in the virginal conception and birth of Christ is based upon a false version and interpretation of the text of Isaiah is a claim that cannot be defended. It is entirely gratuitous, without scholarly support.[24]

The same author confirms that "in regard to Marian doctrine, we can conclude thus: the dogma of our Faith concerning the virginity of the Blessed Virgin Mary in the conception and in the parturition of her divine Son was foretold in this prophecy of Isaiah 7:14."[25]

---

24 Ceuppens, *De Mariologia Biblica*, p. 32. The author rightly finds in the prophecy of Isaiah a basis, authentically biblical, for belief in Mary's virginity, before and during childbirth. His well-thought-out, sound analysis is especially valuable for the dogmatic exposition of Mary's virginal integrity during childbirth.

25 Ibid., p.38. Cf. also the well documented article on the Jewish *Targum* by W.G. Most, *New Light on the Messianic–Marian Character of Isaiah 7:14*, in *Miles Immaculatae* 25 (1989) 54-67.

We too, then, may conclude with Vatican Council II: "This is the Virgin who will conceive and bear a Son, whose name will be Emmanuel."[26]

26 *Lumen Gentium*, no. 55.

3
The Woman in Travail

Micah 5:1–2

And you, Bethlehem of Ephrathah, who are so little to be among the towns of Judah, from you shall come forth unto me one who is to be ruler in Israel; his origins are from of old, from ancient days. Therefore, God will give them over to the power of others until the time when she who is in travail shall bring forth; then the rest of his brethren shall return to the children of Israel.

When the Magi from the East entered Jerusalem, the bright star that had been leading them on their long journey disappeared from their sight. Having lost their way for a moment, they wisely decided to consult local authorities so as to learn the exact place of birth of the long-awaited Messiah, heralded by the star that had been guiding them till then.

At the request of the Magi, King Herod "assembling together all the chief priests and the scribes of the people inquired of them where the Messiah was to be born. They told him, 'In Bethlehem of Judah, for so it had been written by the prophet: "And you Bethlehem, of the land of Judah, are by no means the least among the towns of Judah, for from you shall come a ruler who will govern my people Israel"'" (Mt 2:3–6).

Similarly, in the Gospel of St. John, we read that when the Jews were discussing the question of Christ's origin, some said: "Is the Christ to come perhaps from Galilee? Does not the Scripture say that the Christ will come from the seed of David and from Bethlehem, the village where David was?" (Jn 7:41–42).

Both Evangelists cite precisely this prophecy of Micah: St. Matthew in a more exact and fuller manner, St. John with explicit references to it.[1] Both Evangelists, then, ascribe a properly messianic (and Marian) sense to this prophetic text of Micah foretelling the Mother of the Messiah "in travail," and the exact place of the birth of the Messiah: Bethlehem of Judah.

Fr. Emmanuel Testa in a recent study of this theme writes:

> Both the Hebrew tradition and that of the early Christians were convinced of the messianic meaning of this text.
>
> At the time of the birth of Jesus of Nazareth, the Sanhedrin, asked by Herod where the Messiah was to be born, indicated Bethlehem, referring to this prophecy of Micah (cf. Mt 2:5). The critics of Jesus, known as the Nazarene, referred to the same prophecy, saying that the Messiah must be a Bethlehemite. (Cf Jn 7:41–42). So too, the rabbis of the second and third centuries comment on the text in the messianic sense; typical medieval exegesis such as that of Rashi and Kinki repeat the same point of view.[2]

The prophet Micah was a contemporary of the prophet Isaiah and lived in the days of Jotham, Ahaz, and Hezekiah,

---

1 We may add that St. Luke, although not expressly, also seems to allude clearly to Micah on the two points concerning the birthplace of the Messiah (Bethlehem) and the "woman in travail" (Mary). Thus, St. Luke writes that Joseph and Mary went to Judea "to the city of David, which is called Bethlehem," and that here Mary "gave birth to her firstborn Son" (Lk 2:4–7).

2 E. Testa, O.F.M., "I salvatori apocalittici di Israele: La Partoriente e il suo nato," *Marianum* 40 (1978): 39. Cf. G. Bernini, *Osea, Michea, Nahum, Abacuc* (Rome, 1977), pp. 221–234; A. Fanuli, *Osea il profeta dell'amore. Michea l'uomo della Coscienza profetica* (Brescia, 1984), pp. 150–179 (with the essential and current bibliography).

kings of Judah (cf. Mic 1:1). In Jerusalem, this prophet denounced the corrupt life of the city, its social disorders and cultic aberrations. The situation of the kingdom became progressively more critical before its devastation by the Assyrians, a disaster eventually followed by the Babylonian exile. Upon this stormy, desolate background, there rises like a rainbow the prophecy of "the woman in travail." She will bear the longed-for liberator who will reunite the children of Israel forever into one people.[3]

This Messiah–liberator, the prophet foretells, will be born in the tiny town of Bethlehem in the land of Ephrathah, not the Bethlehem of Galilee. Moreover, in the prophecy it is said that the Messiah's origins are "from of old, from ancient days." The expression from ancient days can also mean everlasting days[4] and thus would expressly indicate eternity, that is, the divine origin of the Messiah rather than merely His long descent from David. The prophet Micah, therefore, would appear to have foretold both the earthly and heavenly places of birth, both the human and divine origins of the Messiah.

This lucid explanation corresponds perfectly with the historic and transhistoric reality of the Word Incarnate. Nonetheless, it does not enjoy the support of the holy Fathers, who though unanimous in affirming the messianic

---

3 This is another example of "prophetic perspective." The prophet Micah juxtaposes the birth of the Messiah and the end of the Babylonian exile. Linking these two events is an effective way of showing that the Messiah is the true liberator and restorer of the kingdom of David. Cf. Rolla, *Il messaggio della salvezza*, pp. 634–635. For a treatment of a very important theme, namely, "the remainder of Israel," one can consult with profit the recent contribution of O. Carena, *Il resto di Israele* (Bologna, 1985, with exhaustive bibliography). An interesting Marian slant on the "remainder of Israel" is offered by S. Cavalletti, "Maria come 'resto' d'Israele," in *Nuovo Dizionario di Mariologia* [hereafter cited as NDM], edited by S. de Fiores and S. Meo (Rome, 1985), p. 514 (particularly in reference to the texts of Isaiah 4:3, 6:3, 10:20ff., 11:1ff.).

4 The Latin text, in fact, reads "a diebus aeternitatis" (from everlasting days). Cf. also Prov 8:23.

sense of Micah's prophecy differ greatly about whether to understand the phrase "ancient days" as indicative of the extra-temporal, divine origin of the Messiah. Testa, in his aforementioned study, concludes his analysis of this point, claiming that the phrase "ancient days" refers "simply to a remote past in antiquity, as is evident in other texts of Micah himself (cf. 7:14–20) and of his contemporaries such as Amos (9:11) and Isaiah (51:9)."[5] But Fr. Vaccari, to the contrary, clearly affirms that "the Hebrew expression can include a divine origin (cf. Is. 9:5) before all time, eternal."[6] This interpretation harmonizes quite well with the divine origin of Christ.

Meriting particular interest is the fact that Micah, rather than directly foretelling the Messiah, foretells His Mother instead, or more precisely, "a Queen–Mother whom God raises up from his people to beget a new king, at a specific place and time and so in reality."[7] Furthermore, in making this prediction, the prophet adopts a phraseology so exact that its meaning must have been perfectly obvious to his listeners: the woman in travail shall bring forth. This brings one to the well-founded supposition that the people were already well acquainted with the prophecy of Isaiah: "Behold, a virgin shall conceive and bring forth a son..." For the prophet Micah, the concise expression, "the woman in travail shall bring forth," was sufficient to make himself understood by everyone.[8]

---

5 Testa, "I salvatori apocalittici," p. 40. The same author cites another study dealing specifically with this text: A. Skrinjar, "Origo Christi temporalis et aeterna. Mic. 5:2–3; Heb. 5:1–2," *Verbum Domini* 13 (1933): 8–16. See also Bernini, *Osea*, p. 302, n. 5:1.

6 *La Sacra Bibbia, I Profeti* 2, Rome 1955, p. 307, note 1.

7 D. Colombo, O.F.M., *Maria nelle attese d'Israele* (Vercelli, 1979), p. 133.

8 The authoritative Fr. Vaccari also writes: "With the words *who shall bring forth...* Micah is certainly referring to the well-known prophecy regarding the virgin..., Isaiah 7:14, a prophecy with which he supposes his contemporaries to be well acquainted" (*La Sacra Bibbia*, vol. 7, *I Profeti* [Florence: 1958], p. 307). The text of Micah, writes B. Boschi, "is not as

P. Pietrafesa writes with considerable insight:

> The mother of the Messiah is unexpectedly introduced without prior warning by the prophet. It is logical, therefore, to think that the listeners were acquainted with this woman–mother of the Messiah. In other words, the expression, the woman in travail shall bring forth, is synonymous with the well-known Marian prophecy: Behold, a virgin shall conceive.... The Oracle of the great Isaiah had by now become so well-known that the merest allusion, e.g., the woman in travail, was enough to recall both prophecy and maternal mission of the woman, the virgin–mother.[9]

Finally, in the light of the prophecy already fulfilled, so in this prophecy as in that of Genesis 3:15 and in that of Isaiah 7:14, the figure of the mother is presented alone with her son. No earthly father of the Messiah–Savior is mentioned in any of the three great Old Testament prophecies. The Mother appears always as virgin mother. The "virginity" of the Mother is the ever-present, luminous backdrop for the event of the Annunciation and that of the birth of the Messiah. This virginity is an evident sign that

---

explicit as that of Isaiah, but it reveals how the idea of the Messiah, linked to the figure of the *mother* of whom the Messiah is to be begotten, is already deeply rooted in Israel" ("Maria nell'Antico Testamento," p. 23). "The majority of commentators," D. Ryan claims, "see a reference to Isaiah 7:14 and the mother of the Emmanuel, and by giving birth to the Prince of Peace (Is 9:6; Mic 5:4) she is most intimately associated with his work," in *A New Catholic Commentary on Holy Scripture* (New York, 1984), p. 711.

9 Pietrafesa, *La Madonna nella Rivelazione*, pp. 53–54. In his exegetical commentary upon Micah, Luciani also writes that the prophet "instead of speaking of an unborn child, speaks of the mother who must bring forth a child. The mother herself is presented veiled by a paraphrase: *She who shall bring forth*, the *jôlèda*. Micah takes the phrase from Isaiah 7:14, as scholars commonly admit today (H. Junker, in *Volume du Congrès* [Leiden, 1957], p. 194), and in this way relives the psychological experience of Isaiah, with whom the phrase originated.... This expression, as W. Wischer notes, *Die Immanuel—Botschaft* (Zollikon, 1955), p. 50, like that found in Isaiah 7:14 (where also no mention is made of a father), shows what importance is attached in the prophecy to the extraordinary birth of 'him who is to be ruler in Israel,' and it demonstrates that the manner of birth as well—not merely the name (Emmanuel) as has been affirmed—is a 'sign,' as Isaiah states in the text cited" (F. Luciani, *Michea, La Sacra Scrittura. I Profeti Minori*, vol. 3 [Turin and Rome, 1969], p. 34).

the Messiah is truly a new creation, the new humanity, the beginning of the salvific era: the Redemption.[10]

* * *

Contemplating the figure of Mary, Mother of the Messiah-Savior, in the three most important messianic and Marian prophecies of the Old Testament (Gen 3:15; Is 7:14; Mic 5:1–2), we may make this inspired and lucid passage from a homily of our Holy Father John Paul II for the Feast of the Birth of Mary our conclusion. It is a concise and marvelous synthesis of divine revelation in the Old Testament concerning Mary all holy:

> This very child, so tiny and fragile, is the 'Woman' mentioned in the first announcement of the future Redemption, whom God opposed to the cunning serpent: 'I will put enmity between you and the woman, between your seed and her seed: she shall crush your head and you shall lie in wait for her heel' (Gen 3:15).
>
> This very child is the 'Virgin' who 'shall conceive and bear a son who will be called Emmanuel, which means: God with us' (cf. Is 7:14; Mt 1:23).
>
> This very child is the 'Mother' who at Bethlehem shall bring forth 'him who is to be ruler of Israel' (Mic 5:1).[11]

---

10 Some have "read" in this absence of the father also the basis of a "miraculous birth," insinuated by the prophet Micah. "One thing is certain. There is only a question of the mother. The father is passed over in silence (cf. Is 7:14ff.). On the basis of such facts a scholar as authoritative as O. Porcksch asks whether Micah has not in this text laid the groundwork for the development of the idea of a miraculous birth. In any case, the arrival of the Messiah will not be simply in terms of a mere historical progression of events, but of that of a miraculous renewal provoked by God" (R. Vuilleumier and A. Keller, *Michée, Nahoum, Habacuc, Sophonie*, 2nd ed. [Geneva, 1990], p. 61.

11 Reported by Bertetto, *Maria nel Magistero*, p. 86. On the link connecting these three important Mariological texts of the Old Testament, see the interesting study of A. Feuillet, "La connexion de la révélation divine avec l'histoire du salut dans l'annonce prophétique du Saveur messianique et de sa Mère. Le Protévangile, les oracles messianiques d'Isaïe et de Michée," *Divinitas* 32 (1988): 543–564.

4
Marian Figures and Symbols

Our Lady, besides being the subject of prophecy, was also prefigured and symbolically represented in the Old Testament in a number of notable texts, particularly appreciated in times past and still present today in the venerable Tradition of the Church, in the Liturgy and in sermons, in pastoral practice and sacred art. In such wise, a preparation for her coming was realized. This was a preparation achieved gradually. It is one that can be discerned in the deeds or more significant personal events in the lives of particular women of the Old Testament. It is also one whose contours are brightly reflected in symbols rich in meaning for the mystery of Mary.[1]

Marian Figures

The Old Testament presents us other exceptional women such as Sarah, Rebecca, Rachel, Miriam (the sister of Moses), Deborah, Ruth, Abigail, Judith, Esther and the Mother of the Maccabees, who played an important role in the divine economy of salvation or in the journey of the Chosen People toward the fullness of time. Pope John Paul II states: "The Old Testament encourages us to admire

---

1 With regard to Marian figures and symbols, it should also be noted that the "*sensus fidei*" of tradition, of the liturgy, and of art truly assures us of a Mariological interpretation transcending the level of a merely pious accommodation. Fr. Pietrafesa writes: "Given the frequency with which Marian figures and symbols appear in the liturgy, in the works of ecclesiastical writers, and in the writings of the holy Fathers, it is only natural to wonder if such Marian symbols or figures are something more than simple accommodations by extension. If one considers that in the liturgy the Church is guided by the Holy Spirit, it does not seem correct to categorize their use in the liturgy as pious accommodations. It is better to call them symbols or figures for lack of better terms" (Pietrafesa, *La Madonna nella Rivelazione*, p. 72).

certain extraordinary women who, prompted by the Spirit of God, participated in the struggles and triumphs of Israel or contributed to its deliverance."[2]

Let us examine each of them briefly. First, naturally, is the figure of Eve, profoundly studied by the earliest Fathers of the Church, presented as the "antithesis" of Mary.[3]

Eve. Emblematic and, biblically speaking, primary is the person of Eve, *"Mother of the living"* (Gen. 3:20). Before the fall into original sin, Eve in fact had been destined to transmit to mankind, via generation, the treasure of grace elevating man to the dignity of divine sonship. But with the fall into original sin, unfortunately, Eve merited the bitter punishment described by Sirach thus: *"In woman was sin's beginning, and because of her we all die"* (Sir 25:23). St. Paul makes this still more precise: *"And Adam was not deceived, but the woman was deceived and was in sin"* (1 Tim 2:14).[4]

The restoration of Eve is brought to pass in Mary Most Holy according to the teaching of St. Irenaeus on the "recirculation" of divine grace.[5] Lost by the sinner Eve after her fall into sin, divine grace once again flourished in the innocent second Eve, Mary, ever immaculate and full of grace. In this sense, one comes to realize that the New Eve

2 John Paul II, *Donne impregnate nella salvezza del popolo*, in *L'Osservatore Romano*, 28 March 1996, p. 4.

3 On the figure of Eve, see the volumes of T. Carizzi, *La Madre di Dio nell'Antico Testamento*, Cerreto Sannita 1938, vol. II; L. Cignelli, *Maria nuova Eva*, Assisi 1966. On the Marian figures in the Old Testament, cf.: D. Barsotti, *Le Donne nell'Antico Testamento*, Turin 1967; G. Ortenzi, *I grandi Credenti della Bibbia*, Casale Monferrato 187; H. Cazelles, *Les figures des Marie dans l'Ancient Testament*, in *Bul. Franc. D'etudes Mar.* 30–31 (1973–1974), Paris 1976; G. Boggio, *Donne nell'Antico Testamento*, in *Parole di vita* 30 (1985) 337–344; E. Green, *Dal silenzio alla parola. Storie di donne nella Bibbia*, Turin 1992; P. Maiberger, *Le grandi figure dell'Antico Testamento*, Brescia 1995.

4 For a brief synthesis of Jewish opinion on the condemnation of Eve, see A. Serra, *Myriam figlia di Sion*, Milan 1997, pp. 20–41. On the text of Sirach see T. Gallus, *A muliere initium peccati et per illam omnes morimur (Sir 25,24)*, in *Verbum Domini* 23 (1943) 272–277.

5 St. Irenaeus, *Adversus Haereses*, III, 22, 4.

restores the old Eve. And in fact the *Fiat* of the first Eve to the request of Satan–serpent (Gen. 3:1–6) was repaired by the *Fiat* of Mary to the request of the Angel Gabriel (Lk 1:30–33). The Old Covenant with God, ruined by the sin of Eve, was restored by the grace of Mary. The pain of childbirth in Eve (*"You will give birth in pain"*: Gen 3:16) was abolished by the painless parturition of Mary at Bethlehem with the birth of the Son of God. Pain is likewise absent in Baptism at the rebirth of the sons of God, according to the interpretation of a verse of St. John's Gospel, 1:13, read in the plural in reference to those to be "baptized."[6] The personal cooperation, active and immediate of Eve in the fall of Adam into original sin (Gen 3:6) was neutralized by the personal cooperation, active and immediate, of Mary in the Redemption wrought by Christ. Hence, it can be said that the former was Eve, *co-sinner* with Adam the *sinner*; the latter was Eve, *Coredemptrix* with the second Adam, *Redeemer*, for our salvation.[7]

Sarah, the spouse of Abram (Gen 17:15–16; 18:9–15). She was the "free" wife of Abraham, unlike Hagar, the "slave." Sarah was sterile. That notwithstanding, she became pregnant by a miraculous intervention of God. She was the mother of Isaac, an only child, who became the father of a great nation.[8] Sarah, the "free," but sterile, spouse, is a figure of Mary, the spouse "free" in virtue of that true freedom from any subjection to sin ("*whoever commits sin is the slave of sin*" [Jn 8:34]). Mary, however, is not a sterile spouse, but a voluntary virgin who conceived

---

[6] On the interpretation of Jn 1:13, see I. de La Potterie, *Maria nel mistero dell'Alleanza*, Genova 1988, pp. 93–143 (Eng. ed. *Mary in the Mystery of the Covenant* [New York, 1992]).

[7] Cf. the interesting study of the biblicist Eugenio Zolli, *Da Eva a Maria*, Frigento 2004, rich in biblical and patristic references on Mary Most Holy as New Eve-Coredemptrix. Cf. in particular the biblicist Fr. G. M. Allegra, *Il Cuore Immacolato di Maria*, Acireale 1991, p. 76.

[8] Cf. Gen 11:29–30, 17:19, 18:9–15, 26:24.

and bore her Son miraculously, that is, virginally, by the working of the Holy Spirit. Further, she was the Mother of Jesus, an only child, who redeemed mankind, becoming Head of the Mystical Body, the "firstborn among many brethren" (Rom 8:29).

Sarah is the shadow of the New Covenant sanctioned by God with Abraham and sealed with the blood of the circumcision. Mary, instead, is the reality of the New Covenant established by Jesus and sealed by Him in His immolation as victim crucified for the Redemption of mankind.[9]

REBECCA, THE SPOUSE OF ISAAC (Gen 24). On many counts, Mary was prefigured by Rebecca, the spouse of Isaac, whose life was so rich in significant events, decisive for the history of the Chosen People.[10]

Abraham ordered his servant Eliezer to seek Rebecca's consent to become the wife of Isaac. In this prefiguration, we discern the plan of God the Father, who ordered the angel Gabriel to request of Mary her consent to the Incarnation of the Word. A special providence arranged all things so that Rebecca would become the bride of Isaac and mother of Jacob. A still more special providence directed history in such wise that Mary, the virgin of Nazareth, would become the ever-virgin bride of St. Joseph so as to be the Virgin Mother of Jesus.

When Rebecca departed her home with Isaac, her brothers addressed their best wishes to her thus: "May you

---

[9] Cf. CARIZZI, *La Madre di Dio*, vol. 2, pp. 9–96; T. KAYLAPARAMBIL, "Figures and Symbols of Mary in the Old Testament," *Biblehas* 3 (1977): 247–248.

[10] On Rebecca, cf. H. MARRACCI, *Polyanthea Mariana* (Cologne, 1710), pp. 569–571 (where is listed the testimony of St. Bonaventure, St. Albert the Great, St. Antonine, St. Thomas of Villanova, et al.); D. RUOTOLO, *Maria... chi mai sei tu?*, (Naples, 1975), pp. 87–91; KAYLAPARAMBIL, "Figures and Symbols," pp. 248–249; D. BARSOTTI, *Le donne dell'Alleanza* (Turin, 1967), pp. 27–34.

increase to thousands of thousands, and may your seed possess the gates of their enemies" (Gen 24:60). These congratulations will come true without limit precisely in Mary, Mother of the new humanity redeemed.

A masterpiece of maternal art, it was a stroke of genius on the part of Rebecca to dress Jacob in the clothes of Esau so that he might obtain for himself and for his descendants (from the moment Esau had sold the inheritance of the firstborn to Jacob) the blessings of his father Isaac. The significant Marian prefiguration of this event is explained thus by Roschini, who bases himself on the teaching of the Fathers: "Mary, with the consent given to the angel, induced the Word of God to clothe himself in human flesh, taking upon himself the iniquities of us all and presenting himself with them to the Eternal Father to gain eternal bliss."[11] Moreover, in this work of mediation between Isaac and Jacob, Rebecca is also a figure of Mary as Mediatrix of men with the new Israel, Jesus Christ, the Incarnate Word.[12]

Rachel, the spouse of Jacob (Gen 29). Rachel, the wife of Jacob, was of a beauty so singular as to enrapture the heart of Jacob. The beauty of Rachel prefigures the beauty beyond compare of her who, full of every grace, "found grace before God" (Lk 1:30), wholly immaculate from the first instant of her conception.[13]

---

11 Roschini, *La Madonna*, vol. 2, p. 102.

12 Cf. P. Mauri, *Maria SS. nella Sacra Scrittura e nei Padri* (Milan, 1912), pp. 44–45.

13 On the figure of Rachel see the numerous pages by T. Carizzi, *La Madre di Dio*, vol. 4, pp. 992; Kaylaparambil, "Figures and Symbols," p. 249; Barsotti, *Le donne dell'Alleanza*, pp. 35–41. In his commentary on Genesis, Ruotolo reflects on how the meeting of Jacob and Rachel occurred, not without special significance, as Rachel led the flocks to the well: "Rachel, in fact, who was leading her little lambs to the well, met Jacob and received from him the tenderness of intimate love. Rachel is a figure of Mary, the beloved little lamb of God and shepherdess of the flock which she guides to the fountain of living water. Mary it was who made Jesus open the fountains of grace with her love. Mary had received from Him the first fruits of the

Rachel was the mother of Joseph, who was sold by his jealous and envious brothers for twenty pieces of silver. But Joseph, conducted by Divine Providence into Egypt as a slave, eventually came by mysterious ways to obtain supreme power under Pharaoh, and so to become the savior of his family and of the people of Israel during the terrible famine of the "seven lean kine" (cf. Gen 41 ff). Joseph prefigures Jesus, the son of Mary, sold for thirty pieces of silver and put to death on the Cross, to become, with His death and Resurrection, the Savior of the entire human race enslaved by the sin of its first parents.

Rachel brought to light two sons, Joseph, her firstborn, and Benjamin. The birth of Joseph was for Rachel a birth in great joy. The birth of Benjamin, instead, was a birth in great suffering, and for this reason Rachel named the babe Benoni, which means son of suffering. Similarly, Mary Most Holy, in bringing her firstborn Jesus to light virginally in the cave of Bethlehem, was filled with ecstatic joy. As universal Coredemptrix, she was filled instead with suffering in bringing all of us, brethren of her firstborn, to the light at the foot of the Cross on Calvary.[14]

MIRIAM, THE SISTER OF MOSES. (Ex 15:20–21) Moses' sister is a figure of Mary, not only in bearing the same name, but for some other particularly interesting considerations. Miriam is the sister of Moses, liberator of the Chosen People, and she is the sister of Aaron, the first priest under the Old Covenant. With Moses and Aaron, she also had the honor of being present in the "Tent of Meeting," where the Lord would descend in the cloud and speak to them.

Redemption in her Immaculate Conception. Mary is ever the Mediatrix of graces and the Mother who brings us near to Jesus Christ and enriches us with his divine and tender love, in mystical communication" (D. RUOTOLO, *La Sacra Scrittura. La Genesi* [Gravina di Puglia, 1931] vol. 1, p. 502).

14 Cf. MAURI, *Maria SS.*, p. 50.

Moreover, she was called prophetess and was the directress of the choir of women chanting the canticle of Moses' triumph, after the miraculous passage through the Red Sea where the army of Pharaoh was completely destroyed.[15]

Very enlightening is the exegesis of Eugenio Zolli on *Miriam* in the "Tent of Assembly," together with Moses and Aaron, prophetess after the passage through the Red Sea. Eugenio Zolli comments on the text of Micah speaking of the people of Israel: "*I have brought you out in the land of Egypt and have redeemed you from the house of slavery, and have commanded you in the presence of Moses, Aaron and Miriam*" (Mic. 6:4). This brief text is of great importance from the typological and Mariological point of view. The work of redemption of the people from Egypt is entrusted by the Lord to Moses of whom a prophet said: "*And through a prophet the Lord drew Israel from Egypt*" (Hs 12:14). Behold how Moses, as on other occasions, is called a prophet and indeed is considered the greatest of the prophets... After the passage through the Red Sea "Miriam the prophetess" intoned, together with the other women of Israel, a hymn of thanksgiving to the Lord. Behold how one comes to understand the reason Micah places all three children: Moses, Aaron and Miriam, on the same level. The work of ransoming the nation Israel is accomplished by the Lord himself, but God also entrusts its execution to Moses... No other woman in the patriarchal context of Israel is ever indicated by the name of "prophetess." Micah places Miriam beside Moses and Aaron as *coredemptrix* of Israel from Egypt.[16]

---

15 Cf. Ex 15:20–21; Mt 6:4.

16 E.ZOLLI, *op. cit.*, pp. 91–92. Interesting and important is this comment on Miriam as *coredemptrix* of the people of Israel alongside Moses, prefiguring Mary as *Coredemptrix* of the new people of Israel alongside Jesus. Also interesting are his particular reflections on Miriam who "effectively from the day on which she saved the life of the child Moses, conducted a work of national coredemption on behalf of Israel... Mary, the Holy Virgin, assisted

"These features," writes Ruotolo,

> are enough to show us that the holy Virgin was obscurely foreshadowed in this woman. Mary is presented in the book of Exodus at the side of Moses and Aaron. The holy Virgin is associated with Jesus Christ not only as His Mother, but also in His work. That implies that as Mary was closely associated with her brother Moses, the lawgiver of the Chosen People, so Mary the Virgin was indissolubly linked to the Supreme Lawgiver Jesus Christ, of whom Moses was a figure and type. So too, the holy Virgin is at the side of Jesus Christ, the High Priest of the New Covenant, of whom Aaron was a figure and type.
>
> The first Mary is presented as a prophetess honored by God; the second Mary, the Blessed among women, is invoked by the Church under the title 'Queen of Prophets.' With the other women, the first Mary repeated the refrain from Moses' triumphant canticle; the second Mary lifts a canticle of praise to the greatness of the Almighty and prophesies, literally, her future glorification by every human generation.[17]

DEBORAH. In extremely dangerous circumstances, Deborah was the energetic woman who saved her people from the Canaanites, leading Barak, with a small army, to victory over the powerful army of Sisera commanded by Jabin. Deborah is above all a figure of Mary Most Holy. For as she had been Barak's active associate in the victory over Sisera in the salvation of her people, so Mary Most Holy similarly is the *alma socia* (beloved helpmate) of Christ in the salvation of mankind through the work of Redemption. With this work Christ, the Redeemer, assisted by Mary, the Coredemptrix, carried out and brought to completion the

---

by Joseph, by means of flight into Egypt, saved the life of the Child Jesus. Miriam, as coredemptrix, assisted her brother in the miracles he performed in Egypt, one of these being the change of water into blood. At the wedding feast at Cana Jesus, at the prayer of Mary, changed water into wine. In the Eucharist the wine becomes the blood of Christ Crucified. From His side flow blood and water" (Ibid. pp. 93–94).

17 RUOTOLO, *Maria... chi mai sei tu?*, p. 82. Cf. also R. LE DÉAUT, "Miryam soeur de Moïse, et Marie, mere du Messie," *Biblica* 45 (1964): 198–219.

plan of Redemption of mankind ruined by the original sin of the first parents. Fr. Pietrafesa writes:

> Deborah cooperated in freeing Israel from the oppression of Sisera and of the Canaanites. Mary Most Holy cooperated with Christ in freeing the entire human race from the slavery of the devil, meriting and satisfying with Him.[18]

Deborah is also a figure of Mary qua prophetess and merciful mother to whom all the children of Israel had recourse in their need. Mary Most Holy is the greatest prophetess. She is the true "merciful mother" whom the Church invokes and to whom all have recourse in hope and trust.

Finally, the hymn of exultation and thanksgiving sung by Deborah for the victory gained over the powerful and proud Sisera will reecho in the Magnificat of Mary who exalts God, the vindicator of the poor and humble over the powerful and proud.[19]

RUTH, THE MOABITE. "The Church sees in Ruth a figure of Mary Most Holy," writes Dain Cohenel,

> and not only in Ruth, but in anything in any way pertaining to this woman. In all the great sanctuaries dedicated to our Lady one can see, often on high, on the ceiling, on the walls, in the windows, a woman with a bundle of grain on her arm, and underneath a simple inscription with the name: Ruth. On the throne is Mary, the woman full of grace: on the walls is her shadow cast from the humble fields of Bethlehem in past centuries.[20]

---

18 P. PIETRAFESA, op. cit., p. 81. See also S. M. MANELLI, *Maria Corredentrice nella Sacra Scrittura*, in AA. VV., *Maria Corredentrice. Storia e Teologia*, Frigento 1998, vol. I, pp. 67–68.

19 Judg 4:4–24, 5. Cf. RUOTOLO, *Maria... chi mai sei tu?*, pp. 93–97.

20 D. COHENEL, *Maria SS. e le prove della vita* (Gravina di Puglia, 1933), p. 30; cf. C. M. GIMENEZ, "La mujer en la Biblia. Transfondo de Ia Anunciación a Maria en el libro de Ruth," *Cultura Biblica* 25 (1968): 230–234; RUOTOLO, *Maria... chi mai sei tu?*, pp. 99–111.

Ruth left her native land, Moab, and her parents, out of love for her mother-in-law, the pious Naomi. Thus, by a providential disposition, she merited becoming the wife of Boaz and mother of Obed, who was the grandfather of David. And so Ruth, an ancestress of David, is numbered among the ancestors of Christ.[21] Mary, too, from infancy, consecrated to God, enclosed in the Temple (according to an ancient tradition included by the Church in the Liturgy for the memorial of the Presentation of Mary, November 21), left her house and her parents. According to the mysterious ways of that plan of love whereby God willed to save mankind, she was prepared by the Lord to become the Spouse of the Holy Spirit.

Ruth declared herself the humble servant of Boaz who had chosen her as his bride. And Mary Most Holy, at the conclusion of her conversation with the angel Gabriel, likewise declared herself the humble "handmaid" of the Lord who had chosen her as His bride to complete the work of the Incarnation and of the universal Redemption.

Ruth, as one who gathered the grain left behind by the harvesters, is also the figure of Mary who succors the dispersed and abandoned. "The Fathers of the Church are of one accord," writes Mauri, "in telling us that Ruth, who gathered the grain left behind by the harvesters, is a figure of Mary who gathers to herself and brings to God the souls even of the most abandoned and despairing of sinners."[22]

---

21 On the figure of Ruth, see C. Lepre, *Il Libro di Ruth*, Naples 1981.

22 Mauri, *Maria SS.*, p. 90. The author explains who the "harvesters" are who abandon the "grain" by quoting a beautiful text of St. Bonaventure: "And who are these harvesters if not the preachers and confessors? O, truly great, then, is the grace of Mary, through whom are gathered under the wings of God's mercy so many of those whom the ministers of the Lord had abandoned as hopeless!" (ibid.).

Abigail (1 Sam 25). Ecclesiastical writers acknowledge several likenesses between Abigail and Mary Most Holy.[23] The name Abigail means exultation of the Father, and it is easy to discover in it what in reality Mary Most Holy is for God, namely, the creature pure and full of grace by virtue of her Immaculate Conception, the Restitutrix of our fallen human nature. Abigail merited the titles of "most prudent and beautiful," perfectly prefiguring Mary, who is universally invoked by the Church as "Virgin most prudent" and "all fair."

Abigail knew how to placate the just anger of David against Nabal, not fearing to "place herself between the anger of David and the iniquity of her husband," writes Mauri,[24] effecting this by her humble, kindly mediation. All the more so did Mary accomplish the same with her sufferings, which, united to those of Christ, placated the just anger of God against a sinful humanity. And today, with her maternal mediation, she still placates the just anger of her Son offended by sinners.

Further, for the riches of her virtue, Abigail was taken as bride by David, placed on the throne and constituted queen of the house of David. So, too, all the more so Mary, all innocent and fair, was chosen by God as Mother of the Word, Spouse of the Holy Spirit, and Queen of heaven and earth.

"Behold your servant ..." (1 Sam 25:41), Abigail said at the announcement of her election to be bride of David. Mary Most Holy at the Annunciation of the angel, who revealed her election to be Mother of God, also exclaimed

---

23 Cf. Marracci, *Polyanthea Mariana*, p. 3; Carizzi, *La Madre di Dio*, vol. 1, pp 9–87; Ruotolo, *Maria... chi mai sei tu?*, pp. 117–121; Kaylaparambil, "Figures and Symbols," pp. 253–254.

24 Mauri, *Maria SS.*, p. 176.

most humbly: "Behold the handmaid of the Lord" (Lk 1:38).

JUDITH. A people at the point of despair and surrender are saved by the bold strategem of a woman, Judith, who energetically and valiantly fights against the enemy Holofernes and triumphs over him, cutting off his head.[25] Judith is a figure of Mary who crushes the head of the serpent, with her Son–Coredemptrix aside the Redeemer, thus saving mankind. This directly recalls the celebrated prophecy contained in the book of Genesis: "*She will crush your head*" (Gen 3:15). Reading in the courage of Judith the courage of Mary, Ortenzi has written that Mary Most Holy "was the truly strong woman, especially on Calvary, such that the history of salvation represents her as Coredemptrix together with her Son for the salvation of all men."[26]

Strength and purity, beauty and courage shone in Judith. For this reason, she was honored with these classic words of praise: "*Blessed are you, O daughter, by the Most High God above all women on earth*; *and blessed be the Lord God, who created heaven and earth and who has guided you to cut off the head of the leader of our enemies*" (Judith 13:18); "*You are the glory of Jerusalem, you are the great boast of Israel, you are the great honor of our people*" (Judith 15:10).

In all these virtues and praises, Judith likewise appears as a figure of Mary, the "*blessed among women*" (Lk 1:42), the strong woman par excellence, the Immaculate, the invincible warrior who crushes the enemy's head with her

25 JUDITH, chaps. 8–16. Cf. also E. HAAG, "Epistola (Jdt 13:22–25; 15:10), Judit como de Maria," in *Asunción de Maria a los cielos, 15 de agosto* (Salamanca, 1967), pp. 39–49; J. ALONSO, "Sentido mariológico del libro de Judit," *Cultura Biblica* 16 (1959): 93–96; CARIZZI, *La Madre di Dio*, vol. "pp. 91–224.

26 G. ORTENZI, *op. cit.*, p. 44. See also: A. VACCRI, *La Sacra Bibbia*, Florence 1943; B. GILLARD, *Maria che cosa dice di te la Scrittura?*, Turin 1983, pp. 105, 109; D. RUOTOLO, *Maria SS. e le prove della vita*, Gravina di Puglia 1933, p. 146.

virginal foot.[27] To her, to the Immaculate, the Church joyfully sings: "*You are all fair, O Mary, and the original stain is not in you. You are the glory of Jerusalem, You are the joy of Israel, You are the honor of our people.*"

Esther. This young Hebrew girl was noted above all for her beauty, for which she found favor in King Ahasuerus' sight, such that he chose her to be queen. Moreover, after the publication of the edict condemning the Hebrew people to extermination, Esther was the sole person excluded from the decree of death passed against her people. Esther's most glorious deed was that of having saved her people condemned to death by the wicked scheming of their enemy, Aman.[28]

For her exceptional beauty Esther is especially a figure of Mary. Mary is "all fair," as the Church has chanted for centuries in Marian celebrations with the *Tota Pulcha es, Maria!* Furthermore, Esther is a figure of Mary because Mary alone did not fall under the universal law governing the contracting of original sin, to which all the descendants of Adam are subject by way of generation. Only Mary had the privilege of the grace of the Immaculate Conception by which from the first moment of her existence rather than being stained by original sin was completely innocent, full of divine grace.

Finally, above all, Esther is a figure of Mary, both because Mary, too, saved her people by triumphing over the infernal enemy through the salvific work of her Redeemer

---

[27] Cf. P. Maiberger, *op. cit.*, p. 116. Another courageous and intrepid biblical woman who can be compared to Judith in reference to Genesis 3:15 is *Jahel* who cut off and nailed to the ground the head of the terrible Sisera, the captain of the army opposing Israel (Judg 4:17–20; 5:24). See also Th. Kaylaparambil, *art. cit.*, p. 253.

[28] Cf. Esther 2:1–18, 4:1–17, 5:1a–8, 7:1–10. Cf. also R. A. Knox, *Esther and Our Lady* (Dayton, Oh., n.d.); Carizzi, *La Madre di Dio*, vol. 4, pp. 95–300.

Son,[29] thus redeeming that people from the condemnation pronounced in Eden, and because Mary, too, in the great need of the Church, the "new Israel," is a powerful Mother and Queen, Advocate and Mediatrix, always ready to intercede for us and grant us graces to escape from danger and punishment.[30] Ortenzi thus summarizes the point: "Esther is queen. She clothed herself humbly and penitentially to be heard by the king. Our Lady calls herself *handmaid* of the Lord so as to take her rightful place in the plan of God and become *Coredemptrix*, *Mother* and *Queen*."[31]

The Mother of the Maccabees (2 Mac 7). Scripture holds up for our admiration the Mother of the Maccabees, who courageously assisted at the martyrial immolation of her seven sons, supporting them in the supreme testimony to their faith in the Savior. The Mother of the Maccabees, in fact, was not only present, but, as the biblical text declares: "exhorted each of them in the language of their forefathers with these words: *I do not know how you came in existence in my womb*; *it was not I who gave you the breath of life, nor was it I who set in order the elements of which each of you is composed. Without doubt… the Creator of the universe in his mercy will give you back both breath and life, because now you disregard yourselves for the sake of his law*" (2 Mac 7:20–23).

The prefiguration in this dramatic event, which the Mother of the Maccabees provides us of Mary Most Holy as *Coredemptrix* at the side of her Redeemer Son, Jesus Crucified, immolated on Calvary is exceptionally enlightening. Mary, in fact was united to Jesus "by a close and indissoluble bond" as Vatican II teaches (*Lumen*

29 Ortenzi, *op. cit.*, p. 42.
30 Cf. P. Maiberger, *op. cit.*, p. 52.
31 Ortenzi, *op. cit.*, p. 42.

Gentium, no. 53). For she had consecrated "herself totally as Handmaid of the Lord to the person and work of her Son, serving the mystery of Redemption under Him and with Him (*Lumen Gentium,* no. 56).

Pope John Paul II also presents the Mother of the Maccabees as a prefiguration of Mary the Sorrowful Mother who shares the passion of her Son and offers Him as propitiatory victim to the Father, cooperating and co-immolating herself for the universal Redemption "with an unshakeable faith, a hope without limits and a heroic courage,"[32] as true "Coredemptrix of mankind."[33]

Abraham and Isaac (Gen 22:1). The coredemptive theme evident in the Mother of the Maccabees as a type of Mary Most Holy is even more apparent in Abraham as a type of the Mother of God on Calvary. Whereas most of the preceding figures of Mary have been women, we now encounter in Abraham a masculine figure or type of the virgin. Indeed in the Litany of Loreto Our Lady is invoked as Queen of Patriarchs: Adam, Noah, and above all Abraham. The Roman Canon of the Mass mentions three Old Testament types anticipating in some way the Redemptive Sacrifice of Christ: the just Abel, the patriarch Abraham and the high priest Melchisedech. Clearly enough Abel typifies Christ as victim; Melchisedech typifies Christ as priest. Abraham however typifies not Christ, but Mary his Mother who offers Him as the true Isaac. Thus the text of Genesis reads: *God said, "take your only son Isaac whom you loved and go into the district of Moriah, and there offer him on the hill which I shall point out to you"* (Gen 22:2–3).

---

32 John Paul II, *La Donna, un'alleata preziosa di Dio*, in *L'Osservatore Romano*, 11 April 1996, p. 4. See also D. Ruotolo, *La Sacra Scrittura. I e II Libro dei Maccabei*, vol. XIX, Naples 1986 p. 329–332.

33 *Insegnamenti di Giovanni Paulo II*, Vatican City 1985, vol. VIII/1, p. 319.

Moriah, which means land of vision, is in fact a part of the mountain on which Jerusalem is built. According to well authenticated tradition it is the exact place where Solomon built his famous temple. Other peaks of the same mountain are that on which David built the city of Zion and that which is known as Calvary. Hence, where Abraham was commanded to sacrifice his dearly beloved heir is the same place where later the Virgin Mary carried out her obedience of faith professed at the Annunciation: *behold the handmaid of the Lord, be it done to me according Thy word.* It becomes clear, therefore, that the typology contained in the figures of Abraham and Isaac, fulfilled in Mary and Christ, is precisely that of *Coredemptrix–Redeemer.* And in view of this the reference to Abraham in the Canon of the Mass is in fact a Marian reference based on the mystery of the Coredemption.

In the text of Genesis it is above all Abraham's faith which is put to test by God. Isaac was conceived miraculously in order that he might receive for himself and his descendants the heritage promised to Abraham, a promise paradoxically only to be realized via sacrifice of himself. In this sacrifice the faith of Abraham is an active influence, without which the promise will not be realized. The faith of Abraham here contrasts with the infidelity of Eve, and anticipates the perfect faith of Mary on Calvary as Coredemptrix, who under and with her Son offers the redemptive sacrifice for the salvation of the rest of his brethren.

Pope John Paul II refers to this typology in an important passage of the Encyclical *Redemptoris Mater*: "Mary's faith can also be compared to that of Abraham, whom St. Paul calls 'our father in faith' (cf. Rom 4:12). In the salvific economy of God's revelation, Abraham's faith constitutes the beginning of the Old Covenant; Mary's faith at the

Annunciation inaugurates the New Covenant.[34] Just as Abraham 'in hope believed against hope, that he should become the father of many nations' (cf. Rom 4:18), so Mary, at the Annunciation, having professed her virginity ('How shall this be, since I have no husband?') believed that through the power of the Most High, by the power of the Holy Spirit, she would become the Mother of God's Son in accordance with the angel's revelation: 'The child to be born will be called holy, the Son of God' (Lk 1:35)."[35]

We find in fact many comments on this Sacrifice of Abraham in the New Testament. Thus St. Paul in chapter 4 of Romans, in Galatians 3:1 – 4:31 and again in Hebrews

---

34 The comments of Feuillet on this point are especially instructive. "With Mary we reach the heights of Christian faith (obviously the human soul of Jesus enjoying on earth the beatific vision could not have the virtue of faith)... More than any other soul Mary experienced the adventure of faith.

"In her life, there is above all the great adventure entailed by her commitment to virginity. With this act she accomplished something more than Abraham in offering his son Isaac. Our father in faith sacrificed his first born, a being who was the better part of himself, but he did not sacrifice his whole self, nor for always. Promising God to remain a virgin, Mary offered herself without reservations and without possibility of return. She offered to God not only her body, but also her noblest faculties, mind and heart, because this is what it means to be a virgin: think only of God, love him alone, and live in the spoliation and ignorance of self, as it were an everlasting holocaust...

"No one before the Blessed Virgin had found the courage to make this kind of oblation, conferring on it so profound a meaning. Abraham opened the series of believers; Mary opened that of perfect believers, of those who after her example would have the courage to risk all for all, because this is the nature of virginity: risk all to meet Him who is All.": A. Feuillet, *Maria, Madre del Messia, Madre della Chiesa* (Milan 2004) pp. 57–58.

35 *Redemptoris Mater,* n. 14. For a commentary on this paragraph of this Encyclical cf. J. Ferrer Arellano, *The Immaculate Conception as Condition of Possibility for the Coredemption*, in *Mary at the Foot of the Cross* V (New Bedford 2005) pp. 128–131. There exist many references in the Papal Magisterium to Abraham and his sacrifice as a type of Mary and her sacrifice, that is to say the sacrifice of the Coredemptrix:, Leo XIII, *Jucunda Semper*, Benedict XV, *Inter Sodalicia*, Pius XI, *Miserentissimus Redemptor*, Pius XII, *Mystici Corporis* and *Ad coeli Reginam*. Cf. L. Deiss, *Mary Daughter of Sion* (Collegeville, MN 1972) p. 21, n. 11. It is interesting that in all of these citations Abraham is primarily a figure of Mary, not of the heavenly Father.

It is not, therefore, the Father who suffers but Mary as Coredemptrix. B. Forte is wrong in using the figure of Abraham to justify his false theory concerning the suffering of the Father at the crucifixion of Jesus. Cf. B. Forte, *Trinità come storia*, (Cinisello Balsamo 1983) p. 37.

11:8–12, 17–19, refers to Abraham's faith in discussing the role of faith in justification. It is obvious that he is not talking about the fiducial faith of Martin Luther, but of an objective faith. The object of this faith, the good work of charity, is to believe and to hope against hope and so carry out the command of God to sacrifice the only apparent natural guarantee of an eternal future. Further, when the typology is realized in the fullness of time (Gal 4:4), it is precisely through the Woman. Her unique contribution makes the difference between remaining in the slavery of sin and infidelity and entering the freedom of the sons of God who thereby share in the fruits of the sacrifice of Abraham–Isaac, of Mary–Christ, of the Coredemptrix–Redeemer. St. James also refers to the same point: ch. 3:20–26, of his letter so often cited as critical of St. Paul. In fact, the two Apostles agree.

Our Lord in Jn 8:48–59 also comments on this famous passage during his reply to violent criticism. He said: "Abraham your father rejoiced that he was to see my day. He saw it and was glad" (v. 56). Moriah, according to St. Jerome, means "land of vision." Therefore the sense is Abraham by faith saw or knew in the typology the mystery of the Redeemer–Coredemptrix. We know even more perfectly by faith: not in the type so much as in the reality symbolized by the type. Thus in beholding the Cross, or better yet adoring the consecrated Host at Mass we, too, see and rejoice.

Our Lady, too, in her *Magnificat* says that "My spirit rejoices in God my Savior." Does not this seem an implicit reference to Abraham believing and seeing Christ's day? The last verse of the *Magnificat* concludes: "Even as he spoke to our fathers, to Abraham and to his posterity forever" (cf. Lk 1:46–55). St. Paul insists (Gal 3:16) that *posterity* is here to be understood first in the singular. Therefore, first Our Lady, and then through Our Lady's maternal mediation, as Pope John Paul II underscores, we share in the blessings promised to Abraham.[36] Fr. Lucien Deiss writes: "It is precisely this central position that Mary's Motherhood holds: it encompasses both the fulfillment of the Old Testament tradition and the inauguration of the messianic era. Mary is to Christ and to the New Testament what Abraham is to Isaac and to the time of promise."[37] Hence, the importance of the genealogies of our Lord in the Gospels of St. Matthew (1:1–16) and of St. Luke (3:23–38). Both Adam (in that of St. Luke) and Abraham (in that of St. Matthew) show how the entire human family and especially the chosen people are linked historically to the Savior and His redemptive Sacrifice on Calvary through Mary.

Marian Symbols

In the dogmatic bull *Ineffabilis Deus*, Pope Pius IX surveys the most significant Marian symbols of the Old Testament applied across the centuries to the Immaculate Virgin in tradition, in the liturgy, and in sacred art thus:

> The Virgin's singular and magnificent triumph, her innocence, her exceptional purity and sanctity, her immunity from every stain of sin, and finally her inexpressible richness and greatness in every grace, her virtues, and celestial privileges the holy Fathers contemplated: in the ark of Noah, which built by command of God remained completely secure and intact in the midst of great disaster; in the ladder, whose summit Jacob saw touching heaven, upon whose steps the angels of God were ascending and descending, and at whose

36 Cf. J. Lemann, *La Vergine Maria, Presentata All'Amore del Secolo XX* (Rome 1901) pp. 437–530. Few commentaries can better the exegetical, theological and spiritual reflections of this priest, a convert from Judaism, with an excellent grasp of the Old Testament in Hebrew.

37 L. Deiss, *Mary Daughter of Sion*, p. 19.

summit God himself was seen; in the bush, which Moses saw all aflame in the holy place, and yet notwithstanding the intense flames the bush, neither consumed nor damaged, remained verdant and in full bloom; in the invincible tower, which no enemy can take and from which hang a thousand bucklers and all the armor of the valiant warrior; in the closed garden, which can neither be violated nor ruined by any artifice or deception; in the shining city of God, resplendent with divine light and full of the grandeurs of the Lord; and lastly in numerous symbols which, according to the teaching of the Fathers, foretell the sublime dignity of the Mother of God, her unsullied innocence, and her holiness free of any kind of stain.[38]

The importance and exegetical value of biblical symbols has recently been articulated clearly and authoritatively by Maurice Cogagnac. He holds that with the language of biblical symbol 'God leads you into the heart of things in order that the theologian and contemplative might penetrate God's own mystery.'[39]

Far from indicating a diminution of content or weakness in meaning, the language of biblical symbol has a consistent value and distinctive incisiveness of expression which cannot not illumine the mind, animate the sentiments and enrich the soul with a more concrete grasp of reality. Every symbol is a word pregnant with understanding of and feeling for what is.

Cogagnac explains: 'the concreteness of the symbol is the very substance of biblical language. The Hebrew language is marvelously apt for this incarnation. In such wise the word of God comes to be articulated fully in each of its potential tonalities. The great mirror of the world and all the facets of the human heart disclose their riches so as to lead man into the presence of God. The Lord who created the world by His Word, makes of all things his word. Thus he formulated

---

38 *Ineffabilis Deus*. Pope Pius IX also mentions other biblical images referring to Mary Most Holy: lily among thorns, virgin earth, splendid, well-tended garden, incorruptible wood, tomb of immortality... (cf. ibid., pp. 47–48).

39 M. Cogagnac, *I simboli biblici. Precorsi spirituali* (Bologna 1998) p. 9.

a message addressed to the whole of man: to his intelligence, to his sensivity, to his sense of beauty.'[40]

Hence, Marian biblical symbolism in the Old Testament serves to enrich suggestively our understanding of the great Marian dogmas and the great truths of faith concerning the mysteries of Mary, illuminating the transcendent enveloping the person and the entire mission of the Mother of God and of men. That symbolism thus confers on Mariology 'a warmth and concreteness lacking in a merely rational elaboration.'[41] As the scholar Mircea Eliade has written, every symbol in fact 'reveals determined aspects of reality, those most profound, those eluding other methods of study.'[42] Or, as R. Riva says: 'the symbol in communication gives expression to the inexpressible,'[43] and can, as L. Murillo maintains, trace a suggestive 'way of beauty' in Mariology.[44]

The riches of biblical Marian symbolism have been assembled and set in relief by various scholars: in addition to those just cited, L. Bartoli,[45] F. Elizondo,[46] Ch. Bernard,[47] S. Babolin,[48] M. Lurker.[49] In a more particular way this symbolism has also been the object of research and of

---

40 Ibid.

41 M. J. Lopez Perez, *Simbolos naturales asociados a la figura de Maria*, in *Ephemerides Mariologicae* 45 (1995) 378.

42 M. Eliade, *Immagini e simboli. Saggi sul simbolismo magico-religioso*, Milan 1981, p. 16 [English Original: *Images and Symbols*, Princeton 1991].

43 R. Riva, *Simbolo*, in *Dizionario di teologia biblica*, Cinisello Balsamo 1989, p. 1478.

44 I. Murillo, *El camino de la bellezza en mariologia*, in *Ephemerides Mariologicae* 45 (1995) 193–205.

45 L. Bartoli, *Lessico di simboligia maria*, Padua 1988. In this work the author presents 233 illustrated Marian biblical symbols. Cf. also for further useful information the larger and more general work by the same author, *La Chiave*, Triest 1986.

46 E. Elizondo, *Simbolos aplicados a Maria*, in *Ephemerides Mariologicae* 45 (1995) 387–394.

47 Ch. Bernard, *Simbolismo*, in *NDM*, pp. 1293–1305. See also by the same author his fundamental work on symbolism: *Teologia Simbolica*, Rome 1981.

48 S. Babolin, *Il languaggio simbolico in Marialogia*, in *Theotokos* 2 (1994) 135–162.

49 M. Lurker, *Dizionario delle immagini e dei simboli biblici*, Cinisello Balsamo, 1990.

direct application to the great truths of faith concerning the mystery of Mary Most Holy, on which it throws a new and suggestive light, a mysterious light capable often of provoking a certain wonderment of the mind and enthusiasm of the heart.[50]

Mary, Ark of the Covenant

Of all the Marian symbols in the Old Testament, certainly the Ark of the Covenant enjoys preeminence. One of the readings used in the revised liturgy of Vatican II for the solemnity of Mary's Assumption body and soul into heaven treats of the Ark of the Covenant. Throughout the centuries, Christian peoples have venerated Mary under the title of Foederis Arca (Ark of the Covenant) in the Litany of Loreto. "The similarities between the Ark and Mary," writes Bressan, "are not merely verbal, and the comparison is rather to Mary's advantage. (Hence, the comparison is a case of extension of the literal sense.)"[51]

In fact, the Ark was the place par excellence of God's presence. The Jews even came to consider the Ark as God himself (Num 10:35), and God's presence was seen between the cherubim placed above the Ark. But the Ark was only a symbol. Mary, instead, is the reality of the *Ark of the Covenant* "which contains in itself not the word of God written on stone (the tablets of the Law), but the very Word of God, the *Logos*, made flesh, become her Son; which carries in herself 'not the flowering rod of Aaron, but

---

50 See also the essay of S. M. Manelli, *Maria nella simbologia biblica*, Castelpetroso (IS) 1999, in which are presented "a number of symbols richer in expressive value" applied to the fundamental truths of faith concerning the mystery of Mary. These are "the Divine Maternity, the perpetual Virginity, the Immaculate Conception, the universal Coredemption, the universal maternal Mediation, the Assumption in soul and body to heaven and the Queenship" (p. 12).

51 Bressan, "L'arca nel tempio di Dio," in Homiletica *La parola per l'assemblea festiva* (1972), no. 63, p. 65.

the root of Jesse'[52]; which contains in itself not the manna, figure of the Eucharist, but the very Body, Blood, Soul and Divinity of the Eucharistic Christ, adored by the golden Cherubim!"[53]

In her, God was really present, so much so as to become her Son. It is precisely "this presence of Christ, the Man-God, in Mary," Crocetti points out, "that brought the early Christians to consider Mary as the Ark of the New Covenant. In fact, the infancy Gospel of St. Luke (1:39–44) applies to Mary all that was said of the Ark in 2 Samuel 6:2–11. Compare, for example, 2 Samuel 6:9 with Luke 1:43 and 2 Samuel 6:11 with Luke 1:56."[54]

Finally, in the mystery of Mary's Assumption into heaven, in the splendor of glory, is realized most fully the incorruptibility of the Ark, perennial dwelling place of God.

Mary, Ark of Salvation

The ark of Noah has rightly been considered the ark of salvation for mankind when stricken by the universal flood on account of its corruption. "*The earth was corrupt in the sight of God, and it was filled with violence... for all men lived corruptly on the earth*" (Gen 6:11–12).

Submerged by the torrential waters of the flood, the whole earth and all mankind underwent the dramatic chastisement sparing nothing and no one. Only the *ark of Noah* and those who have found refuge there saved their lives and could commence their lives again on earth after

52 M. Lurker, *op. cit.*, p. 20.

53 S. M. Manelli, *op. cit.*, p. 13.

54 G. Crocetti, "La festa dell'Arca dell'Alleanza," in Homiletica *La parola per l'assemblea festiva* (1972), no. 63, p. 73. See also F. Elizondo, *op. cit.*, p. 392, with references to St. Athanasius and St. Maximus of Turin; S. M. Manelli, *op. cit.*, p. 13, with references to St. John Damascene and St. Andrew of Crete.

the waters of the flood had receded, and a most merciful God had made a new covenant with man (cf. Gen 7–9).

It is not difficult to perceive in the ark of Noah a twofold Marian symbolism linked to salvation. The first regards the person itself of Mary Most Holy, the only daughter of Adam and Eve conceived immaculate and full of grace. Only she, in fact, in the shipwreck of all mankind corrupted by sin, both original and personal, was fully saved by her Immaculate Conception, placed well above the tempestuous and destructive waters of the flood, "like that *ark of Noah* which sailed upon the tempestuous seas, the bearer of life and salvation in the midst of the devastating theory of the flood. So states the dogmatic Bull *Ineffabilis Deus* on the Immaculate Conception as a truth of faith."[55]

The second Marian biblical symbol here pertains especially to the salvific mission of Mary Most Holy on earth, as universal Mother Coredemptrix, on Calvary gathering about herself at the feet of the Redeemer the sons of Israel and bringing them salvation, just as the *ark of Noah* brings salvation to all those who found refuge in it. The teaching which this symbolism gives us is highly salvific: "Whoever takes refuge in the *Ark*, or gives and entrusts himself to Mary, will find salvation, recalling the verse of *Proverbs* applied by the Liturgy to Mary Most Holy: '*Who finds me, finds life*' (Prov 8:35)."[56]

---

55 S. M. Manelli, *op. cit.*, p. 18.

56 Ibid. On the symbolic riches of the Ark and of the flood, see J. Danielou, *Sacramentum futuri: études sur les origins de la typologie biblique*, Paris 1950. Particularly important is the assertion that the Ark of Noah symbolizes the Church, outside of which there is no salvation (cf. 1 Pet 3:19–21); so teach St. Cyprian, *De unitate Ecclesiae*, 6, PL 4, 503; St. Jerome, *Ep. 15 ad Damasum*, 2, PL 22, 355; St. Augustine, *Contra Faustum* 12, 14, PL 42, 262.

Mary, the virgin earth

Fr. Testa has written: "This is not merely one of many titles given Our Lady to underscore one of her privileges or virtues, but one indicating a hidden vein fecundating Mariology... This title has also influenced Marian devotion, above all in the Mother Church of Jerusalem."[57]

Suggestive in fact is the biblical exegesis of the *incipit* of St. Matthew's Gospel: *"Biblos ghenéseos Jesu Christu"* (Book of the generation of Jesus Christ). It is possible to find in this *incipit* of St. Matthew a correspondence with the expression *Biblos ghenéseos* adopted by the *Septuagint* in regard to the creation of the world (Gen 2:4) and of the creation of mankind (Gen 5:1), implying that the generation of Jesus Christ is also intended for us to be a new creation, a new generation. If, then, on this basis Jesus Christ is a new progenitor of a renewed humanity, the womb of Mary is the new *Virgin Earth*[58] which has made Him (*"Factum ex muliere"*: Gal 4:4).

The *virgin earth* from which was made the first Adam *directly* symbolizes, one might say, the *Virgin Earth* or Mary, from whom was made the Second Adam, Jesus Christ. The early Fathers of the Church, in fact, present and defend the Marian symbolic value of the *Virgin Earth* against the errors of their day, inseparably uniting Christ and Mary, His *Virgin Earth*, far more important than the first Eve taken from the side of Adam.[59] In particular, furthermore, the *Virgin Earth* symbolizes the Virgin Mary conceived

---

57 E. Testa, *Maria Terra Vergine*, vol. I, Jerusalem 1985, p. 2.

58 Cf. A. Feuillet, *L'Esprit Saint et la Mère du Christ*, in *Etudes Mariales* 25(1968) 40–45; A. Serra, *op. cit.*, pp. 64–65.

59 See the *Enchiridion Marianum biblicum patristicum*, Rome 1974, edited by D. Casagrande, wherein are found texts of St. Irenaeus, *Adversus Haereses* I, ch. 21; Tertullian, *De Carne Christi*, ch. 17; Methodius, *Convivium decem virginum*, ch. 4; St. Ephrem, *Evangelii concordantis expositio*, ch. 2; St. Augustine, *De genesi contra Manichaeos*, II, ch. 24. Also St. Proclus of Constantinople, *Sermo de nativitate Domini*, PG 65, 845.

immaculately and full of grace to conceive the New Adam as man–God.

Meriting particular attention is St. Irenaeus who explained theologically the Marian symbolism of the *Virgin Earth*, showing the primacy of the Second Eve over the first Eve. Fr. Lethel observes how "the theme of Mary as the new earth enjoys a priority literarily and theologically over that of Mary as New Eve."[60] Later St. Bonaventure takes the same position. Fr. Fehlner writes that Bonaventure "correlates Mary with the Virgin Earth as a figure preceding Adam, and correlates Eve with the Church depending both on Adam (principally)—cf. Gen 2:8–14—and on the earth (subordinately) for her existence. Here is contained not only the transcendence of Christ over Adam and Mary over Eve, but also the absolute primacy of the New Adam and the New Eve in respect to our first parents."[61]

Mary, Paradise of God (Gen 2:8–14)

In the ancient Liturgy *of St. James the Apostle* Mary Most Holy is called "Paradisus spiritualis secundi Adam" (spiritual Paradise of the second Adam), as Bartoli writes.[62] According to a great Father of the Church, St. John Chrysostom, as the first Adam "was formed from the earth which then became for him Eden or a garden of delights, so the new Adam was miraculously formed from the

60 F.M. Lethel, *Connaître l'amour du Christ qui surpasse toute connaissance*, Venasque 1989, p. 84.

61 P.D. Fehlner, *Il cammino della veritá di Maria Corredentrice*, in Aa.Vv., *Maria Corredentrice. Storia e teologia*, vol. V, Frigento 2002, p. 75, note 51 [Eng. original: *Immaculata Mediatrix: Toward a Dogmatic Definition of the Coredemption*, in *Mary Coredemptrix, Mediatrix, Advocate, Theological Foundations II* (Santa Barbara, CA 1997) pp. 259–329, here pp. 292–294 and notes 49, 50. The Italian translation is a revised and slightly enlarged version of the English.]

62 L. Bartoli, *op. cit.*, p. 171.

immaculate Virgin Mother who then became His Paradise and that of the entire Trinity."[63]

St. Germanus, famous Bishop of Constantinople, speaks of this Marian symbol "Paradise of God" in his impassioned homilies.[64] Otherwise in the Tradition of the Church "Paradise" has become a Marian symbol "eminently patristic," writes Roschini, citing in confirmation a number of Fathers of the Church such as St. Leo the Great and St. Proclus, St. Andrew of Crete and St. John Damascene.[65] Mankind lost the earthly paradise through Adam's sin (cf. Gen 3:24) but God the merciful Father had prepared another "Paradise" in the ever-virginal womb of Mary Most Holy.[66]

In biblical Marian symbolism, Bartoli informs us, the ever-virginal womb, or the womb ever integral and intact, is precisely an image of Paradise. It is sufficient to reflect, as regards this point, that the Hebrew root of the word *Paradise* means precisely a garden *enclosed, fenced, sealed.* Paradise and Virginity seem therefore to call out for one another, to attract one another and to unite. For this reason St. Basil of Seleucia can call Mary Most Holy *"Paradisus florentissimae virginitatis"* (Paradise of a most flourishing virginity).[67]

Mary, Gate of God—Gate of Heaven

In the Litany of Loreto we invoke Our Lady as "*Janua Coeli*: *Gate of Heaven*": the Virgin Mary, in fact, is the "gate" through which Christ came to us and through which

---

63 P.D. FEHLNER, *op. cit.*, l.c.

64 ST. GERMANUS OF CONSTANTINOPLE, *Oratio I in Praesentatione Deiparae*, 15, PG 98, 306.

65 G. ROSCHINI, *Maria Santissima, "Paradiso di Dio,"* in *Miles Immaculatae* 13.

66 Cf. S.M. MANELLI, *op. cit.*, p. 17.

67 L. BARTOLI, *op. cit.*, l.c. Cf. also C. BIESTRO, *The Enclosed Garden*, in *Mary at the Foot of the Cross* III (New Bedford 2003) pp. 172–222.

we go to Christ. The symbolism of the "gate" illustrates the truth of the "mediation" of Mary Most Holy who gives Christ to us and us to Christ, who therefore reopened, it may be said, entrance into the Kingdom of God. The Ambrosian Liturgy, in this regard, has an antiphon rich in depth and beauty, even if simple in its formulation: *"The Gate of Paradise was closed because of Eve; through Mary it was again opened."*[68]

The text of Ezekiel 44:1–2, states:

> *And he brought me back to the way of the gate of the outward sanctuary, which looked towards the east, and it was shut. And the Lord said to me: This gate shall be shut, it shall not be opened, and no man shall pass through it, because the Lord the God of Israel hath entered in by it, and it shall be shut.*

The Marian interpretation of the Fathers reads in this passage of Ezekiel the truth of the Perpetual Virginity of Mary Most Holy. The virginal womb of Mary always kept intact its virginal seal, as a sealed door kept ever closed.[69] St. Jerome writing at a time when that virginity was under attack says: "Some quite emphatically understand this closed gate through which only the Lord God of Israel passes… as the Virgin Mary, who remains a Virgin before and after childbirth. In fact, she remains always a Virgin, in the moment in which the Angel speaks with her (Lk 1:35) and when the Son of God is born."[70]

68 As cited by L. Bartoli, *op. cit.*, p. 176.

69 "A very large number of Holy Fathers, Doctors and ecclesiastical writers," writes Spadafora in regard to Ezek 44:1–2, "delight in interpreting this text in terms of the Perpetual Virginity of Mary Most Holy" (F. Spadafora, *La Sacra Scrittura. Ezechiele* [Turin, 1961], p. 327). This author cites expressly St. Jerome, Theodotus of Ancyra, St. Ambrose, St. Thomas Aquinas, St. Lawrence of Brindisi.

70 St. Jerome, *Commentarium in Evangelium Lucae*, PL 25, 430. Among modern exegetes, Ruotolo writes simply and clearly confirming the Mariological interpretation of the Fathers: "The eastern gate which remains closed to all because God is to enter through it, is, as the Fathers say, a figure of the Most Holy Virgin, who remained an immaculate virgin even after childbirth. For she had conceived and given birth to the very Son

In the teachings of the Greek homilists of the fifth century, the virginal childbirth preserving integrally the physical virginity of Mary Most Holy "is affirmed by all, without distinction," as Toniolo observes, and "they prove it biblically with the text of Ezechiel 44:1–2 (a text repeated concordantly)."[71]

"The vision of the prophet Ezekiel (44:1ff.), writes Lurker, "in which the gate of the sanctuary faces east and in which only the 'prince' can stand, is referred by tradition to Mary; of her Ambrose says: 'She is closed because she is a virgin; she is a gate, because Christ has entered through her.... This gate faces east, because she has given birth to him who rises, the sun of justice.'"[72]

St. Ambrose says further: "Mary is the good gate that was closed and was not opened. Christ passed through it, but did not open it."[73]

Hesychius of Jerusalem makes reference to this passage of Ezekiel (44:1–2) while commenting on the account of the presentation of the child Jesus in the Temple according to the prescriptions of the law of Moses: "Every male that opens the womb shall be called holy to the Lord" (Lk 2:23) and writes that Christ "precisely as Legislator fulfills His own law in a manner transcending that law: He does not in fact open, but leaves closed the virginal gate, removes not the natural seal, injures not the Mother of God, but leaves intact her virginal honor."[74]

---

of God become flesh" (D. Ruotolo, *La Sacra Scrittura. Ezechiele*, vol. 16 [Naples, 1986], p. 506).

71 E. Toniolo, "Padri della Chiesa," in *NDM*, p. 1067.

72 M. Lurker, *Dizionario delle immagini e dei simboli biblici* (Cinisello Balsamo, 1990), p. 163.

73 St. Ambrose, *De Institutione Virginis*, 8, 57. PL 16, 334.

74 Hesychius of Jerusalem, *Homily I on the Presentation,* PG 93, 1467–1478, quoted in *Testi mariani del primo millennio*, ed. by G. Gharib, E. Toniolo, L. Gambero, G. Di Nola, vol. 1 (Rome, 1988), p. 535 (to be cited hereafter as *Primo millennio*).

And in his turn, St. Proclus of Constantinople states that Jesus "as God does not break the virginal seals: in such wise He exits the womb as He entered there through the ear; thus He was born, as He was conceived: without passion He entered, without corruption He exited, according to the prophet Ezekiel who says: 'This gate will remain closed.'"[75]

In a hymn of the Eastern liturgy, we read: "Hail, gate of the King of glory, which only the Most High has passed (Ez 44:1–3) and alone has been preserved sealed for the salvation of our souls."[76]

Mary Most Holy, therefore, is the "Gate of God." The virginal Gate. The sealed Gate. The Gate ever closed. Through this "Gate" ever closed, God, the Word become man, came to us as Jesus the Redeemer. He passed through the virginal "Gate" of Mary, not only without injury to her virginity, leaving it integral, but, what is more, sanctifying her and making her shine with the brilliance of the fullness of grace, just as the rays of the sun passing through crystal do not break it, but rather make it luminous and shine with brightness.

Indeed, via the prayer over the gifts assigned for the first Holy Mass of the Common of the Blessed Virgin Mary, the liturgy, in its customary sober and limpid style, teaches us that Jesus "in being born of the Virgin did not diminish, but consecrated the virginal integrity of His Mother." In other words, not only in being born did Jesus not touch and not take from His Mother the seal of physical, virginal

---

75 St. Proclus, *Homily I on the Mother of God*. PG 65, 679–692, quoted in *Primo millennio*, vol. 1, p. 562.

76 Quoted in *Primo millennio*, vol. 1, p. 930. De Fiores also states that the great Fathers of the Church—St. Hilary and St. Jerome, St. Augustine and St. Peter Chrysologus, St. Proclus and St. Gregory the Great—liken the "Gate ever closed" that is the intact virginity of Mary to the "closed Door" through which Jesus passed and made Himself present among His disciples in the Cenacle. Cf. S. de Fiores, "Vergine," in *Nuovo Dizionario di Mariologia*, p. 1458.

integrity, but, on the contrary, precisely by being born, he enriched it and rendered it still more precious with divine graces, conserving it miraculously intact.[77]

Nor could it have been otherwise. It is not conceivable, in fact, that the Son should deprive His Mother of that concrete "sign" of virginity, which more than any other expresses both the totality of her consecration and belonging to God, and the truth of the virginal conception worked by the Holy Spirit. It could not be a "style worthy of God" to damage in His Mother the beauty and honor of her virginal integrity. Quite the contrary, we must believe that the Son would have done anything, performed any miracle, to guard in His Mother that pearl of virginal integrity. Just so, in fact, Severus of Antioch, one of the ancient Fathers, wrote that with the birth of Jesus the virginity of Mary "remained sealed by virtue of a miracle befitting the style of God."[78] Exactly: the miracle of the virginity of Mary Most Holy, preserved intact even in childbirth, fits characteristically the "style of God."

In addition to connoting the ever-intact virginity of the Mother of God, "gate" in biblical usage also symbolizes Mary Most Holy as the "Gate of heaven." Christian piety has employed this title in the Litany of Loreto, invoking Mary as *Janua coeli*, or "Gate of heaven," through which, with the Incarnation and Redemption, it is again possible for men to enter into the Kingdom of heaven.

Indeed, Anastasius the First of Antioch expressly calls our Lady "Gate of Paradise."[79] And the reflection of

---

77 Cf. *Roman–Franciscan Sacramentary* (New York, 1974), p. 768. Our translation adheres more exactly to the original Latin of this prayer and to the Italian version used by the author.

78 Severus of Antioch, *Octoechos. Hymn 117*, PG 6, 156–157, quoted in *Primo millennio*, vol. 1, p. 630.

79 Anastasius I of Antioch, *Homily II on the Annunciation*, PG 89, 1385c-1389b, quoted in *Primo millennio*, vol. 2 (Rome, 1989), p. 78.

Severus of Antioch is significant: "To you all of us address our prayer, to you who are the gate of heaven.... Through it we who had been expelled and put out, have again been brought on high.[80]

The two biblical passages commented on in this sense by the Fathers across the centuries are: "This is no other but the house of God and gate of heaven" (Gen 28:17), and "This is the gate of the Lord, the just shall enter through it" (Ps 117:20).

Evidently, then, the symbol of the "gate" can be referred both to the integral virginity of Mary to express the mystery of the Incarnation via the miracles of the virginal conception and virginal maternity, and to the very person of Mary as the mystery of grace, true "Gate of heaven" through which the Savior comes to us and men go to God.

Noteworthy, for their theological content, are the three antiphons assigned for the Mass of The Blessed Virgin Mary, "Gate of Heaven," included in the new Marian Sacramentary. The first, the entrance antiphon, proclaims: "Hail, O Virgin Mother, Hail, O Gate of Paradise: in bringing God into the world you have unlocked for us the gate of heaven." The second antiphon, at the Gospel, underscores the link between this gate and Paradise: "The Gate of Paradise," declares the antiphon, "closed by the sin of Eve, is reopened by you, O Virgin Mary." The antiphon for Communion, instead, sings thus of the Blessed Virgin: "Blessed be you, O Virgin Mary, resplendent Gate of light; through you Christ, the light of the world, came to shine on us."[81]

---

80 Severus of Antioch, *Octoechos*, 156–157, 161–162, quoted in *Primo millennio*, vol. 1, pp. 632, 633–634.

81 Cf. *Collection of Masses of the Blessed Virgin Mary*, vol. 1, *Sacramentary* (New York, 1992), p. 268; vol. 2, *Lectionary* (New York, 1992), p. 195.

Likewise in the celebrated hymn *"Ave, maris stella,"* our Lady is called *"Felix coeli Porta* [Blessed Gate of heaven]," through which all of us are encouraged to pass to enter happily into the Kingdom of heaven. And in the hymn *"O gloriosa Domina,"* our Lady is called *"regis alti ianua et porta lucis fulgida* [gate of the Most High King and shining Door of light]" to signify explicitly that through her has passed and comes to us the very King of Kings who wished to save us and bring us into His Kingdom. So, too, in the great antiphon *"Alma Redemptoris Mater,"* the Blessed Virgin is invoked as one who remains the *"pervia caeli porta* [the accessible gate of heaven]."

It appears clearly, therefore, that patristic exegesis and liturgical exegesis have interpreted the symbol "Gate of heaven" in a Mariological sense, specifically with salvific import for men, called to pass through this "Gate of heaven" to save themselves and so enter into the Kingdom of heaven.

Other Mariological Passages

It is useful, to indicate here other passages from the Old Testament that are interpreted in a Marian sense, even if their importance as to content and meaning is not as great as that of the principal texts.

Of all these passages, the more important are certainly the following texts: Isaiah's on the *Rod from the Root of Jesse* (11:1) and Jeremiah's on the *Woman Who Shall Compass a Man* (31:32). Both texts have been interpreted in a Marian sense by a fairly good number of holy Fathers and Catholic exegetes. They have seen Mary both in the "root of Jesse" from which the Messiah sprouted and in the "woman who shall compass a man," that is, who shall bear the Messiah in her virginal womb. It seems certain, however, that the Marian sense of these biblical passages is only implicit.[82]

Another significant text is that from Proverbs on the Strong Woman, interpreted in a Marian sense because of the impressive and splendid description it gives of the woman rich in many virtues, all found in Mary in an incomparably high degree.[83] Moreover, among the figures of Mary in the Old Testament, one should not overlook Anna, the mother of Samuel,[84] and Jahel, who transfixed the head of Sisera.[85]

Among the many lesser Marian symbols of the Old Testament, it is proper to recall some in particular, more expressive of the person of Mary Most Holy and of the mission played by her in the history of salvation of the human race. These are symbols employed in Tradition, in the Liturgy, in sacred arts here and there, some more others less, but a certain insistence and continuity across the centuries of Christian history to illustrate and celebrate, never to lament, the mysterious and ineffable reality of Mary Most Holy. We note with rapid stroke only a few.

---

82 Cf. Roschini, *La Madonna*, vol. 2, pp. 80–83, 85–88; D, Squillaci, "La Vergine Madre del Messia in Geremia 31:22," *Palestra del Clero* 38 (1959): 456–460; D. Bertetto, *La Madonna oggi* (Rome, 1970), p. 70. The importance sacred art places upon the "rod from the root of Jesse" is significant: cf. J. Fournée, "Les themes iconographiques de l'Immaculée Conception en Normandie," *Virgo Immaculata*, vol. 15 (Rome, 1957), pp. 46–60. In regard to the text of Jeremiah (31:22), Fr. Boschi writes: "St. Jerome understood it as directly related to 'personal messianism' with its explicit prefiguration of Mary's virginal conception. In this interpretation he was followed by such luminaries as St. Bernard, St. Thomas, St. Bonaventure, and various modern authors as well (Knabenbauer, Fillion, Roschini)" (Boschi, "Maria nell'Antico Testamento," p. 23).

83 Cf. S. del Paramo, S.J., "La Santissima Virgen, la Mujer fuerte de los Proverbios," *Estudios Marianos* 32 (1969): 109–124.

84 1 Sam 1:2, 1:9–20, 2:1–10. Cf Kaylaparambil, "Figures and Symbols," pp. 250–251; Barsotti, *Le donne dell'Alleanza*, pp. 89–96.

85 Judg 4:17–20, 5:24. Cf. Kaylaparambil, "Figures and Symbols," p. 253.

The DOVE with the Olive Branch gracefully symbolizes Mary who brings to a world torn by sin the olive branch of peace, Jesus, the "Prince of Peace" (Is 9:6).[86]

The RAINBOW is a sign of the end of a storm and symbolizes Mary whose coming into the world signaled the end of sin and the beginning of an era of redemption for mankind.[87]

The BURNING BUSH symbolizes Mary who in her virginal womb, as the burning bush that was not consumed, bore the Incarnate God, preserving integral and immaculate her virginity.[88]

The ROD OF AARON flowered without the intervention of natural causes and so symbolizes Mary's virginity, fecund without the cooperation of man. And even though she conceived and bore Jesus, she remained intact. Hence, she is called the "lily of the valley" (Song 2:1).[89]

The CLOUD bringing life giving water to the parched land of Samaria symbolizes Mary who bore in her womb the source of redemptive grace, the Word Incarnate, to restore life to the desert of this world.[90]

In addition, other symbols of Mary Most Holy are the *Golden Candlestick* (Ex 25:31–40), the *Fleece of Gideon* (Judg 6:36–40), the *Tower of David* (2 Sam 5:17), the

---

86 Gen 8:8ff. Cf. ROSCHINI, *La Madonna*, pp. 132–33. The author refers to Marracci, who "collected about 150 passages of the Fathers and ecclesiastical writers concerning the title 'Dove' in reference to Mary" (ibid., p. 131, no. 1) C. also CARIZZI, *La Madre di Dio*, vol. 5, pp. 19–26: KAYLAPARAMBIL, "Figures and Symbols," p. 255.

87 Gen 9:11–17. C. ROSCHINI, La Madonna, pp. 134–135; CARIZZI, *La Madre di Dio*, vol. 5, pp. 27–34.

88 Ex 3:1–11, Cf. L. CUBILLO, O.S.A., "Figuras Marianas en el Antiguo Testa mento. La zarza ardiente (Ex 3:3 sq)," *Cultura Biblica* II (1954): 271–274; CARIZZI, *La Madre di Dio*, vol. 5, pp. 47–58.

89 NUM 9:16–24. Cf. ROSCHINI, *La Madonna*, pp. 141–42 Carizzi, *La Madre di Dio*, vol. 5, pp. 75–84.

90 1 KINGS 18:42–45. Cf. ROSCHINI, *La Madonna*, pp. 143–44.

Throne of Solomon (1 Kings 10:18–20), the *Ladder of Jacob* (Gen 28:12), the *Golden Crown* (Ps 21:4), the *Crown of Stars* (Apoc 12:1), the *Moon* (Song 6:10).[91]

For the many references they make to Mary Most Holy, the Psalms could only be adequately treated in a separate chapter. Significant allusions to these have been retained in the present revised liturgical rites. It suffices here to remark how from the earliest Christian centuries the Greek Fathers[92] and the Latin Fathers[93] found in the Psalter, especially in certain psalms or specific verses,[94] lines of thought expressive of Mariological themes. These have ever since served to nourish efficaciously the Marian devotion and piety of the faithful.

In his study of the Latin Fathers of the second to sixth centuries, Fr. Calabuig notes that the Mariological interpretations of the holy Fathers "often assumed a cultic

---

91 For these and other symbols, cf. Carizzi, *La Madre di Dio*, vol. 5, *passim*; S. M. Manelli, *op. cit.*; Kaylaparambil, "Figures and Symbols," pp. 255–258; J. M. Calabuig, "Liturgia," in *Nuovo Dizionario di Mariologia*, vol. 3, pp. 775ff.

92 Cf. R. Masson, O.P., "L'interprétation mariale des psaumes chez les Grecs Pères," in *De primordiis cultus Mariani*, vol. 3 (Rome, 1970), pp. 242–262. The author concludes his study saying that the Mariological interpretation of the Psalms given by the early Greek Fathers, even though restrained, is nevertheless "significant when one relates that interpretation to the other, considerably richer Marian writings of these Fathers, and when one keeps in mind that the Psalms read in the light of patristic Christology in fact deal with the presence of the Mother of the Savior" (ibid., pp. 259–60).

93 Cf. M. J. Calabuig, O.S.M., "Repertono di interpretazioni mariologiche del Salterio presso i Padri Latini," in *De primordiis cultus Mariani*, vol. 3, pp. 263–90. In the conclusion of this study, the author points out that "during the second to sixth centuries the mystery of Mary occupied an important place in the Christian interpretation of the psalter. The almost seventy 'Marian' verses indicated in the repertoire demonstrate that this is so" (ibid., p. 289).

94 Cf. M. F. Moos, O.P., "Pourquoi l'Eglise appliqué-t-elle certains psaumes a la Sainte Vierge?," *Vie Spirituelle* 98 (1958): 186–208; L. Herran, "Maria en el ambiente de los salmos," *Sal Terrae* 53 (1965): 483–504; A. Peña Martínez, "Interpretación Mariana del Salmo XLIV, en La Tradición Patristica Latina de los ocho primeros siglos," Regina Mundi 29 (1969): 5–17; C. Bissoli, "Sta la regina alla tua destra," in homiletic *La parola per l'assemblea festiva* (1972), no. 63, pp. 106–16; R. Cavedo, A. Serra, and E. M. Peretto, "I canti dell'umile serva. Salmi 44 (45), 84 (85), 95 (96), 112 (113), 131 (132), 146 (147); 1 Samuele 2; Giuditta 16; Luca 1, 46–55," in *Il Lezionario Mariano* (Brescia, 1975), pp. 174–213.

character both in virtue of their form (homilies, euchological texts) and in virtue of their content (expressions of praise and admiration for Mary, exhortations to imitate her)." He concludes saying that "the time-consuming labor involved in listing all the verses in the Psalter referring to Mary is without doubt one of the more important contributions that the Fathers made toward the development of Marian devotion."[95]

Finally, from among the many Marian symbols of the Old Testament, it is only right to recall several others particularly expressive of the person and mission of Mary Most Holy in the history of salvation. They are symbols that tradition, the liturgy, and sacred art have constantly used, here and there, some more, some less, for the purpose of illustrating the ineffable reality of Mary Most Holy.

Lastly, one should also ponder the rich and suggestive Marian symbolism of the psalms. In this regard, Fr. Calabuig has written that "the vocabulary of the Marian verses and the imagery contained in them will help enrich euchological terminology and the Marian symbolism (earth, cloud, bridal chamber, sun, tabernacle, city, enclosed valley, hall, seat, rod…) of the liturgy, literature, and art."[96] More recently, the same author referred to the "Mariological interpretations of the Psalter as a patrimony" that remains "still normative in the Roman liturgy"[97] and, we may add, in the pastoral practice of important sectors of the Church.

* * *

Considering the immense Marian mosaic offered us by the Old Testament, so rich in prophecies, figures, and

95 Calabuig, "Repertorio di interpretazioni mariologiche," vol. 3, pp. 289–90.

96 Calabuig, "Repertorio di interpretazioni mariologiche," vol. 3, p. 290.

97 Calabuig, "Liturgia," pp. 773–75.

symbols foretelling, prefiguring, and symbolizing Mary, we may conclude, repeating with Fr. Roschini: "These are the chief figures and symbols of Mary. Beautiful are the prophecies foretelling her. Magnificent are the persons prefiguring her. Attractive are the symbols foreshadowing her. But the reality is incomparably more beautiful, more magnificent, and more attractive. It is like the sun that makes the pale, weak light of dawn vanish."[98]

---

98 Roschini, *La Madonna*, p. 147.

5
Marian Passages in the Liturgy

The liturgy is an important theological *"locus."* And above all, it is to the certainly not insignificant value of this theological "locus" that we are indebted for the Marian sense of other texts of the Old Testament. The liturgy reformed by Vatican II adopts a modest number of these Old Testament texts for use in Marian solemnities, feasts, memorials, and recurrences.[1]

To reduce, however, as some do, the use of such Old Testament texts to the level of mere accommodation not only does little honor to the liturgy, but also contrasts sharply with the genuine theological sense of the liturgy, which weighs and adopts each biblical passage of the Old or New Testament for liturgical use in the light of the revelation of Christ, of the fulfillment of redemption, and of the *sensus fidei* of the Church, teacher of truth.[2] "Mariology," Le Déaut affirms,

> cannot rest satisfied in regarding the Old Testament merely as a rich source of images applicable to the Virgin in an accommodated sense, more or less appropriate. The Old Testament contains a precise revelation about the Mother of the Messiah, even if it be in outline only. It is a revelation

---

1 Cf. A. Miorelli, S.M., *L'Uso della Scrittura nelle feste liturgiche mariane* (Turin, 1968); *Il Lezionario Mariano*.

2 On this subject, cf. C. Vagaggini, *Il senso teologico della liturgia* (Rome, 1958), pp. 354ff. (Eng. ed.: *Theological Dimensions of the Liturgy* [Collegeville, MN, 1976], pp. 455–486); A. M. Triacca, "Bibbia e Liturgia," in *Nuovo Dizionario di Liturgia* (Rome, 1984), pp. 175–197; A. Nocent, "La lettura della Sacra Scrittura," in *Assemblee* (Brescia, 1986), pp. 198–221. One should carefully note what *Dei Verbum* says of the Church as being always solicitous "*above all in the Sacred Liturgy to nourish* herself with the bread of life from the table either of the word of God or of the body of Christ, and to offer it to the faithful" (no. 25-italics ours).

> that appears in the New Testament, the fulfillment of the Old, and in the traditional interpretation of the Church.[3]

Sacred Scripture, the Church, and the liturgy always stand together, organically united in fruitful, vital ties by way of that Faith which saves man.

In treating the theological value of Marian devotion, G. Roschini appropriately observes that

> the liturgical prayer of the Church [her worship] is an expression of the Faith of the Church, a Faith that precedes liturgical prayer or worship, and therefore becomes a pledge of that Faith.
>
> Consequently, it is not the liturgy (with its forms of prayer and worship) that produces the Faith or the truths of Faith, but the Faith that produces the liturgy, i.e., the expressions of prayer and worship, as the tree produces the fruit, and not contrariwise.[4]

For this reason, it has rightly been written that "the liturgical interpretation of the scriptural texts has a theological importance of the first order,"[5] because it is a vehicle of the true Faith of the Church, and hence "Marian–liturgical formulae of worship, i.e., Marian prayer, do nothing else but express and manifest the Faith of the Church in the various truths relative to Mary Most Holy."[6]

---

3 R. Le Déaut, "Mane et l'Ecriture dans le Chapitre VIII," *Etudes Mariales* 22 (1965): 61. "If there is an area where the Church is certain of the Holy Spirit's assistance, it is precisely in the fundamental structure of her liturgy. Now, there is nothing so much in common to all Christian rites as this bond between Old and New Testament," writes D. C. Jean-Nesmy, "Per una lettura cristiana della Bibbia," *Communio* no. 87 (1986): 48.

4 G. Roschini, O.S.M., "Il valore teologico e l'efficacia pastorale del culto mariano," *Marianum* 39 (1977): 86.

5 I. H. Dalmais, "La liturgia e il deposito della fede," in *La Chiesa in preghiera*, vol. 1 (Brescia, 1984), p. 306. See also A. G. Martimort, "Struttura e leggi della celebrazione liturgica," in *La Chiesa in preghiera*, vol. 1, p. 160; Eng. ed.: *The Church at Prayer* (New York, 1968).

6 Roschini, "Il valore teologica," p. 86. Immediately afterward, the author refers to the example of Pope Pius XII, who in the encyclical *Mediator*

Thus, among the Old Testament texts adopted and interpreted in a Marian sense by the liturgy, besides the three basic texts of Genesis, Isaiah, and Micah, there are at least six others of major import. Of these, two have also been cited and interpreted in a Marian sense by Vatican Council II: the text on the "poor of Yahweh" and the text on "the daughter of Zion."[7]

Among the "Poor of Yahweh"

In the eighth chapter of *Lumen Gentium*, it is stated: "She [Mary] stands apart among the humble and poor of the Lord, who confidently await and receive salvation from Him."[8]

Various psalms describe the reality of the "anawim" of God, the true "poor of Yahweh."[9] They are the children of Abraham, humble and God-fearing, oppressed by men, but confident in the Lord who saves them. In the sadder events of the Chosen People, in the tragedy of the deportations and of the Babylonian exile, the "poor of Yahweh" realized the highest forms of Old Testament asceticism, and their proven fidelity made them that "remnant of Israel" from which was to come the renewed Chosen People, the Church of Christ.

Dei cited "as an instance of the famous principle: 'rule of prayer, rule of faith,' the fact that Pius IX, in defining as a dogma of Faith the Immaculate Conception of Mary most holy, included in the documentation a consideration drawn from the liturgy" (ibid.).

7 In regard to the two expressions "the poor of Yahweh" and "Daughter of Zion," it has rightly been observed that in the conciliar text "neither of the two expressions is accompanied by a reference. The two phrases express in fact a commonplace of Old Testament piety concerning 'the Daughter of Zion,' figure of the Chosen People, who will bring the promise to fulfillment in the fullness of time" (G. Philips, *L'Eglise et son mystère au deuxième Concile du Vatican. Histoire, texte et commentaire de la Constitution "Lumen Gentium,"* vol. 2 (Paris, 1968), p. 231.

8 *Lumen Gentium*, no. 55.

9 See, e.g., Psalms 9, 10, 11, 12, 34, 37.

In the Magnificat, our Lady placed herself precisely among the humble favored by God, who "has looked upon the humility of his handmaid" (Lk 1:48) and who "has exalted the humble" (Lk 1:52). At the Annunciation, while speaking with the angel and at the very moment when she accepted the sublime mission of divine motherhood, the Virgin Mary pronounced her *fiat* as a poor "handmaid of the Lord" (Lk 1:38). Socially and economically, our Lady was poor, living in a small town of no account ("Can anything good ever come from Nazareth?" [Jn 1:46]), hidden and ignored by all.

Vatican II itself notes that in the Temple, because of her poverty, Mary Most Holy had to make the offering of the poor.[10] This exterior poverty was a sign and figure of the great interior poverty that made her par excellence "the humble virgin," the model and teacher of the poverty of spirit the Lord Jesus in the Sermon on the Mount declared a beatitude: "Blessed are the poor in spirit, for theirs is the kingdom of heaven" (Mt 5:3).[11]

The Exalted Daughter of Zion

We read in *Lumen Gentium*: "After long expectation of the promise, the times were at length fulfilled in her, the exalted Daughter of Zion, and the new dispensation was inaugurated, when the Son of God took of her human nature, that He might through the mysteries of His flesh free man from sin."[12]

---

10 *Lumen Gentium*, no. 57.

11 On this point, cf A. Gelin, *Il povero nella Sacra Scrittura* (Milan, 1956), pp. 121–123 (Eng. ed.: *The Poor of Yahweh* [Collegeville, MN, 59641, pp. 121–123; F. Uricchio, O.F.M. Conv., "La povertà di Maria nella Sacra Scrittura," *Miles Immaculatae* 12 (1966): 175–184; da Spinetoli, *Maria nella Bibbia*, pp. 111–31; E. G. Mori, *Figlia di Sion e Serva di Iahvé* (Bologna, 1970), pp. 301–449.

12 *Lumen Gentium*, no. 55.

Zion is the "motherland" of those "poor of Yahweh" who made up "the remnant of Israel," from which was to arise "the new Israel." Mount Zion is a figure of Yahweh's eternal kingdom renewed in a new people, as announced through the prophet Micah: "In that day, says the Lord, I will assemble the lame, gather the dispersed, and those whom I treat harshly. Of the lame I will make a remnant, and of the dispersed a strong nation. And the Lord will reign over them on Mount Zion, from this time forth and forevermore. And you, O tower of the flock, hill of the daughter of Zion, to you shall it come, the former dominion shall come, the kingdom of the daughter of Jerusalem" (Mic 4:6–8).

Mary is "the exalted daughter of Zion," that is, it was precisely she who was chosen from among the humble and poor of the Lord to fulfill the ancient promises of salvation, establishing the "new economy," wherein mankind is ransomed, redeemed from sin, and "the former dominion" is restored.[13]

Originally, Zion was a fortress overlooking Jerusalem. It was the fortress conquered by David, who there built his royal palace and who also transferred there the Ark of the Covenant.[14] For this reason Zion was called "the city of David" and "the dwelling place of Yahweh." Later with King Solomon, Zion also began to be called the Mount. It was here that he had built the new temple and the new palace, just north of Jerusalem.[15] Finally, the word Zion came to indicate the whole of Jerusalem and the entire people of Israel, as is the case in various Old Testament passages,[16] other than that of Micah cited above.

13 Cf. Joel 2:21–27; Zeph 3:14–17; Zech 9:9.

14 Cf. 2 Sam 5:6–7, 5:9–11.

15 Cf. Is 18:7; Jer 26:18.

16 Cf. Is 37:32, 46:17, 52:1–2; Jer 26:18, 51:35, Ps 142:2.

As the "exalted daughter of Zion," Mary contains in herself the fulfillment of the salvific plan of God and becomes herself the personification of the new Israel, the true "dwelling place of God," via the Incarnation of the Son of God, who is to restore the kingdom of Israel with a rule to have no end.

In view of all this, the implications of the theme of Mary, "the exalted daughter of Zion" finds its richest, most joyful expression in the texts of Zephaniah (3:14–17) and of St. Luke (1:29–33).[17] In both, messianic rejoicing finds its outlet in the joyful cry: "exult." Zephaniah foretells the future coming of God: "Exult, daughter of Zion..." (3:14). In St. Luke, on the other hand, the angel announces to Mary the joy of the arrival of the Word of God about to take flesh in her womb: "Exult, O full of grace..." (Lk 1:28).[18]

Mary Most Holy and Wisdom

Certainly among the more sublime pages of the Old Testament are to be counted those describing Wisdom as a personification of God, as the Word of the Father preexisting and presiding over the entire work of creation.

---

17 Cf. Bertetto, *La Madonna oggi*, pp. 65–66.

18 The very interesting theme of "the Daughter of Zion" studied in relation to the New Testament, specifically Lk 1:26–38, has engaged and continues to engage the attention of the best qualified scholars in the biblical and Mariological fields. Their conclusions, however, do not always agree, as is clearly demonstrated in N. Lemmo's exhaustive review: "Maria, 'Figlia di Sion,' a partire da Lc 1, 26–38. Bilancio esegetico dal 1939 al 1982," *Marianum* 45 (1983): 175–258. See also G. M. Papini, O.S.M., "La Vergine Maria, figlia di Sion, modello della Chiesa e dell'unità del popolo di Dio," *Marianum* 37 (1975): 301–325; F. C. Correira, "Maria Filha de Sião. Alcance eclesio-mariólogico e dimensão ecumenica do titulo," in *Theologica* 4 (1969): 437–455. Of considerable importance is the attempt to present the theme of "Daughter of Zion" as "the biblical backdrop for the New Testament figure of Mary," as I. de La Potterie has done: *Maria nel mistero dell'alleanza* (Genoa, 1988), (Eng. ed.: *Mary in the Mystery of the Covenant* [New York, 1992]).

For this reason, these pages of Sirach and of Proverbs have been used by the Church, with appropriate distinctions, ever since the seventh century for the Feast of the Assumption of Mary Most Holy (Sir 24:3–21) and since the tenth century for the Feast of her Birth (Prov 8:22–35), whereas with the new Liturgical reform these were inserted into the Lectionary of the *Common of the Blessed Virgin Mary*, under the heading "*Mary, Seat of Wisdom.*"[19]

In particular, the passage of Proverbs, with its solemn beauty and sublime expression, images, and concepts, leads us to contemplate the origin of Mary in the eternal thought of God. Wisdom is transposed, by participation and reflection, to Mary, the Mother of the Word of God.[20]

A question is often raised at this point, however, whether such texts are referred to the Virgin Mary only on the basis of accommodation, or by virtue of some other more properly biblical sense, or at least whether this should not be considered altogether inappropriate. The opinion of those authors, who so decisively categorize this usage as mere liturgical accommodation to stimulate devotion, strikes us as overly hasty, and indeed odd. For they are well aware that Mary Most Holy was predestined by God from all eternity "in one and the same decree" with the Word Incarnate, as the bull *Ineffabilis Deus* clearly affirms, explicitly applying to Mary the words about Wisdom.[21]

---

19 *Lectionary for Mass, Common of the Blessed Virgin Mary*, (New York 1976) p. 828.

20 A. Romeo, "Maria e il Verbo Incarnato nei libri poetici e sapienziali del V. T.," *Tabor* 23 (1958): 323. Cf. also D. J. Alonso, "Marie et la Sagesse divine (Prov 8, 22–35)," in *Assemblées du Seigneur*, no. 80, pp. 19–28.

21 The original text of the papal bull is as follows: "Hence the very words wherewith Sacred Scripture speaks of uncreated Wisdom and represents its eternal origins the Church is accustomed to use both in ecclesiastical offices and in the Sacred Liturgy and to transpose to the origins of the Virgin who by one and the same decree was predestined with the Incarnation of divine Wisdom." Cf. T. Plassmann, O.F.M., "Uno eodemque decreto," in *Virgo Immaculata*, vol. 3, pp. 174–197.

Msgr. Romeo writes:

> Because of her intimate, active participation in the Incarnation of the Word of God, she [Mary} is clothed in certain measure with the mission and the prerogatives of the hypostatic Wisdom who 'has dwelt among us' (Jn 1:14). It is not a question of arbitrary accommodation, but of the 'full' sense postulated by the mystery of the Incarnation. Uncreated Wisdom, becoming incarnate in Mary, made her the center of the Truth and of the Life (Seat of Wisdom).[22]

Furthermore, it is truly difficult to admit that the liturgy, qua "rule of prayer," so closely linked to the "rule of faith," would, under the action of the Holy Spirit, make use of merely pious accommodations in order to enlighten and sanctify the faithful.

The remarkable fact, rather, is the constant application of these biblical passages over so many centuries to Mary Most Holy; a fact that "cannot be explained," as Fr. Pietrafesa rightly stated,

> at a level of 'simple accommodation' more or less appropriate, but must be evaluated at the theological level, precisely because of their use in the liturgy. This is to read the Bible with Christian eyes in the light of the wonders that God has accomplished in Christ and in the Virgin Mary. Hence, it is not surprising to find that the Bible contains a much richer, more extensive, and more profound sense unrecognized by the hagiographer and his contemporaries. This sense obviously presupposes the literal, but at the same time transcends it, enlarges upon it and enriches it.[23]

It is certainly not correct to write that "the Liturgical reform no longer inserts the passages on wisdom personified

22 Romeo, "Marie e il Verbo," pp. 327–328.

23 Pietrafesa, *La Madonna nella Rivelazione*, p. 64; note the important references there to some authoritative scholars, such as Bea, Vagaggini, Scheeben, Dillenschneider (ibid., p. 65, nos. 7–10). For a more extensive and documented coverage of the point, see E. Catta, "Sedes Sapientiae," in *Maria. Etudes sur la Sainte Vierge*, vol. 6 (Paris, 1961), pp. 688–866; D. Colombo, O.F.M., *Maria nei libri sapienziali* (Vercelii, 1979).

among the public readings approved for celebration in honor of the Mother of God,"[24] when exactly the opposite is the case. It suffices to examine superficially the biblical *Lectionary* for Masses of the *Common of the Blessed Virgin* as well as the *Lectionary* for the *Collectio Missarum De Beata Virgine Maria* to find therein the two main readings: Proverbs 8 and Sirach 24.[25] This is surely significant, because the Liturgy, a *locus theologicus* of great value, is indicated as an area of vitality and living expression for believers nourished and sustained by their *sensus fidei*.

"Thou Art All Fair"

Song of Songs is an allegorical poem on love. But what love? To whom is it addressed? The bride in Song of Songs "according to the most reliable interpretations of modern exegesis," wrote Fr. Bertetto,

> and confirmed by patristic and medieval tradition, designates metaphorically either the Daughter of Zion, or the people of Israel, in relations of love and fidelity with Yahweh, the bridegroom; or the Catholic Church, a continuation of the people of God of the Old Testament; or also every faithful soul, a member of the Church, and so in a particular way Mary Most Holy, to whom some verses of the Canticle are applied and referred in the typical sense of Scripture according to the patristic and theological tradition: *hortus conclusus* (enclosed garden), *fons signatus* (sealed fount)

24 G. Odasso, *Percorsi dell'esegesi e della teologia biblica: prospettive per la Mariologia*, p. 38, note 79. The author, contrary to more than thousand years old liturgical tradition, refuses to admit in any way and any instance the possibility of such readings in Marian celebrations and writes severely that "it is not possible even in the level of popular piety, to read texts which speak of Divine Wisdom as though they were speaking of the Virgin Mary" (ibid., p. 38). Unfortunately, there is always someone to whom it seems licit to not agree with and also to criticize liturgical dispositions. Nonetheless, the Liturgy continues to support the validity of a Mariological interpretation of these readings.

25 See E. Manfredini, *Analisi tematica del legionario per le celebrazione*, in Aa. Vv., *Il Messale Romano Vaticano II. Orazionale e Legionario*, vol. II, Turin 1981, pp. 85-159; P. Sorci, *Testi biblici non mariani applicati alla Vergine nella Liturgia*, in *Theotokos* 8 (2000) 644.

(Song 4:12), in support of Mary's virginity; and *tota pulchra es* (you are all fair) (Song 4:7) in support of the absence of sin in Mary.[26]

Taken as a whole, therefore, the Song of Songs expresses by way of rich, poetic allegory the reality of God's love for His chosen bride, without sin or blemish, all fair and innocent. This "bride" is the "new Israel," that is, the Church "without spot or wrinkle" (Eph 5:27); this "bride" is every Christian soul giving itself to God in purity and sanctity; this "bride," in a perfect and eminent way, is Mary Most Holy and only she, the Immaculate, who is "all fair" par excellence and "without spot" par excellence.

It is interesting to note that the *sensus fidei* of the Church as expressed by the liturgy when applying to Mary the passages of the Song of Songs, is in full accord with the Mariological interpretation supported by such Fathers and ecclesiastical writers of the Church as St. Hippolytus, St. Ephrem (above all), St. Ambrose, St. Jerome, St. Epiphanius, St. Sophronius, St. John Damascene, St. Germanus, St. Peter Damian, Rupert of Deutz, Alan of Lille, etc.[27]

In the Constitution of Vatican Council II on the Sacred Liturgy, it is stated that the Church "admires and exalts in Mary the most perfect fruit of the Redemption, and in her the Church contemplates with joy, as in a most pure image, that which she herself wholly desires and hopes to be."[28] This "most pure image" the liturgy presents to us as the spotless "bride" of the Song of Songs, to whom the Lord addresses words impregnated with the longing of ecstatic

---

26 Bertetto, *La Madonna oggi*, p. 66.

27 Cf. the precise and extensive study of A. Rivera, C.M.F., "Sentido mario lógico del Cantar de los Cantares," *Ephemerides Mariologicae* 1 (1951): 437–682 (1952): 25–42.

28 *Sacrosanctum Concilium*, no. 103.

love: "Arise, my love, my fair one, and come! ... O my dove, you who stay in the clefts of the rock, in the coverts of the cliffs, let me see your face, let me hear your voice, for your voice is sweet and your face comely" (Song 2:10–14).[29] And again: "All fair are you, my love: in you there is no spot! Come with me from Lebanon, my bride, come!" (Song 4:7–8).[30]The *sensus fidei* of the patristic tradition and of the liturgy would have us read Song of Songs as though Mariologically watermarked, bringing us to a transparent contemplation of the bride, Mary. She is all fair and without spot, and by her original purity—in contrast to the adulterous infidelity of Israel—she recapitulates, reflects, and sublimates in herself the "new Israel," i.e., the Church, and every soul, bride of the Lord.[31] At this point, a brief comment is required on the well-known verse 9 of chapter 6: "Who is she who rises like the dawn, fair as the moon, bright as the sun, terrible as an army set in array?" The figure of Mary here described in terms of the more attractive works of the universe (the dawn, the moon, the sun) and the power of men (an army on the attack) evokes prophetically the "great sign" of Revelation, the "woman clothed with the sun, with the moon under her feet, and on her head a crown of twelve stars" (Rev 12:1) in victorious battle against the infernal dragon. The similar imagery

---

29 The text is cited in the responsorial psalm of the Mass for the *Visitation of the Blessed Virgin*.

30 On the delicate and evocative theme of Mary "spouse of the Word Incarnate," see A. Rivera, "Maria Sponsa Verbi en la tradición biblico-patristica," *Ephemerides Mariologicae* 9 (1959): 461–478; A. Piolanti, "Sicut Sponsa ornata monili bus suis," in *Virgo Immaculata*, pp. 181–193.

31 Laurentin has written: "The apparently hyperbolic statement made by King Yahweh to Israel: There is no spot in you, was verified to the letter only in that new creation begun with the Immaculate Conception of Mary. Since this literal sense was objectively realized, and has been abundantly acknowledged as such (even if often with defective reasoning) by tradition, the theologian is justified in viewing this statement as a kind of full sense or ultrasense matching the intentions of God, the principal author of Scripture" (Laurentin, *La Vergine Maria*, p. 179, n. 3). Cf. also Romeo, "Maria e il Verbo," pp. 318–323.

present in the two texts and linking them identifies, as it were symbiotically, the Bride of Song of Songs with the woman of Revelation. And in fact, the liturgy, together with medieval tradition, understands both texts as referring directly to the Virgin Mary.[32]

32 Cf. P. de Ambrogio, *Il cantico dei cantici* (Rome, 1952), p. 211; G. Nolli, *Cantico dei cantici* (Rome, 1968), p. 34; D. Colombo, *Cantico dei cantici* (Rome, 1983), p. 22.

6
Mary in the Old Testament: A Portrait Sketched

An overall view of the content and value of the Mariological texts of the Old Testament is enough to make one realize their importance as a source of knowledge about the Virgin Mary in God's salvific plan. If to this overview a careful study of the meaning and deeper implications of the inspired word be added, the importance of such scriptural texts stands in even greater relief, rendering clearer the divine plan for man's salvation and Mary's active presence in the history of salvation. Finally, if such study be developed and sustained by a biblical–theological exegesis, as this has been conducted in the Church and guaranteed by the Church via tradition and the Magisterium, the liturgy and the *sensus fidelium*, then the Mariology of the Old Testament evidently assumes a primacy and indispensability for delineating the figure and work, the personality and mission of Mary in the divine plan of universal Redemption.

We can affirm, then, at once that the Mariology of the Old Testament has all the essential characteristics of a Mariology at its "roots." In that Mariology are contained in fact the "roots" of that unique, precious plant that is Mary Most Holy. From those "roots" has sprung, in the New Testament, the one 'full of grace" (Lk 1:28), the Mother of God and of the new humanity. In these Mariological texts of the Old Testament are discovered the "roots" of the mystery of Mary, predestined "in one and the same decree" (*Ineffabilis Deus*) to be the "woman," Mother of the New Adam, with whom she is united in the same "enmity" for the serpent whose head is to be crushed (Gen 3:15). This "woman" is the Virgin Mother of Emmanuel, that is, of "God with us" (Is 7:14). She is the "woman in travail" bearing God made man, the Savior of the "remnant of Israel," of the people of God (Mic 5:1–2).

The two mysteries of the Incarnation and of the Redemption, foreshadowed in these prophetic oracles, are intimately linked to the mysteries of the Immaculate Conception (Gen 3:15), the divine and virginal maternity (Is 7:14), and the Coredemption (Gen 3:15) attributed to the "woman in travail" of Bethlehem (Mic 5:1–2).

Together with these three fundamental Mariological texts, we also find in the Old Testament an abundance of minor texts that converge to give to those "roots" a certain consistency in prefiguring and symbolizing the extraordinary personality of Mary. Thus, we discover the "roots" of Mary in the "daughter of Zion" (Mic 4:8), in "the poor of Yahweh" (Ps 9), in "the strong woman" (Sir 26:2) who works for the regeneration and salvation of the people. We find her prefigured by Sarah, Rebecca, and Rachel, by Miriam, the sister of Moses, by Deborah, Abigail, and Ruth, by Judith and by Esther. We can read of the virtues and sanctity of Mary in the various and richly allusive biblical symbols, such as the burning bush, the fleece of Gideon, the holy ark, the rainbow, Jacob's ladder, and in many others. We can penetrate the very heart of Mary on the wings of that sublime poetry of love in Song of Songs and with the inspired, prayerful voice of so many psalms.

The Mariological reading of this scriptural data carried out in the Church, in continuity with tradition,[1] the

---

1 Cf. D. Casagrande, *La Madonna nel mistero della salvezza* (Rome, 1975); and his very important repertoire: *Enchiridion Marianum biblicum patristicum* (Rome, 1974), with the patristic texts commenting on the Marian passages of the Bible.

Magisterium,[2] the liturgy,[3] and art,[4] has pervaded and nourished the sensus fidei of the Christian people in their praise and love, veneration and imitation of the Blessed Virgin Mary. Not only may no exegete prescind from this reality and this historic patrimony of lived faith, but on the contrary he must "scrutinize the sensus ecclesiae," writes Alves, "as the lodestar of his interpretation."[5]

To vary the metaphor, it might also be said that the biblical Mariology of the Old Testament taken as a whole is an accurate "sketch" of that wonderful portrait drawn afterward in the New Testament, from the Gospel of St. Matthew through the Revelation of St. John. In the sketch, we already find the basic elements, the general lines, the perspective, the colors, the profile, and the principal features of the figure of Mary, her poses and her movement. All this is alluded to and outlined there. The transition from sketch to portrait can be observed in the proportions, the volume and space, the figurative details, and in the completeness of the final touches and shadings, particularly the decorative, which lend to the whole a delicate beauty and appropriate tone.

We find, then, the Mariology of the New Testament already "sketched" in that of the Old, on the basis of a reading

---

2 The dogmatic bull *Ineffabilis Deus*, for example, applies to the Immaculate a number of Old Testament symbols: the ark of Noah, Jacob's ladder, the burning bush, the impregnable tower, the enclosed garden, the lily among thorns, the coffer of immortality, etc.

3 See the excellent synthesis of Calabuig, "Liturgia," in *NDM*, Rome, 1985, pp. 767–787 (with the essential bibliography). It would also be useful to examine all the biblical periscopes in the lectionary, in the missal, and in the liturgy of the hours for Marian solemnities, feasts, and recurrences.

4 Note, for example, the paintings on cloth and on wood depicting the Immaculate Virgin surrounded by a crown of biblical symbols to illustrate her sanctity and her mission. See the brief essay by P. Amato, "Arte/ Iconologia," in *NDM*, pp. 138–154 (with bibliography), and the interesting work of L. Bartoli, *Simbologia mariana* (Padua, 1987).

5 M. I. Alves, "Esegesi per la Chiesa," *Communio*, no. 87 (1986): 58; the author directly refers to *Dei Verbum*, no. 23.

carried out "in the light of Christ and of the Church."[6] The figure and mission of Mary are already limned in the prophecies, in the figures, and in the symbols of the Old Testament. The prophecies foretell her and describe her personality, outlining its primary characteristics: Mary's freedom from original sin because of her enmity with the serpent, her Divine Maternity as the Mother of "God with us," her virginal maternity as the virgin "in travail," the universal Coredemption because of her victory over the serpent whose head is crushed.

The figures and symbols make it possible to perceive the various threads outlining the more personal and dynamic features of Mary's mission, at times delicately described (e.g., the gentle figure of Ruth, the Moabite, and the rainbow symbol), and at other times forcefully and dramatically illustrated (e.g., the figure of Judith and the symbol of Noah's ark). These figures and symbols embellish the personality of Mary concretely and dynamically, showing her more clearly to be a "living creature," as Garofalo writes, "with all the force of her mystery and humanity, in the very lively panorama of the story of salvation narrated in the Bible."[7]

The pilgrimage of faith in the word of God has carved this path of literal and spiritual exegesis for the interpretation of biblical data. This is how the Church has read these texts "from of old." Thus, the Church has nourished the people of God, constantly verifying that "symbolic language is the appropriate vehicle of popular

6 Pontifical Biblical Commision, *The Hebrew People and its Sacred Scriptures in the Christian Bible*, n. 7.

7 S. Garofalo, *La Madonna della Bibbia* (Milan, 1958), pp. 10–11. Nor ought one overlook the distinctive structure of the Hebrew language, which reflects a mentality essentially active, expressed via image and symbol in a more immediate, forceful manner. Cf. E. Jacob, *Théologie de l'Ancienne Testament* (Neuchâtel, 1968), pp. 103–109.

piety," as C. A. Bernard writes,[8] for "by symbolic language all the faithful more easily grasp the religious message being communicated to them"[9] and are concretely moved to incorporate it into their lives. Hence, "the figure of Mary and all the other symbols enriching an understanding of her figure, contain in themselves a dynamic moving the faithful to relive personally the mystery they represent."[10]

Biblical–theological exegesis supports and carries forward this Mariological interpretation of the prophecies, figures, and symbols of the Old Testament, that first firm root of the Faith of the Church, "the pillar and bulwark of the truth" (1 Tim 3:15). "Scripture must be interpreted according to the Spirit," wrote J. A. Moehler, "because it is the work of the Spirit; this Spirit enlivens the Church of Jesus Christ who gives us the Spirit…, the Church that has come down to us in perfect continuity; thus whoever

---

8 C. A. Bernard, "Simbolismo," in *Nuovo Dizionario di Mariologia*, p. 1303.

9 *Ibid.*

10 *Ibid.*, p. 1304. In recent times, however, many have imprudently yielded to pressures to eliminate in one fell swoop the entire patrimony of Marian biblical exegesis, embracing the figures and symbols of the Old Testament, a patrimony guarded and cultivated by the Church for nearly 2,000 years. Further, too many contemporary Mariologists seem to allow only a very limited place for the prophecies of Gen, Is 7:14, and Mic 5:1–2, not to mention those who interpret these so reductively, obliquely, or implicitly of Mary that one is hard put to find even a minimal Mariological sense in these prophecies.

In regard to the figures and symbols of the Old Testament, apart from references to "the daughter of Zion" and to "the poor of Yahweh" (cited by *Lumen Gentium*, chap. 8), many of these Mariologists hold that such figures and symbols should be discarded as being of no worth in grasping the mystery of Mary. This position is the fruit of a biblical exegesis reduced to mere philology. Such a methodology is all the more incongruous today, when the "theology of symbols" and pastoral practice focused on "signs" are being reaffirmed, either in theory or in practice: liturgical, catechetical, artistic. Regarding this, see the important work of a specialist on this subject, C. A. Bernard, *Teologia simbolica* (Rome, 1981). The author examines the more important studies of J. Goetz, M. Eliade, P. Ricoeur, H. de Lubac, H. U. von Balthasar, P. Evdokimov, G. Gusdorf, G. Durant, J. Chevalier, and others. Also useful is the work of L. Bartoli, *La chiave* (Trieste, 1986), on the significance of sacred symbolism.

contradicts her must be accounted as in error."[11] It has been also correctly written that the first Christians "began to read the text of the Old Testament *in the spirit of Jesus*, namely beginning with *faith* resting on Him. The Fathers very quickly concluded that so long as in a text of Scripture this *spiritual* sense had not been found, that text had not yet revealed its truest meaning."[12]

A biblical exegesis that does not take account of the Church's Faith is certainly off-track, not only because it minimizes the theological dimension of faith in the word of God, but also because it runs the risk of deviating from that very faith. Fr. Ignatius de la Potterie has magisterially shown how so-called scientific modern exegesis in its foundation rest on Spinoza and its immanentism. Consequently, as de La Potterie writes, "biblical science has become exclusively a matter of philology and history. Exegesis can be only be governed by such criteria; it must exclude any other dimension, ignore any opening on the transcendent, prohibit any introduction of faith. Hence, as has been recently said, a radically critical exegesis is 'methodologically atheist' (J. Borella)."[13]

From the study made so far, we can affirm that a biblical exegesis minimizing or repudiating the Mariological interpretation of the prophecies, figures, and symbols of the Old Testament cannot be the exegesis so "highly recommended by the Council," as *Dei Verbum* declares

---

11 Cited by I. de La Potterie, S.J., "La lettura della Sacra Scrittura 'nello Spirito': il modo patristico di leggere la Bibbia è possibile oggi?," *Communio*, no. 87 (1986): p. 26 (Eng. ed.: "Reading Holy Scripture 'in the Way of the Spirit': Is the Patristic Way of Reading the Bible Still Possible Today?," *Communio* [1986]: 308–325).

12 Th. Spidlik–I. Gargano, *La spiritualità dei Padri greci e orientali. Storia della spiritualità*, vol. 3/a, Rome 1983, p. 157.

13 De la Potterie, *art. cit.*, p. 32: with a few lucid and telling witticisms, de La Potterie has said everything essential in order to understand the damage and failure of a biblical exegesis divorced from the faith of the Church.

(no. 10), because it is an exegesis that parts company with the living tradition and constant Magisterium of the Church, thus breaking "the connection between Bible and Church."[14]

This, in fact, is the net impression gained from study of that modern exegesis according to which the majority of biblical texts of the Old Testament referring to Mary Most Holy and used by the Church in her liturgy and catechesis either make hardly any sense or are altogether out of place. The prophetic texts of Genesis 3:15, Isaiah 7:14, and Micah 5:1–2 certainly have not been understood by the Church in her liturgy and catechesis (we may also add: in dogma and art) as the modern exegetes have understood them. Here is a case in point. Modern exegetes not only do not identify Mary with the "woman" of Genesis 3:15 but they rather tend to exclude her altogether from that passage or they include her only in the "seed" of the "woman" (intending the term "seed" in a collective sense), or at the most they see her only indirectly, in obliquo, with respect to Eve.

By contrast, Pope John Paul II, in a homily for the Feast of the Birth of Mary, said: "This very child, still so small and fragile, is the 'woman' of the first proclamation of future redemption, whom God placed in opposition to the cunning serpent: 'I will put enmity between you and

14 P. Toinet, *Pour une théologie de l'exegèse* (Pans, 1983), p. 40, cited by de La Potterie ("La lettura," p. 37), who in turn discusses the "rupture" between exegesis and faith, between exegesis and dogmatics, brought about by that modern "autonomous exegesis" directly reflecting the "total separation of the Jesus of history" and the "Christ of faith." As a consequence, it also reduces the basic events of our Faith (for example, the virginal conception, the miracles, and the Resurrection of Jesus) to the level of "a mere construction of the Easter faith" of believers, to a simple "theologoumenon" (cf. ibid., pp. 32–34). Such seems to be present also in the research of the so-called new "procedures of exegesis and of biblical theology," fundamentally linked to that reductive old-testament rabbinic exegesis surely without "the light of Christ and of the Church."

the woman.'"[15] Do we not hear in the Supreme Pontiff's words the perennial voice of the Church, which continues to affirm thus simply that Mary is to be identified with the "woman" of the famous oracle of Genesis?

Of what use, then, is an exegesis that contradicts or dissents from the constant Magisterium of the Church? True exegesis can never find in Sacred Scripture "anything in contrast with the Church's convictions," affirms Moehler, and consequently, "to explain Scripture according to the doctrine of the Church has never been considered an obstacle for the exegete."[16] On the contrary, as Pope Pius XII clearly taught, "the work of research, including that in the area of Mariology, will proceed more securely and fruitfully insofar as everyone keeps in mind the proximate and universal norm of truth for every theologian in questions of faith and morals, i.e., the sacred Magisterium of the Church."[17] And the authoritative document of the Pontifical Biblical Commission, the interpretation of the bible in the Church, expressly teaches that exegesis "must permit itself to be illumined by theological research...

---

15 Cited by Bertetto, *Maria nel Magistero*, p. 86. Even more important is the recent catechetical instruction of the Holy Father given on December 17, 1986, at a general audience: "Il Protoevangelio della salvezza," in *L'Osservatore Romano* (December 18, 1986): 4. Here, as in so many other instances, it is clear that the constant doctrine of the Church, more specifically as found in *Dei Verbum*, on the necessity of harmonizing exegesis with tradition, the Magisterium, and the *sensus fidelium*, has "met opposition," writes Alves, "where methodological harmony between exegesis and the theological-pastoral use of Sacred Scripture is wanting." Such "opposition" is always unavoidable if the exegete fails "to take the mind of the Church," as Alves notes, "as the focus of his interpretation" ("Esegesi per la Chiesa," pp. 53, 58).

16 See above, no. 10. Hence, de La Potterie rightly states that it is necessary "once again to use both the Jewish and the Christian type of exegesis, which does not divorce Bible and tradition" ("La lettura," p. 40). And Jean-Nesmy adds that exegesis must become "a prayer, under the action of the Holy Spirit, guided by the Church and by her tradition" ("Per una lettura," p. 52). That is true of any exegetical method: be it fundamentalist or critical-historical, be it historical-literary or structuralist. Cf. also *The Navarre Bible. St. Mark's Gospel*, pp. 22–25.

17 Radio Message "Inter Complures" to the Second International Mariological Congress, *AAS* 46 (1954): 677.

The scientific study of the Bible may not prescind from theological research nor from spiritual experience and the discernment of the Church."[18]

We can, therefore, conclude our present study affirming that according to biblical–theological exegesis, which integrates the literal and spiritual interpretation of the word of God,[19] the Mariological reading of the three prophecies:

Genesis 3:15, Isaiah 7:14, and Micah 5:1–2, of the figures, symbols, and other passages of the Old Testament analyzed in the course of this study, has enjoyed and will continue to enjoy in the Church and in the faith of the people of God the right of citizenship, even if not with the same weight and value in each case. It seems to us rather that the Mariological reading of these texts, cultivated by the Church over the centuries, reveals the essential characteristic of authentic exegesis, the one Laurentin has described as "an interior penetration of the text, written for believers and by believers who were inspired according to their experience of God."[20]

For the rest, in the New Testament, the entire Mariological content of the Old Testament is found to be fulfilled in the reality of the person and life of Mary, as the "woman," as the "virgin," as the "mother" of the Emmanuel, as the exalted "Daughter of Zion," as endowed with those sublime gifts and virtues of the more admirable

---

18 *The Interpretation of the Bible in the Church*, Enchiridion Biblicum, no. 1489.

19 In regard to this point basic to biblical–theological exegesis, one should read the succinct critique of de La Potterie on the "opinion common today which claims that a search for the 'spiritual sense' of Scripture does not form part of genuine exegesis." This scholar concludes that in order to have an authentic biblical exegesis, "it would certainly be necessary to rediscover the patristic method of reading the Bible: we must read it in the spirit of the Fathers. It was in this spirit that it was read in early tradition; and today it is this which is recommended to us by Vatican II in *Dei Verbum*, no. 12" ("La lettura," pp. 37, 40).

20 Laurentin, *Come riconciliare l'esegesi e la fede* (Brescia, 1985), p. 10.

women of the Old Covenant, and by the more suggestive, poetic symbols employed by the sacred writers. The great St. Augustine, therefore, was right when he wrote that "in the Old Testament is hidden the New, and in the New the Old becomes clear."[21] That is especially true of Mariology, which has sprouted and flowered in the New Testament, as it were, from its "roots" in the Old. Mariology has developed from an admirable Old Testament "sketch" to that still more admirable portrait painted in the New.

St. Andrew of Crete (d. 740?) once wrote that our Lady is "the seal of the Old and of the New Testament; she is clearly the fulfillment of every prophecy."[22] And at the close of this first section of our study, while contemplating the mosaic of Mariological texts contained in the Old Testament (which could be multiplied *ad abundantiam*), we too can verify the magnificent truth formulated by Pope Pius XII:

> There are many sublime things which Holy Scripture reveals to us about the most Blessed Virgin in the books both of the Old and New Testament. Indeed, in Holy Scripture there is found an explicit affirmation of her more illustrious privileges and gifts: that is, of her virginal maternity and undefiled sanctity. There we find vividly described the image and features of the Virgin herself.[23]

21 Cf. St. Augustine, *Quaestiones in Heptateuchum*, 11, 73.

22 St. Andrew of Crete, *On the Nativity of Mary*, Sermon 5, PG 97, 663a.

23 Radio Message "Inter complures," p. 678.

PART TWO

The New Testament

- *The Gospels of the Infancy*
- *The Virgin Mary and the Origins of Jesus*
- *The Annunciation*
- *The Visitation*
- *The Magnificat*
- *St. Joseph's Anxieties*
- *The Birth of Jesus*
- *The Announcement to the Shepherds*
- *The Presentation in the Temple*
- *The Magi in Adoration*
- *The Flight into Egypt*
- *The Slaughter of the Innocents*
- *Return to Nazareth*
- *The Finding of Jesus in the Temple*
- *The Marriage Feast at Cana*
- *Mary in the Public Life of Jesus*
- *Behold your Mother… Behold your Son*
- *With Mary the Mother of Jesus*
- *The Woman Clothed with the Sun*
- *Synthesis of the Biblical Mariology:*
  The Immaculate

7
The Gospels of the Infancy

The first two chapters of St. Matthew's Gospel and of St. Luke's Gospel are known as the "gospels of the infancy." They cover a period of time that extends from the Annunciation to the finding of the child Jesus in the Temple and His return to Nazareth. The two Evangelists, although differing in their presentations and views, do, however, complement one another, thus providing us with a sufficiently complete picture of the events that preceded, accompanied, and followed the mystery of the Incarnation of the Word up to the time of His public life carried out in the land of the Near East.[1]

And with that, a very basic question arises: On what sources did the Evangelists draw to write their "gospels of the infancy," that whole series of narratives, some of which are so rich in detail? Historical and textual criticism have aimed at indicating possible links between the Evangelists and the probable dependence of one Evangelist upon the other in view of those links. This line of research has entailed hypotheses describing how the Evangelists drew on possibly existing earlier writings and collections of factual data. The results of such studies do not agree with one another and do not seem to be as securely grounded as one might desire. The methodology and approach involved apparently do not get beyond "plausible" hypotheses and leave wide margins of doubt and contradiction, not only

1 The bibliography on the Infancy Gospels is immense: see S. Muñoz Iglesias, *Los Evangelios de la Infanzia*, 4 vols., Madrid 1986–1990: AA. VV., *Evangeli dell'Infanzia* (a cura di A. Serra - A. Valentini), *Ricerche Storico-bibliche* 4, 1992.

about the content, but about the very authors of the gospels of the infancy.[2]

Laurentin, in his recent, weighty study of the subject, forcefully reaffirms the unity and the identity of authorship: "Literary analysis has established the unity of authorship:

Matthew 1–2 certainly belongs to Matthew and Luke 12 to Luke. There has been little success in any attempt to reduce these narratives to fabricated models or to legendary or mythical processes. The never-ending attempts to do so have yielded only inconsistencies and contradictions."[3]

Yet the answer to our question can only be this: the unique source of information for the gospels of the infancy was Mary Most Holy. No one else could have knowledge

---

2 Fr. Stramare writes thus in his most recent and far ranging study: "notwithstanding numerous studies dedicated in recent years to the gospel accounts of the infancy and hidden life of Jesus, one must confess that the results are disappointing": T. Stamare, *Vangelo dei Misteri della vita nascosta di Gesù*, Bornato in Franciacorta (BS) 1998, p. 13. For a summary outline of the different questions see A. Valentini, *A proposito dei Vangeli dell'Infanzia*, in *Theotokos* 3 (1995) 3-11.

3 R. Laurentin, *The Truth of Christmas beyond the Myths* (Petersham, Mass., 1986), p. 450. [Italian translation: *I Vangeli dell'infanzia di Cristo* (Turin, 1985), p. 599. The Italian edition used by Fr. Manelli will be cited where it contains material omitted from the English version; otherwise page references will be to the English Trans.] This study by Laurentin is already justly considered a "classic on the subject of structural analyses" (C. Marcheselli-Casale, "Luca racconta, in *Ecclesiae Sacramentum* [Naples, 1986], p. 139). Fr. E. Testa, in his monumental study *Maria terra vergine* (Jerusalem, 1985), 2 vols., states that the unity of Matthew 1-2 and Luke 1-2 is also confirmed by "structuralism" (vol. 1, pp. 259, 269, 274). Cf. also G. Leonardi, *L'Infanzia di Gesù nei vangeli di Matteo e Luca* (Padua, 1975), p. 5.

See also R. Brown's long introduction to his book *The Birth of the Messiah. A Commentary on the Infancy Narratives in Matthew and Luke* (New York, 1977), pp. 25-41. The author's positions, here and elsewhere in this work, are often not acceptable. Cf. A. Bottino's long and critical reviews in *Marianum* 55 (1982): 645-657, and those of F. Spadafora in *Lateranum* 48 (1982): 138-154. See particularly Testa, *Maria terra vergine*, vol. 1, who criticizes not only this volume of Brown (pp. 105-154), but also the volume *Mary in the New Testament* (Philadelphia, 1978), written by him in collaboration with an ecumenical group of Catholics and Lutherans, and the issue of *Concilium*, no. 19, (1983), with an article by McKenzie (pp. 155-98). The accurate criticism of Fr. Testa (pp. 209-21) of the positions and unacceptable conclusions of such authors, victims of a typical, long outdated Kantian-Hegelian idealism, is important.

of those episodes known so well to her. "In the final analysis, Mary is the only possible source of an episode like the annunciation, and the most appropriate source for several others," writes Laurentin; "otherwise, the gospels of the infancy would be fiction and in contradiction with Luke himself (prologue 1:1–4)."[4] Guidetti also writes that "Mary was the only and authoritative witness of this almost entirely unknown period."[5]

Laconi affirms, even more strongly, that Mary Most Holy was "the evangelist, therefore, of old and hidden events."[6] And Garofalo, considering "the nature of the

---

4 LAURENTIN, *Truth of Christmas*, p. 461. The "numerous other" episodes of the infancy to which the author refers are: the visitation, the circumcision of John the Baptist, the Nativity, the presentation, and the finding of Jesus in the Temple (cf. ibid.).

Elsewhere (pp. 28–33) the author has analyzed the diverse hypotheses and attempted reconstructions of a "source" of the gospels of the infancy, made by several scholars (Resch, Conrady, Reitzenstein, Völter, Erdmann, Dornseiff, Geyser, Winter, Resenhoeft, Sahlin, Gaechter), concluding, however, that "these reconstructions, which are incompatible one with the other, seem to be unrelated among themselves like tapestries woven, each according to the most diverse grids and inspiration.... Hence the hypotheses make no progress and get bogged down. The text resists these contradictory dismantlings" (p. 32).

5 A. GUIDETTI, S.J., *Conoscenza storica di Gesù di Nazareth* (Milan, 1981), p. 159. Immediately before, the author writes: "It is unthinkable that Mary, during her long sojourn among the Apostles, from the resurrection to the ascension of her Son (Acts 1:4), while living in the house of John in Jerusalem (Jn 19:26), would not have been questioned and would not have responded to the questions regarding the life of Christ, preceding His public manifestation at His baptism by John" (ibid.). Leonardi, reporting the views of B. de Solages, also says that "both traditions, Matthew's as well as Luke's, would have their common source, above all for the virginal conception, in the confidences given by Mary to the disciples in the first years of the Church" (LEONARDI, *L'Infanzia di Gesù*, p. 12, no. 2).

6 M. LACONI, "I vangeli dell'infanzia nella duplice presentazione di Matteo (12) e di Luca (1–2)," *Rivista di Ascetica e Mistica* 13 (1968): 43. Even Brown, as regards Lk 1–2, is forced to admit the possibility "*a priori* that she [Mary] was the source of material for the Lucan narrative of the infancy that describes facts of which she would still remain the most probable witness" (*Birth of the Messiah*, pp. 29–30). Cf. also M. MIGUENS, O.F.M., "Servidora del señor," in *Maria in Sacra Scriptura*, vol. 4 (Rome, 1967), pp. 74–75 (For Fr. Miguens' position, in English, see his *The Virgin Birth. An Assessment of the Scriptural Evidence* [Westminster, Md., 1975] and *Mary "The Servant of the Lord"* [Boston, 1978]); J. DANIELOU, S.J., *Les évangiles de l'enfance* (Paris, 1967), pp. 65–66 [Eng. ed.: *The Infancy Narratives* (New York, 1968)].

events relative to the infancy of Jesus and the exact variety of details," has no doubt in concluding "that the primary source of St. Luke's narrative was the most holy Virgin herself."[7] And elsewhere, very beautifully, the same author expressed his thought thus:

> From whom was Luke able to learn about the intimate and recondite events that he narrates? Zechariah and Elizabeth, already well advanced in age at the time of the annunciation of the birth of the Baptist, had been dead for many years when St. Luke wrote between 60 and 63. Of the shepherds who had seen the newborn God only the youngest could be alive, and how could they be found? Simeon, the just man who had embraced the Consoler of Israel, though he need not be thought decrepit as he is popularly imagined to be, was already then awaiting death. Anna was eighty-four years old, when in the Temple, in testimony to her faith and piety, she recognized the Desired One. Dead were the doctors who had debated with the wise twelve-year-old; already dead, by the beginning of Jesus' public ministry, was His legal father Joseph.
>
> And who, on the other hand, could ever have related what had happened in the sacred and inviolate intimacy of Mary's house at the time of the betrothal and of the hidden life? Who could have been privy to the secrets of Zechariah's, Elizabeth's and Simeon's hearts and witness to their words? Who could have known about the anxiety of the Mother during the loss of Jesus? Who would have dared to affirm that on that occasion Mary and Joseph did not comprehend the sense of the Child's answer?
>
> Twice, in the brief course of this history, the Evangelist notes that the Virgin carefully kept in her heart all that she heard and all that happened in regard to Jesus: the first time after the visit of the shepherds to Bethlehem: 'Mary kept all these things and meditated upon them in her heart,' and the second at the end of the infancy narratives: 'His Mother kept all these things in her heart.' It is a sensible way of indicating

[7] S. Garofalo, *Le parole di Maria* (Milan, 1962), p. 18.

to readers the source from which the author obtained his information.[8]

From this source, then, originated the gospels of the infancy, and it appears evident that the presence of Mary, in the series of episodes described by St. Matthew, and even more by St. Luke, in the first two chapters of their Gospels, was determinative, since she was placed at the center of the events, next to her Son, who, with the Incarnation, inaugurated the new period in the history of salvation.

A second question must now be posed, to be answered with the help of philological and theological exegesis: Are the gospels of the infancy narratives historical in character, even in respect to their minor details, or were they reworked by the Evangelists, who embellished them with symbolic elements (the angels, the star, the Magi, etc.) useful in elaborating or dramatizing the event narrated? The question is important, because if everything in the narratives of Jesus' infancy is not historical, it obviously would be necessary to free the basic historical facts from accretions in any way legendary or mythical in character.

On this subject, non-Catholic scholars support the most radical thesis possible according to which the infancy narratives, as a whole, are to be relegated to the category of myths and fables void of any historical worth.[9]

---

8 *Ibid.*, pp. 14–16. See also A. Feuillet, Maria: *Madre del Messia, Madre della Chiesa*, Milan 2004, p. 38.

9 In an interesting note, Pietrafesa thus denounces this radical thesis as untenable: "The historicity of the narratives of the infancy is questioned because at the time of their composition, supposedly, it was usual to envelop the great personages of antiquity in a halo of legend, especially the obscure period of their infancy. But this generic consideration has no bearing on the gospels of the infancy, since neither Matthew nor Luke indulge in the prodigious, nor do they exalt their hero by way of the sensational; rather they set in relief His lowliness, His poverty, His suffering. In the narrations of the two Evangelists all is set forth in a tone of simplicity and nothing suggests an imaginary construction made up of marvelous events" (Pietrafesa, *La Madonna nella Rivelazione*, pp. 107–108, n. 3).

The greater number of Catholic exegetes, instead, have supported the historicity of the gospels of the infancy, as a whole and in their details as well.[10] This is a thesis of classical exegesis "for two thousand years," writes A. Ory in a recent essay.[11] Now

> if classical exegesis admits the historicity of the narratives of the infancy, that means that the angel Gabriel, in fact, really is an angel who brought a message from heaven to Mary, a virgin in body, who is to remain a virgin while becoming a mother, and that Joseph is the putative father of Jesus. A host of angels sang on the night of the Nativity, and the Magi came from the East with their gifts. The children of Bethlehem were slaughtered while the Holy Family fled to Egypt and later settled in Nazareth where they led a hidden life.[12]

Some modern Catholic exegetes, however, dissent from this classical position, claiming that the gospels of the infancy belong to the literary genre known as haggadic midrash,[13] a genre halfway between history and historic fiction, between history and theology, a combination of real facts and of fictionalized accretions or idealized models.[14]

---

10 Such as the great biblicists Lagrange, Durant, Buzy, Garofalo, Spadafora, McHugh, Schmid, Benoit, Spicq, Sabourin, Laurentin, and Danieli. Cf. Pietrafesa, *La Madonna nella Rivelazione*, p. 108. And in this regard it is to be noted expressly, that the Pontifical Biblical Commission had already asserted the historical authenticity both of Matthew 1–2 (June 19, 1911) and Luke 1–2 (June 26, 1912). Further, Vatican II, in *Dei Verbum*, confirms in precise terms both the apostolic origin (no. 18), and the historicity (no. 19) of the four Gospels (and therefore also of Mt and Lk 1–2). Cf. F. Spadafora, "Origine apostolica e storicità degli Evangeli nella *Dei Verbum*," *Renovatio* 2 (1967): 578–581.

11 A. Ory, *Riscoprire la verità storica dei Vangeli* (Milan, 1986), p. 72.

12 Ibid.

13 The term *midrash* (plural *midrashin*) is an Aramaic word meaning "interpretation" or "comment." Midrash could be either *haggadic*, i.e., historic-narrative, or *halakhic*, i.e., moral; there were also "allegorical," "apocalyptical," "liturgical" midrashin. Cf. R. Bloch, "Midrash," in *Dictionaire de la Bible. Supplement* (1957): 1263–1280; Wright, *The Literary Genre Midrash* (New York, 1967), and the critical review of R. Le Déaut, "A propos d'une definition du midrash," *Biblica* 50 (1969): 394–413.

14 Cf. Ortensio da Spinetoli, O.F.M. Cap., *Introduzione ai Vangeli dell'Infanzia* (Brescia, [967), pp. 20ff.; X. Leon Dufour, "Libro della Genesi di Gesù

Now, against this thesis, whose supporters do not agree among themselves on many issues, very serious difficulties arise, showing it to be without foundation or even without minimal plausibility.[15]

The solid, clear, precise observations of J. Leal in an important study serve to underscore an initial, essential distinction:

> That Luke could have been able to describe the infancy in the form of midrash is certain. That he, in fact, did describe it in that way must be proved. If midrash is understood to mean simply that history is presented for parenetical, catechetical and religious ends, there is no difficulty in saying that all the Gospels are midrash, historical narratives written for such purposes. But this is not the proper sense of midrash. Midrash supposes an elaboration, a reflection on the past (the Old Testament) and on new phenomena, hence, an explicit comparison. But all this comparative substructure is totally lacking in the infancy narratives, nor is it found in the rest of the Gospel, or in the Acts of the Apostles.
>
> Here everything is set forth in expository, narrative form, with the simplicity of the historian. To speak of a Judeo-Christian midrash closer to the days of Pentecost would imply that the gospel of the infancy reflects the mentality, the sentiments of faith of the first Christian converts, who saw the life of Jesus, His death, His resurrection and ascension. But this mentality nowhere appears in Luke 1–2. All the characters in it, all its religious background, are of a period and of a mentality prior to Jesus' public ministry, death and resurrection. We find in these narratives a surprising, marvelous fidelity to history... Therein is reflected not a Judeo–Christian midrash, but a history of Christian origins.[16]

Cristo," *Rivista Biblica* 13 (1965): 223; S. Muñoz-Iglesias, "El Evangelio de la infancia en S. Mateo," in *Sacra Pagina* II (Gembloux, 1959), pp. 120–49.

15 On this subject see the critical study of U. E. Lattanzi, "Il Vangelo dell'Infanzia è verità storica o mito?," in *De primordiis cultus Mariani*, vol. 4, pp. 31–46.

16 J. Leal, S.J., "El Evangelio de la Infancia," in *La Sagrada Escritura, Nuevo Testamento*, vol. 1, *Evangelios* (Madrid, 1961—Biblioteca de Autores Cristianos, vol. 207), pp. 539–552. (The text cited is taken from Spadafora's

Moreover, the historical fact that a Christian midrash did not appear until after the Gospels at a much later date should not be overlooked. "The midrashin that have come down to us were put down in writing only in the fifth century A.D.," writes Leonardi.[17] Now to extrapolate backward across four centuries solely on the basis of a presumed oral tradition, seems to us, frankly, to build on a void. Fr. Ortensio da Spinetoli, himself a supporter of the midrashic theory, has to admit that "at present it is not always easy to determine if current events, true and objective, simply coincide with past episodes, or instead, if old models have imposed their form upon recent events. The problem is clear, but the answers up to the present date are not equally such."[18]

In rebuttal of the position of Fr. Ortensio, Guidetti, among others, has rightly noted that "the meditation of Mary 'on all these things' (Lk 2:19)—and the text refers directly to all that the shepherds recounted: the apparition of the angel who announced the Savior and the signs by which to recognize Him and the hosannas of the angels singing (Lk 2:8–14)—does not permit the second hypothesis [midrash] here or elsewhere."[19]

---

review of Brown, *Birth of the Messiah*, pp. 140–41). In his latest, imposing work of scientific Mariology, Fr. Testa also rejects the hypothesis of midrash as false (*Maria terra vergine*, vol. 1, p. 246).

17 *L'Infanzia di Gesù*, p. 27. This is also the reason why Fr. Testa holds as untenable the hypothesis of midrash, which at that time did not as such exist. He maintains that "it cannot be understood at all why one must ascribe so much value to the Jewish midrashin and none to the apocrypha of the second century, when it is known that chronologically the second are much more ancient and that they are no more theological, sectarian and heretical than the first" (Testa, *Maria terra vergine*, p. 214).

18 da Spinetoli, *Introduzione ai Vangeli*, p. 102.

19 Guidetti, *Conoscenza storica*, p. 166. Garofalo also notes that St. Luke attaches the second text: "*His Mother kept all these things in her heart*" (2:51), precisely "to the end of the narrative of the infancy": "a clever indication to the readers revealing the source from which he has drawn his information" (Garofalo, *Le parole di Maria*, p. 16; see also his *La Madonna della Bibbia* [Milan, 1958], p. 13).

In reality, it is incomprehensible why exegetes who affirm a midrashic genre in the infancy narratives should not consider and learn from later history, including recent and contemporary, in such a way as to acknowledge the factual character of the extraordinary events described in the gospels of the infancy, and elsewhere, without seeking to empty them of meaning by appealing to more or less plausible hermeneutics or presumed theological models reflecting only "the profound meditations of an adult community."[20]

With regard to the extraordinary elements entwined with the events surrounding the Incarnation of the Word, Guidetti states very concretely that

> in the final analysis, coincidences and not forms borrowed from events of old are found in similar events read about in the biographies of the saints: apparitions of angels (and of the Virgin) accompanied by fear, dialogue and a message; prodigious and prophetic dreams (St. John Bosco). The celestial phenomenon of the star guiding the Magi is rather insignificant compared to the solar phenomenon promised by the seers of Fatima, that occurred at the exact hour predicted, and was witnessed by over fifty-thousand persons. We are reminded, too, of the star that guided St. John Capistran on his journey from the city of Aquila to Rome.[21]

---

20 Leonardi, *L'Infanzia di Gesù*, p. 32.

21 Guidetti, *Conoscenza storica*, p. 166. Mention should be added here of the extraordinary facts associated with the stigmatization of St. Francis of Assisi (cf. Thomas of Celano, *First Life of St. Francis*, nos. 94–96; St. Bonaventure, *Legenda Minor*, chap. 6, Lec. 1–9; for English versions consult *St. Francis of Assisi. Omnibus of Sources* [Chicago, 1972], pp. 225–355, 789–831); and St. Padre Pio of Pietralcina (cf. *Epistolario*, vol. 1 [S. Giovanni Rotondo, 1977], pp. 1092–1095); the extraordinary episodes of St. Gemma Galgani's guardian angel (cf. Germano di S. Stanislao, *Santa Gemma Galgani* [Rome, 1972], pp. 206–17; Eng. ed.: *The Life of Gemma Galgani* [London, 1913], pp. 207–216); the phenomena of the bleeding sacred images in the home of Teresa Musco (cf. G. Roschini, *Teresa Musco* [Rome, 1979], pp. 181ff.). See also Laurentin, *Truth of Christmas*, p. 391 (Ital. ed.: p. 508), with references to the "extraordinary events" in the lives of St. Teresa of Avila, St. Bernadette, the seers of Fatima, Beauring, and Banneaux (see also p. 534, n. 5; Ital. ed.: p. 620, n. 6).

As for the doctrinal content embedded in every event mentioned in the accounts of Jesus' infancy, it is similarly incomprehensible why, according to these exegetes, such theological content should have to be supported by mythical and legendary factors, rather than rest directly on the historical reality of these facts with their details, as described by the Evangelists limpidly, simply, and without a trace of artificiality.[22] Fr. Leal writes:

> It is true: exegetes should strive to penetrate the entire thought of the inspired author, and certainly, in his narrative, St. Luke intended more than can be expressed by the commonplace sense of the words. But we doubt very much that these undercurrents are not equally found in the rest of the Gospel and that they can vindicate the claim of the infancy Gospel as being of the midrashic genre. We doubt as well that the early readers of Luke, such as the distinguished Theophilus, were aware of all these profundities and that the exegesis of the Gospels is so difficult and so mysterious.[23]

"If it is evident," writes Pietrafesa, "that the events of Jesus' infancy have a theological import, it is not less

---

22 Cf. G. Danieli, "Matteo I-II e l'intenzione di narrare fatti accaduti," *Rivista Biblica* 16 (1968): 187–199. Lattanzi rightly regards as absolutely offensive the application of midrashic genre to St. Luke, who expressly professes, in the prologue of his Gospel, the desire to present a careful, orderly, historical work, after having "investigated all things carefully" (Lk. 1:3). With unerring critical sense, Lattanzi writes that "the pretext of wishing to find in the Gospel of Luke an 'historical nucleus' and a 'midrashic embroidery' is as unjust as it is false: false because it is based on a false presupposition; unjust, because it is offensive to Luke. The pretext implies, in fact, nothing less than that the prologue of Luke is the prologue of an imposter. I maintain than any attempt to soften the insulting aspect of this assessment of St. Luke, implicit in the exegesis of the 'midrashic school,' is simply impossible" ("Il Vangelo dell'Infanzia," p. 44). Cf. also Pietrafesa, *La Madonna nella Rivelazione*, p. 110. Laurentin also writes plainly that "the hypothesis of a literary, dramatical fiction does not square with what we know of Luke, nor with the statement of intent laid out in his prologue, nor with the overall consistency of his work. It does violence to the text" (*Truth of Christmas*, p. 461).

23 Leal, "El Evangelio," p. 589. H. Schurmann also states that in Luke 1–2 "there is no comment (or exercise), or exegesis of this kind," with the features of the midrashic kind and hence "it is better not to describe... Luke 1–2 as midrashic, because the description is imprecise and really says nothing at all": H. Schurmann, *Il Vangelo di Luca*, Brescia 1993, pp. 102–103.

clear that the Evangelist intended to recount real events that took place. Theological intent does not exclude the will to narrate historical events, even if it is a question of history different from that to which our modern mentality is accustomed."[24] And Danieli stated incisively that in the gospels of the infancy "all is also theology," that is, not only history (in the sense of chronicles), but "also" theology.[25]

> The Gospels also contain doctrinal teaching: in other words, the Evangelists were not only concerned to record mere facts for posterity; they sought also to explain what those facts meant in God's plan of salvation, and how man is supposed to respond to them.
>
> For example: the Evangelist Matthew reports that when St. Joseph was puzzled on finding that Mary was expecting a child, 'an angel of the Lord appeared to him in a dream, saying: "Joseph, son of David, fear not to take Mary, your wife, for that which is conceived in her, is of the Holy Spirit. She shall bring forth a son: and you shall call him Jesus. For He shall save His people from their sins."' But St. Matthew does not limit himself to a mere retelling of the event, because there next follows: 'Now all this was done that it might be fulfilled which the Lord spoke by the prophet, saying: Behold a virgin shall be with child and bring forth a son: and they shall call His name Emmanuel, which being interpreted is, God with us.' So the description of the event is followed by the explanation: God has already announced, by means of Isaiah, the future virginal birth of the Savior, and now the divine oracle is coming true. Showing that the promise of God has come true is not, obviously, a matter

---

24 Pietrafesa, *La Madonna nella Rivelazione*, p. 109. Laurentin, for his part, writes that "the religious intent of St. Luke... cannot be disassociated from a concern to express the truth about events relating to the real person of Christ.... He wanted his history to be truthful, solid, rigorous" (*Truth of Christmas*, p. 318).

25 G. Danieli, C.S.J., "I Vangeli dell'infanzia," *Credere oggi* 4 (1982): 40. The "discomfort," then, claimed by Perrot in contemplating the "wonders" of the infancy gospels appears unjustified and unfounded, and his discussion of the midrash does not seem very convincing. Cf. C. Perrot, *I racconti dell'infanzia di Gesù. Matteo 1–2, Luca 1–2* (Turin, 1977), pp. 8, 10–16.

> of anecdotal interest, but an invitation to the readers to respond in faith, and to commit their lives to Jesus Christ.[26]

Moreover, those who accept the thesis of midrashic genre, applied to the gospels of the infancy, must address all the complex problems involved in defining the criteria appropriate for distinguishing and separating what is history from what is historical fiction, what are facts from invented details, the events that really occurred from their interpretation as expressed through those narratives or details. Using such a premise, it is impossible for exegetes of an extremist bent and those more balanced not to arrive at conflicting assessments that confuse even more matters so delicate and important.[27]

Lastly, still more complicated is the problem of reconciling the midrashic genre with biblical inerrancy, since midrash introduces fictional elements of a legendary

---

26 *The Navarre Bible. Saint Mark's Gospel*, p. 41. In regard to the interpretation of the figure of Mary in Sacred Scripture, it is well known that there are two principal trends in the field of exegesis, as Laurentin notes: "that which holds Mary (and the biblical texts concerning her) as 'historical' and that which regards her as purely 'symbolic'" ("Bulletin sur Marie Mere du Seigneur," in *Revue des Sciences Philosophiques et Théologiques* 62 [1978]: 99). On this question, see the well-documented article of F. Spadafora, "L'Evangelo dell'infanzia," *Renovatio* 16 (1981): 46–71.

27 "In any historical assessment," says Peretto, "it is necessary to distinguish between the reality that the author wishes to affirm as true, and the modalities of the descriptions, i.e., precisely the interpretations of that reality" (E. M. Peretto, O.S.M., "Ricerche su Matteo 1–2," *Marianum* 35 [1969]: 140–247). But this is exactly the point at which exegetes collide. Who can determine where history concretely ends and modality and interpretation begin? St. Matthew, for example, is rich in Old Testament quotations suggestive of attractive parallels and coincidences, and yet "we are still far from the day," writes da Spinetoli, "when one might take for granted as well-founded the paralleisms discovered by scholars" (*Introduzione ai Vangeli*, p. 91). Laurentin, on his part (following Perrot), speaks of a turned-around midrash "that no longer defines events in the light of Scripture, but redefines Scripture in the light of Christ" (*Truth of Christmas*, pp. 90–91, also pp. 45, 451), and rests his case on "the reuse" of some Old Testament texts by St. Luke, of which only some, "by unanimous consent," would be certain (for example, 2 Sam 7:14; Mic 5:1; Mal 3; Dan 9), and advises "increasing this sum total" of "these identifications" (p. 45). Sustaining the contrary is U. E. Lattanzi, "Il Vangelo dell'Infanzia," pp. 39–42.

or mythical kind. The problem is a weighty one and difficult to resolve.

In conclusion, we wish to take as our own the Catholic position, the one not admitting the presence of the midrashic genre in the accounts of Jesus' infancy. We wish to affirm this expressly with regard to matters or particular details described by the Evangelists: the angels, the Magi, the star, the dreams, the grotto. We agree with Guidetti: "For us the details also share the historical character of the account: the biblical citations, and the numerous allusions, as well as the forms on which they are patterned, derive from the Mother of Jesus who, by her own testimony, 'kept all these things in her heart' (Lk 2:51b). Not only that, but 'she carefully kept all these things, pondering them in her heart'" (Lk 2:19).[28]

> On this point a passage of Feuillet strikes us as lucid and convincing: '... how can we believe that an Evangelist, who evidently intends to recount real facts, would have intentionally inserted false episodes in his narrative? One or the other of these two must be true: or he did not do this knowingly, and thus our confidence in him is seriously compromised, or he did this intentionally. But we must prove this latter convincingly. One must at the same time also show that so doing the Evangelist intended to trick or to deceive no one, even though he took no pains to note this expressly, or indicate how the narrative belongs to a literary genre so special that we are authorized to treat it in a manner apart. This is not all. Once on this path, how can we stop?...
>
> In reality, once one admits as present in the Gospels even one purely fictitious account, the exegete finds himself in a hellish bind. Why admit one and not another? The same reasons for calling the historicity of a passage into question

---

28 Guidetti, *Conoscenza storica*, p. 163. See also Laurentin, *Truth of Christmas*, pp. 386–398, where the author presents an interesting critical discussion on the "wonders" of the gospels of the infancy in relation to "wonders" in the religious experience of modern persons and in current events.

can continue to present themselves in relation to other passages, and so in fact has it happened. Initially it was the historicity of the accounts of the infancy to be attacked, then the resurrection, next the baptism of Jesus, the transfiguration and naturally the miracles. We supposedly do not know with certainty whether Jesus actually spoke the words of institution of the Eucharist… all is called into question. This slide into doubt becomes unstoppable and denial inevitable, as experience proves. Skepticism runs wild, a skepticism ruinous of faith, a ruin which little by little includes anything relative to the fundamental events of salvation history. In regard to the multiplication of bread, with some critics in the past sought to transform into a banal picnic rather than acknowledge a miracle, Fr. Lagrange once made this witty observation (as told to me): 'the miracle was invented, why not regard the whole event as a complete fiction? One can imagine anything.' Effectively the position of the extreme critics, excluding nothing from denial, at least has the merit of logic. As regards, for example, the accounts of the infancy in St. Matthew and St. Luke, a thoroughly logical negation would consist in refusing to believe everything *en bloc*, including the virginal conception of Jesus, on the grounds that it belongs to an autonomous literary genre. This genre consists in a clever exegetical, theological and symbolic montage, constructed with purpose of illustrating the singular greatness of Jesus, by introducing into the Gospel bits and pieces of the Old Testament. But by what right do we refuse some parts of the account and accept the rest?…

Hence, how can I distinguish in the narrative historical and non-historical elements? I will be condemned by this method to everlasting doubt. It is prudent, then, to ponder the words of Fr. Lagrange: 'one can imagine anything,' everything, including the apparitions of Christ Crucified. (If, as is often said, the details of the apparitions of the Risen Christ were invented, why not consider the fact of the

Resurrection fictitious as well?) What certain datum in such a scenario could support a firm conviction to the contrary?'[29]

[29] A. FEUILLET, *Maria Madre del Messia, Madre della Chiesa*, Milan 2004, pp. 15–17.

8
The Virgin Mary and the Origins of Jesus

Jesus has a dual origin. The first is his eternal generation—"from days of eternity" (Mic 5:1)—as the Word of the Father (Jn 1:1). The second is His generation in time from the Virgin Mary, as the *Incarnate* Word. His generation from *eternity* is in the bosom of the Father. His generation *in time* is in the womb of the Virgin Mary.

In the New Testament, the origins of Jesus Christ have been described by St. Paul and by the Evangelists St. Matthew, St. Luke, and St. John. Though briefly and schematically, St. Paul (Gal 4:4) and St. John (1:13–14) have clearly indicated the origins of Jesus both from the Father and from Mary. St. Matthew and St. Luke, on the other hand, have recorded the temporal origin of Jesus in its human, historical context by way of a genealogy descending from Abraham down to Jesus, according to St. Matthew (1:1–16), and a genealogy ascending from Jesus to Adam, according to St. Luke (3:23–38).

Only St. Matthew speaks of Mary by name in the genealogy of Jesus (1:16) St. Luke says nothing expressly about her in his genealogy. St. Paul does not name Mary, but explicitly talks about the "woman" who "made" Jesus (*factum ex muliere*). So too, St. John does not name Mary, but speaks in equivalent terms about the "virginal birth" of Jesus (1:13–14).

The presence of Mary, in any case, is beyond question in the record of the temporal origin of Jesus, because she, and she alone, by the work of the Holy Spirit, without any cooperation of man, is the human origin of Jesus. She has linked the Word of God to human flesh and to the history of mankind. She has *"made"* Jesus (Gal 4:4); and from her *"Jesus was born"* (Mt 1:16); she is the *"Mother of Jesus"* (Jn 2:1). Detailed study of these three biblical passages will contribute to a fuller and deeper knowledge of Mary, the one person always with her Son *from His birth* and, in a certain sense, from *eternity* as well.

I

But when the fullness of time was come, God sent His Son, born of a woman, born under the law, to redeem those who were under the law, that we might receive the adoption of sons (Gal 4:4–5).

The Apostle of the Gentiles mentions Mary only once.[1] He gives no data concerning her, nor does he even record her name. Nevertheless, for all his brevity, he succeeds in presenting her as an active participant in the mystery of the Incarnation of the Word and of the Redemption of men called to the *"adoption of sons."* Mary is the *"woman"* who has made Jesus (*factum ex muliere* as the Vulgate reads), from

1 "This is the only passage of St. Paul," writes A. Poppi, "which contains an allusion to the Mother of Jesus. Hence, it is given a certain priority in the lists of Marian texts, because it is one of the oldest of these" ("I nuovi figli di Dio," with D. Pezzetta, *Il Lezionario Mariano*, p. 230). In fact, it seems inadequate to categorize as a simple "allusion" a text so rich in content. It is preferable to call it a clear "reference," fleeting indeed, but important and incisive. In regard to its alleged dating prior to the Gospels, R. Laurentin rightly states: "Is it even certain that the Gospels were written after the Pauline epistles and the year 70? Robinson has demonstrated the weakness of the generally held consensus on this question, and no one has refuted the view which places their composition between 50 and 60" (*Truth of Christmas*, p. 410). See, for confirmation, the important article of F. Spadafora, "Data di composizione degli Evangeli," *Divinitas* 30 (1986): 78–84, where the author reviews three recent and important studies by J. A. T. Robinson, C. Tresmontant, and J. Carmignac. Of great value is the more recent study of Ph. Rolland, *L'origine et la date des évangiles*, Paris 1994.

whom Jesus was *"born"* in the *"fullness of time"* appointed for the Redemption of mankind.[2]

In the text, St. Paul speaks of the Incarnation in terms that "characterize its exclusively feminine mode," writes Laurentin, "a curious paradox if one considers that the very apostle reputed by many to be misogynous has emphatically reserved this role to the woman."[3] The picture sketched by St. Paul reveals the most fundamental point of God's salvific plan: the Incarnation of the Son of God will make men the adoptive "sons" of God, ransoming them from the slavery of the law. "We see in his theology," writes Koehler, "an indispensable frame of reference for correctly understanding the divine plan and the place of Mary in the history of salvation."[4] The Mother of the Son of God, the "woman" Mary, is here introduced primarily to guarantee the reality of the Incarnation in its human dimension, to guard against any temptation to docetism.[5] Moreover, in view of the expression *"born of a woman,"* unusual and inexplicable in terms of the Semitic mentality regularly describing a person as *born of a man*,[6] it cannot be doubted that St. Paul wanted to affirm and confirm directly the absence of a human father of Jesus,[7] and implicitly,

---

2 Concerning the philological discussion of the terms "natum" and "factum," see A. Vanhoye, S.J., "La Mère du Fils de Dieu selon Gal.," *Marianum* 40 (1978): 238–240.

3 Laurentin, *Truth of Christmas*, p. 408 (Ital. ed., p. 544).

4 T. Koehler, S.M., *Maria nella Sacra Scritura* (Vercelli, 1970), p. 45.

5 Mary "is the one who guarantees the true humanity of the Son of God among us" (Pezzetta, "I nuovi figli," p. 236).

6 "A quite striking expression," writes Laurentin, "which refers Him to a mother and not to a human father (Gal 4:4). It would have been more natural and more obvious to say: 'begotten of a man'" (*Truth of Christmas*, pp. 408–409). Laurentin himself cites the detailed study of A. Vicent Cernuda, "La genesis humana de Jesu Cristo según S. Pablo," *Estudios Biblicos* 36 (5978): 57–77, 267–289.

7 The expression "*born of a woman*," explains Laurentin, "reveals the intention of avoiding any allusion linking Jesus to a human father" (*Tutte le genti*, p. 22). Vanhoye points out that "the formulation employed by St. Paul harmonizes without difficulty with the tradition of the infancy narratives, for it presents the Christ as the Son of God, on the one hand, and as "born

therefore, but unequivocally, "to lay the grounds" not only for the *virginal maternity* of Mary in regard to Christ,[8] but also for her *Divine Maternity* in regard to the Son of God[9] and her *Spiritual Maternity* in regard to the "adoptive" sons of God:[10] the pauline text is indeed thus pregnant in expressing, even in outline form, the primary and profound content of the mystery of Christ and Mary.

It is surprising that there are still exegetes who try to deny any unequivocal reference, even implicit, to the virginal maternity of Mary, in the *"woman"* of Galatians 4:4. "It is inappropriate," claims A. Poppi, "to force the sense of 'made by a woman' so as to deduce from it a Mariological doctrine without basis here. Paul has absolutely no intention here of setting in relief the virginal conception of Jesus."[11] That St. Paul, in Galatians 4:4, does not want "to set in relief" the virginal conception of Jesus, is clear enough. Nevertheless, that the virginal conception is here asserted implicitly, but unequivocally, is equally clear, because the expression *"born of a woman,"* in excluding the presence of a human father, clearly describes an event, the conception and birth of Christ, that is *virginal*: evidently and necessarily in view of the description. Hardly "groundless,"

---

of a woman" on the other, without any mention of a human father" ("La Mere du Fils," pp. 243–244).

8 For the history of the exegesis of Gal 4:4 regarding the virginal maternity, see E. de Roover, "La maternité virginale de Marie dans l'interprétation de Gal 4, 4," *Studiorum Paulinorum Congressus*, vol. 2 (Rome, 1963), pp. 17–37. Only since the nineteenth century have exegetes formed four schools of thought on this point (ibid., p. 30).

9 The expression "*his Son*" (literally "the Son of him") appears "precisely defined," writes Vanhoye; "it is in the singular, with the article and with a personal pronoun connoting God; it is predicated of a real person who enters human history. No text of the Old Testament speaks of the Son of God in so precise a fashion" ("La Mère du Fils," p. 243).

10 Laurentin speaks of orientation "towards a conception of spiritual maternity" (*Tutte le genti*, p. 22); Pietrafesa recognizes in Gal 4:4 "a rather important hint concerning the Spiritual Maternity of the Blessed Mother for all the redeemed" (*La Madonna nella Rivelazione*, p. 106).

11 Poppi, "I nuovi figli," p 232.

therefore, is the Mariological doctrine resting on this text in relation to the virginal maternity of Mary Most Holy.[12] Thus the authoritative A. Feuillet could write recently that "according to a good number of Catholic and also Protestant commentators, St. Paul shows himself aware of the virginal maternity of Mary, because he gives absolutely no hint of a father of Jesus, born of the Woman."[13]

In this regard particularly significant is the fact that the new *Catechism of the Catholic Church* associates the passage of Galatians 4:4 with that of the Annunciation in St. Luke (Lk 1:26–38): "the Annunciation of Mary inaugurates the 'fullness of time' (Gal 4:4), viz., the fulfillment of the promises and of the preparation" (§ 484).

In particular, with reference to the *virginal maternity* of Mary in the context of St. Paul's Christological thought, we agree with the conclusion of A. Vicent Cernuda quoted by R. Laurentin:

---

12 Laurentin affirms that Pauline theology regarding the origin of Christ neither ignores nor denies His virginal conception, but, on the contrary, it "contains some surprising traits which harmonize with it" (*Truth of Christmas*, p. 409). Likewise Pietrafesa, who refers to other exegetes who "think that Paul by saying 'born of a woman,' instead of a man, wants to affirm the virginity of the Blessed Mother" (*La Madonna nella Rivelazione*, p. 106). Ruotolo, too, in Gal 4:4, understands the Word to have assumed "human nature from the most pure womb of Mary, without the cooperation of any man" (*La Sacra Scrittura*, vol. 22C [Naples, 1981], p. 54). F. Amiot cites in support of this reading Pelagius, Comely, Steinmann (*S. Paolo. Epistola ai Galati. Epistole ai Tessalonicessi* [Rome, 1964], p. 584). M. Sales cites also Durand and Brassac (*La Sacra Bibbia. Nuovo Testamento*, vol. 2 [Turin, 1949], p. 257). "The text of Gal. 4:4 probably assumes that St. Paul had knowledge of the virginal birth, though he does not treat that point directly," writes J. Bligh, *La Lettera ai Galati* (Rome, 1972), p. 653 (original Eng. ed.: *Galatians. A Discussion of St. Paul's Epistle* [London, 1969]). See also F. Manzi, op. cit., p. 672, where the author explains how St. Paul does not speak expressly of "the virginal birth of Jesus, not because he is unaware of it, but simply because his attention in focused rather on the paradoxical dynamic of the Incarnation of the Son of God." For this reason the text of Gal 4:4, even though extremely concise from a Mariological point of view, remains nevertheless "open to the Gospel details on the virginal maternity of Mary" (p. 686).

13 A. Feuillet, Maria: *Madre del Messia, Madre della Chiesa*, Milan 2004, p. 12. The author also refers to his study: *Le Sauveur messianique et sa mère dans les récits de l'enfance de saint Matthieu et de saint Luca*, Vatican City 1990.

> St. Paul knew of the virginal conception and transmitted it... as an integrating element of the Incarnation. If it is true that this mystery does not by itself constitute a prominent feature of Pauline theology, it is no less true that the stylized allusions (analyzed above) reveal the depth of the Apostle's meditation on this theme in its two aspects:
>
> —the assumption of a concrete humanity (by Christ, etc.);
>
> —its virginal actuation.
>
> He is proposing... [this] Christology in admirable outline... as it were, abbreviated. His archaic formulae confirm that the virginal conception, considered mythical by many exegetes, belonged to the oldest strata of Christian tradition.[14]

It might seem that such deductive argumentation draws too much from this simple expression *"born of a woman."* In reality, all of the inferences are found in that expression without forcing the text in any way. Quite the contrary, they are supported by the general tenor characteristic of Pauline thought as a whole, which in this passage is directed to give evidence of the Incarnation of the Son of God. This Son, not directly, but *ex muliere,* through a woman, reaches the human family in order to assume it and redeem it by making men sons of God "by adoption," that is, His brothers and co-heirs, as elsewhere St. Paul himself says (cf. Rom 8:17; Eph 1:11), making them pass "from a state of subjection to a state of emancipation," as Manzi writes.[15] "The text of Galatians 4:4 has a great importance for Mariology," writes Koehler, "because it synthesizes very well the belief of the first Christians in the historical fact of the Incarnation and the theology that for Paul provides the

---

14 CERNUDA, "La genesis humana," p. 289, quoted by Laurentin, *Truth of Christmas*, p. 409. At the end of his study, Vanhoye concludes that "the phrase of Gal 4:4 is, in virtue of the genre used, positively open to complementary affirmations of the infancy narratives on the subject of the human birth of the Son of God" ("La Mere du Fils," p. 247).

15 F. MANZI, *Tratti mariologici del "Vangelo" di Paolo*, in *Theotokos* 8 (2000) 659.

context for proclaiming this event of salvation."[16] Mary, the "woman," appears here as the necessary link, or better, as the vital point of insertion of the divine in the carnal, historical, human reality assumed by the Word in her and from her, for the Redemption of all men.[17]

Thus, even if implicit or indirect, subordinated or dependent, the presence of this "woman": Virgin Mother, here appears inseparable both from the Son of God by nature and from the sons of God by "adoption," from the Redeemer and from the redeemed humanity, and finally, from Christ and from the Church. In Galatians 4:4 can be caught a precise glimpse of the Virgin Mother of Christ and of the Church.[18]

"Besides a generation according to the flesh," D. Pezzetta concludes, "we find here in Mary a generation of the Son of God by faith and love. In this sense she is the first, unique member of the Church of which Christ is the Head, and so, Mother of all the new sons of God."[19]

---

16 Koehler, *Maria nella Sacra Scrittura*, pp. 45–46. It should be noted that St. Paul "experienced difficulty," writes Laurentin, "in trying to express the Incarnation, which he perceives in terms of contrast as an abasement and 'kenosis' (whereas St. John finds glory in the flesh and in the Cross itself)" (*Truth of Christmas*, p. 408; Ital. ed.: p. 545). "In Galatians 3:13–14 and 4:4," writes Vanhoye, "Paul in this way seeks to give a fully satisfying explanation of the Redemption. His objective rather is to underscore the astounding, the supra-rational dimensions. The Redemption is a divine work: God upsets the calculations of men. The Incarnation of the Son of God and His death as a criminal are among the follies of God. (cf. 1 Cor 1:18, 23)" ("La Mere du Fils," p. 245).

17 "God sent (*exapesteilen*) His Son," writes Poppi, "preexisting from eternity, to assume our flesh. He 'becomes' man, being born of a woman (*genômenon ek gynaik ôs*), that is: he really joins the human family. Furthermore, by being born under the law (*genòmenon ypò homôn*), he shares its history, becoming profoundly one with the destiny of men" ("I nuovi figli," p. 231).

18 Cf. the profound, well-documented study of C. Pozo, S.J., *Maria en la Escritura y en la fe de la Iglesia* (Madrid, 1978).

19 Pezzetta, *I nuovo figli*, p. 237.

II

Jacob begot Joseph, the Spouse of Mary, of whom was born Jesus called the Christ (Mt 1:16)

The first appearance of Mary's name in the Gospel of St. Matthew occurs in the first chapter, verse 16, precisely on the first page of the Gospel.

Mary is inserted here in a genealogy originating with Abraham. She is the penultimate link in the third group or series of fourteen persons just before Jesus, who terminates the genealogy, a genealogy structured by St. Matthew according to the style of that time, dominated by the symbolism of numbers, so popular among the Hebrews.

"The fourteenth personage of the third series," notes Leonardi, "is Jesus: in order to reach the fourteenth, one needs to count, besides Joseph, Mary too. This is a rarity in a Hebrew genealogy, where the father only, and not the mother, figured in the computation. The rarity, however, is intentional here, to underscore the extraordinary character of the virgin birth of Jesus from Mary by the work of the Holy Spirit."[20]

Interestingly, St. Matthew, although elsewhere in his Gospel stressing almost exclusively the role of men in the work of salvation, here reveals himself very solicitous about placing Mary at the key point in the dynasty of the Messiah. St. Luke, instead, though recording far more extensively

---

20 LEONARDI, *L'Infanzia di Gesù* (Padua, 1975), p. 37; the author also cites (ibid., n. 25) X. LEON DUFOUR and S. CAVALETTI (the second in regard to the symbolism of numbers). "In reality," notes G. SALDARINI (citing D. Buzy), "the emphasis in the last verse (v. 16), puts Mary in an exceptional place" ("La genealogia di Gesù," in *Introduzione alla Bibbia*, vol. 4 [Turin, 1973], p. 226). According to A. Ory, Mt 1:16 has much value as a "reasonableness test" in favor of the physical virginity of Mary Most Holy at the conception of Jesus. In concluding his analysis, Ory affirms that in this verse there is "a proof of silence, extraordinarily convincing, of the physical virginity of Mary" (*Riscoprire la verità*, p. 104).

the activity of women in his Gospel, does not mention Mary at all in the genealogy of Jesus (3:23–38). Further, St. Matthew includes in his genealogy four other women: Tamar, Rahab, Ruth, and Bathsheba (although they do not constitute genealogical links in their own right, but only in union with their husbands).[21]

The presence of these four in the genealogy has been variously interpreted. Thus, there has existed a tendency to regard these four women, or at least some of them, as public sinners, to show that the Messiah came to save sinners. Likewise they have often been viewed as foreigners (non Israelites), to demonstrate the universalism distinctive of the salvific plan of the Redeemer Messiah.[22] Further, these four women may be considered as mothers who became such in an irregular, though not a sinful way, and thus were inserted in the salvific plan guided from on high, in order to prepare or prefigure the maternity of the Mother of Jesus, miraculous in every respect.[23]

Finally, the presence of these four women in the genealogy underscores the fact that "they played an extraordinary,

---

21 Of interest are the observations of R. Laurentin on this point: "Here Matthew is unusual and differs from Luke. Though the latter has brought the women of the Gospel into broad daylight, he does not, strangely enough, breathe a word about Mary in his genealogy (3:23–38). It is a genealogy without a mother. He who has spoken better of Mary than anyone else (Lk 1:26–56, 2:5–7) does not name her at all and omits, in this context, any reference to her lineage.

"Then, why does Matthew, who seems more inclined to the masculine prejudices, give to Mary a key position? And why does he include four other women, Tamar, Rahab, Ruth, and the wife of Uriah, Bathsheba, who became the wife of David? (The questions are related.) Why has he chosen these women and not Sarah, nor Rebecca, nor Leah and others, who figure more prominently in the history of the origins of the Chosen People in accordance with Jewish tradition?" (*Truth of Christmas*, pp. 339–340).

22 Cf. J. Schniewind, *Il Vangelo secondo Matteo* (Brescia, 1977), pp. 26–27; Laurentin, *Truth of Christmas*, pp. 340–341; Leonardi, *L'Infanzia di Gesù*, pp. 37–38; A. Poppi, *Sinossi dei quattro vangeli. Commento* (Padua, 1988), p. 26; A. Lancellotti, *Matteo* (Rome, 1986), pp. 39–40.

23 This is the thesis proposed and defended especially by A. Paul, *Il Vangelo dell'infanzia secondo San Matteo* (Rome, 1986), pp. 28–38. See also Saldarini, "La genealogia di Gesù," p. 227; Poppi, *Sinossi*, p. 26.

personal role in the history of Israel, and, more specifically in the history of the dynasty."[24] Thus, TAMAR prevented the extinction of the tribe of Judah, by providing her father-in-law messianic posterity (Gen 38:15–16, 29–30). RAHAB facilitated for the Hebrew people the conquest of Jericho, making easier their entrance into the promised land (Jos 2:1ff.; 6:17ff.). RUTH, the Moabite, married Boaz, the closest relative of her dead husband, and begot Obed, the grandfather of David (Ruth 3:1; 4:13, 15). BATHSHEBA secured from David that her son Solomon should become the heir promised by God according to the word of the prophet Nathan (2 Sam 7:8–16).[25]

Now, "if Matthew," observes Laurentin, "who usually gives women a marginal role, mentions these four at the beginning of his Gospel, he does so in order that they might prefigure the unexpected, and *different,* role of Mary,"[26] that is, Matthew affirms "the bewildering fact (which was scarcely credible to his contemporaries) that Mary was the sole human origin of Christ."[27] This is the reason why, therefore, Mary "is counted as the second to the last of the fourteen links between the two begotten non-begetters: Joseph, the legal father, and Christ, the last link. She is another unusual link (disconnected from Joseph, referred to God alone: 1:18–20), indispensable to the manifestation of a mystery, which bewilders the wisdom of sages and the order of this world."[28] It is certain, nevertheless, that the

24 LAURENTIN, *Truth of Christmas*, p. 341.

25 R. SEEBERG synthesizes very well the significance of these women "by recalling how they stand at the principal junctures of Israel's history: Tamar at the beginning of the genealogy, Rahab in the conquest of the promised land, Ruth as a progenitor of David's house (Ruth 4:17), Bathsheba, wife of the first king" (quoted from SCHNIEWIND, *Il Vangelo*, p. 27). See LAURENTIN, *Truth of Christmas*, p. 341; the author also cites studies of Jeanne d'Arc Soveur, A. PAUL, and J. MASSON (ibid., pp. 9, 10, 11).

26 Ibid., p. 341.

27 Ibid., p. 346.

28 Ibid., p. 347.

genealogy of St. Matthew is ended exactly by the triad Joseph–Mary–Christ. It is this earthly "trinity" that marks the beginning of the creation of the new humanity from the virginal womb of Mary made fecund by the Holy Spirit.

In regard to Mary's own genealogy, however, little can be said with certainty. Some claim to discover the genealogy of Mary in the genealogy compiled by St. Luke (3:23–38): she would figure here as the daughter of Eli (Eliakim, or Joachim).[29] "In Matthew we are told the legal descent of Jesus, via his foster father Joseph," states G. Saldarini,

> while in Luke we have the natural one, via Mary. The two genealogies remain, in this way, perfectly consistent with the scope of each Evangelist. Matthew, who wants to affirm more expressly that Jesus is the Messiah, makes use of a legal genealogy, based on the paternal line of the foster father; Luke, instead, who wants to show Jesus as the Savior of all men, employs His natural genealogy from Adam, based therefore on the maternal line. The validity of this hypothesis rests on the verification of one condition: that Mary would have been, if not the only daughter, at least the heiress. In fact, nothing is ever mentioned in the New Testament about brothers of Mary. In John 19:25 there is a possible reference to *sisters,* but not necessarily older ones; who may well be sisters only in the wider sense of the term.[30]

All this still remains at the level of hypothesis and research, in no wise affecting the truth of these genealogies or their substantial value and meaning for theology.[31]

---

29 See Leonardi, *L'Infanzia di Gesù*, p. 48; Severiano del Paramo, *Vangelo secondo Matteo* (Rome, 1970), who in support cites the exegetes Vogt, Heer, Mangenot, Didon, Le Camus, Ruffini, Simon-Dorado (ibid. p. 47, n. 5). According to some recent authors, instead, Matthew should be considered as reporting the genealogy of Mary, and therefore the Joseph in 1:16 would be the father of Mary (cf. H. A. Blair, "Matthew 1:16 and the Matthean Genealogy," *Studia Evangelica* 2 [1964]: 149–154).

30 Saldarini, "La genealogia di Gesù," p. 231.

31 For the whole, intricate question, see the well-written and documented studies by Masson, *Jésus fils de David*; Saldarini, "La genealogia di Gesù," pp. 223–232. Regarding difficulties, which, however, do not affect the

It is clear, in any case, that the place of Mary in Matthew's genealogy as mentioned above is a privileged one, even syntactically, because exactly where the final link between David and Jesus, that is, Mary, must be inserted, St. Matthew makes use of a passive verbal form, instead of an active one (*"Mary of whom Jesus was born"*), indisputably clear evidence for the mystery of Jesus' divinity.[32]

Of particular significance, therefore, is the fact that at the very inaugural of God's salvific plan on the very first page of the Gospel, 1:16, we "meet joined for the first time the three names of Jesus, Mary and Joseph, so dear to Christian piety."[33]

III

Who not from blood, nor by will of the flesh, nor by will of man but of God has been begotten (Jn 1:13).

The Incarnation of the Word, His virginal conception, and virginal birth are contained in verse 13 of the prologue of St. John's Gospel, if the verb "has been begotten" (*eghennéte*) is read in the singular, thus referring to Jesus, rather than in the plural: "have been begotten" (*eghennéatesan*), *referring* to believers in Christ and to their baptismal rebirth, as is the case when the verb is read in the plural.[34]

---

importance and the historical value of the two genealogies of Matthew and Luke, cf. also the pages of Laurentin, *Truth of Christmas*, 354–357.

32 Cf. M. Masini and G. Antonioli, "Risalendo alle origini," in *La Madre di Dio*, edited by M. Massini (Brescia, 1975), p. 263; *The Navarre Bible. St. Matthew's Gospel* (Dublin, 1988), p. 29.

33 Del Paramo, *Vangelo secondo Matteo*, p. 48.

34 For the whole question, quite complicated and delicate, see the fundamental studies by P. Hofrichter, *Nicht aus Blut sondern monogen aus Gott geboren. Text kritische, dogmengeschichtliche und exegetische Untersuchung zu Joh 1, 13–14* (Würzburg, 1978); J. Galot, *Etre né de Dieu. Jean 1, 13* (Rome, 1969); *idem*, "Maternità verginale di Maria e Paternità divina," *La Civiltà Cattolica* 139 (1988): III, pp. 209–222. By reading the verb in the singular ("has been begotten") "the text refers to the virginal birth of Christ... rather than to the baptismal rebirth of Christians" (D. Crossan, O.S.M.,

The translation used here is that in the singular, the one adopted by the *Jerusalem Bible,* which is the reading unanimously preferred in antiquity.[35] The plural, first used by Valentinian heretics (agnostic sect) was later adopted by the Church, in order to oppose the error of the Docetists' denial of the reality of the humanity of Christ.[36]

> An important confirmation of the preference to be accorded the version in the singular of verse 13 of the Prologue of St. John comes from a study of Bernadette Escaffre Ladet,[37] where it is asserted that, although there are really few manuscripts or codices with verse 13 in the singular—'no Greek manuscripts transmit a reading in the singular. Only two manuscripts of the *Vetus Latina* do so (the *codex Veronensis* of the 5th century and the "*liber comicus,*" the lectionary of the church of Toledo ascribed to St. Ildephonse...)'—nonetheless, the witness of Fathers and writers such as St. Ireneaus, Origen, Tertullian, St. John Chrysostum, St. Jerome, Sulpitius Severus and St. Augustine, is without exception in support of the singular, nor is the possibility to be excluded that St. Ignatius of Antioch and St. Justin 'are among the Fathers in favor of the reading in the singular.' On the other hand one should not overlook the fact that while the version in the plural has only witnesses in the region of Alexandria, the version in the singular enjoys witnesses from many more

"The Marian Significance of John 1:12–13," in *Maria in Sacra Scriptura*, vol. [Rome, 1967], p. 99).

35 Study of the Fathers of the second century shows "the first witnesses unanimously in favor of the singular for Jn 1:13" affirms J. Galot, *Etre né de Dieu*, p. 80. The same has been stated, more recently, by R. Robert, "La leçon christologique en Jean 113," *Revue Thomiste* 87 (1987): II. See also de La Potterie, *Maria nel mistero*, p. 124 (Eng. ed.: *Mary in the Mystery*, pp. 97–98): "The most ancient witnesses are all in favor of the singular." (Hereinafter all page references will be to the English edition of this work).

36 Besides the three studies cited in note 33, see also I. de La Potteire, "La Mere de Jesus et la conception virginale du Fils de Dieu. Etudes de théologie johanique," *Marianum* 40 (1978): 41–90, especially pp. 64–65, 70–72. Two longer, more detailed studies were subsequently published by the same author, including an analytical exposition of each point in question set within the framework of a solid, integrated vision: "Il parto verginale del Verbo incarnato: 'Non ex sanguinibus..., sed ex Deo natus est' (Jn 1, 13)," *Marianum* 45 (1983): 127–174; *Mary in the Mystery*, pp. 96–141.

37 *L'Evangile de Jean fait-il reference a la conception virginale?*, in *Ephemerides Mariologicae*, 43 (1993) 349–365.

areas: Gaul (Irenaeus); Alexandria (Origen); North Africa (Tertullian); Syria or Palestine (Letter of the Apostles); and perhaps Rome (Justin) and Antioch (Ignatius of Antioch)."

Still more decisive, finally, seems to be the fact that the writings of the Fathers with the version in the singular are older that the Greek manuscripts and codices where the reading in the plural is found: 'on the other hand the writings of the Fathers here cited, witnessing to the reading in the singular, are older than the Greek codices. Only the papyrus could be contemporary with Irenaeus, Tertullian and the Letter of the Apostles. One is thereby justified in calling into question the authenticity of the reading proposed by the Greek manuscripts.'[38]

The singular form, supported by a considerable number of contemporary exegetes,[39] sets in relief the Christological and Mariological content of verse 13, above all, the profound link between the mystery of the Incarnation of the Word and the mystery of His virginal conception and His virginal birth of Mary.

St. John the Evangelist, who has transmitted no details of the genealogy and the infancy of Jesus in the prologue to his Gospel, instead has synthesized and transmitted truths that are at the basis of the Incarnation, that is, the eternal preexistence of the Word[40] and His "making Himself flesh" in Mary and by Mary[41] via the *virginal* conception and

---

38 *Art. cit.*, pp. 351–353.

39 Cf. DE LA POTTERIE, "La Mère de Jesus," pp. 60–61; "Il parto verginale," p. 128, n. 21.

40 "The fact John does not provide a genealogy," writes Laurentin, "and brings up the human origin of Christ only through the objections of adversaries (1:46; 6:42; 7:42–52), manifests a breakthrough more radical than Matthew's eagle-eye perspective rises to the eternal pre-existence of the Son of God made man" (*Truth of Christmas*, p. 363).

41 G. Segalla makes an interesting observation on this verse of the Prologue: "*and the word became flesh and dwelt among us*," in which verse "is hidden the living presence of the Mother. One may in fact ask: *how* did the word become flesh and dwell among us? Obviously through his Mother, included in this singular event whereby the only-begotten Son reveals God the Father (Jn 1:18)": G. SEGALLA, *La "Madre degli inizi" nel Vangelo di Giovanni*, in *Theotokos* 8 (2000) 774.

birth. Concisely, yet organically, John 1:13, together with verse 14, contains the following articles of faith concerning the mystery of the Incarnation of the Word:

1. Jesus, the Son of God, born of Mary, *"has been begotten of God"* (v. 13), *"the only-begotten of the Father"* (v. 14). This is an affirmation of the *unique* origin of Jesus, or of the *paternity of the Father.*[42]

2. *Jesus "has been begotten of God"* in the sense that Mary has conceived Him not *"by the will of the flesh, nor by the will of man"* (v. 13), but *virginally.* It is an affirmation of her *virginity before childbirth.*[43]

3. Jesus *"made himself flesh"* (v. 14), being born of Mary virginally and *"not from blood"* (v. 13), that is, being born without the pain and afterbirth that accompany natural delivery. This is an affirmation of her *virginity during childbirth.*[44]

---

42 "Contrary to Matthew and Luke, our text attributes the conception of Christ, not to the Spirit, but to God, and this, immediately after the exclusion of a human father, which discreetly introduces the idea of the divine fatherhood": De La Potterie, "La Mère de Jesus," p. 78. "It is God himself who has been presented as the Father of the Incarnate Word" (*idem*, p. 131). Nevertheless, "with regard to the man Jesus, God does not act as father in the physical sense," but in the creative one (*idem*, p. 138). "The conception of Jesus is new creation," says J. Ratzinger, *Introduzione al Cristianesimo* (Brescia, 1969), p. 221 (Eng. ed.: *Introduction to Christianity* [New York, 1970], p. 206). About the radical incompatibility of two paternities for Jesus: one of the Father and one of Joseph, see de La Potterie, "parto verginale," p. 139, where he quotes, in support, J. Ratzinger, J. Ledit, R. Virgoulay, against R. Brown and others, off-base; in *Mary in the Mystery*, he also cites in support von Balthasar, Laurentin, McHugh, Martelet, Barth (pp. 132–133, 138).

43 Laurentin writes that in Jn 1:13 "the virginal conception is explicitly referred to" (*Truth of Christmas*, p. 406). The "will of the flesh" connotes carnal desire proper to the sexual instinct; the "will of man" connotes the role of the man who wills procreation: cf. de La Potterie, *Mary in the Mystery*, pp. 105–106.

44 "The negation 'not from blood,' then, signifies that, when He was given birth by His mother, there was no afterbirth, that it was a *virginal birth*": de La Potterie, "Il parto verginale," p. 150. Also important is the documented explanation of the meaning to be assigned the plural "bloods" instead of "blood" (ibid., pp. 139–147, 150–158), in reference also to Lk 1:35 (pp. 163–171). On pp. 148–50 this author replies to the weak objections of J. Galot and J. Winandy against this interpretation in favor of the virginal birth; see also *Mary in the Mystery*, pp. 100–116.

The absence of the three specific elements *blood, flesh, man,* necessary in every natural human generation, helps to demonstrate the reality of the Incarnation of the Word conceived and delivered by Mary *virginally,*[45] that is, miraculously, without opening the womb and without afterbirth, and nevertheless in a very proper and real sense of the term a fully "corporeal," human generation.[46] "Each of the three negatives in the verse," observes de La Potterie,

> has a specific value. The third negation excludes the intervention of a man in the conception of the Incarnate Word (it is what later will be called *virginity before childbirth*). By means of the first negation, John says that the childbirth itself took place without the bodily pain usually followed by afterbirth blood (*virginity during childbirth*). According to this reading, John speaks both of the virginal conception and of the virginal birth of the Word made flesh.[47]

Precisely this "virginal" conception and birth are the effective "sign" of the *divine filiation*: of Jesus, begotten of God, as the *"only-begotten of the Father."* "If the man Jesus," continues de La Potterie, "is truly born 'without afterbirth,' if He has truly been conceived without the intervention of a 'will of man,' then we have in this a 'sign' that He *'has been begotten by God.'* God Himself is His Father, and He is the *only-begotten Son* from that Father (v. 14)."[48]

---

45 "The triple negation," writes J. Galot, "is not a redundancy. It excludes with exactitude all that must be excluded from the virginal birth of Christ" (*Etre né de Dieu*, p. 118).

46 The expression "was begotten" has "clearly a corporal sense: it deals both with conception and with birth, that is to say, with the flesh of the Word Incarnate" (De La Potterie, "La Mère de Jésus," p. 83).

47 De La Potterie, "Il parto verginale," p. 142. The polemical character of the Evangelist's triple negation directly against those denying the virginal conception and birth of Jesus should be noted. The same author continues: "The triple negation, certainly, reveals polemical intent; it is directed, however, not against heretics who rejected the reality of the *Incarnation*, but against those denying the virginal *conception* and birth of Jesus" ("La Mère de Jésus," p. 74).

48 De La Potterie, *Mary in the Mystery*, p. 131.

An important detail to be noted, however, concerns the active presence of the "will" of the Virgin Mary, to whom the Evangelist does not explicitly allude. Yet it is a detail that seems connatural to the dynamism of the act of conceiving proper to a free and judicious woman such as Mary was under the divine action, as depicted in Luke 1:26–38. "In calling attention to the virginal birth," notes J. Galot,

> the Evangelist took care not to exclude the will of the woman. He knew that Mary had accepted the divine invitation to become the mother of a child who would be the Son of God. He did not mention this cooperation of the woman because his purpose was to stress the divine filiation. Thus can be understood the difference and complementarity between the account of John and that of Luke, according to which Jesus is born of the Holy Spirit and the Virgin Mary. According to John, Jesus is born of God without the cooperation of the will of man. Nevertheless, though silent about the role of the woman, the Evangelist in effect did consider it in a special way: it is the only human cooperation he has not excluded from the birth of Jesus. Hence, a woman permitted the Son of God to belong to the human family by means of an authentic human birth.[49]

So interpreting verses 13 and 14 of the prologue, we have in St. John a witness of the highest caliber to the mystery of the Incarnation, revealed both in its metahistorical and transcendent, as well as historical and physical (corporal) dimensions. The Fatherhood of God and the divine filiation of the Word, the Divine Maternity of Mary and the virginal conception and birth of Jesus from her, are contained, both explicitly and implicitly, in these two verses of John's prologue.[50] Further, these dimensions are

---

49 Galot, "Maternità verginale," p. 219.

50 Thus, the thesis of those who deny to St. John knowledge of the virginal conception becomes untenable: cf. J. McHugh, *The Mother of Jesus in the New Testament* (New York, 1975), p. 266. It remains a fact, however, that this is "the only text of the fourth Gospel that mentions explicitly the virginal conception" (De La Potterie, "La Mère de Jésus," p. 59).

so correlated that the corporal virginity of Mary, before and during the childbirth, is the concrete, effective *sign* of the divine filiation of Jesus.[51]

In perfect harmony with these two verses is verse 12, which deals with the birth of Christians through faith and baptism, a prolongation, we might say, of the Incarnation of Christ and an unveiling of His eternal generation from the Father. Laurentin writes that "it is through 'power' given Christians to 'become children of God' by faith in Him who 'was not begotten of blood, nor by the will of flesh, nor by the will of man, but was born of the will of God' that the eternal birth is known."[52] Consequently, the close link between the divine filiation of Jesus and the filiation by faith of the baptized clearly postulates on the part of the baptized just as close a link with the maternity of Mary, embracing Son and children, Christ and the Church.

"Because our supernatural childhood parallels the divine childhood," explains de La Potterie, "the maternity of Mary in reference to us will parallel her maternity in reference to Jesus."[53] Furthermore: "If Mary is the Mother of the God made man, our model, she will have a role to play in the repetition of this 'incarnation' in the souls of believers. The maternity of Mary initiating the Incarnation of Jesus, prolongs itself in the life of Christians."[54]

---

51 Cf. de La Potterie, "La Mère de Jesus," p. 85: "*The corporal virginity of Mary*, when she conceives and gives to the world her child, is the sign and the manifestation of the divine filiation of Jesus"; *idem*, *Mary in the Mystery*, pp. 131–132.

52 Laurentin, *Truth of Christmas*, p. 408. "Between our divine birth and the earthly birth of Jesus," summarizes de La Potterie, "there is an intimate, essential relation" ("La Mère de Jesus," p. 80). D. Crossan understands in v. 13 "the plural as reflective of the singular idea, i.e., baptismal rebirth described in terms of the virginal birth of Jesus": ("The Marian Significance of John 1:12–13," in *Maria in Sacra Scriptura*, vol. 5, p. 104). The author defended this thesis as a "harmonizing" of the plural and singular readings of v. 13; but his opinion gained no support.

53 De La Potterie, *Mary in the Mystery*, pp. 118–119.

54 Ibid.

Thus, verses 12 to 14 of St. John's prologue provide us with a very synthetic, complete view of the Incarnation of the Word, minus any factual narrative, as in St. Matthew and St. Luke. The divine and virginal maternity of Mary is presented sensitively, like a delicate watermark, both as it touches the Incarnate Word and those redeemed by Him, the Son and the "Sons in the Son," *filii in Filio,* as a classical formula of theology has encapsulated the sense of the mystery of the Word Incarnate and of the Church.

9

The Annunciation

Luke 1:26–38

St. Luke is the true artist of the Virgin Mary. We should be grateful to him because he has sketched for us the sober, lovely features of our Lady, recounting for us those important episodes that illumine the ineffable mystery of the Incarnation. As a diligent and faithful historian, he carefully researched the events and stories reported in his Gospel, thus guaranteeing that what we read truly occurred and is solidly documented.[1]

But what were the sources of the information contained in the first two chapters of the Gospel of St. Luke? The one certain response is this: only Mary Most Holy was the protagonist and depository of the events narrated in the "infancy Gospel." She was the "eyewitness," says Laurentin.[2] Only she, then, is the source; only she is the matrix of the narratives reported in the first two chapters of St. Luke and of St. Matthew: "Mary was the only witness of the Annunciation," writes Testa, "the principal protagonist of the other events."[3]

---

1 "From the beginning," writes Caba, "Luke shows himself to be an authentic historian, not only because he prefaces his work with a prologue, a common technique of other historians like Flavius Josephus and Dionysius Halicarnassus, but above all because he claims to have gathered detailed information and that he wishes to follow a precise order in his work" (J. Caba, *Dai Vangeli, al Gesù storico* [Rome, 1974], p. 243).

2 Laurentin, *Truth of Christmas*, p. 356.

3 Testa, *Maria terra vergine*, vol. 1, p. 315. Even more categorical is Guidetti, who says: "The author of the accounts is for us without a doubt Mary, the Mother of Jesus" (Guidetti, *Conoscenza storica*, p. 159). "In reference to the origin of the factual matter narrated in Lk 1–2 and above all in Lk 1:26–38, we admit that the original source of information is the most Blessed Virgin; the principal reason is that many of the details are so intimately personal and the rest in every way so private, that without her contribution

Would St. Luke have known our Lady personally? Could he have heard from her directly the accounts of the infancy? It is possible; perhaps even probable, at least as a working hypothesis. Thus Garofalo claims it not only to be possible, but that "one or more meetings of the physician–Evangelist with the Mother of Jesus in order to learn more of her secrets"[4] can be considered "probable." No more than this, however.[5] On the other hand, it is certain that the information in the infancy Gospels originates only from Mary Most Holy, either directly or indirectly (perhaps through St. John).[6]

* * *

In the sixth month (v. 26).

This is a chronological notation relating the announcement to Mary with the pregnancy of St. Elizabeth. The precursor, St. John the Baptist, is older than Jesus by— six months.

The angel Gabriel (v. 26).

This is the same angel who appeared to Zechariah. The identity of the angel expresses the unity of the salvific

---

as source they would have remained forever a secret of God" (MIGUENS, "Servidora del Señor," p. 74; see also his *Mary "The Servant of the Lord."*

4 GAROFALO, *La Madonna della Bibbia*, p. 15.

5 Cf. LAURENTIN, *Truth of Christmas*, p. 569 [Ital. ed.1, where the author claims that every "reconstruction" of the actual shape of the source for Lk 1–2 is "pure fantasy without value." (See also pp. 28–33, Eng. ed.).

6 Some scholars have attempted to support a hypothesis according to which St. John, when younger, wrote an account of events utilized by St. Luke and St. Matthew, cf. E. BURROWS, *The Gospel of the Infancy and Other Biblical Essays* (London, 1940); A. FEUILLET, *Jésus et sa Mère dans les rêcits lucaniens de l'enfance et d'aprés Saint Jean* (Paris, 1974), pp. 79–91. [Eng. ed.: *Jesus and His Mother* (Still River, Mass., 1984), pp. 66–78.] Other scholars attempt the impossible project of determining how an earlier written source could have come into the hands of St. Luke: cf. GAECHTER, *Maria im Erdenleben*; but "the reconstruction belongs in the realm of science *fiction*," LAURENTIN writes ironically, *Truth of Christmas*, p. 32.

design and the close union between St. John the Baptist, the precursor, and Jesus, the Messiah.[7]

Was sent by God (v. 26).

The plan of salvation originates with God, who sends His messenger to announce the arrival of the Savior. After that of the precursor, there follows the announcement of the Messiah awaited by the people. The actualization of the plan regularly records its progressive steps. The events, are closely linked to one another, interdependent, yet at the same time quite distinct.[8]

Into a city of Galilee called Nazareth (v. 26).

Nazareth: that is, into a poor village of about five hundred inhabitants, situated on a hill (349 meters, or 1,134 feet above sea level) in the mountains of Galilee.[9] Nazareth

---

7 "It is evident that Luke 1–2 depends on Daniel 7–9," says Laurentin. "The name Gabriel alone would suffice to guarantee this link, as the only two OT texts where this name figures are Dan. 8:16 and 9:21" (ibid., p. 48). See the "coincidences" between St. Luke and Daniel: ibid., p. 49.

8 "Between the two events," Pietrafesa points out, "there are many points of similarity: the time factor (sixth month from the announcement to Zechariah), the same angel, the two announcements regarding the same Messianic work. Nevertheless, points of contrast are equally prominent: the announcement to Zechariah occurs in the Temple, that to our Lady in her own house. There it is Zechariah who (in a certain sense) approaches the angel; with Mary, it is exactly the opposite, because the center stage of divine action is not in the Temple of Jerusalem, but in her house. The announcement of the Precursor takes place in official form, made to a priest in the course of his ministry; the announcement to Mary takes place in the most disconcerting simplicity. The announcement to Zechariah appears in a Hebraic perspective; that to Mary suggests a universalistic view [of salvation] stressing gratuity and interiority" (PIETRAFESA, *La Madonna nella Rivelazione*, p. 129). It should also be noted that Zechanah "goes up to meet the angel, but it is the angel who comes down to meet Mary in that much despised province [Nazareth]: 'The lesser goes to the greater,' as A. Gueuret remarks" (LAURENTIN, *Truth of Christmas*, p. 16).

9 Cf. B. BAGATTI, O.F.M., *Gli scavi di Nazareth* (Jerusalem, 1967); E. TESTA, *Nazareth Giudeo-Cristiana* (Jerusalem, 1969).

We note immediately, that Nazareth (an insignificant town) is called a "city" by St. Luke. Why? "By reason of the fact that Mary lives there, the great consignee of the divine message, and there the great mystery is fulfilled." So respond G. SALDARINI and L. MORALDI, "Le due annunciazioni," in *Introduzione alla Bibbia*, vol. 4, p. 255.

appears to be so insignificant that it is never mentioned in all the books of the Old Testament. *"Can anything good come from Nazareth?"* exclaimed the pious Nathaniel (Jn 1:46). "God's way of acting," writes Leonardi, "is different from man's: the greatest event in the lowliest place."[10]

In any case, the name "Nazareth" probably means "shoot." And Jesus, in being called the "Nazarene," fulfills the prophecy of Isaiah (11:1) who called the Messiah a "shoot": *"A shoot shall come forth from the stump of Jesse, and a branch shall grow out of his roots."*[11]

To a virgin (v. 27).

The Greek term *parthènos* (virgin) had already been used by the Septuagint for translating the Hebrew word *almâh* in the celebrated prophecy of Isaiah (7:14). St. Luke presents Mary precisely as the *"virgin,"*—that virgin foretold by the prophet. "Certainly," Leonardi affirms, "Luke deliberately used this term here in order to prepare his readers for the prophecy of Isaiah 7:14, so important to the conversation of Gabriel following."[12]

---

10 LEONARDI, *L'Infanzia di Gesù*, p. 135. On these chronological and topographical details (sixth month, Galilee, Nazareth), Ferraro makes a brief but accurate reflection: "The temporal and spatial frame, upon which Luke insists, shows that the theological value and the salvific importance of the facts are inseparably connected with human history; the plan of God is inscribed and realized among the rhythms and vicissitudes of human history, assuming dimensions characteristic of that rhythm" (G. FERRARO, *I racconti dell'infanzia nel Vangelo di Luca* [Naples, 1983], pp. 25–26).

11 Cf. A. ROLLA, "Nazareth," in *Enciclopedia della Bibbia*, vol. 5 (Turin, 1971), p. 73. According to others, however, the name Nazareth does not mean "sprout" (from *neser*), but "sentinel" (from *nasar*). The analyses and reflections of Fr. Testa on the contrast between Jerusalem and Nazareth are interesting: "Jerusalem is the city of the Law (Lk. 2:22, 23, 24), the place of the Temple (Lk. 1:27, 37–46), which stands on high, where one must go up (*anabasis*) and where the hierarchy, the High Priest, and royalty (2 Sam. 6:17–20) are to be found. By contrast, Nazareth is the city where Christ is conceived by the grace of God (Lk. 1:28, 30–38), the place that is below where one must go down (*katabasis*) and where the powerful, the rich and kings are humiliated and cast down from their thrones (Magnificat)" (TESTA, *Maria terra vergine*, vol. 1, p. 259).

12 LEONARDI, *L'Infanzia di Gesù*, p. 136. The allusion to Isaiah 7:14 has been noted by many. See, e.g. H. Schurmann, *Das Lukasevangelium*, I Part

Betrothed (v. 27).

This expression (a participle of the Greek verb *mnesteuô*) has been the subject of much discussion. Consensus about the entire verse has so far never been achieved. All agree, though, that the celebration of betrothal among the Jews was in fact a true marriage and that the fiancée was in fact called "spouse."[13]

After the betrothal, for a certain time (at most a year), the fiancée remained among her relatives; and on the day the bridegroom brought the bride into his home, the nuptials were solemnly celebrated for several days and they began to live together. At the announcement of the angel, was Mary already living with Joseph? The point is disputed. Ancient and modern authors affirm it. Others deny it. Difficulties exist for both positions.[14]

(Commentary on chapters 1:1–9, 50), Freiburg in Br.-Basel-Viena 1990, p. 42; F. Bovon, *Das Evangelium nach Lukas* (Lk 1:1–9, 50), Zurich-Neukirchen-Vluyn 1989, pp. 72–73.

13 Moreover, if the betrothed man died, the betrothed woman was considered a widow; if a child was conceived, it was considered legitimate; if the betrothed woman was unfaithful, she was stoned as an adulterous spouse; finally, to break an engagement, a true and proper divorce was required. C. Ceuppens, *De Mariologia Biblica*, p. 57, n. 1. Fundamental is the work of H. Strack and K. Billerbeck, *Kom mentar zum Neuen Testament aus Talmud und Midrash*, vol. 2 (Munich, 1924), pp. 372–400.

14 The opinion denying cohabitation rests on the expression of St. Matthew *antequam convenirent* (in Greek the verb *synelthein*: 1:18), which may mean "before they lived together"; and *accepit coniugem suam* (in Greek *paralabein*: 1:24), which may mean "he took his spouse" into his house. The opinion defending their living together, on the other hand, rests on the term "espoused" adopted by St. Matthew (1:18) and by St. Luke (1:27; 2:5). In Luke 2:5 this very term certainly connotes "spouses who have lived together," and most probably has the same significance in Mt 1:18 and Lk 1:27 as well. Cf. Ceuppens, *De Mariologia Biblica*, pp. 56–60; F. Zorell, *Lexicon Graecum Novi Testamenti* (Rome, 1931), p. 850; D. Frangipane, Utrum B.V. Maria ab angelo salutata in domo Joseph coniux fuerit?," *Verbum Domini* 25 (1947): 99; Leonardi, *L'Infanzia di Gesù*, pp. 54–55, 136; Laurentin, *La Vergine Maria*, p. 28, n. 6.

To a man whose name was Joseph, of the house of David (v. 27).

The Davidic descent of the Messiah was legally guaranteed by St. Joseph, who was "of the house of David."[15] It is not stated, however, that the parenthetical clause *"of the house of David"* should not be referred to Mary as well, or perhaps in this instance should be referred only to Mary, since in chapter 2:4, St. Luke clearly asserts the Davidic descent of St. Joseph. The custom of marrying among members of the same tribe; the necessity or at least the convenience of attributing to the Messiah a Davidic descent, not only legal, but also biological, of Davidic blood; and finally, the clear, precise affirmation of St. Paul to the Romans: *"[Jesus] who was born from the seed of David, according to the flesh"* (1:3), that is, the flesh of His Mother Mary, leads one to hold as true what tradition has well-nigh constantly affirmed—the Davidic descent of Mary Most Holy.[16]

The virgin's name was Mary (v. 27).

For the second time, St. Luke speaks expressly of the *"virgin."* This underscoring is to be connected with the celebrated prophecy of Isaiah regarding the *"virgin"* who would be the virgin mother of the Emmanuel (Is 7:14),[17]

---

15 That St. Joseph belonged to the house of David is also affirmed by Mt 1:16, 20, and by Lk 2:4.

16 Cf. J. Fischer, "Die davidische Abkunft der Mutter Jesu. Eine biblischpatristische Untersuchung," *Wiedenauerstudien* 4 (1911): 1–115 (the author demonstrates the "unanimity" of tradition). A wide-ranging and exhaustive study (also in reference to the relationship of Mary to St. Elizabeth, of the priestly line of Aaron) is that of Judant, "Maria figlia di Levi," pp. 303–329, 451–471; the author plainly asserts that Mary belonged to the house of David. More recently, in a study on the genealogy of Jesus, the Davidic descent of Mary has been defended, once again, by Masson, *Jesus fils de David*. So, too, the editors of The Navarre Bible. St. Matthew's Gospel, p. 29. Laurentin, *Truth of Christmas*, pp. 342–345, follows a different line (but without convincing arguments).

17 Colombo writes: "Luke accents at least twice the fact of the virginity of Mary, her 'parthenia': surely, Luke wanted to use this term here to

and it is to be taken in the sense of a proposal of virginity on the part of Mary, which the Evangelist St. Luke desires in some way to anticipate, in accord with the style characteristic in the use of the literary figure called precisely "allusive anticipation."[18]

The name of Mary, first borne by the sister of Moses, was widely used at the time of our Lady and was interpreted to mean, respectively, according to Egyptian, Hebrew, and Ugaritic etymologies: *beloved of God, beautiful, lady,* and *highness.*[19]

Being come in (v. 28).

The remarkable, objective, concrete character of the apparition of the angel to Mary, as described here by St. Luke, counts strongly against those who would speak only of interior locution and dialogue between Mary and the angel. "It is noteworthy," writes Pietrafesa, "that the account of the Annunciation cannot be categorized as an *imaginary vision.* St. Luke speaks of the angel *'being come in to her... of the angel who departs from her.'* Such language in no way suggests a merely subjective vision."[20]

---

introduce the prophecy of Isaiah 7:14; there the corresponding Hebrew word is 'Almah,' already translated in the LXX precisely by the term 'virgin' (*parthenos*) recurring here" (Colombo, *Maria nelle attese d'Israele*, pp. 9798).

18 Cf. O. Battaglia, *La Madre del mio Signore. Maria nei vangeli di Luca e Giovanni*, Assisi 1994, pp. 49, 51.

19 Cf. O. Bardenhewer, "Der Name Maria," in *Biblische Studien*, vol. 1 (Freiburg, 1895), pp. 1–61; E. Vogt, "De nominis Mariae etymologia," *Verbum Domini* 26 (1948): 163–168; R. Laurentin, "Traces d'allusions étymologiques en Luc 5–2," *Biblica* 37 (1956): 435–456, and 38 (1957): 1–23.

20 Pietrafesa, *La Madonna nella Rivelazione*, p. 128, n. 4. The same author continues thus: "Moreover, because the account was certainly narrated by the protagonist, Mary Most Holy, it is not admissible that she would permit the early Church and the Evangelist (as some critics maintain) to mythologize or distort the episode of the annunciation, falsifying it in the retelling" (ibid.).

The angel said "Hail" (v. 28).

The Greek term adopted by St. Luke is *chaire.* Etymologically, *chaire* means "rejoice." Nevertheless, as this word is currently translated, it undoubtedly corresponds to the Hebrew greeting *shalom,* meaning "peace," and to the Latin *ave,* meaning "hail," "I greet you," a reverent and very courteous greeting the angel Gabriel addresses to Mary "as a subject to his queen."[21]

Basically, however, one cannot and ought not rule out the possibility that with *chaire* St. Luke also wanted to record in the formula of reverent greeting the joy experienced at the arrival "of the long-awaited Messiah, already, in that precise sense, foretold by the prophets Zephaniah, Joel, Zechariah, and Micah."[22]

Full of grace (v. 28).

The angel Gabriel calls Mary with an expression identifying her and unveiling her hidden most being: she is the *Full of Grace.* In Greek, the expression is a past participle (*kecharitomene*), not easily translatable. Other proposed translations are these: "highest in grace," "most

---

21 Ibid., p. 130. One must also take into account the fact that to greet a woman—according to the Talmud—was a gesture totally unbecoming. (Cf. PERROT, *I racconti dell'infanzia*, p. 44).

22 In fact, Leonardi writes: "Currently for many exegetes it seems that Luke precisely intended, with all its allusions and implications, the etymological sense; it would seem, in fact, that the Evangelist had been meditating on Zephaniah 3:14–18; Joel 2:21–27; Zechariah 2:14 and 9:9–10 (cf. Micah 4:14–18); where in the Septuagint our 'chaire' occurs. With this term, the prophets address the *daughter of Zion* (Jerusalem, the Hebrew nation) and invite her to *rejoice and be glad* because of the announcement that Yahweh will come to reside in her womb as King and Savior" (LEONARDI, *L'Infanzia de Gesù*, pp. 138–139). See S. ZEDDA, "El chaire di Lc. 5:28 alla luce di un triplice contesto anticotestamentario," in *Parola e Spirito* (Brescia, 1982), pp. 273–292. Cf. also I. DE LA POTTERIE, S.J., "L'annuncio a Maria Lc. 1:26–38," in *Parola Spirito e Vita*, vol. 6, *La Madre del Signore* (Bologna, 1982), pp. 60–62; VARÓN VARÓN, *Sagrada Escritura*, p. 41; E. DELEBECQUE, "Sur la salutation de Gabriel a Marie," *Biblica* (1984): 352–355; LAURENTIN, *Truth of Christmas*, p. 53 (Ital. ed., p. 77). Decisively contrary to such an interpretation instead are others: cf. G. C. BOTTINO-N. CASALINI, *Maria nella storia della salvezza in Luca-Atti*, in *Theotokos* 8 (2000) p. 741, note 21.

beloved," "privileged," and "gratified."[23] The Vulgate translation *full of grace* is certainly a good one, but does not fully express all of the nuances of the Greek.[24] The fullness of grace here meant is, obviously, a fullness above all spiritual, but not excluding that which is physical,[25] in the sense of sanctifying grace (*gratia gratum faciens*) and not in the sense of a *gratia gratis data.*[26]

The exceptional character of the angel's greeting to Mary consists not so much in the single phrases, also found elsewhere in the Old Testament, as in the linking of the two expressions, "Rejoice" and "full of grace," as a form of address. No similar instance of this in relation to any other creature can be verified in the Old or New Testament. Hence, Origen could write: "Because the angel greeted Mary with new expressions, which I have never encountered elsewhere in the Scriptures, it is necessary to comment on this. I do not, in fact, recall having read in any other place in the Sacred Scriptures these words: *Rejoice, O Full of Grace.* Neither of these expressions is ever

23 Cf. Leonardi, *L'Infanzia di Gesù*, p. 139; Pietrafesa, *La Madonna nella Rivelazione*, pp. 133–134.

24 The Greek verb *charitaô* in the active sense means "to enrich with grace"; in the passive sense, it means "to be enriched with grace"; in the sense of the perfect passive participle, it means "to be enriched with grace in a firm and stable way": cf. Ceuppens, *De Mariologia Biblica*, p. 62. Cf. also Roschini, *Maria Santissima*, vol. 3, p. 30, where the author bases himself on the authoritative study of Stummer; Laurentin, *Truth of Christmas*, pp. 18–19.

25 There are three other biblical texts of the Old Testament in which the same term *kecharitomene* is found: cf. Eccl 9:8, where it connotes physical beauty, feminine grace; Ps 18:26, where it indicates moral goodness; Sir 18:17, where it indicates grace, both physical and moral. In St. Paul, Eph 1:6, the term refers to Christians in the grace of God. Cf. M. de Tuya, "Valoración exegetico-teológica del 'Ave gratia plena,'" *Ciencia Tomistica* 43 (1956): 9–27. It appears evident, in any case, that "whereas the parents of John the Baptist are eulogized for their practice of the *law*, Mary is praised by virtue of grace alone," so writes Laurentin, *Truth of Christmas*, p. 17.

26 Cf. I. de la Potterie, "Maria 'piena di grazia' (RM 7–11)," *Marianum* 50 (1988) 113–132 (against J. Fitzmyer): pp. 122–125.

addressed to a man: such a special greeting was reserved only for Mary."[27]

St. Luke, moreover, also makes it clear, even if not expressly, that Mary had had the "fullness of grace" from the first moment of her conception. In fact, the use of the past perfect participle (*kecharitomene*) is to indicate something already true of the subject in the past, and hence possibly extending even to the very first moment of her existence.[28] Here can be recognized one of the implicit foundations for the truth of the Immaculate Conception, which excludes from the very beginning of her existence any presence of sin, and which alone with perfect exactitude is "fullness of grace."[29]

The Lord is with thee (v. 28).

The third section of the angelic greeting is completed by this phrase, not the expression of a wish, but the affirmation of a present reality: "The Lord is with thee." At the same

27 Origen, PG 13, 1815–1816. The felicitous, penetrating observation of the great Origen effectively rebuts the sophisticated opinions of those who speak instead of "stereotyped" expressions adopted by the angel in his greeting to Mary. Cf. E. M. Peretto, O.S.M., "Contenuti e limiti dell'Annunciazione," in *Identità dei Servi di Maria* (Rome, 1975), pp. 35–45.

28 Cf. Varón Varón, *Sagrada Escritura*, p. 43; Leonardi, *L'Infanzia di Gesù*, p. 140. One should also ponder the fact that the angel in a certain sense gives a new name to Mary, calling her "full of grace": "It is, as it were, the proper name of the Virgin, which the angel pronounces" (Ceuppens, *De Mariologia Biblica*, p. 64). Mary is she who is "full of grace" par excellence, in the most perfect and unique sense, by which she is always such, from the beginning of her existence: "For the fullness of grace is neither perfect, nor uniquely Mary's privilege, unless coinciding with the very first moment of Mary's personal existence" (ibid., p. 64).

29 Ceuppens, at the end of his accurate examination of the term *kecharitomene*, states: "Whence we may conclude that the dogma of the Immaculate Conception of Bl. Mary is insinuated by Lk. 1:28, not however expressly asserted" (ibid., p. 64). Cf. also Roschini, *La Madonna*, pp. 32–33; Saldarini and Moraldi, "Le due annunciazioni," p. 260 and n. 9 (with reference also to the Assumption); M. Jugie, *L'Immaculée Conception dans l'Ecriture Saint et dans la Tradition orientale*, Rome 1952.

time, implicit in this formula is the promise of a special divine assistance to accomplish a great mission.[30]

In fact, in sacred Scripture, such an expression is relatively rare and is only addressed either to the people of God, in need of special assistance, or to an individual person called to carry out a demanding task.[31] Regarding Mary, then, the angel makes clear that to her is entrusted an important and difficult mission, the divine and coredemptive maternity to be accomplished with the special help of the Lord, for the salvation of the people of God, whom she now represents at the inception of the New Covenant.[32]

At these words she was troubled and asked herself what manner of greeting this might be (v. 29).

The exceptional significance of the words spoken by the angel was perceived immediately, even if generically, by the humble Virgin, who remained troubled, fearful, and who reflected on them to discover immediately their exact implications. Her familiarity with Sacred Writ must have allowed her quickly to grasp that the angelic greeting was the premise of something great to which she was being called; precisely she who, so rooted in humility, remained deeply embarrassed on hearing such magnificent praise: O Full of Grace![33] Mentally, however, she remained serene and recollected, indeed spoke to herself (*dialogizeto*) about

---

30 Pietrafesa rightly points out that "while the qualification of being graced or full of grace regards the past, *the Lord is with you* refers to the present with an eye toward the future as a guarantee of special divine help" (*La Madonna nella Rivelazione*, p. 136). Also...de La Potterie writes that "it is oriented toward the future": "L'annuncio a Maria," p. 65.

31 The most expressive examples are those of Jacob (Gen 28:13–15), Moses (Ex 3:12), Jeremiah (Jer 1:8), Gideon (Judg 6:12–16).

32 Cf. U. Holzmeister, "Dominus tecum, Lc. 1:28," *Verbum Domini* 23 (1943): 260–261; *The Navarre Bible. St. Luke's Gospel* (Dublin, 1987), p. 37.

33 It is precisely a quality of humble souls, as St. Thomas observed long ago, to marvel at and be embarrassed by praise (cf. *Summa Theologica* III, q. 30, a. 4, ad 1). One should remember, further, that in this instance it is a most delicate virgin, about 14 years old, who is involved.

the significance of such an extraordinary greeting.[34] How long her reflection lasted is not known. But the angel did not delay in putting her at ease.[35]

The angel said to her: "Do not fear, Mary, for you have found grace before God" (v. 30).

While she was troubled, Mary did not reply to the angel's greeting. A truly prudent virgin, before responding she wished to understand the deepest sense of the angelic words. But humility left her unable to overcome embarrassment and fear over the great things of which the words of the angel gave her a foretaste.

At this point, the angel intervened to calm her using a certain familiarity, calling her by name (*"Do not fear, Mary"*), and to reassure her on God's behalf because in addition to being already "full of grace," she will enjoy a unique, divine strength and aid in order to accomplish a great mission. And then, before revealing the content of the divine message, the angel guarantees the humble Virgin that she will find God disposed to show her every kindness and support, in order to accomplish the heavy responsibility being entrusted to her.[36]

---

34 "Mary is profoundly acquainted with the Sacred Scriptures," Varón Varón observes; "as she shows in her canticle, the Magnificat, and realizes that the angelic salutation contains a profound messianic mystery. Mary suddenly is brought face to face with the depth of the mystery, but she is not disorientated. Rather she reflects. She does not lose that inner poise which prudence gives her, and so she thinks before speaking" (*Sagrada Escritura*, p. 44). Laurentin rightly notes that while Zechariah, at the announcement of the angel, "is passive under the shock: 'fear fell UPON HIM.' Mary instead acts, reflects. The word *dialogizeto* derives from the same root as *dialogue* and *dialectic*" (*Truth of Christmas*, p. 20).

35 According to some exegetes, Mary's discomfort is to be contrasted with that of the sinner Eve; and indeed, in the two scenes—of Genesis (original sin) and of St. Luke (the Annunciation, grace)—"the two women are contrasted so strikingly that it hardly seems rash to ascribe to the Evangelist an insight into this" (Nolli, "Maria nella Bibbia," p. 391).

36 In the stories of Noah (Gen 6:8), of Moses (Ex 33:17), of Gideon (Judg 6:17) are found three examples of a unique divine assistance expressed by the words "*you have found grace*" before God.

A significant example from the past is that of Queen Esther, who saved her people from massacre, because *"she found grace and favor"* in the sight of King Ahasuerus (Esther 2:6). How much more has Mary *"found grace before God"* in order to inaugurate the era of the universal Redemption?

Behold thou shalt conceive in thy womb and shalt bring forth a son, and thou shalt call his name Jesus (v. 31).

Here begins the object of the divine message, expressed in terms of a true prophecy.[37] Mary will conceive and bear a son, to whom she will give the name Jesus (which means Savior). The expression employed by the angel evidently refers to the text of Isaiah: *"The virgin shall conceive and bear a son: and his name shall be called Emmanuel"* (Is 7:14).[38] St. Matthew, moreover, had in his Gospel already expressly recalled and quoted the celebrated prophecy of Isaiah (Mt 1:22–23) in confirmation of the virginal conception effected in Mary.

The name is given the Child by his Mother. That is contrary to the norm, according to which the father is expected to name the son. This is done to indicate precisely the active and unique role the Mother played in this event.[39]

He shall be great and shall be called the Son of the Most High; the Lord God shall give him the throne of David

---

37 Cf. Ceuppens, *De Mariologia Biblica*, p. 66.

38 Both Luke (1:27) and Matthew (1:23) "use the word parthenos with reference to Is. 7:14" (Laurentin, *Truth of Christmas*, p. 404). Some scholars (Lyonnet, Laurentin, Ortensio da Spinetoli, Mori) would also like to refer Luke 1:31 to Zephaniah 3:14–17. But the reference would seem superfluous: cf. Leonardi, *L'Infanzia di Gesù*, pp. 142–143, n. 46. On this much-disputed subject see the exhaustive presentation of Lemmo, "Maria 'Figlia di Sion,'" pp. 175–258.

39 On this point, however, see Laurentin, *Truth of Christmas*, p. 22.

his father (v. 32) and he shall reign over the house of Jacob forever and his reign will have no end (v. 33).

With some adaptations, the angel describes the extraordinary personality of the Son of the Virgin Mary, recalling simultaneously the prophecy of Nathan to David (2 Sam 7:12–16) and that of Isaiah (9:6)[40] regarding the future Messiah, royal descendant of David.[41]

The idea of the "greatness" and of the duration "forever" of a reign that "will have no end" possesses an extratemporal–transcendent content not predicable of mortal creatures and terrestrial realities, as exceptional as they may be.[42] There is more: the expression "will be great," without further specification, was applicable in biblical language uniquely and only to God. The point becomes quite evident in the contrast with John the Baptist, who the angel said would be great "before God" (v. *is*), while of Jesus he says simply that He will be *"great, the Son of the Most High."*[43]

At this the Virgin, enlightened and amazed, has begun to understand the immensity of what is upon her: to

40 Here are the texts of the prophecies: "I will raise up thy seed after thee and I will establish his kingdom. I will establish his throne forever... I will be to him a father and he will be to me a son.... Your house and your kingdom shall be firm before my face: your throne will endure forever" (2 Sam 7:12–16). "To give an everlasting peace to the throne of David and to his kingdom... now and forever" (Is 9:6).

41 On the subject of royal messianism, see the fundamental study of Coppens, "Le messianisme royal," pp. 483–490.

42 "The infinite does not fall within the purview of human affairs," writes Ceuppens, summarizing Fr. M. J. Lagrange (*De Mariologica Biblica*, p. 68).

43 Cf. de La Potterie, "L'Annuncio a Maria," p. 66; Leonardi, *L'Infanzia di Gesù*, p. 46; Ferraro, *I racconti*, p. 31. "Hence it is our opinion," writes Ceuppens, "that the expression Son of the Most High, by reason of its immediate context, must be understood in the strict sense of natural, divine filiation, of the divinity of the Son of Mary" (*De Mariologia Biblica*, p. 68). We note with Laurentin that "Jesus is called 'Son of God' in Lk 1:32a before he is called 'Son of David' in 1:32b, a sequence which announces the Johannine notion of pre-existence" (*Truth of Christmas*, p. 327). In all of this, as *The Navarre Bible. St. Luke's Gospel*, p. 38, states, "Mary, who knew Sacred Scripture, clearly understood that she was about to become the Mother of God."

become the Mother of the *"Son of the Most High"*; that is, the Son of God makes Himself her Son. The troubling of soul, first felt on the extraordinary greeting of the angel, was in fact a presentiment of something exceptional, which she is now beginning to understand: nothing less than the Divine Maternity.

As Battaglia discerningly notes "Jesus is called great in the absolute sense, in the way God is called 'great' by David after receiving the Messianic promise, recalled immediately thereafter (2 Sam 7:22). Greatness is an attribute of God and pertains to him alone (Dt 10:17). Further, the greatness of Jesus is defined by the attribute which follows: 'he will be called Son of the Most High.' This renders explicit clearly and in terms of divinity the promise made by God to David concerning the future Messiah: 'I will be his Father and he will be my Son' (2 Sam 7:14). The son of Mary will also be Son of God."[44]

Then Mary said to the angel: "How shall this be? For I do not know man" (v. 34).

Confronted by this wondrous announcement, however, the Virgin finds herself embarrassed; not because of the sublime greatness of the maternity announced to her, but rather for the way in which such a maternity might be realized. The embarrassment would seem inexplicable because, on any reasonable grounds, she is precisely a woman in ideal conditions to conceive a son. She is the young spouse of Joseph. What young spouse would not be inclined to desire a beautiful son?[45] It is obvious, therefore, and must be acknowledged that Mary's difficulty stems

44 O. Battaglia, *op. cit.*, pp. 65–66.

45 Rightly Laurentin speaks of a "response causing amazement in a betrothed woman, at a time when betrothal already implied all of the rights of matrimony" (Laurentin, *La Vergine Maria*, p. 28). See also Danieli, "I Vangeli dell'infanzia," p. 202.

from a precise commitment, vow or promise, not to "know man," that is, to be and remain a virgin. St. Augustine rightly says, that "Mary certainly would not have spoken those words if she had not vowed her virginity to God."[46] In fact, only by admitting Mary's virginal consecration to God, can it be understood why she found herself facing an unsolvable dilemma: How to reconcile her virginal offering to God with the request of maternity on the part of God? How could she become a mother without betraying a promise of virginal consecration to God?[47]

---

46 St. Augustine, *De Sacra Virginitate*, PL 40:398; 38:1096; 38:1318. P. Vaccari also affirms that "her words ('I do not know man') are a sure indication that she had decided to remain a virgin, and she had promised such to God and that, being betrothed, as such her proposal was fully agreed to by her spouse Joseph" (*La Sacra Bibbia*, vol. 8, p. 196). This is "the most common interpretation among Catholic exegetes," writes Leonardi (*L'Infanzia di Gesù*, p. 145); and no other is tenable. Some claim that our Lady meant only "*now* I do not know man," or that she wished to deny already having conceived, as she seemed to have understood the angel to imply. But in both instances it is enough to consider that the angel speaks in terms of the future: "you *will* conceive." Others hold that the words "I do not know man" signify a proposal the opposite of virginity (that is: "How is that possible, because in that case I would have to know man?"), or even that they are merely words employed by St. Luke for the sole purpose of initiating a theological discussion of virginal conception. In these two instances, there is quite plainly a complicated and inadmissible forcing of the text (as can be examined in J. Ernst, *Il Vangelo secondo Luca*, vol. I [Brescia, 1985], p. 98). Laurentin says well that "except by straining the text, one must interpret it as follows: Mary, inspired by God, had decided not to know man in the biblical sense of the expression" (*La Vergine Maria*, pp. 28–29; see also the long chapter in *Structure et theologie de Luc 1–2* [Paris, 1956], pp. 17ff.; and lastly, his *I Vangeli dell'infanzia di Cristo* [Rome, 1985], pp. 555–556). Cf. also Varón Varón, *Sagrada Escritura*, pp. 47–49; Pietrafesa, *La Madonna nella Rivelazione*, pp. 141–149; R. Marmion, "De Virginitate Beatae Mariae Virginis apud Evangelium Annunciationis," in Maria in *Sacra Scriptura*, vol. 4, pp. 465–474; Leal, "El Evangelio," pp. 110–112; Saldarini and Moraldi, "Le due annunciazioni," p. 264, where these authors strongly affirm that the "I do not know man" of Mary "is to be taken in the absolute sense: as a proposal of perpetual virginity"; also B. Rinaldi, more recently, vigorously affirms that verse 34 "can only be taken to mean a vow of chastity" ("Mariologia, situazione negli anni '80, prospettive per il 2000," *Ephemerides Mariologicae* 35 [1985]: 393); *The Navarre Bible. St. Luke's Gospel*, p. 39.

47 "Mary certainly was disposed to obey God," Ceuppens pointedly notes, "and to accept the Divine Maternity. There existed, however, a serious obstacle, not depending, it seemed, on her will. Otherwise, it could easily have been removed—assent could have been given immediately to the divine will. It was rather a question of an obstacle not depending on her alone, but also on God, namely, of her virginity, which she had consecrated perpetually to God" (*De Mariologia Biblica*, p. 73).

Some scholars find such a dilemma implausible, because a proposal entailing virginal life in those days seems inconceivable. But Laurentin convincingly refutes this and affirms that in any case "Mary was so spiritually endowed as to be in the vanguard undertaking such an engagement."[48] On the other hand it has been remarked that the reply of Mary is equivalent to taking a firm and clear stand. In fact, Battaglia writes that "the objection of Mary is peremptory because formulated in the present indicative, which in Greek indicates a continuing action, not one momentary and episodic… This is possible only if we understand that the two [spouses: Mary and Joseph] had together decided, after their marriage, to lie both in virginity… Of this vow of virginity in marriage Luke is certainly thinking when he presents Mary from the beginning, insistently, as 'virgin espoused to a man of the house of David, called Joseph' (Lk 1:27)."[49]

As for any point concerning the vow or proposal of virginity on Mary's part, we must consider convincing and definitive the wide-ranging and detailed study of G.

48 Laurentin, *La Vergine Maria*, p. 56; *Idem*, *Truth of Christmas*, pp. 417–418. See also Leonardi, *L'Infanzia di Gesù*, pp. 146–147. Read also the pertinent reflections of Varón Varón (*Sagrada Escritura*, pp. 48–52) on the value of the virginity of Mary in relation to the mystery of the Incarnation and of the Redemption. Cf. L. Scheffczyk, "Les trois moments de la virginité de Marie," *Communio* 3 (1978): 20–31 R. Laurentin, "Sens et historicité de la Conception virginale," in *Mélanges Balic* (Rome, 1971), pp. 515–42; De La Potterie, *Mary in the Mystery*, pp. 123–154.

49 O. Battaglia, *op. cit.*, pp. 69–69. The author poses the question: if Mary had decided to remain a virgin, why is she espoused? "The reply to this legitimate question is found in the environment in which Mary lived. Here it was the custom to destine a child for a future spouse from the tenderest years. The choice and destination was made in mutual agreement by the parents of the children, and the marriage to follow later on this basis was an obligation from which neither could withdraw… On the other hand the marriage was part of that divine plan which Mary was called to realize. God chose for his Son a genuine human family because, as a complete man, He would lack none of that warmth and riches of a natural environment indispensable to His sound and balanced growth" (ibid., pp. 71–72).

Graystone.[50] His solid, final conclusion is this: "After much reflection we believe that the 'traditional' interpretation [that is, on the subject of Mary's virginity], as we have argued it above, offers the only reasonable and satisfying explanation of Mary's words."[51]

The angel answered her: "The Holy Spirit shall come upon thee, and the power of the Most High shall overshadow thee" (v. 35a).

Immediately, the angel calms the Virgin, solving her dilemma with few but sublime words, revealing to her the reality of the virginal conception that will be accomplished in her by the work of the Holy Spirit.

Jesus is the new Adam, the new creature made by God through the Virgin Mary. The "Holy Spirit" is the "power of the Most High": it is God, One and Triune, who intervenes in the Incarnation, but the work is attributed "by appropriation" to the third Person of the Most Holy

---

50 G. Graystone, *Virgin of All Virgins. The Interpretation of Luke 1:34* (Rome, 1968). This was a thesis for the doctorate in sacred Scripture, defended before the Pontifical Biblical Commission.

51 Ibid., p. 139. See also the essay by the same author: "Virgin of all Virgins. The Interpretation of Luke 1:34," *Ephemerides Mariologicae* 21 (1971): 5–20. In agreement with this position of Graystone are S. Lyonnet, F. Ceuppens, R. Laurentin, G. Roschini, G. Saldarini, L. Moraldi, B. Rinaldi, C. Ghidelli, A. Lancellotti, D. Bertetto, J. Galot, M. Zerwick, J. Neves, E. Lauras, S. Garofalo, J. Leal, P. Pietrafesa, Varón Varón, the exegetes of *The Navarre Bible*, and many others. Cf. E. Vallauri, "L'esegesi modema di fronte alla vergiitâ di Maria," *Laurentianum* 14 (1973): 455–456. I. de La Potterie, on the other hand, would admit in Mary only a "tendency to virginity" in the context of a normal matrimonial obligation to St. Joseph, almost dramatizing in her heart the coexistence of the "desire of virginity" with the marriage already "contracted." What is involved here, more than anything else, is an allusion to an ordinary psychological fact, normally present in a woman who marries and experiences within herself a conflict between the tendency toward virginity and that toward maternity: on the one hand she would like to remain always a virgin, on the other she aspires toward maternity. But none of that appears in Mary from the Lucan text, and the interpretation of de La Potterie (which is a reelaboration of R. Guardini) would conclude by denying, in substance, precisely the "interior virginity" of Mary, something utterly untenable. Cf. *Mary in the Mystery*, pp. 25–29, 144–148.

Trinity.[52] St Luke is the Evangelist of the Holy Spirit. Here the Holy Spirit, the power of the Most High, intervenes for the incarnation of the Word in the Virginal womb of Mary. It is precisely Mary, then, who is the first, through the angelic message, to receive the revelation of the mystery of the Most Holy Trinity[53] and the "descent" of the Holy Spirit. "For the Virgin," writes Danieli, "that moment is an anticipated Pentecost, a supreme moment of grace and holiness."[54] And the ineffable operation of the Holy Spirit in the virginal conception of the Word Incarnate made Mary "Spouse of the Holy Spirit."[55]

The verb "to overshadow," then and the metaphors "shadow" and "cloud" have a characteristic meaning in biblical language, connoting the *"presence of God"* in the meeting tent (Ex 40:34–35) and in the Temple of Yahweh where the Ark was kept (1 Sam 8:10–11). Mary also, "overshadowed" by "the power of the Most High," is

---

52 Cf. St. Thomas, *Summa Theologica* III, q. 32, a. 1. On the specific operations of the Holy Spirit in Mary see the brief and compact synthesis of Testa, *Maria terra virgine*, vol. 1, pp. 454–457.

53 "The annunciation, besides being the sublime moment in which 'the Word became flesh,' is the chosen instant when God reveals for the first time to a creature the mystery of the Most Holy Trinity" (H. de Azevedo, "La Vergine e l'Eucaristia," *Studi Cattolici* 29 [1985]: 164).

54 G. Danieli, "L'Annunciazione a Maria," in *Il messagio della salvezza*, vol. 6 (Turin, 1979), p. 320. Just previously the same author, in order to dispel the doubts of those who question whether the phrase "Holy Spirit" in Lk.1:35 should be understood in the sense of the third Person of the Blessed Trinity, writes that "the Holy Spirit understood in the specifically Christian sense is too important in all of the Lucan work, not to be meant in that sense here as well. Now, because the term frequently recurs in all St. Luke's writings and generally enjoys a meaning beyond question, it seems correct to give it the same meaning here too, since the Evangelist does not offer any sign to the contrary." See also K. Stock, "Lo Spirito su Maria," *Parola Spirito e Vita* 4 (1981): 88–98; Laurentin, *Truth about Christmas*, pp. 6–7.

55 Cf. G. Arnaiz, S.J., "Maria Sponsa Spiritus Sancti (Lc. 1,35)," in *Maria in Sacra Scriptura*, vol. 4, pp. 123–128. De La Potterie ("L'Annuncio a Maria," p. 70), reflecting on the "difficulty" of Mary and on the "response" of the angel, rightly holds that the safeguard for Mary's virginity extends not only to the conception, but also to the parturition: the angel, namely, assures Mary that her *virginal integrity* will *never* be touched or compromised and she will remain always a virgin enjoying "complete preservation" of her virginity.

transformed into a true "tabernacle" of the Most High, into a sanctuary of the living presence of God who also makes Himself her Son.[56]

Therefore, he who is to be born of you shall be holy and shall be called the Son of God (v. 35b).

By the presence and the operation of the Holy Spirit in the virginal womb of Mary, the new conception will not only be miraculous but "divine," that is to say, it will have as its fruit a child not only exceptional, but also "holy" and the "Son of God."[57] We are dealing, then, with the human generation of the Son of God.[58]

---

56 Cf. S. Lyonnet, S.J., "Il racconto dell'Annunciazione e la maternità divina della Madonna," in *La Scuola Cattolica* 82 (1954): 411–446. "The divine shadow," writes Laurentin, "designated by the characteristic word *episkiásei*, recalled the cloud that was the sign of the presence of Yahweh. This cloud was manifested for the first time at the moment of the institution of the Mosaic cult. It had *covered with its shadow* the Ark of the Covenant, while the glory of God, that is, God himself, rested within. Mary, in her turn, would be the object of this double manifestation: presence from above, that signifies transcendence, and the interior presence of the Lord of glory" (Laurentin, *La Vergine Maria*, p. 37). Cf. also *idem*, *Truth of Christmas*, p. 54; Leal, "El Evangeio," p. 113; Varón Varón, *Sagrada Escritura*, p. 56; Ferraro, *I racconti*, p. 33; A. Serra, "Aspetti mariologici della Pneumatologia di Lc. 1, 35a," in *Maria e lo Spirito Santo* (Rome, 1984), pp. 148–154; *The Navarre Bible. St. Luke's Gospel*, pp. 39–40.

57 On the grammatical and syntactical connection of the individual words of this verse 35b, see the wide-ranging and accurate analysis made by S. Zedda, "Lc. 1, 35b, 'Colui che nascerà santo sarà chiamato Figlio di Dio,'" *Rivista Biblica* 33 (1985): 29–43, 165–189. On these two terms *holy* and *Son of God*, to be understood in the transcendent sense of "divinity," see Laurentin, *Truth of Christmas*, pp. 69–70, nn. 95, 96; pp. 196–197 (Ital. ed.: p. 80, n. 25, pp. 100–101, 269–271). It is interesting to note that the revelation of Jesus "Son of God" is made for the first time by an angel (cf. Perrot, *I racconti dell'infanzia*, p. 36). It is to be remarked, moreover, that at the origin of Jesus is found, not the Father, but the Holy Spirit: "a designation of God in Hebrew feminine, in Greek neuter. This significant datum, which radically excludes every theogamic model, has escaped notice!" (Laurentin, *Truth of Christmas*, p. 404; Ital. ed.: p. 537). See also Testa, *Maria terra virgine*, vol. 1, p. 247.

58 Against the interpretation of Maldonatus, who understood the expression "Son of God" in the sense of a man made by God and not by man—as in the case of Adam–Lyonnet pointedly responds that "in effect, created directly by God, Adam was not 'conceived by the Holy Spirit.' The present case is quite different. Further, for Luke, the term 'Son of God' applied to Christ has a very precise meaning. It is clear in his thought, that the angel understood it in the same sense. In reporting the term or in putting it on the lips of the angel, he surely intends to affirm that this child will be He whom the

The two terms *"holy"* and *"Son of God"* are an even more explicit reaffirmation of the divinity of Christ. In reality, for the virginal conception of a man, a simple intervention of the divine power would have been enough (as in the analogous case of the sterile Elizabeth again made fecund); but, for the virginal conception of a man–God, God's presence itself was necessary in the maternal womb, as happened precisely in Mary with the descent of the Holy Spirit. Laurentin has written very well on this point: "The function of the intervention of the Holy Spirit for the virginal conception [...] is less to bring about this generation than to guarantee the divine Sonship of Him who was in no way born of man (Lk 1:34; cf. Jn 1:13). This is different from the other characters mentioned above who have a natural filiation and who are then more or less adopted by God."[59]

The same expression *"he will be called Son of God"* has not only a logical, but also an ontological value in confirming the divinity of the Son of Mary, from the moment that *"he will be called"* is seen to mean in biblical language "he really will be and will be recognized as the Son of God."[60]

In such wise, the only-begotten Son of the Father, "the Word," as St. John calls Him (1:1), really became the only, begotten Son of Mary. The mystery of the Incarnation was realized thus, with the joint divine and human action of

---

primitive community, notably St. Paul, will name the Son of God, this in the same sense, namely, the proper sense" (S. Lyonnet, "L'annunciation et la mariologie biblique," in *Maria in Sacra Scriptura*, vol. 4, p. 67). Cf. also ZEDDA, "Lc. 1, 35b," pp. 187–189. See, to the contrary, ambiguous as ever, BROWN, *Birth of the Messiah*, p. 316, n. 56. For a critical synthesis of the older and more recent formulation of the problematic centering on the virginal conception, see LAURENTIN, *Truth of Christmas*, pp. 399–431.

59 LAURENTIN, *Truth of Christmas*, p. 147. "It is for the sake of so exceptional a child," writes Pietrafesa, "that it was necessary for the Holy Spirit to descend upon her, and not simply for the virginal conception, for which a mere divine intervention would have sufficed" (PIETRAFESA, *La Madonna nella Rivelazione*, p. 153).

60 ZEDDA, "Lc. 1, 35b," p. 187.

the Holy Spirit and of Mary, as we profess in the Creed: "By the work of the Holy Spirit, He was made flesh in the womb of the Virgin Mary and became man."

It cannot be doubted, at this point, that the Virgin Mary understood, much more profoundly than anyone else, all the essential content of the discourse of the angel to be fulfilled in her, that is: her election as Mother of the Son of God, Messiah and Savior of men, and the virginal conception of the Son of God by the work of the Holy Spirit. Not to have understood this real and essential content of the angelic message, would have meant, on Mary's part, not to give a true *assent* to the angel's request, not to exercise any *faith* at all in that mystical reality, and in the final analysis not to become in any way the *Mother of God,* but merely a simple and unwitting "incubatrix" of the Word Incarnate.[61]

---

61 On this key point, we consider beyond question Fr. Harrington's synthesis in the American biblical commentary: *A New Catholic Commentary on Holy Scripture* (New York, 1984), p. 997. The author's exegesis, as solid as it is incontrovertible, shows that had Mary Most Holy, at the Annunciation not understood the Incarnation of God in her womb (and therefore, not understood the "divinity" of the Son to be conceived), she would not effectively have grasped "the very essence of the angelic message," and therefore, she would have been unable either to consent to the objective request of the angel or exercise any act of faith (however obscure) in the Incarnation of the Word. Here is Fr. Harrington's text: "In Mary's consent we may see a true pattern of her humility. If she had been troubled and if she had asked a question it is because she had been perplexed. Now that she knows the divine purpose, she accepts that purpose unhesitatingly and with perfect simplicity. Mary now knew the divine purpose—but did she 'understand it'? Above all, did she realize that the child to be born of her would be divine? If we look to the essentials of Luke's narrative we find that his attention first bears on the child whose birth he announces, then on the Motherhood of Mary and lastly on the manner of her maternity. In other words, the central fact, and the source of the others, is the Incarnation and this, by definition, means that God became man. It forms the kernel of the angel's message, and if Mary had not grasped this she had not really understood the message. But, according to the principles of the literary form in question, she ought to have understood the message before the departure of the angel, and Luke's treatment of the matter implied that she had. We may maintain, therefore, not gratuitously but with sound reason, that at the moment of the Incarnation, Mary knew that the child then and there conceived in her womb was divine. This, however, is not to claim that she was fully enlightened (cf. 2:50; 2:19, 51); and we are told that her 'Fiat' was essentially an act of 'faith' (1:45)—which includes, in its object,

Exactly and correctly de Azevedo has written:

Maternity is distinguished from mere generation or reproduction—a phenomenon occurringthroughout the animal kingdom—by the rational and voluntary character that distinguishes man from animal, the factor precisely specifying human nature.

Where consciousness or willingness is wanting, there exists neither true maternity nor paternity nor filiation. Even if the new being has the same nature as the one who has procreated him, he is not, however, a true son if he is not born of persons as such, but of their flesh and of their animal impulses. That human fecundity might give rise to a maternal or paternal relation, spiritual activity is indispensable, that is, a prior and unconditional welcoming of the person begotten: a welcoming that may be generic and virtual, but must exist. Otherwise, the procreators are not true parents. It happens frequently, in fact, that the parents do not want the son, to the point that they kill him before birth. Many times their welcome is no more than mere resignation to accept the child. In such cases, only God knows whether such acceptance is at least virtual, and so constitutive of true paternity, or if it is no more than a form of adoption of a human being whom the parents did not desire or did not succeed in killing, and who ends up being treated *as if he were* a son, not being such in fact.

Mary did not adopt Jesus. She is the true Mother of God. This means that Mary consented, with full consciousness and volition, to the Incarnation, in her virginal womb, of the second Person of the Most Holy Trinity.

Otherwise, she would not have been the Mother, but only the biological cause of the body of Christ. Therefore, it is necessary to affirm that she was perfectly conscious of accepting a Divine Person. If she had thought that she was simply about to generate a man, she would have erred and

---

the divinity of Christ, but seen in the darkness that is a necessary feature of faith."

the real Person born of her most pure womb would not have been her true son.[62]

For this reason *Lumen Gentium,* in a brief and incisive phrase, states that the Virgin Mary "at the announcement of the angel accepted in her heart and in her body the Word of God," where the term "heart" clearly indicates the seat of intelligence and of the will, as well as of human affectivity, in the most genuine of biblical senses (no. 53). And in *Redemptoris Mater,* Pope John Paul II writes that at the Annunciation, Mary *"believed* that by the power of the Most High, by the work of the Holy Spirit, she would become the Mother of the Son of God" (no. 14).[63]

Behold, thy cousin, Elizabeth, also has conceived a son in her old age; and this is the sixth month for her who was called barren (vv. 36–37).

To confirm the possibility of an event so extraordinary as the divine and virginal maternity, the angel spontaneously

62 De Azevedo, "La Vergine e l'Eucaristia," p. 164. Compared to these, and similar reflections, the contrary opinions of some scholars, including Catholics, appear fragile and unconvincing (in particular, Galot). Hence, not only biblical scholarship and the constant teaching of tradition and of the Magisterium, but sound psychology as well render untenable the hypothesis of a Mary Most Holy "unaware" of the Incarnation of the Word in her womb.

63 On Mary's certain knowledge of the divinity of her Son, see the extensive studies of D. Unger, O.F.M. Cap., "Utrum secundum Doctores Ecclesiae Virgo Maria Filium suum Dei Filium esse nuntio angelico cognoverit," in *Maria in Sacra Scriptura*, vol. 4, pp. 347–420; "Mary's Knowledge of Her Son's Divinity at the Annunciation. The Papal Tradition," *University of Dayton Review* 5 (1968): 33–48. Cf. also Enrique del Sagrado Corazón, O.C.D., "Vida teologal de la Virgen Maria: en la linea del Concilio Vaticano II," *Revista Española de Teologia* 26 (1966): 195–231; J. A. Grispino, "When Did Mary Learn That Her Son Was Divine? (Lk. 1:30–35)" in *Ephemerides Mariologicae* 15 (1965): 126–130; P. C. Landucci, *Maria SS nel Vangelo* (Rome, 1954), pp. 59–66; Varón Varón, *Sagrada Escritura*, pp. 59–60; Laurentin, *La Vergine Maria*, p. 42, where the author holds that Mary had a knowledge of the divinity of the Son "more real, less notional," because she understood "more intensely and more vitally than we, the essentials"; E. Galbiati, *La fede nei personaggi della Bibbia* (Milan, 1979), pp. 133–136; Saldarini and Moraldi, "Le due annunciazioni," p. 270, where they conclude the *excursus* on v. 35 with these words: "The angel gives to Mary's question the only satisfactory response: her maternity must be virginal, because it will be a divine maternity."

offers Mary a "sign." The "sign" in question is a prodigious one: the "sign" is Elizabeth's maternity, Mary's elderly relative,[64] afflicted for so many years with sterility, and now "six months" pregnant with John the Baptist. The "sign," it is clear, is in relation to the divine omnipotence now pledged to accomplish in Mary the virginal conception of the Word, an event so much more extraordinary than that accomplished in Elizabeth.[65]

And Mary said: "Behold the handmaid of the Lord; be it done to me according to thy word." And the angel departed from her (v. 38).

This Annunciation differs in its underlying structure from others of the genre[66] precisely at its final conclusion, that is, by the "consent" that Mary gives to the message of the angel.[67] Such "consent," given by Mary, is not merely private, but expresses the willing participation of man, of humanity, in the work of salvation. In the freedom of Mary, at that instant, were contained all the desires, fears, and hopes of man in need of redemption. And the new Eve spoke her full, total *yes* to the angel of light, just as the first Eve had once spoken her *yes* to the angel of darkness.[68]

Moreover, the response given by Mary to the angel also expresses, in addition to her consent, a humble and unconditional dedication to the plan of God entrusted to

---

64 On the relationship between Mary and Elizabeth, see note 16 above.

65 Such a "sign," obviously, would not have made any sense if Mary's conception did not have to be "virginal," as Lyonnet points out: "The evident parallel (cf. v. 34) with the sterility of Elizabeth underscored by Luke (vv. 7 and 25) makes no sense at all if the conception of Jesus is natural" ("L'annonciation et la mariologie biblique," p. 64).

66 See the "table" of annunciations in Brown, *Birth of the Messiah*, p. 156.

67 Cf. Nolli, "Maria nella Bibbia," p. 389.

68 "From the text,"... writes Leonardi, "it appears that God respects the personality of Mary, her human liberty: he proposes to her an act of obedience, but leaves her free; through her, by way of her free 'yes,' depended the present plan of Redemption" (*L'Infanzia di Gesù*, p. 557).

her. Such a dedication reveals the incomparable faith of Mary, a faith that would call forth the inspired exclamation of Elizabeth and offers the perfect model of obedience, animated by the noblest charity, for the salvation of others. "Mary has the last word," write Saldarini and Moraldi.

> Hers is an act of obedience, but above all an act of faith in God's word. As the economy of the promise begins with Abraham's act of faith (Gen 15:6), so that of the New Testament is inaugurated at that instant when Mary pronounces her '*fiat*' and conceives Jesus, who recapitulates within Himself all humanity and the universe. It is not improbable that Luke, expressing the 'yes' of Mary with the same verb used to express the creative command of God (Gen 1:3, 6, 14), wanted to suggest that it was the moment of a new creation.[69]

Further, the expression used by Mary, *"handmaid of the Lord,"* explicitly recalls the celebrated passage of Isaiah concerning the Messiah, the "servant of Yahweh." Indeed, it is the exact "feminine equivalent of the expression servant of Yahweh," as Danieli affirms.[70] This reference establishes two important truths: first, the close union of the "handmaid of the Lord" with the "servant of Yahweh" in the unique work of the "suffering servant"; and second, the sharing of the painful events of the "suffering servant," immolated for the Redemption of men (Is 53:2ff.). The Virgin Mary, in using that expression, did not so much accept as give her all to the redemptive work,[71] as the humble associate of the *"man*

69 SALDARINI and MORALDI, "Le due annunciazioni," p. 271. A. Serra has done a good analysis of Lk 1:38a, noting that Mary's response illumines the parallel with the Covenant of Sinai (*Maria secondo il Vangelo* [Brescia, 1987], pp. 7–23).

70 Danieli, "L'Annunciazione a Maria," p. 322.

71 de La Potterie, in an already quoted study ("L'Annuncio a Maria," p. 72), rightly points out that Mary gave her consent, not grudgingly, but with full generosity so that the salvific plan of God might be quickly realized (so the use of the Greek optative *genoito* makes clear). See also LEAL, "El Evangelio," pp. 115–116.

of sorrows pierced for our offenses, bruised for our iniquities" (Is 53:3–5).[72]

* * *

In conclusion, we have discovered while reflecting on the Lucan pericope of the Annunciation an inexhaustible wealth of content, above all *Christological,* centered on the Incarnation in the virginal womb of Mary; next, *Mariological,* evidenced by the announcement made to Mary, "Full of Grace," called to be the Mother of God; and *eschatological* or apocalyptic, given utterance by Mary who inaugurates the last times, unveiling the light of the mysteries of salvation.[73]

Meditating on the gospel episode of the Annunciation, we become in the final analysis more and more aware of this reality, which, better than all others, the Virgin Mary has understood: that her Son is the Son of God, that His Father is God the Father, and that this Son of Mary has so come upon the earth in human form, by the work of the Holy Spirit, as to suffer and die upon the Cross and thus to save His people from sin. Like Mary, and through Mary, we too must not so much accept the fact as give ourselves to the redemptive work with the same faith and obedience of the Immaculate Handmaid, the perfect fruit of a perfect Redemption, whose faith leads to the beatitude

[72] In chapter 8 of *Lumen Gentium*, we find these elements well summarized: "The Daughter of Adam, Mary, consenting to the Word of God, became the Mother of Jesus, and committing herself whole-heartedly and impeded by no sin, to God's saving will, she devoted herself totally, as a handmaid of the Lord, to the person and work of her Son, under Him and with Him, serving the mystery of the Redemption, by the grace of Almighty God" (no. 56). On this subject see the extensive article of Miguens, "Servidora del Señor," pp. 73–110 (in English, cf. his *Mary "The Servant of the Lord,"* and the study of S. Garofalo,"Ancilla Domini," in *De Mariologia et Oecumenismo*, pp. 49–57.

[73] E. G. Mori's synthesis "Annunciazione del Signore," in *Nuovo Dizionario di Mariologia*, p. 80, where the author cites the specialized studies of A. Feuillet (for the "Christological" content), of K. Stock (for the "Mariological" content), and of L. Legrand (for the "eschatological" content).

of the resurrection. *"Blessed is she who hath believed that the things spoken to her by the Lord will be accomplished in her"* (Lk 1:45).

10
The Visitation

The account of the visitation of Mary to her relative Elizabeth is to be reckoned among the richest and most suggestive of the Gospel. The colors of St. Luke's palette deepen the tone and perfect the careful shading of a delicately balanced portrayal of events, wherein the ineffable reality of grace and charismatic experience interplay.[1] Here we contemplate the mystery of the Incarnation, sensitively traced. Inaugurated at the Annunciation, it is now made present *with* Mary and operative *through* Mary in the house of the Precursor of the Messiah.

Many exegetes call attention to a suggestive and solidly based parallel[2] between the journey of the Ark of the Old Covenant from the house of Abinadab to that of Obededom and to Jerusalem (2 Sam 6:1–15), and this journey of Mary—the true Ark of the New Covenant—from the house of Nazareth to the house of Zechariah in the hills of Judea, toward Jerusalem. The comparison of the two "journeys" is certainly significant, both for the wealth of parallel details harmonized with astonishing accuracy,[3]

1 Laurentin sees in this episode of the "visitation" of Mary to Elizabeth "a 'protopentecost' (Lk 1:41 and Acts 2:4) demonstrated by an outpouring of prophetic charisms and thanksgiving" (*Truth of Christmas*, p. 99).

2 Burrows has explained such a parallel in his *Gospel of the Infancy*, p. 47. But the scholar who has done the most profound study is R. Laurentin, *Structure et théologie*, pp. 79–81; *Truth of Christmas*, pp. 56–58, 154–159. Other exegetes holding this view are A. Feuillet, P. Pietrafesa, G. Leonardi, G. Ferraro, Varón Varón, H. Muñoz, J. Ernst. The new liturgy celebrates the Feast of the Visitation with this biblical theme as backdrop: cf. D. Sartor, "Visitazione," in *Nuovo Dizionario di Mariologia*, pp. 1480–1481.

3 One could consider, for example, the following parallels: the two "journeys" take place in Judea; the shouts of jubilation of the people and of Elizabeth; David and John the Baptist "exult for joy"; the presence of the Ark and that of Mary are a blessing for the house; the Ark and Mary remain in the house for three months. Cf. H. Muñoz, "Beata te che hai creduto," in *Parola Spirito e Vita*, vol. 6, pp. 96–98.

and for the profoundest themes made plain in the passage from Old Testament *shadow* to New Testament *light,* from the *figure* of the Ark in the Old Covenant to its *reality* in the New, to Mary *theophora* (she who carries God).[4]

Another luminous lesson of the "visitation" narrative is the truth about the salvific-missionary aspect of Mary's journey, above all in the person of Mary *associated* with her Son, *entirely one* with Him in the work of Redemption. Elizabeth and John, receiving Mary into their house, receive the Messiah Savior, who fills them with joy and the Holy Spirit. Mary thus becomes the first "evangelatrix" of the Kingdom of God in the heart of man, she to whom are first applied the words of the prophet Isaiah: *"How beautiful upon the mountains are the feet of the messenger of glad tidings who announces peace, the messenger of goodness who announces salvation, who says to Zion: 'Thy God reigns'"* (Is 52:7).[5]

And Mary rising up in those days, went into the hill country with haste into a city of Judea (Lk 1:39).

Why did Mary set out on a journey? Why did she go in haste into the town of Elizabeth? The mystery of the Incarnation had just been accomplished in her. Mother and

---

4 See the thorough and detailed study of G. Aranda Perez, *La Visitacion: el arca nuovamente en camino*, in *Ephemerides Mariologicae* 43 (1993) 189–211, where the author attentively notes how Mary can be called in truth "*Ark of the Covenant*" only if one admits that she really does carry in her womb the "*Son of God*" of whom St. Luke writes in 1:35c. If in the expression "*Son of God*" of St. Luke one reads "the expression of transcendent divine sonship of the Child in the womb of Mary, in that case the Virgin can be likened, according to the same text, to the Tabernacle or Ark"; whereas if she carries in her womb only a davidic messiah (not divine), "she cannot be considered in this scene as Tabernacle or Ark of the Covenant" (ibid., p. 194; in note 15 the author cites S. Lyonnet, R. Laurentin, J. McHugh).

5 *Lumen Gentium*, too, has expressly recognized this truth in the "visitation": "This union of the Mother with the Son in the work of salvation is made manifest... first when Mary, arising in haste to go to visit Elizabeth, is greeted by her as blessed because of her belief in the promise of salvation, and the Precursor leaped with joy in the womb of his mother" (no. 57).

Son are totally one. But why was the Word made flesh? To work the Redemption of mankind, bringing the Kingdom of God into the heart of every man. The Redeemer wishes to commence the work at once, by bringing His Kingdom into the heart of His Precursor. Mary cooperates, always united and active. She moves; indeed "she hastens." She is the bearer of the Messiah Savior. She has within her the fountain of grace. She is already the "dispensatrix" of grace. Mary's motive for traveling in haste is the most exalted possible. It is supernatural charity, the motive of the salvific mission of the Son, who operates through the Mother associated with Him, ever inseparable from Him.

Exegetes also suggest other considerations, prevalently psychological in character, which moved Mary to hasten to her relative Elizabeth. One such is the desire to rejoice with Elizabeth over the grace of maternity, which had freed her from the disgrace of sterility. Another is that of lending assistance to an elderly relative during the delicate and difficult period preceding childbirth. Yet another motive is that of being able to confide to Elizabeth the mystery of the Incarnation of the Son of God that had occurred on the day of the Annunciation. For Mary was sure of being understood by her elderly, holy cousin.

Surely to be rejected as motivation is a desire on Mary's part to confirm her faith by *verifying* the *sign* given her by the angel. Such a motive would irreparably compromise Mary's *obedience of faith* and could in no way be reconciled with Elizabeth's cry at the greeting of Mary: *"Blessed is she who has believed…"* Laurentin writes, correctly, that Mary moves "only to share, not to verify, as the rest of the narrative shows. Her haste arises from the Holy Spirit, who plays the role of motivator throughout the Gospel (and in the Acts of the Apostles)."[6]

Exactly where was Mary going? St. Luke employs the generic expression "into the hill country," without any other specification. The most probable hypothesis based on tradition speaks of Ain Karim, a village about 7 kilometers [4 miles] to the west of Jerusalem and 150 kilometers [95 miles] from Nazareth.

The journey must have lasted about five days. Most probably Mary, a young girl of scarcely 14 or 15 years, traveled with one of the caravans that were usually formed on that route toward Jerusalem;[7] she was probably accompanied by some member of her family, perhaps by her mother, St. Anne.[8]

---

6 Laurentin, *Truth of Christmas*, p. 154. "Mary visits Elizabeth, but not to dispel a doubt or to verify the truth of the words of the angel," writes C. Ghidelli, *Luca* (Rome, 1981), pp. 72–73.

Among authors preoccupied about proving a need to "verify" the sign offered to Mary by the angel, is Ortensio da Spinetoli, O.F.M. Cap., *Maria nella tradizione biblica* (Bologna, 1967), p. 112, n. 3; *idem*, "Il segno dell'annunciazione o il motivo della visitazione," in *Maria in Sacra Scriptura*, vol. 4, pp. 315–345 (a conference delivered at the Mariological Congress of Santo Domingo in 1965); *idem*, Luca (Assisi, 1982), pp. 80–84. A. Martinelli, O.F.M., has given a thorough response to Fr. Ortensio in his *"Maria nella Bibbia." Note critiche e dilucidazioni* (Rome, 1966). This concise critique sets in relief the unfounded and extravagant character of Fr. Ortensio's thesis. See also P. Pietrafesa, *La Madonna nella Rivelazione*, pp. 165–171, with its pointed reflections in this regard.

7 Cf. G. Roschini, *La vita di Maria* (Rome, 1948), p. 140; Ceuppens, *De Mariologia Biblica*, p. 92; Gaechter, *Maria im Erdenleben*, p. 103. That explains why the Evangelist says that Mary set out "in those days" and not immediately: precisely to wait for a passing caravan.

8 Cf. Leonardi, *L'Infanzia di Gesù*, p. 170. Certainly the presence of St. Joseph must be excluded, at least to Ain-Karim, "because in that case," explains Pietrafesa, "he would have comprehended from the plain diction of Elizabeth, the mystery of the Divine Maternity and would not have suffered the cruel anxieties that afflicted him at the first signs of the maternity of his spouse" (Pietrafesa, *La Madonna nella Rivelazione*, p. 172, n. 12). Cf. also Garofalo, *Le Parole di Maria*, pp. 74–75.

She entered into the house of Zechariah and saluted Elizabeth (v. 40).

The description is minimal. Mary enters and salutes. The words of greeting, which the Evangelist does not record, were probably the usual ones: "Peace be with you." The greeting might also have included an embrace and a kiss.[9] But the Evangelist does not even hint at that. "One needs to keep in mind," notes Ernst, "the desire of the author to be concise in the narration in order to concentrate attention on that which is essential."[10] It appears evident that what is essential here is not the greeting between Mary and Elizabeth, but the amazing, extraordinary effect that such a greeting produces, for which, far from being something ordinary and banal, it takes on an exceptional importance.[11]

When Elizabeth heard the salutation of Mary, the infant leaped in her womb. Elizabeth was filled with the Holy Spirit (v. 41).

In the announcement to Zechariah, the angel had said that his son John would be *"full of the Holy Spirit even from his mother's womb"* (1:15). This prophecy is now realized in the fact that the child, at the appearance of Mary, "leaps" in the womb of his mother Elizabeth. The leap

9 Cf. Laurentin, *Truth of Christmas*, p. 155. See in particular the interesting n. 38 on the somatic value of the greeting (the embrace and the kiss) between Mary and Elizabeth: "For the visitation," concludes this author, "this element is neither excluded nor indicated." Ruotolo, on the other hand, maintains that it is appropriate to admit it, and writes that Elizabeth embraced Mary and "pressed her to her heart almost with maternal effusion, since she was already advanced in age," and precisely "in pressing her [Mary] she felt in her something divine, she understood by grace the mystery of her Divine Maternity" (D. Ruotolo, *La Sacra Scrittura. Vangelo secondo Luca* [Naples, 1979], p. 39).

10 J. Ernst, *Il Vangelo secondo Luca*, p. 110; in the note this author quotes H. Schurmann, *Das Lukasevangelium* (Freiburg, Basel, and Vienna, 1969), p. 66.

11 Cf. H. Balz-G. Schneider, *Dizionario esegetico del Nuovo Testamento*, 1, Brescia 1995, p. 460.

in question here is joyful, as Elizabeth herself will clarify shortly afterward in verse 44.[12] The entrance and salutation of Mary, in fact, have set in motion the operation of the Holy Spirit in the infant and in his mother. The infant, enclosed in the womb, manifests as far as he is able—with the "leap"—his joy at the outpouring of the Holy Spirit, who reveals to him, in Mary, the Mother of the "God who saves." Battaglia writes: "The voice of the Mother is the vehicle of the voice of the Son. The Handmaid of the Lord is the prime instrument for the transmission of the Gospel as announcement of joy. She has indeed preceded the Baptist as prime 'voice.'"[13] John's mouthpiece, it can be said, is his mother Elizabeth herself, who is also *"filled with the Holy Spirit,"* because she is wholly one with the son enclosed in her womb.[14]

And she cried out with a loud voice: "Blessed art thou among women, and blessed is the fruit of thy womb" (v. 42).

Elizabeth's emotion is great. In view of the sequence of events she perceives in those very moments, the

12 One may ask: Is the "joyous leap" of the infant in the womb of his mother also a "sign" of his sanctification or of the presence of divine grace that has eliminated original sin? Pietrafesa holds that the "sanctification" of John the Baptist in the maternal womb is "based expressly on tradition" (*La Madonna nella Rivelazione*, p. 174). This seems obvious to us, once the infant is recognized as *"full of the Holy Spirit from his mother's womb."* Ceuppens also states clearly: "Exegetes agree that the text of Luke 1:15 and 41 must be understood as a purification from original sin in his mother's womb. This doctrine, although not defined, is nonetheless commonly held in the Church, and cannot be denied without temerity" (*De Mariologia Biblica*, p. 94). In support of this truth, Ceuppens cites such great biblicists as M.J Lagrange, D. Buzy, L. Marchal, F. Ogara (ibid., n. 1). See also J. Leal, *Vangelo secondo Luca* (Rome, 1972), p. 117; Landucci, *Maria SS. nel Vangelo*, Rome 2000, p. 88.

13 O. Battaglia, *op. cit.*, p. 96.

14 Cf. Laurentin, *Truth of Christmas*, p. 155 (Ital. ed.: p. 220), where the author points out that "in this description of her pregnancy mother and child are totally one. Luke, in saying that Elizabeth is filled with the Holy Spirit, does not work a transposition from son to mother, but identifies them as one living being."

working of the Holy Spirit makes her respond to Mary's salutation "with a loud voice." Enlightened about the Divine Maternity of Mary, she "cries out." It is part of the psychology of the human creature to "cry out" in the face of great things: the acclamation of joy or amazement at extraordinarily happy things; a cry of sorrow or of horror at extraordinarily sad things. Elizabeth now finds herself before the Mother of God. Embarrassment and emotion might have overwhelmed her, but the same Spirit who has filled and enlightened her now places in her "cry" words of blessing and beatitude: "solemn and rhythmic words," writes Leonardi, "which some consider a true canticle."[15]

"Blessed art thou among women": as if to say that Mary is the only blessed one or the blessed one par excellence among all women.[16] *"Blessed,"* that is, enriched with grace, filled with heavenly treasures in the divine Son she is carrying in her womb.[17]

---

15 Leonardi, *L'Infanzia di Gesù*, p. 171.

16 It is safe to say that nearly all exegetes have interpreted the exclamation of St. Elizabeth in the superlative sense. See, for example, Pietrafesa, who speaks of "the Most Blessed" (*La Madonna nella Rivelazione*, p. 178); J. Ernst speaks of "a superlative expressing the maximum dignity" (*Il Vangelo secondo Luca*, p. 111). G. Leonardi points out that St. Elizabeth makes us clearly understand how she considers Mary "superior to herself, though chosen to be the Mother of the Precursor" (*L'Infanzia di Gesù*, p. 172); F. Ceuppens explains that the expression "'Blessed among' is a semitism equivalent to a superlative" (*De Mariologia Biblica*, p. 95); J. Leal, "El Evangello," p. 117, says the same; B. Gillard concludes that Mary "is not 'blessed'; she is blessing" (*Maria che cosa dice di te la Scrittura?* [Turin, 1983], p. 37).

17 Why is the exclamation of St. Elizabeth addressed first of all to Mary, the Mother, and then to Jesus, the Son? Laurentin explains precisely by referring to a sort of "communication of idiom" that occurs in the pregnant woman: "During pregnancy, Luke considers mother and son as indistinct; the mother, alone visible and active (whether in reference to Mary or Elizabeth), appears simply as a sign of the hidden child, in the final analysis, the most important figure. That relation is expressed in the text by means of a curious communication of idiom between the Son and the Mother" (*Truth of Christmas*, Ital. ed.: p. 221). No less illuminating on this point is Ruotolo when he writes that if Mary "were only a channel through which the Redeemer passed, as the Protestants say, Elizabeth, filled with the Holy Spirit, would not have addressed her as blessed among women, and called her fruit the Redeemer, the fruit from a most pure plant, which, evidently, only she, such a plant, could produce. The plant is not a simple

It has been observed, rightly, that the acclamations of Elizabeth suggest or recall those of the priest Uzziah to Judith, the admirable woman who saved her people from Holofernes:

"Blessed are you, O daughter before the Most High God, above all women on earth, and Blessed be the Lord God who created heaven and earth" (Judith 13:18). The reference is highly suggestive. The transition from figure (Judith) to reality (Mary) is enlightening. The words addressed to Judith reappear in those addressed to Mary, but transformed by the reality of the Divine Maternity and of the presence of God Incarnate. Judith and the Lord God in the Old Testament passage may be seen as forming a bridge to Mary and the Word Incarnate. Laurentin affirms that this link of the words of Elizabeth to those of the priest Uzziah "imply the identification of Mary with Judith and, moreover, of her Son with the Lord God. Therefore, in the succeeding verse Elizabeth calls Jesus 'Lord' (anticipating Lk 2:11)."[18]

To what do I owe that the mother of my Lord should come to me? (v.43).

This is a most important verse. Elizabeth, face to face with the Mother of God, notes her own littleness and the greatness of the honor done her. It is clearly evident that she proclaims here "in a loud voice" the Divine Maternity of Mary; and that she was the first to proclaim it.[19]

---

channel of the fruit; it generates it, nurtures it, and without the plant it is impossible to harvest it" ("Vangelo secondo Luca," p. 40).

18 LAURENTIN, *Truth of Christmas*, Ital. ed.: p. 221. Cf. also VARÓN VARÓN, *Sagrada Escritura*, pp. 64–66; Ferraro, "I racconti," p. 44; M. GALIZZI, *La scelta dei poveri, Vangelo secondo Luca*, vol. 1 (Turin, 1985), p. 41. On the reference to Jahel and to Judith see O. BATTAGLIA, *op. cit.*, pp. 99–101.

19 "She proclaims her, for the first time in human history, solemnly and with humility, Mother of God (v. 43) and bearer of grace (v. 44)," writes P. TERMES, "Visita di Maria ad Elisabetta," in *Enciclopedia della Bibbia*, vol. 6 (Turin, 1971), p. 1189. Elizabeth "is the first to proclaim the Divine Maternity of

There are still to be found some who would argue over the exact significance of the word "Lord" used by St. Elizabeth. Does it mean "God," or simply "Messiah"? The reply to this question is critical, because one's affirmation of belief or lack thereof on the part of Elizabeth in the Incarnation of the Son of God, Messiah and Savior, is determinative of one's understanding of much else in the pericope.

Quite obviously, it would be a grievous error to think that the Holy Spirit would have *"filled"* Elizabeth inclining her to believe that the person of the Messiah might be only human, that is to say, giving her an erroneous faith precisely in regard to the very *person* of the Son of God, who was made man in Mary. The Holy Spirit is the Spirit of truth, not of deceit or error (as a certain kind of exegesis concludes). "Mary of Nazareth," Pope John Paul II has written, "presents herself at the threshold of Elizabeth and Zechariah's house as the Mother of the Son of God. This is Elizabeth's joyful discovery: 'The Mother of my Lord comes to me'" (*Redemptoris Mater,* no. 13).[20]

Further, for a correct exegesis of the passage, it is enough to examine the whole first chapter of St. Luke,[21] where, a good seventeen times, the Evangelist uses the

---

the Most Blessed Virgin," writes D. SQUILLACI ("Riflessioni bibliche circa la missione di Maria," *Miles Immaculatae* 6 [1970]: 285).

20 G. Aranda Perez clearly affirms that in the Gospel of St. Luke we encounter the proclaimation of Jesus as Son of God united with the descent of the Holy Spirit at the Jordan (cf. Lk 3:22) and with the divine presence in the cloud in the Transfiguration (Lk 9:35). In Lk 1:35 both the Spirit and the divine Presence appear working in Mary to actualize the conception of the Son of God: the Holy Spirit as divine Spirit Creator (cf. Gen 1:2); the power of the Most High covering Mary with its shadow as the cloud in the book of Exodus": G. ARANDA PEREZ, *art. cit.*, p. 193.

21 One should read attentively on this subject G. ROSCHINI, "La 'Madre del mio Signore,'" in *Miles Immaculatae* 7 (1971): 256–258: this article is a brief but profound exegetical exposition, exact and lucid in affirming the Divine Maternity of Mary, formulated in the words of Elizabeth to Mary "Mother of my Lord."

term "Lord," always meaning "God."[22] In particular, then, when Elizabeth says "Mother of my Lord" in verse 43, and shortly after, in verse 45, says, *"Blessed is she who has believed in the fulfillment of the words of the Lord,"* it is evident that the term "Lord" has the same meaning in one and the other verse, both of which have issued from her mouth. Now, it is evident that Mary believed the word of God at the Annunciation—and not of the Messiah—transmitted by the angel. Hence, the term "Lord" can only signify "God" in the expression "Mother of my Lord." "Otherwise," remarks Roschini, "the term 'Lord' used by Elizabeth in the first instance (v. 43) would have one sense (that of 'Messiah') and in the second (v. 45) would have a quite different one (that of 'God'): something exegetically impossible, merely by reason of the context itself."[23]

---

22 Roschini writes: "Thus, for example, one speaks of the apparition of the 'Angel of the *Lord*' (1:11), that is to say, of the Angel of *God* (not yet the angel of the Messiah); Elizabeth, after having conceived the Baptist, exclaims: 'Behold, thus has the *Lord* dealt with me' (1:25), that is to say, *God* (not yet the Messiah, who was still to come). The Angel Gabriel greets the Virgin, saying:'The *Lord* is with you' (1:28), i.e., '*God* (not yet the Messiah) is with you'; and the Virgin exclaims 'My soul magnifies the Lord' (1:46), i.e., God (not yet the Messiah). And it is to be noted that this exclamation of the Virgin ('My soul magnifies the Lord') immediately follows on Elizabeth's exclamation full of wonder: 'And whence the grace for me that the mother of my *Lord* should come to visit me?' (1:43). If the 'Lord' of whom Mary speaks (echoing Elizabeth) is 'God,' it follows that the 'Lord' of whom Elizabeth herself had already spoken is also 'God.' Now, if in all of chapter 1 of St. Luke's Gospel the term 'Lord' means 'God' (and not Messiah), it follows that the expression 'Mother of the Lord' is perfectly identical with the expression 'Mother of God'" (ibid., p. 257).

23 Ibid. See Ferraro, *I racconti*, p. 45, persuasively expounding 2 Sam 6:9 ("How shall the Ark of the Lord come to me?") as "confirming thecomparison of Mary 'Mother of the Lord' to the 'Ark of the Lord' and leading us to understand the title 'Lord' given to the Son of Mary in the transcendent, divine sense." See the interesting excursus "Christ the Lord" (2:11) by Laurentin, *Truth of Christmas*, pp. 185–187, where he maintains that the word "Lord" signifies "God": this author cites A. George and I. de La Potterie (p. 186) in support. Cf. also Varón Varón, *Sagrada Escritura*, p. 66; Pietrafesa, *La Madonna nella Rivelazione*, pp. 174–176 (a reelaboration of R. Laurentin, *Compendio di mariologia* [Rome, 1956], pp. 34–35). Also in the more recent *The Navarre Bible. St. Luke's Gospel*, it is affirmed that "Elizabeth is moved by the Holy Spirit to call Mary 'Mother of my Lord,' thereby showing that the Virgin is Mother of God" (p. 42).

"With these inspired words," as Ruotolo has so truly written, "testimony to the Divine Maternity of Mary and to her ineffable greatness has been carved in stone for all ages,"[24] confirmed and transmitted immediately from the first centuries by St. Irenaeus, Tertullian, St. Hyppolite of Rome, Origen, St. Athanasius, St. Ambrose.[25]

For behold, as soon as the voice of your salutation sounded in my ears, the infant in my womb leaped for joy (v. 44).

Now it is the turn of Elizabeth herself to speak of the joyful leap of the Baptist, directly linked to the sound of the "voice" of Mary. Thus it is clear that the "voice" of Mary has stimulated in the infant that joyful "leap" which the Evangelist describes in the terminology of "dancing."[26] One may speak, then, of a current of grace that, originating with the Word Incarnate enclosed in the maternal womb, reached the Precursor by means of the "voice" of Mary and aroused in him joy. "At the Visitation there are distributed through Mary the gifts of the Messiah Savior: the pouring

---

24 D. Ruotolo, *Vangelo secondo Luca*, pp. 39–40. And we may well reflect that if Elizabeth knew the mystery of the Divine Maternity of Mary, who can say "therefore, what understanding, what awareness Mary herself must have had" (A. Nicolas, *La Vergine Maria secondo il Vangelo* [Turin, 1938], p. 197). At this point it is clear that a consistent and believing exegesis cannot accept the pseudo-exegesis of those who affirm that Elizabeth by using the term "*Lord*" testified only to a faith in the "messiah" son of Mary, ignorant of and unbelieving therefore in regard both to the divinity of Jesus and to the Divine Maternity of Mary. Such faith in St. Elizabeth obviously would have been an "erring" faith, anything but admirable, besides being inadmissible in her who was "*full of the Holy Spirit*" (v. 41). To say that it is St. Luke or the Church with a "post-Easter" faith to place "on the lips of Elizabeth" that title of "Lord" (which means "God"), without Elizabeth in fact having believed or said it, cannot but falsify and offend genuine exegesis, as well as the historical truth of the fact. Cf. B. Maggioni, *op. cit.*, p. 20; O. Battaglia, *op cit.*, p. 103.

25 Cf. L. Gambero, *Antiche riletture patristiche di Lc 1, 39–45*, in *Theotokos* 5 (1997) 25–52.

26 Cf. Laurentin, *Truth of Christmas*, p. 57 (Ital. ed.: p. 84): "The charismatic movement of John the Baptist 'filled with the Holy Spirit from his mother's womb... is described as a dance analogous to that of David before the ark."

out of the Spirit on Elizabeth and the joy of the future Precursor (cf. Lk 1:41)."[27]

This joy is a conscious joy, evidently a messianic joy, soteriological, a joy at the coming of the Savior, the expected of the people.[28] And in this joy is to be discovered the direct link that unites Jesus and the Baptist, even before birth. Some have interpreted the "leap of John the Baptist in the womb of Elizabeth, at the sound of Mary's voice and in her presence, as an indication of the future mission of the Precursor of the Son of Mary."[29]

Moreover, by reflecting on the events of grace and joy that occurred in the house of Zechariah on the arrival of Mary, it becomes strikingly evident that "with this outpouring of gifts, Mary initiates her role as Mediatrix of grace so as to lead all to salvation through the intervention of her Son whom she makes known to mankind."[30] And indeed, it is well to add here that the Mariological doctrine of the Church has constantly seen in the "visitation" one

---

27 *The Virgin Mary in Intellectual and Spiritual Formation*, Letter of the Congregation for Catholic Education (Rome, March 25, 1988), no. 8. "The leap of John," writes Ceuppens, "is attributed to the greeting and presence of Mary. Hence, the greeting and presence of Mary in some way contributed to the exultation and purification of the babe in his mother's womb" (*De Mariologia Biblica*, p. 94). There have been and there are theologians who, in the visitation, see not only "moral," but also "physical" and "ministerial" causality in the mediation of Mary, precisely because in the encounter with Elizabeth, "the sanctification of John, expressed through the phenomena of exultation perceived by the pregnant woman, is effected 'at the voice' of the greeting of Mary: God, that is, makes use of her voice to sanctify the Precursor. This fact is usually considered representative of a general principle" (Cf. Lo Giudice, "Riflessioni sulla mediazione di Maria SS.," *Miles Immaculatae* 22 [1986]: 112). See also G. Roschini, "De natura influxus B. M. Virginis in applicatione Redemptionis," in *Maria et Ecclesia*, vol. 2 (Rome, 1959), pp. 223–235; *The Navarre Bible. St. Luke's Gospel*, p. 42, speaks expressly of the "sanctification" of John the Baptist from original sin.

28 Cf. A. Feuillet, "La Vierge Marie," p. 36; Squillaci, "Riflessioni bibliche," pp. 283–284.

29 Ferraro, *I racconti*, p. 46, where the author notes an effective parallel with the sons of Rebecca, Esau and Jacob, who, in the maternal womb, "struggled with each other." (The use of the same verb skirtân in St. Luke and in Gen 25:21–23 is significant.) Cf. also Perrot, *I racconti dell'infanzia*, p. 48.

30 P. Pietrafesa, *La Madonna nella Rivelazione*, p. 174.

of the biblical bases for the dogmatic definability of Mary's mediation in the distribution of grace for the salvation and sanctification of souls. Emblematic, therefore, is the very "sanctification" of John the Baptist worked by Christ through the "presence" and the "voice" of Mary.[31]

And blessed is she who has believed in the fulfillment of the words of the Lord (v. 45).

Elizabeth has proclaimed Mary "Blessed" (*benedicta,* in the sense of "praised"—v. 42) and now she proclaims her "Blessed" (*beata,* in the sense of "happy").

The blessedness of verse 45 is that of faith. The first of the theological virtues, faith, inaugurates the New Covenant with Mary, just as the Old Covenant began with the faith of Abraham (Gen 15:5).[32]

What was the object of Mary's faith at the Annunciation? It is not difficult to determine. From the dialogue with the angel of the annunciation, we understand what the objects of Mary's faith were:

– the *mystery of the Most Holy Trinity:* the angel *"sent by God"* (the Father) speaks to her of the Son of God and of the Holy Spirit;

---

31 See the interesting publication of the studies of two pontifical commissions on the "definability" of the mediation of Mary, in particular, the study of the Belgian Commission, "De definibilitate mediationis beatae Virginis Mariae tribuenda disquisitio et vota," *Marianum* 47 (1985): 95, under the signatures of the theologians C. M. J. Van Crombrugghe, M. J. Lebon, B. H. Merkelbach (ibid., p. 174). See also Lo Giudice, "Riflessioni sulla mediazione," pp. 95–117 (*passim*); *The Navarre Bible. St. Luke's Gospel*, p. 42.

32 For a parallel between Abraham's faith and that of Mary, cf. G. Huyghe, *Conduits par l'Esprit. Une école de la foi* (Paris, 1965), pp. 60–130. Of importance is the specification that Mary is proclaimed "blessed" not for the great things that will take place in her, but for her faith in those superhuman events of grace. "Mary is declared blessed," writes Ceuppens, "not in view of the fulfillment of what the angel has announced to her, namely, her virginal conception, but by reason of her faith in the divine promises; Mary firmly believed what the angel had announced to her, notwithstanding their extraordinary and plainly supernatural character" (*De Mariologia Biblica*, pp. 96–97).

- the *mystery of the Incarnation:* the angel proposes to her the conception and birth of the Son of God, by work of the Holy Spirit;
- the *mystery of the Redemption:* the angel informs her that the Son will be called "Jesus," which means "God saves," because He will be the Savior;
- the *mystery of the Divine Maternity:* the angel tells her that the son to be conceived and born is the Son of God; and
- the *mystery of the virginal maternity:* the angel explains to her that she shall conceive virginally, "overshadowed," rendered fruitful by the Holy Spirit.[33]

Nonetheless, this affirmation of the fundamental content of the faith of Mary is not a reason for denying that she continued to grow in faith through each of the events in the life and mission of her Son. Rather, one cannot but admit that if Mary knew the redemptive plan of God overall, she did not, however, know all the "steps" and "details" of the plan, upon which, precisely as the Evangelist says on more than one occasion, she continued to "meditate in her heart" via what transpired (Lk 2:19, 51), experiencing even the darkness of faith that causes one

---

33 Transposed into theological formulae, the following can be said of the Blessed Virgin, that she believed above all, with pure faith, the two greatest mysteries of our Creed: 1. the unity and Trinity of God; 2. the Incarnation, Passion, death, and Resurrection of our Lord Jesus Christ. Moreover, she believed the two mysteries of the Divine Maternity and of the virginal maternity, which regarded her personally. Cf. DE AZEVEDO, "La Virgine e l'Eucaristia," p. 164. F. SUÁREZ, S.J., wrote in his time: "It is evident the Virgin's faith was most perfect... whereby she believed distinctly the mysteries of the Trinity and Incarnation and whatever else pertained to the divinity and humanity. So teach the Fathers Ambrose, Epiphanius, Augustine, Bernard, Rupert" (*Opera Omnia*, XIX, 297, Disp. 19,1). Recently, in his apostolic letter *Mulieris Dignitatem*, Pope John Paul II spoke of Mary's awareness of the mystery of the Most Holy Trinity at the Annunciation: "The self-revelation of God, that is, the inscrutable unity of the Trinity, is contained in its essentials in the *Annunciation of Nazareth*" (no. 3).

"to live intimately with the mystery," as Pope John Paul II says in *Redemptoris Mater* (no. 17).

Finally, it is to be remarked that however sublime and profound Mary's faith, it surely was not given expression in an academic or scientific mode, as is ours normally, but in an essential and sapiential one, at the level of the most pure and ineffable contemplation.[34]

In this brief verse, then, we find expressed the initial realization of the prophecy Mary herself would utter immediately after: *"All generations will call me blessed."* St. Elizabeth was the first to know and to proclaim the Divine Maternity of Mary. St. Elizabeth was also the first to proclaim the Virgin Mary "blessed," thereby inaugurating the choral chant of blessing and praise for the Mother of the Lord to be continued from generation to generation until the end of time. Lastly, St. Elizabeth, moved by the Holy Spirit, has also offered us the first example of "veneration" of the Blessed Mother of God: "veneration" uninterrupted thereafter throughout the entire two-thousand-year history of the liturgy and devotion of the whole Church.[35]

---

34 Cf. Laurentin, *La Vergine Maria*, p. 42. Here also it is necessary to free oneself from the "reductionism" of a sophistical exegesis which concludes by confusing *belief* in God one and triune, *belief* in the redemptive Incarnation of the Word of God, *belief* in the divine-virginal Maternity (as every Christian who knows the Catechism consciously believes) with *understanding* of deepening the divine mysteries in their content. This *understanding* of the divine mysteries may progress, grow and elevate itself so as to believe *ever more* in God one and triune, in the redemptive Incarnation of the Son of God and in the divine-virginal Maternity, but the *understanding* does not mean a passing from *non-belief* to *belief*. Who does not believe knowingly in the divine mysteries is *without faith*, is an *unbeliever*, and when he begins to believe passes from unbelief to faith. Now then Mary was full of faith in the divine mysteries of the unity and trinity of God, of the redemptive Incarnation of the Word of God, of her divine-virginal Maternity, and was full of faith from the beginning, without hesitations, always growing into the *maximal understanding* of the divine mysteries in their infinitely transcendent content. This is her *blessed* faith, supreme and incomparable model for all believers. Cf. A. M. Apollonio, *Maria modello di fede?*, Frigento 1998: quaderno di apologetica.

35 "The greeting of Mary," writes Ernst, "contains a first, timid beginning for the Christian veneration of Mary" (*Il Vangelo secondo Luca*, p. 111).

It could not have been so "timid," however, if Elizabeth spoke "in a loud voice." Nicolas writes in fact: "Elizabeth exclaimed 'in a loud voice,' with a voice so loud and so strong that it resounds throughout the centuries to follow and is still heard in the Gospel" (*La Vergine Maria*, p. 198). Cf. also Leal, *Vangelo secondo Luca* (Rome, 1972), p. 122; *The Navarre Bible. St. Luke's Gospel*, p. 42.

11
THE MAGNIFICAT

Luke 1:46–56

The account of the visitation culminates in the canticle of the Magnificat. This canticle has not only engaged the attention of exegetes and theologians in every era, but also that of artists and men of letters. It can be stated without fear of contradiction that the Magnificat is the canticle par excellence among all of the Old and New Testament canticles.[1]

The literary genre of the Magnificat is one of praise and thanksgiving, expressed in the form of a hymn, with an abundance of biblical reminiscences from the sacred hymns of Israel.[2] The reminiscences, nevertheless, are not

---

1 The most recent, authoritative, and thorough studies on the Magnificat are: G. ROSCHINI, O.S.M., "Il 'Magnificat,' cantico della Vergine," *Marianum* 31 (1969): 260–323; A. VALENTINI, S.M.M., "La controversia circa l'attribuzione del Magnificat," *Marianum* 45 (1983): 59–93; *idem*, "Il Magnificat e l'opera lucana," *Rivista Biblica* 33 (1985): 395–423; S. MUÑOZ IGLESIAS, *Los canticos del Evangelio de Ia Infancia según San Lucas* (Madrid, 1983), pp. 71–103; R. COSTE, *Il Cantico di Maria*, Rome 1988; LAURENTIN, *Truth of Christmas*, pp. 3–11, 379–383, *idem*, *Il Magnificat*, Brescia 1993 [French Original: *Magnificat: action de grâce de Marie*, Paris 1991]. Other up-to-date studies are found in *Ephemerides Mariologicae* 36 (1986), issue 1–11, by S. MUÑOZ IGLESIAS, G. ARANDA PEREZ, A. MOLINA PRIETO, E. VILLAR, P. FRANQUESA, R. SCHNACKENBURG, with extensive bibliography, older and newer, included in each of the articles; and the number of the review *Theotokos* 5 (1997) with various studies, among which two of A. VALENTINI, *Approcci esegetici a Luca 1, 46b-55*, pp. 403–422; *Il problema dell'attribuzione del Magnificat*, pp. 643–674, in addition to the editorial (pp. 391–402) and a note on *Il senso degli aoristi in Luca 1, 51–53*, pp. 725–729.

The study of Roschini, wide-ranging and solid, treats the history, art, and exegesis of the Magnificat and includes an ample bibliography. The essays of Valentini and the monograph of Muñoz Iglesias deal with the historical problem of authorship of the Magnificat. Laurentin, utilizing the latest reesearch, forcefully defends the attribution of the Magnificat to Mary on the basis of semiotics, as well as of history and tradition

2 For the biblical references and allusions in each verse of the Magnificat, cf. any edition of the Bible citing these in the margin of the text (e.g., *The Jerusalem Bible* [London, 1966]) or at the foot of the page.

so expressed as to render the Magnificat an "imitation" of Old Testament canticles. It is not a question of "imitation," but rather of "creation."[3]

The Virgin Mary glorifies the Lord for the works of mercy and power accomplished by Him in herself (vv. 48–50), in the poor and little ones (vv. 51–53), and in the people of Israel (vv. 54–55). In this interpretation, the Magnificat is above all the canticle of praise and hope of the Chosen People, through Mary. "In fact, in her," writes Feuillet, "is incarnated the better part of Israel with its eschatological hopes."[4]

If, further, one would comprehend the profound solicitude animating the whole canticle, anticipating an ever-wider salvation, it is preferable to examine the Magnificat from a threefold point of view: that of the *personal,* concerning Mary alone; that of the *community,* in regard to all people awaiting salvation; and that of the *cosmic,* embracing the whole history of redeemed humanity, "the new Israel."[5]

***Then Mary said* (v. 46a).**

The traditional attribution of authorship of the canticle to Mary remains solidly grounded and unshaken, notwithstanding hypotheses attempting to ascribe it to Elizabeth,[6] or to a not further specified "primitive Judeo-Christian community," or to a group of "anawim."

---

3 "Not imitation, but a new creation," as Gaechter so precisely puts it, *Maria im Erdenleben*, p. 139.

4 Feuillet, "La Vierge Marie," p. 39.

5 Cf. Ferraro, *I racconti*, p. 51.

6 On this "ascription" of the Magnificat to Elizabeth without any serious grounds, see Valentini, "La controversia," pp. 55–93, and his more recent study: *Il problema dell'attribuzione del Magnificat*, in Theotokos 5 (1997) 643–674; Muñoz Iglesias, *Los canticos*, pp. 71–103 Laurentin, *Truth of Christmas*, pp. 3–11, 379–382, where the author also rejects the attribution of the Magnificat to Elizabeth on the basis of structural analysis.

Clearly, these hypothetical alternatives to the traditional view affect and alter the very substance of the canticle. In none of them would Mary be, in fact, the authoress or the proclaimer of the canticle. The more insidious are those ascribing the Magnificat to a primitive Judeo-Christian community or to the community of anawim, from which St. Luke would have received it, to put it then on the lips of Mary at the time of the visitation.

This theory leaves only a faint suspicion that the canticle may somehow have been Mary's, whereas in reality, she would neither have composed it nor ever have even proclaimed it. Only the genius of St. Luke could have grasped the value of this canticle of the Judeo-Christian community or of the anawim and found an opportunity to place it on the lips of Mary as her response to the praises of Elizabeth. It would, in a word, be a construction of the Evangelist and nothing else. The hypothesis is obviously unacceptable; and indeed, Laurentin is quite correct when, in regard to this proposal to ascribe the Magnificat "to poor and hungry Christians of the first Christian generation," the so-called anawim, he writes that "this theory departs from the precise data of the text (Lk 1:28–46), in the interest of a contrived and groundless hypothesis,"[7] and when he states, in regard to the presumed, generic "creative Christian community," that this is but a "lovely myth."[8]

The thought of Laurentin is well summarized by Testa, *Maria terra vergine*, vol. 1, p. 251, n. 37.

7 Laurentin, *Truth of Christmas*, p. 380; see also p. 9. Against those (e.g., Brown, Benoit) who support such hypotheses solely on the basis of "imaginary" or emotional exegesis, cf. also Roschini, "Il 'Magnificat,'" p. 281 (who agrees with Feuillet); Leonardi, *L'Infanzia di Gesù*, p. 176, n. 115. The artistry of St. Luke would also in such hypotheses be the equivalent of "fictionalizing," seriously compromising his obligation to be the attentive and loyal historian, as he states in the prologue of his Gospel.

8 Laurentin, *Truth of Christmas*, p. 380. See also Roschini, *La Madonna*, pp. 265–266, where the opinion of Fr. Lagrange is reported. Just as unsupportable appears the more recent hypothesis of Muñoz Iglesias, according to whom the author of the Magnificat would be an "unknown

Nor may one overlook the ethnic character of Mary, daughter of a Semitic people, of that people, in whose blood, as it were, flowed the inspiration of song and poetry, the capacity both to improvise and memorize with great ease.[9] "The faculty of improvising songs in particular circumstances," Garofalo summarizes well,

> is characteristic of the Semites... Jewish poetry does not have iron laws, tending to mortify the imagination; its fundamental and elementary rule, the balancing of ideas between two members of each verse, above all allows anyone familiar with other poetic texts, to improvise similar chants with facility. In this matter, women, indeed, have special aptitudes. Notable from early Israel are the examples of Anna, of the prophetess Deborah, and of Judith, with which comparable phenomena still occur today among Arabic tribes.... Facile improvisation among the Semites is complemented by a remarkable ability to memorize a text, even a very long one, after having heard it only once, without referring to the script.[10]

Now, it would seem truly strange to deny to Mary what is conceded to Deborah and Judith (not to mention the Arabic women of today): that is, to deny to Mary the capacity to improvise a hymn of joy and thanksgiving, keeping in mind, as Lagrange accurately notes, that Mary, after the Annunciation, had a period of several days to meditate and compose in her heart the canticle of the

---

Jew"—whence the various "semitisms"—Who wrote the gospels of the infancy, afterward borrowed by St. Luke, translated by him into Greek and incorporated into his Gospel: see S. Muñoz Iglesias, "Genesis histórico-literaria del Magnificat," *Ephemerides Mariologicae* 36 (1986): 9–27.

9 Cf. Roschini, "Il 'Magnificat,'" p. 287. Laurentin writes, in turn, that in those times "women, almost all of them illiterate, had only their memories for a prayer book" (*Truth of Christmas*, Ital. ed.: p. 505).

10 Garofalo, *Le parole di Maria*, pp. 80–81. Cf. G. Ricciotti, "La Madonna nel Vangelo," in *Mater Christi* (Rome, 1957), p. 87; Roschini, "Il 'Magnificat,'" p. 287; Pietrafesa, *La Madonna nella Rivelazione*, p. 189; Leal, *Vangelo secondo Luca*, p. 119; G. Amorth, *Dialoghi su Maria* (Padua, 1987), pp. 74–77.

Magnificat, proclaimed, afterward, at Ain–Karim in response to the praises of Elizabeth.[11]

In reference to the Annunciation, further, one must keep in mind this important particular: St. Luke does not say that Mary spoke the Magnificat *"filled with the Holy Spirit,"* as happened with Zechariah (1:68) and would happen with Simeon (2:30) in proclaiming their hymns. For this reason, some maintain that Elizabeth would have proclaimed the Magnificat, she who indeed was said to be *"filled with the Holy Spirit."* But just here is the special, unique character of the continuous operation of the Holy Spirit in the Virgin Mary. It is enough to bear in mind that she has already received, at the Annunciation, the Holy Spirit who made her the Mother of the Word and had enriched her with a prophetic charism. That charism, here, at Ain-Karim, after days of reflection and meditation, makes her burst forth with the canticle of the Magnificat in pure exaltation of spirit. Not only this, but it must also be added that "Elizabeth," as Laurentin points out, "attributes to Mary's greeting the outpouring of the Holy Spirit (1:43) with whom both she and her son (1:42 and 1:15) are filled."[12]

11 Cf. M. J. Lagrange, "Le récit de l'Enfance de Jésus dans S. Luc," *Revue Biblique* 4 (1895): 160–185. Above all therefore, there is no need to invoke some miracle to explain how Mary Most Holy could have composed and proclaimed the wonderful canticle which is the *Magnificat*. The natural gifts of an ordinary woman of Palestine would have been sufficient, let alone the natural gifts of Her who was "*full of grace*"! But this "plausible" solution is discounted without batting an eyelash by the biblical exegesis of the closet rationalists. The consequently necessary recourse to a "miracle" is then refused, as it were, *absolutely*, as though such cannot be permitted in the case of Mary. Thus, a two thousand year old conviction of Tradition which recognizes instead in Mary the true and only author of the *Magnificat* is radically rejected. (For a study of the patristic tradition, see A. Gila, *Riletture patristiche*, in *Theotokos* 5 (1997) 423–461.

12 Laurentin, *Truth of Christmas*, p. 7. See also G. Aranda Pérez, "El Magnificat, el Evangelo proclamado por María," *Ephemerides Mariologicae* 36 (1986): 33, where the author writes expressly that the "specific action of the Holy Spirit produces in Mary the Messianic maternity and prophetic charism which moves her to express the salvific action of God with a depth as great as the strength of the Holy Spirit infused in her." Also interesting is n. 24,

The position, then, of those holding that the Magnificat came from the heart and lips of Mary Most Holy, and was composed under the inspiration of the Holy Spirit who had already filled her at the Annunciation, is well grounded.

Such, however, does not preclude that St. Luke, in the Greek transcription and translation, may have colored with his own style the original text of the Magnificat, without however altering "the substance of Mary's thought and sentiments,"[13] respecting, rather, the characteristic Semitic cadences, as Garofalo observes.[14]

The same may be said of the eventual, and perhaps inevitable, variations in the canticle, bound up with an exclusively oral transmission, as was the custom in those times of extensive illiteracy. Oral transmission usually may introduce some retouching or minor changes, but not a transformation capable of altering the content of a message. "In the oral transmission of the prayer," writes Laurentin, "ecclesial and communitary mediation has, without doubt, played an essential role in the way this text has been handed down. But to transmit is not to create."[15]

---

p. 36, where the author illustrates philologically the difference between a joyful cry that is "spontaneous and immediate" and the cry of Mary, one of joy "experienced and pondered."

13 Roschini, "Il 'Magnificat,'" p. 284. "It should cause no surprise," confirms Laurentin, "that the final written form should bear the mark of Luke" (*Truth of Christmas*, p. 382), and just afterward, the same author illustrates this very effectively by comparison with a recent instance, a text of Baudelaire (ibid., Ital. ed.: p. 506). Against those who have considered the Magnificat a composition too elaborate and developed, reflecting a mastery beyond the capacities of a young girl like Mary, see Roschini, "Il 'Magnificat,'" pp. 282–284, in agreement with Albarelli, Forestell, Lagrange, Pelaia, Garofalo, Gaechter (ibid., nn. 71–75).

14 Garofalo, *Le parole di Maria*, p. 19.

15 Laurentin, *Truth of Christmas*, p. 381. The hypothesis that Mary might have proclaimed the canticle not during the "visitation," but much later, after the Resurrection of Christ, also is incapable of proof, because it "relies on fictitious presuppositions" (ibid., p. 534, n. 23). See also Roschini, "Il 'Magnificat,'" pp. 281–282, where the author, in accord with Feuillet, responds to Gaechter on this same point. Also in regard to other hypotheses of interpretation and of dating the Magnificat, cf. Laurentin, *Truth of Christmas*, p. 532, nn. 20 and 21.

It must be affirmed, then, that Mary really did compose and proclaim the Magnificat. But it is also to be admitted that the canticle has not come from the exultant soul of Mary complete and exactly as we have it today, without any "mediation" that might have entailed stylistic retouching or embellishment—at least on the part of the translator, the Evangelist Luke—as though Mary had dictated it word for word to a copyist for transmission.[16]

On reflection, we may say that the two points harmonize well, that is, that the Magnificat is certainly the genuine creation of Mary, but in its present form it has been "mediated" through the normal channels of transmission, one of which certainly is the Evangelist Luke who received it, translated it, and transmitted it in Greek.

To conclude this discussion of authorship, we quote a concise passage of Leal: "On the whole, the ascription of the canticle to Mary may be considered certain. Its entire content reflects the inmost psychology of Mary, and what is more, prior to the events in the life, passion and resurrection of her Son."[17] The majority of the exegetes agree with this,[18] and we may add, finally, that

---

16 Cf. Laurentin, *Truth of Christmas*, p. 380.

17 Leal, *Vangelo secondo Luca*, p. 119. A. Molina Prieto has also written that "the canticle perfectly reflects a lively awareness of the mystery of which Mary is the protagonist at the Annunciation during the colloquy with the Angel (Lk 1:26–38), and above all from the moment she gives her consent to the Incarnation of the Word in her virginal womb" (A. Molino Prieto, "Mensaje liberador del Magnificat y surgerencias marginales," *Ephemerides Mariologicae* 36 [1986]: 61–62).

18 Even recently, in fact, on the subject of the attribution of the Magnificat to Mary, proclaimed by her at Ain-Karim during the visitation to Elizabeth, it has been asserted expressly that "the majority of exegetes reply with Zerwick in the affirmative" (Prieto, "Mensaje liberador," p. 61). More than a few, however, continue to maintain that it is "impossible" to ascribe to Mary the composition and the proclamation of the Magnificat, as E. Peretto, for example, expressly holds ("Magnificat," in *Nuovo Dizionario di Mariologia*, p. 855), as does Serra (*Maria secondo il Vangelo*, p. 1, where he claims that "Luke placed the Magnificat on the lips of Mary"). These exegetes still prefer, in the words of Laurentin, to depart from "the precise data of the text (Lk 1:28–46) in the interest of a contrived and groundless hypothesis,"

the Magisterium of the Church itself; including the more recent and solemn documents *Lumen Gentium, Marialis Cultus,* and *Redemptoris Mater,* continues unfailingly to confirm the ascription of the Magnificat to Mary, citing verses of the canticle as the words of Mary.[19]

> In confirmation of what has been stated and explained up to this point, we consider the teaching of Laurentin set out in his new volume on the Canticle of Mary Most Holy to be a precious guarantee. We reproduce here only brief excerpts, apologetic in character, but among the more important and valuable contents of this book:[20]
>
> 'What is most damaging to the *Magnificat* is the fact that a large majority of exegetes do not ascribe this canticle to Mary. It is rather, so they say, a late composition of a Judeo-Christian community which out of devotion attributed it to the Virgin. A similar conclusion is reached on the basis of philosophical and cultural prejudice which we shall examine...
>
> The elegant surgical operation by which the clear attribution of the *Magnificat* to Mary by the Evangelist Luke is challenged, depends on *a priori* assumptions. All the properly historical arguments converge in confirming (and not in weakening) everything Luke, the most historical of the Evangelists, says and in disqualifying other hypotheses as without any support...

justifying themselves on the basis of a "lovely myth" of an unknown and vague "creative Christian community" (see above, nn. 7 and 8).

19 Cf. Roschini, "Il 'Magnificat,'" p. 279; Prieto, *"Mensaje liberador,"* p. 62. In addition there is the authoritative confirmation in a decree of the Pontifical Biblical Commission (June 26, 1912) on this point (cf. H. Denzinger–A. Schönmetzer, *Enchiridion Symbolorum*, Barcelona 1967, n. 3571). Also important is the conclusion of the International Scientific Committee for "the Greek New Testament" which states: "The Committee was impressed by the overwhelming weight of external evidence, as well as by the balance of international probabilities, and therefore preferred to read *Mariam* as the subject of *eiper*": B.M. Metzger, *A Textual Commentary on the Greek New Testament*, London–New York 1971, p. 131.

20 R. Laurentin, Il *Magnificat*, Brescia 1993.

The worst feature of the affair is that Mary's authorship is not denied directly. Those who excluded are careful not to force the issue. They eliminate her authorship bit by bit, without being overly insistent. The *Magnificat* is a work of a 'professional' (so they claim) and not a poor girl of Galilee: to think otherwise is a pious illusion.

And they hasten to add: whether the *Magnificat* be by Mary or not, changes nothing. The canticle remains the same. It is equally beautiful... This changes nothing. But indeed. This changes much!

When a painting attributed to Rembrandt is recognized as false, the painting remains beautiful as before, but immediately loses its prestige and market value in astronomic proportions. If a historical fact is proven false, it loses its probative power for the people whose inheritance depends on it.

If the *Magnificat* is not by Mary, the text remains the same, without doubt. But it does not have the same value of witness, of bonding, of recollection. Its sounds hollow, if we detach it from the sonorous background constituted by the Woman *blessed among women* (Lk 1:43–48); the canticle loses its roots and the chant its harmony. If it is no longer a thanksgiving of Mary, Mother of Jesus, in virtue of this event, basis of salvation, all becomes disconcerting, incoherent, unexplainable.'[21]

All objective indices strengthen the ascription of the *Magnificat* to Mary as attested by Luke. Refusal to agree stems not from objective considerations, but from the *a priori* prejudices which we have rapidly reviewed... To refuse Mary authorship of the *Magnificat,* and, more broadly, to refuse to ascribe the infancy Gospel to her recollections, means to condemn oneself to incoherence. Exegesis then embarks on a never-ending cycles of tenuous hypotheses each contradicting one another...

---

21 *Op. cit.*, pp. 10. 11. 12. 13.

> If Mary is the source for the account of the Annunciation (of which she is the only witness), as well as for the account of the Visitation and of the *Magnificat*, all is perfectly consistent on the biblical and historic, interior and spiritual levels. We understand the inspiration and the simple depth of the canticle, and its links with the biblical context of that time.[22]

My soul magnifies the Lord and my spirit exults in God my Savior (vv. 46–47).

Numerous indeed are the biblical reminiscences in these first words spoken by Mary in the canticle, as she directs the praise received from Elizabeth entirely to God.

One notes immediately the three parallels: *"soul"–"spirit," "magnifies"–"exults,"* and *"Lord"–"God,"* expressing well Mary's profound joy in glorifying God. She desires to *"magnify"* (that is to say, philologically, "make great") God with all her *"soul,"* and she *"exults"* with her whole *"spirit"* in glorifying God who is her *"Savior."*[23]

There are three particular details in this verse to be set in relief:

1. The pronoun *"my"* characterizes the content of the verse in a personal sense, making evident first of all the merciful action of God in regard to Mary. This personal form renders intelligible the importance of Mary in herself, with respect to the Chosen People and with respect to the universe, both cosmic and human. Mary, that is, in her own right, occupies

---

22 *Op. cit.*, pp. 148. 152. 153.

23 About these two terms "soul" and "spirit," Leal writes: "*Soul—nefesh*: is the principal of corporal life, the seat of the sensible emotions. *Spirit—ruah*: is the superior part of the soul, the seat of the intellectual and religious life. Both of the terms may indicate the whole human being. Here, in virtue of the law of parallelism, 'soul' and 'spirit' are identified and are used to signify the whole person of Mary" (Leal, *Vangelo secondo Luca*, p. 121). Cf. also Roschini, "Il 'Magnificat,'" p. 289; C. de Ambrogio, *Il Vangelo di San Luca* (Turin, 1977), p. 53.

in the plan of creation and of universal salvation a public place uniquely hers.[24]

2. The verb form *"exults"* (in some translations *rejoices*) is an aorist in the Greek text, that is to say, a past tense. The Vulgate text adopts the present perfect tense (*exultavit*). The past tense in both texts indicates a very important fact. Garofalo writes: "My spirit 'exulted' in the remote past—in Greek aorist, instead of present—is a manner of expression recalling, as it were, the moment of the announcement."[25] The Virgin Mary proclaims the Lord great now, in the house of Elizabeth, but she had already exulted, or "had begun to exult"[26] in Him from the Annunciation.

3. The word *"Savior"* corresponds to the Hebrew term *"Jesus,"* used by the angel in speaking to Joseph: *"You shall call him Jesus: for he shall save his people from their sins"* (Mt 1:21). And hence, in the words of Mary, expression is given to the ineffable exultation of her spirit in God her *"Savior,"* that is, in her *"Jesus,"* carried in her womb.[27]

---

24 Ernst writes: "The very personal note expressed by the pronoun 'my' merits a certain attention. The first part of the canticle does not refer, therefore, to the great salvific work that Yahweh completes in the history of Israel, but exclusively to the personal grace that has been granted to Mary" (Ernst, *Il vangelo secondo Luca*, p. 114). And Varón Varón clarifies God's taking possession of Mary thus: "God has taken full possession of Mary and in her exists nothing deviating from God and from His interests" (*Sagrada Escritura*, p. 68).

25 Garofalo, *Le parole di Maria*, p. 83. Also Varón Varón writes that "according to Saint Anthony and other Doctors Mary speaks in the past tense and refers to the moment of the Incarnation" (*Sagrada Escritura*, p. 69).

26 Thus Pérez points out ("El Magnificat," p. 35, n. 19) that "the aorist égalliasen has the sense of an ingressive aorist: 'has begun to exult.'" Ceuppens speaks of a Hebrew "conversive future," which ordinarily connotes the past, but which after a verbal form indicating the present, also assumes the meaning of the present" (*De Mariologia Biblica*, p. 97).

27 Cf. Roschini, "Il 'Magnificat,'" p. 290. In fact, the same verse in Habakkuk 3:18 is translated in the Vulgate as "in God my Jesus." Cf. also Laurentin, *Truth of Christmas*, pp. 163, 220–221. A fortiori this serves to refute the view that the Magnificat could have been proclaimed by Elizabeth, and neutralize the use made of an absence in the Magnificat of references, at least implicit, to the Word Incarnate whom Mary was carrying in her womb. On this subject, it is helpful to quote Msgr. Cristiani: "In her canticle the mystery of the Incarnation is not mentioned. But it is present in each word, from first to last!" (L. Cristiani, *La Vierge Marie et les Evangiles* [Geneva, 1964], p. 173). And The *Navarre Bible. St. Luke's Gospel* says that in

But in what sense does Mary speak of *her* Savior? Certainly not in the ordinary sense of one who saves or liberates from contracted sin as this commonly applies to all other men, because "the salvation freely given to Mary," notes Leal, "must not be understood negatively as liberation of Mary from evil, but positively: the fulfillment in her of 'great things' (v. 49)."[28]

Because he has regarded the humility of his handmaid. From this day on all generations shall call me blessed (v. 48).

A kind of counterpoint is clearly featured in this verse: humility and littleness on the one side, beatitude and glorification on the other. *Tapeinosis* (lowliness) and *makariousis* (blessedness) by reason of their contrast mutually imply one another, in degrees of direct proportionality: the greater the *tapeinosis,* the greater the *makariousis.*[29] *But the ultimate ground for such a correlation is the regard of God alone.*[30] *Transformation of tapeinosis* into *makariousis* is effected by the "regard," the "look" of God. Mary exults, in fact, because God who "has looked upon" her *tapeinosis* will bring about her *makariousis* by

---

the first verse of the Magnificat, "Mary glorifies God for having made her Mother of the Savior" (p. 43).

28 Leal, *Vangelo secondo Luca*, p. 121. See also Ferraro, *I racconti*, pp. 54–55.

29 "It is evident, first of all," writes Roschini, "from the text itself and from the context, that the Virgin contrasts her exaltation (they will call me blessed) with her humiliation (wretchedness)" ("Il 'Magnificat,'" p. 293). Miguens confirms this in a long article, speaking of a "contrast between the humility (*tapeinosis*) and the new state that is going to be produced among all peoples and for all times" (M. Miguens, O.F.M., "Beatam me dicent," in *De primordiis cultus mariani*, vol. 2, p. 2).

30 There is a look of God that "enriches," a look of God that "judges," a look of God that "chastises": cf. Laurentin, *Truth of Christmas*, p. 470, n. 15. Regarding the importance of this "look" of God upon Mary, it has justly been written that "if anything really capital has ever happened in the entire history of mankind, it is precisely this 'look'" (M. Adinolfy, *Maria di Nazareth* [Jerusalem, 1966], p. 81).

all generations. In what sense, however, is *"humility"* to be taken?[31] Certain interpretations are to be excluded:

1. That it connotes the *virtue* of humility. It is obvious that our Lady, precisely because she was most bumble, could not proclaim or extol her own humility.[32]
2. That it connotes the humiliations Mary had to endure from her companions because of her irreprehensible conduct, truly angelic. This opinion excessively narrows the meaning of "humility."
3. That it connotes the condition of being a virgin, since virginity was considered a humiliation for a Jewish woman. But for Mary virginity was a state freely chosen in love and joy.[33]

The best-founded interpretation of *tapeinosis* is the one defining it as the recognition of one's own condition as a creature radically dependent upon the Creator in whom all of us *"live, move and have our being"* (Acts 17:28).[34] We might say that *tapeinosis* connotes here the metaphysical condition of the human creature, understood as human

---

31 For general orientations, cf. F. Rivera, "El concepto biblico de tapeinosis e nel Magnificat," *Revue Biblique* 68 (1958): 70–72.

32 Cf. Roschini, "Il 'Magnificat,'" p. 295; Garofalo, *Le parole di Maria*, p. 87.

33 This point Leal illustrates very well: "The exegesis of Gaechter does notseem acceptable to us. He perceives, in the 'littleness' of Mary her oppression on the part of the Nazarenes. Nor does that of Lyonnet, who perceives in it an allusion to her liberation from voluntary virginal sterility, precisely because this sterility was embraced and preserved joyfully, and because the Messianic maternity was accepted not to overcome this sterility, but rather in obedience to the will of God" (Leal, *Vangelo secondo Luca*, pp. 121–122).

34 The term *tapeinosis* "corresponds, in the Septuagint, to the term 'anawah' of the Old Testament, one connoting the spiritual poverty and the dependence of a creature upon his Creator, because of which he has trust in Him and not in himself" (Leonardi, *L'Infanzia di Gesù*, p. 179). Another author identifies the *tapeinosis* with the "fear of God" proper to the anawim (Pérez, "El Magnificat," p. 40). Perhaps the *tapeinosis* of Mary, the Mother, might be correlated with the *kenosis* of Jesus, the Son.

finitude, radical dependence, the littleness and lowliness of a "handmaid" and "slave" before the Lord.[35]

The beatitude: *makariousis,* of Mary, instead, which begins with the inspired cry of St. Elizabeth and is to continue through the ages until the end of time, stems from the divine regard (look, glance).

Already during His public life, a woman's voice would one day cry out to Jesus: *"Blessed is the womb that bore thee and the breasts that gave thee suck"* (Lk 11:27). And Jesus would respond: *"Yea, rather, blessed are they who hear the word of God and keep it"* (Lk 1:28). "Jesus not only does not contradict the praise of the woman," comments Garofalo, "but He confirms it and suggests where, in a higher sphere, transcending the simply natural, one must search and discover the greatness of His Mother."[36]

In these words of Mary, *"all generations shall call me blessed,"* we find utterance given to one of the most marvelous and significant prophecies of sacred Scripture. "What could be more precise than this oracle?," asks Nicolas. "And, after it has been pronounced, what could be naturally more impossible than its fulfillment?"[37]

---

35 *Tapeinosis* designates "a humble condition, a natural abasement" (Ceuppens, *De Mariologia Biblica*, p. 98); it is "to be understood in the sense of human littleness before the greatness of God" and "it matches the phrase: 'Behold the handmaid of the Lord' (v. 38)" (Leal, *Vangelo secondo Luca*, p. 121). Cf. also Ernst, *Il vangelo secondo Luca*, pp. 114–115 Ferraro, *I racconti*, p. 56; Pietrafesa, *La Madonna nella Rivelazione*, p. 191. Also interesting is the "semiotic point of view" (Laurentin, *Truth of Christmas*, pp. 5–11). Roschini notes that the *tapeinosis* acknowledged and accepted by Mary is in radical contrast with the proud "I will not serve" of Lucifer ("Il 'Magnifcat,'" p. 295).

36 Garofalo, *Le parole di Maria*, p. 88. In a note, the author points out that "the same Evangelist who has recounted the prophecy of Mary intends to show us, in this episode, its first verification."

37 Nicolas, *La Vergine Maria*, p. 219. Anyone denying Mary Most Holy composed and proclaimed the *Magnificat* should ask how ever would St. Luke have made such a pretentious "prophecy" and placed it on the lips of Mary? Could the author of such a "prophecy" been St. Luke? Or the Judeo-Christian community? Or one of the "anawim"?

This oracle is clearly eschatological in character and is linked clearly to and dependent upon the other oracle pronounced by the angel about the Kingdom of the Son *"of which there will be no end"* (Lk 1:33).[38] This intrinsic connection reveals the primary reason for the perpetuity of Marian devotion: she will be praised and blessed for her Divine Maternity until the end of time, because she is the Mother of Jesus.[39]

The Almighty has done great things in me and holy is his name (v. 49).

Mary proclaims that she has been the singular, personal (*"in me"*)[40] object of exceptional deeds (*"great things"*)[41] worked by the onmipotent and holy God. Therefore, we must believe that she had an understanding and a view of the *"great things"* done by God to her. Certainly, among these *"great things"* are included the virginal conception and the Divine Maternity.[42]

But it is certain that Mary also refers to all the *"great things"* of the past and for the future in God's plan. Her eternal predestination with the Son "by one and the same decree" (bull *Ineffabilis Deus*), the Immaculate Conception, the Coredemption and spiritual Motherhood of humanity, the glorious Assumption of body, and soul, the coronation

38 Cf. Pérez, "El Magnificat," pp. 42–43.

39 Cf. Leal, *Vangelo secondo Luca*, p. 122; Roschini, "Il 'Magnificat,'" p. 296; Varón Varón, *Sagrada Escritura*, p. 72.

40 Cf. Pérez, "El Magnificat," p. 44, where the author links this personal, individuating detail with that of the Annunciation: *"Be it done to me" (genoito moi)*, in Lk 1:38.

41 *"Great things,"* in Greek *"tà megála,"* which for the Septuagint corresponds to the Hebrew *ghedholoth*, with its more precise sense of "prodigies" (cf. Leal, *Vangelo secondo Luca*, p. 122; Roschini, "Il 'Magnificat,'" p. 297).

42 F. Ceuppens writes on the subject: "The great things which divine omnipotence has done for Mary are the virginal and supernatural conception whereby Mary is constituted Mother of the Messiah and Mother of the Son of God" (*De Mariologia Biblica*, p. 99). Cf. also Leal, *Vangelo secondo Luca*, p. 122; Varón Varón, *Sagrada Escritura*, p. 73.

as Queen of heaven and earth:[43] all of these *"great things"* are connected with the omnipotence and holiness of God, because only God—with whom *"nothing is impossible"* (Lk 1:37), who is the Holy One, absolutely transcendent[44]—can work these *"great things."*

His mercy is from generation to generation upon them that fear him (v. 50).

With this verse, the perspective of the Magnificat shifts from the plan of God regarding the person of Mary, to the communal plan[45] regarding all men awaiting salvation, that is to say, those who fear God (v. 50), the humble (v. 52), the poor (v. 53).[46]

Mary is the bearer of the "mercy" of God. The Incarnation signals the *"fullness of time"* (Gal 4:4) in the salvific plan of God. Now the messianic mercy[47] is poured out upon humanity for all ages: *"from generation to generation,"* and for all who accept it, that is to say, for men who *"fear him,"*

---

43 Cf. Roschini, "Il 'Magnificat,'" p. 297, where the views of St. Lawrence of Brindisi and St. Thomas are cited; Pietrafesa, *La Madonna nella Rivelazione*, pp. 192–193, where Hugh of St. Victor is cited. Likewise interesting is the interpretation of the expression "in me," also translated "*for me*" and "*by means of me*," to connote the "mediation" of Mary in relation to the creation and the Redemption: cf. Varón Varón, *Sagrada Escritura*, p. 73.

44 "*Holy*: in biblical usage 'sanctity' designates the absolute transcendence of God" (Leal, *Vangelo secondo Luca*, p. 122). Also noteworthy is the fact that Mary says "*holy is his name*," rather than God is holy. But "the Hebrew language, which avoids the adjective 'divine,' accepts as synonymous the names 'Yahweh' and 'Holy" (Laurentin, *Truth of Christmas*, p. 482, n. 76). Cf. also Roschini, "Il 'Magnificat,'" p. 298.

45 "This passage from the particular instance to the universal is frequent in biblical poetry," writes Pérez, "El Magnificat," p. 46.

46 Roschini points out that in this second part of the Magnificat (four verses: 50–53), Mary Most Holy "expresses four laws according to which divine government in the world is conducted: 1) the 'law of mercy' for all those who fear Him (v. 50); 2) the 'law of dispersion of the proud' (v. 51); 3) the 'law of deposing the powerful hostile to Him and of the exaltation of the humble' (v. 52); 4) the 'law of impoverishment of the rich and of enrichment of the poor' (v. 53)" ("Il 'Magnificat,'" p. 299).

47 On the concept of messianic "mercy," not understood—except where reductionism is operative—as compassion or benevolence towards the poor, but as "fidelity to the Covenant," see Prieto, "Mensaje liberador," p. 65.

obeying and serving Him in the faithful fulfillment of His wishes.[48] Garofalo writes correctly that "Mary has a clear perception of the consequences the Incarnation of the Word in her womb will have for all times and for all men."[49] The Incarnation is the highest "mercy" which, like a perennial stream, flows out upon God-fearing men and those who believe in Him, beginning with the humble Mary, the handmaid of the "Fiat."

Let us always remember that "the fear of God and trusting recognition of His mercy," as Ferraro notes, "constitute the great praises of His glory, the motive for His exaltation and for exultation in Him, with which the canticle of Mary begins."[50]

He has shown the power of his arm; he has scattered the proud in the conceit of their heart (v. 51).

An initial consideration about this verse, and about the next two, concerns the six verbs in the past tense: six Greek aorists, the translation of six Hebrew perfect tenses. Now "the *Hebrew perfect,"* notes Leonardi, "has a vast range of nuances, to be selected on the basis of their context. Here the six verbs connote the past conduct of God in the history of the Chosen People, a conduct, however, in the present and in the future as well.... They are, then, *gnomic* aorists: they express that which God does in every age, even

48 "*Those who fear God*: to fear God, in the Old Testament, is synonymous with serving Him, obeying Him" (Leal, *Vangelo secondo Luca*, p. 122). Cf. Varón Varón, *Sagrada Escritura*, p. 76. Ceuppens writes that the salvific mercy of God is offered to all men "provided that they fear God; acknowledge the God of love and holiness, love Him with genuine filial respect, serve Him always and everywhere faithfully" (*De Mariologia Biblica*, p. 99).

49 Garofalo, *Le parole di Maria*, p. 89.

50 Ferraro, *I racconti*, p. 57. "The *mystery fearful and fascinating* of God holy and sublime," writes Ernst, "becomes accessible in the mystery of mercy, in the richness of mercy... As leitmotif, this idea is developed throughout the Gospel of Luke" (*Il Vangelo secondo Luca*, pp. 115–116).

if Mary has in mind specifically the preceding history of the people of God."[51]

In verse 51, with an anthropomorphism: *"the power of his arm,"* Mary describes the operative plan of God unfolding according to criteria quite different from those of man and of the world, as is clear from the history of the Chosen People. God not only is not disposed to save the proud man, confident and self-satisfied, but has decided, at the opportune time, to disperse and eliminate him. As examples from history illustrative of the point, we may recall here the cruel Holofernes and the giant Goliath, eliminated respectively by an unarmed woman (Judith) and by a young shepherd (David).[52] Reflecting further, we can admire even more the divine "power" in the heroic strength given by God to the legions of martyrs, virgins, and apostles, and to the pontiffs who have governed the Church in the most difficult times.[53]

Mary speaks of the *"proud in the conceit of their heart."* The seat of thought for the Jews is the *"heart."* The proud who cultivate haughty thoughts, presumptuous ambitions, vainglorious projects are the enemies of God and, sooner or later, will be dispersed by Him.[54]

---

51 Leonardi, *L'Infanzia di Gesù*, p. 181. Cf. Leal, *Vangelo secondo Luca*, p. 123; Pérez, "El Magnificat," p. 46; Prieto, "Mensaje liberador," pp. 68–71; Ernst, *Il Vangelo secondo Luca*, p. 116. Roschini also writes that these verbs "embracing the past, present and future, are as it were temporal" ("Il 'Magnificat,'" p. 299, n. 100).

52 In an interesting note, Roschini briefly examines some biblical episodes illustrating this action of the "arm" of God ("Il 'Magnificat,'" p. 301, n. 103). "God has shown the power of His arm, above all against Egypt, the great human power, worldly and inimical. This theme runs throughout all of the Old Testament" (Ferraro, *I racconti*, pp. 57–58).

53 Varón Varón in fact writes: "The divine Arm is marvelously displayed in the host of martyrs, of virgins; in the conversion of sinners; in those chosen to transmit His message (the charism of the Apostles), in the perpetuity of the Church, etc." (*Sagrada Escritura*, p. 76).

54 "Why this hatred for the proud?," asks Roschini. He replies, explaining that, in contrast to other vicious men, the proud man "offends the universal (cosmic) order in virtue of which the creature is obliged to recognize his Creator as the source of all that he is and has" ("Il 'Magnificat,'" p. 301).

Garofalo reads in these words of Mary a particular "allusion to the vain pride of men who dare to judge the work of God par excellence: the Incarnation of the Word. Who ever thought that the Son of the Most High should have had to take flesh in the womb of a poor little creature like all the sons of men?"[55] Choosing the poor and unknown Mary, God shows precisely that he takes no one into account and ignores any creature reputed important. That means that for us, Mary constitutes the model of humble union with God and of trusting acceptance of His plan.[56]

He has put down the mighty from their thrones, he has raised up the humble (v. 52).

"The history of Israel," writes Garofalo, "is rich in examples of rash kings and princes who, inebriated by earthly glory, betrayed God, who cast them from their thrones, and of obscure but virtuous men and women, who unexpectedly shone forth to restore the desecrated throne."[57] The angel Gabriel had said to Mary that her Son would occupy *"the throne of David his father"* (v. 32). Proclaiming verse 52 of the Magnificat, Mary must have thought of the powerful Saul, cast from the throne, and of the little shepherd David, raised to the throne.[58] Much

55 GAROFALO, *Le parole di Maria*, p. 92. Cf. also CEUPPENS, *De Mariologia Biblica*, p. 100. Laurentin, on the other hand, does not read "*in*," but "*by*" the thoughts of their hearts, and explains that God confounds the proud "not by a violent action, but by 'the imagination of their hearts,' since pride is a false type of *knowing* which leads to self-destruction" (*Truth of Christmas* p. 157).

56 On this matter, read the pointed reflections of PÉREZ, "El Magnificat," p. 49.

57 GAROFALO, *Le parole di Maria*, p. 95. Cf. also VARÓN VARÓN, *Sagrada Escritura*, p. 77. The two parallel terms expressed in this verse—the mighty (*dynástai*) and the humble (*tapeinoi*)—are counterpointed. The mighty "pertain, par excellence, to the category of proud in virtue of the thoughts of their heart. Compared to them, the humble are those who are in a condition similar to Mary's.... For this God intervenes, given that they are poor and have accepted Him": so writes PÉREZ, "El Magnificat," p. 50.

58 Cf. ROSCHINI, "Il 'Magnificat,'" p. 302.

more, however, must she have remembered the glorious and proud Davidic dynasty, also fallen, and now raised up again forever by her Son Jesus, the meek and humble *"lamb of God"* (Jn 1:29).[59] Precisely in Mary, then, God realizes His most disturbing and definitive intervention in history, raising an obscure, humble descendant of David to the paternal throne, to rule a kingdom that *"will have no end"* (Lk 1:33).[60]

Notwithstanding so clear a meaning, this verse, together with the preceding and following ones (vv. 51 and 53), has recently occasioned rivers of ink in support of the so-called *liberation theology*, wherein the Magnificat is expounded as a true "hymn of the revolution," the religious expression for every movement of radical, social restructuring, those especially provoking so much blood and cruel affliction in many parts of the world.[61] As far as any legitimate exegesis is concerned, these three verses of the Magnificat (51–53), when interpreted and applied reductively by liberation theology, are twisted beyond recognition and so such an interpretation is untenable,[62] above all in terms of the

59 Cf. Leonardi, *L'Infanzia di Gesù*, p. 181.

60 "The intervention of God," comments Pérez, "raising up the Messiah in the womb of Mary, has begun this reversal of positions. Mary, the chantress of the hymn has seen this—in the faith and the words of Elizabeth—fulfilled in her, and now proclaims it to be realized for all the humble" ("El Magnificat," p. 1). It should not be forgotten that Mary—the "*handmaid*" (servant), the "*tapina*"—also will be raised and seated upon the throne beside her Son, as Queen Mother of the King of the heavens: cf. Roschini, "Il 'Magnificat,'" p. 303.

61 See the important document of the Sacred Congregation for the Faith, *Instruction on Certain Aspects of the Theology of Liberation* (Rome, 1984). A well-documented and analytic study is that of Prieto, "Mensaje liberador," pp. 57–88. More generic, on the other hand, and less convincing, is the article of E. Villar, "El Magnificat en la Teología de la liberación," *Ephemerides Mariologicae* 36 (1986): 89–112. It is above all v. 52 of the Magnificat that has become, in a certain sense, the revolutionary banner of liberation theology. Prieto notes explicitly: "I think that it is no little exaggeration to take the expression of Luke 1:52 ... as the central point and the exclusive key for discovering the role of God such as it is revealed in history" (p. 58).

62 Again, Prieto speaks expressly of "exorbitant excesses, doctrinal deviations and some more or less conscious manipulations" (ibid., p. 58).

logic inherent in the revealed soteriology and illustrated by biblical theology.

On this point, it is sufficient to note that the general line of thought pursued by liberation theology in expounding the Magnificat is nothing more or less than a revival of the ancient aspirations of the Jewish people for liberation from the oppressions of their Roman overlords, for a recovery of civil and political liberty, and for the restoration of the temporal kingdom of David. Hence, liberation theology is a strictly naturalistic, secular approach and exposition. It is but a regression to an ancient error concerning the Messiah and His Kingdom, decked out as revolution or reversal of worldly fortunes. Liberation theology constitutes a very grievous mistake in perspective as well as content.

Mary, on the other hand, proclaims a messianic liberation that is in essence freedom from that true *slavery* far more burdensome and degrading for every man: the *slavery* of sin, of death, of the flesh, of the devil.[63] Mary enjoyed this freedom in its fullness, *from her beginning*, from her Immaculate Conception, fruit of a preservative redemption, in view of the foreseen merits of her Son.[64]

We know as well, moreover, that Mary, like Jesus himself, was born poor, lived poor, died poor. But who can ever dream of having her "riches"? Evangelical *poverty* is blessedness: *"Blessed are you poor!"* (Lk 6:20). Earthly

---

63 "This liberty," writes Prieto, "as a total Messianic gift, supposes and brings with it the liberation from sin, from death, from slavery of the flesh and the dominion of Satan. That which Mary proclaims is an effusive torrent of liberating mercy" (ibid., p. 73). A little further on, the same author affirms that messianic liberation "demands and deepens an experience of personal conversion, of glad acceptance" (p. 74). If there is not this "personal conversion" and this "glad acceptance," there are no true poor, no *tapeinoi*—like Mary—at all, but only poor revolutionaries without God on their side.

64 "The Virgin announces, in global terms, the imminent Messianic liberation of which she feels eminently favored and the privileged bearer" (ibid., p. 73).

wealth, worldly and carnal well-being are misery and ruin: *"Woe to you rich!"* (Lk 6:24).

The "revolutionary" language of Christ and Mary is understood only by *"those who fear God"* (v. 50).

He has filled the hungry with good things: and the rich he has sent away empty (v. 53).

Fr. Lagrange once said that this verse of the Magnificat is to be explained against the backdrop of Eastern courts and their customs, where access was denied the poor because they had nothing to give, while it was permitted the rich who presented themselves with hands full of gifts to offer their sovereigns, who always repaid them with regal munificence.[65]

Mary proclaims here a reversal on God's part: at the divine court, the poor man, the hungry man, he whose hands are empty, is satisfied and filled with good things. The rich man, instead, he whose hands are full, is sent away without receiving any of the good things of God. But to what good things is reference made? The answer is decisive: "messianic" goods, those spiritual goods of the Kingdom of God, such as grace and freedom, the Holy Spirit and the sacraments, interior peace and joy of spirit, sanctity and eternal life.

Jesus would one day say: *"Blessed are you that hunger now, for you shall be filled"* (Lk 6:21) and *"blessed are they that hunger and thirst after justice, for they shall have their fill"* (Mt 5:6). He speaks here of those who have "the desire," explains Garofalo, "to realize the ideal of being good and, more than good, perfect."[66]

---

65 Lagrange, "Le récit de l'Enfance," pp. 160–185; Ceuppens, *De Mariologia Biblica*, p. 101.

66 Garofalo, *Le parole di Maria*, p. 99. Roschini speaks of hunger and thirst "for spiritual riches, for general uprightness of life, for holiness (that

It is not a question, then, of a simple transposition or reversal in the social and economic order, whereby the materially poor become rich and the rich become poor.[67] It is, instead, a matter of an assignment of goods totally different: to the rich, a surfeit of earthly and passing goods, with the privation (*"empty hands"*) of spiritual and eternal goods; to the hungry and indigent, on the other hand, privation of earthly goods, but with the fullness and wealth (*"filled"*) of spiritual and eternal goods.[68]

"The supreme model," writes Roschini, "and the closest to us of these poor ones, hungry and thirsty for justice and for sanctity, is precisely Mary."[69] Truly, Mary had always been poor in earthly goods, while she had been rich in every heavenly good. This, in substance, is the teaching proclaimed with remarkable force by the Blessed Virgin in the Magnificat. She is revealed here as the active and enlightened woman, ready, courageous and forthright in proclaiming to all in what consists true freedom, authentic greatness, and the imperishable wealth of man.[70] And if

---

constitutes the greatest riches of this world)" ("Il 'Magnificat,'" p. 304).

67 That which today the "emotional" exegesis of liberation theology would claim as true, has long since been considered and rejected by Lagrange, who in his time wrote that "the immediate relationship between God, on the one side, and the poor and the rich on the other, demonstrates well that there is no question here of a social revolution designed to put the one (the poor) in the place of the other (the rich), but of an attitude of God toward those who humbly ask and those who believe it their right to demand (because they pretend to have given). The sequel then suggests that it is a question of Messianic goods, not at all desired by those who are satisfied with their position in the world" (text quoted by Roschini, "Il 'Magnificat,'" p. 304). See also the reflections of Ceuppens, *De Mariologia Biblica*, p. 101, and of Ernst, *Il Vangelo secondo Luca*, p. 117.

68 This was precisely the extraordinary experience—emblematic it can be said—of St. Francis of Assisi, the Little Poor Man (*Poverello*), who rid himself of earthly goods in order to possess heavenly, and who wanted his friars (and his followers) to be "poor in temporal goods, rich in virtue" (*Definitive Rule* [1223], c. 6).

69 Roschini, "Il 'Magnificat,'" p. 304.

70 This attitude of Mary as an active and courageous woman, in no way passive or remissive in proclaiming what is true, what is just, what is noble, has been set in relief by Pope Paul VI in *Marialis Cultus*, no.37.

certain supporters of liberation theology reconstruct the Magnificat to present Mary as a "theological locus" and exemplary archetype of *liberation* for all humanity,[71] they utter a great truth, but then commit a gross error, reducing this "theological locus" and Marian exemplarity to a laundry list of social complaints and demands.[72] In such wise the vision and reality of the Kingdom of God—which *"is not of this world"* (Jn 18:36)—are deformed and reduced to the level of a kingdom of man stuffed with material foods and bloated by earthly goods.

"Wealth," we conclude with Garofalo, "is not that which is possessed materially and linked to the fate of a world dying every instant; wealth is that which has become ours in the very depths of the soul, that can quench our thirst for eternal life and unending happiness."[73]

He has come to the help of Israel his servant, being mindful of his mercy (v. 54).

In this verse also is contained a reaffirmation of the promise of the Messiah Savior, initially made by God to our first parents, Adam and Eve, for the entire human race (Gen 3:15), and then expressly confirmed with Abraham, father of the Chosen People (Gen 17:1–14).

"He has come to the help of Israel": "The past tense," says Leal, "refers, rather than to the entire history of Israel, to the

---

71 Villar writes thus: "Mary, as a theological locus, is also a prophetic locus, archetype of all humanity" ("Teología de la Liberación," p. 107), and a little further on: "Mary represents not only Israel, but all of humanity" (p. 108; see also p. 109).

72 In his study of this subject, Prieto warns precisely of this "temptation" of liberation theology to interpret the Magnificat in such a manner as to "reduce the Gospel of salvation to a mere collection of social wants or protests" ("Mensaje liberador," p. 80).

73 Garofalo, *Le parole di Maria*, p. 101. And "only the message of Jesus," writes Varón Varón, "can satiate human understanding and the heart of man" (*Sagrada Escritura*, p. 78).

immediate fact of the Incarnation."[74] The true, definitive "help" is only He, the Word Incarnate in Mary.

"Israel his servant": the people of Israel were chosen by God as His "servant," that is to say, as the people that would have served God, advancing His worship in belief and in deed—monotheism and monolatry—in the midst of all other polytheistic and idolatrous peoples, in expectation of the Messiah Savior.[75]

"Being mindful": is another biblical anthropomorphism. Applied to God, it signifies that He never fails, but in due time realizes, in fact, the promise He has given.[76]

"Of his mercy": namely, His fidelity to the covenant stipulated with Abraham, based on the promise to send the Messiah Redeemer to work the salvation awaited from age to age, proclaimed by prophet after prophet, continuously prepared across centuries so often afflicted with cruel sufferings.[77]

Now, "the realization of the promise," writes Ferraro, "consists in the sending and the presence of the Messiah

---

74 Leal, *Vangelo secondo Luca*, p. 124. "Has come to the aid": translates the Greek *antelábeto*, which means "has taken" care and "has taken" us in His arms. The Vulgate, in fact, translates it: "*Suscepit Israel puerum suum*"—God has taken Israel in His arms "as a father takes his son," writes Leonardi, *L'Infanzia di Gesù*, p. 182.

75 Interesting is the commentary of Garofalo on the historical development of the plan of God according to the Covenant He himself established: *Le parole di Maria*, pp. 101–107.

76 Cf. Leal, *Vangelo secondo Luca*, p. 124; Leonardi, *L'Infanzia di Gesù*, p. 183.

77 "*Mindful of his mercy*": Leal writes that "the phrase as a whole could be paraphrased thus: 'actualizing the mercy promised by sending the Messiah'" (*Vangelo secondo Luca*, p. 124). It is certain that the language closely recalls the Old Testament; nevertheless "the Old Testament phraseology should not be so stressed as to obscure the New Testament perspective of the canticle, which, in Israel's acceptance, contains the total salvific event up to its eschatological completion," remarks Ernst, *Il Vangelo secondo Luca*, p. 118.

in Mary. This is the great, culminating, definitive act of salvific history."[78]

As he promised to our Fathers, to Abraham and to his seed forever (v. 55).

This verse delineates the historical and prophetical "memory" of God's salvific project carried out through the *"Fathers,"* through *"Abraham,"* through the *"lineage"* of Abraham, until the end of time. The line of development of the redemptive plan begins with Adam and Eve, our first parents, is channeled through Abraham and through the Davidic lineage, and terminates in Mary, the Mother of the Messiah Redeemer.[79]

The particular importance of this verse, however, consists above all in an affirmation of the "universality" of salvation, which is not confined within the limits of the Chosen People of Israel according to the flesh, but is opened and extended to all the people who form Israel according to the spirit (the Church), for all times, according to a prophetic allusion contained in the promise of God to our first parents (cf. Gen 3:15), and according to an explicit promise made to Abraham: *"In thy seed shall all the nations of the earth be blessed"* (Gen 22:18).[80]

It is to be observed, nevertheless, that the term *"seed,"* or lineage, interpreted by St. Paul, means in the strict sense and in the final analysis only Christ: *"To Abraham were the promises made,"* says St. Paul, *"and to his seed. Scripture does not say 'to his seeds' as if referring to many, but, speaking of one*

---

78 Ferraro, *I racconti*, p. 61. Cf. also Garofalo, *Le parole di Maria*, pp. 101–107; Pietrafesa, *La Madonna nella Rivelazione*, p. 196; De Ambrogio, *San Luca*, p. 55. Roschini asks: "In what way has God 'come to the aid of Israel' and been mindful 'of His mercy'?... [and he replies:] By means of Mary's virginal conception of the Messiah" ("Il 'Magnificat,'" p. 306).

79 Cf. Garofalo, *Le parole di Maria*, pp. 101–107.

80 Cf. Roschini, "Il 'Magnificat,'" pp. 307–308; De Ambrogio, *San Luca*, p. 55; Leonardi, *L'Infanzia di Gesù*, p. 183.

alone, says: 'and to your seed,' which is Christ" (Gal 3:16).[81] In Christ the Redeemer, then, is centered the new Israel, the Church, to which all of humanity and the cosmos itself is called: because only Christ is *"the Alpha and the Omega"* of the universe (Rev 1:8), because all was made *"in him"* (Col 1:16), and only in Him do *"all things hold together"* (Col 1:17). The historic Christ, the mystic Christ, the cosmic Christ: this is the true *"seed,"* now present in the virginal womb of God's Mother who *"magnifies the Lord."*[82]

And Mary remained with her about three months. And she returned to her own house (v. 56).

This verse precedes the description of the birth of John the Baptist, and suggests, seemingly, that Mary departed from the house of Elizabeth before the birth of the Precursor.

Exegetes find difficulty in reaching agreement about what might be the most correct interpretation of this "closure" of St. Luke completing the typology of the Ark, which also remained "three months" in the house of Obededom (cf. 2 Sam 6:11). The majority of exegetes, however, seems to support a stay of Mary in the house of Elizabeth even during the birth of John the Baptist. And that for various reasons.

First, it is the style of St. Luke to make use of the so-called "anticipation method," whereby he concludes one event before narrating another. Verse 56 in fact concludes

---

81 PÉREZ writes precisely that, according to St. Paul, "the true seed of Abraham, in the proper and strict sense, according to the letter of the Scriptures, is Jesus Christ, and beginning with Him, all those who make up the new Israel, the Church" ("El Magnificat," p. 55). Cf. also ROSCHINI, "Il 'Magnificat,'" pp. 307–308.

82 Therefore, the Magnificat has "cosmic value in relation to all times and to the universal vicissitudes of humanity;... and becomes a paradigm for the mystery of salvation that embraces and comprises all" (Ferraro, *I racconti*, p. 51).

the account of the visitation of Mary to St. Elizabeth,[83] although Mary's departure may have occurred after the birth of the Precursor.

Second, the very fact that Mary lived with Elizabeth for *"about"* three months, that is to say, a time span that is approximative, seems to insinuate that the reason for describing her stay there in approximative terms was directly connected with the expectation of the birth of Elizabeth's child.[84]

Third, it would seem truly strange that Mary, hastening to visit Elizabeth to congratulate her on her miraculous pregnancy, would then take leave of her relative just before the joyous birth of the child occurred.[85]

Fourth, if Mary assisted Elizabeth during the months of gestation, how much more would she not have aided her during the trials of delivery? How could her leaving the house of Elizabeth on the vigil of delivery be justified?[86]

Other reasons of a psychological kind or of a type entailing appropriateness, seem, nevertheless, to argue against a stay of Mary until the birth: the custom of

---

83 Cf. Leal, *Vangelo secondo Luca*, pp. 52–53. On pp. 53–59, the author gives a series of texts illustrative of the "method of elimination." See also Roschini, *La vita di Maria*, pp. 168–170. Laurentin also affirms that St. Luke "usually disposes of the principal character at the end of a sequence which concerns that character" (*Truth of Christmas*, p. 158).

84 Cf. Leal, *Vangelo secondo Luca*, pp. 52–53, where the author says that the expression "about" three months "favors Mary's presence at the birth and circumcision of John." Laurentin, for his part, writes: "The three months of Mary's stay thus extend to and, we would argue, include the birth of John" (*Truth of Christmas*, p. 158). See also A. Merk, S.J., "La figura di Maria nel Nuovo Testamento," in *Mariologia*, ed. by P. Sträter, vol. 1 (Rome, 1951), p. 58.

85 Cf. Leal, *Vangelo secondo Luca*, pp. 52–53: "To this reason is added a motive psychological in character: Mary, who had gone to Elizabeth to congratulate her in her joy, could not be absent at its culminating moment."

86 Pietrafesa writes: "Elizabeth could not have been left alone at the moment when she had the greatest need" (*La Madonna nella Rivelazione*, p. 197); the author, nevertheless, presents this as uncertain. Leonardi, on the other hand, maintains that "the service of charity was even more urgent in the days after the birth of the child" (*L'Infanzia di Gesù*, p. 185).

excluding the presence of virgins at delivery (Lagrange and others), the reserve and modesty of Mary (Prat), the probability that Elizabeth would have spoken of Mary *"Mother of the Lord"* to the friends who came to rejoice with her over the birth of the child (Landucci).[87]

The concluding remark: *"She returned to her own house,"* is not uniformly interpreted by exegetes. Some find in these words a confirmation that Mary "did not cohabitate" yet with Joseph, and therefore had to return to *"her own house"* and not to the house of Joseph.[88] Others, instead, read in these words a confirmation that Mary already "lived" with Joseph, for whom the house of Joseph was already *"her house."*[89]

The visitation of Mary to St. Elizabeth concludes with verse 56. It is an event of exceptional grace, enriched by the extraordinary charisms that filled the house of Elizabeth. Ferraro writes:

> Mary's travelling when the scene opens, from her own house to the house of Elizabeth, and her return journey are presented from the start of the account as the journey of the ark of the covenant, as an illustration of the mystery of the presence of God among men, a presence in Mary that is no longer bound to one material locale alone such as the Temple, but passes through the mountains and through the streets of this world to spread the blessing of salvation.[90]

---

87 Cf. Ceuppens, *De Mariologia Biblica*, p. 103; Leal, *Vangelo secondo Luca*, pp. 52–53; p. C. Landucci, *Maria SS. nel Vangelo* (Rome, 1954), p. 82.

88 Cf. Pietrafesa, *La Madonna nella Rivelazione*, p. 197; Leonardi, *L'Infanzia di Gesù*, p. 185; Laurentin, *Truth of Christmas*, pp. 157–158.

89 Cf. Lagrange, "Le récit de l'Enfance," p. Ceuppens, *De Mariologia Biblica*, p. 118, where the author concludes that "from that expression nothing can be deduced, whether Mary was only espoused, or whether she was already married.

90 Cf. Ferraro, *I racconti*, p. 47.

12
St. Joseph's Anxieties

After recording the *"genealogy of Jesus Christ, Son of David, Son of Abraham"* (Mt 1:1), the Evangelist Matthew describes the *"birth of Jesus Christ"* (v. 18), beginning with the drama lived by St. Joseph on discovering that Mary, his virginal spouse, was with child.[1]

That drama must have begun upon Mary's return from Ain–Karim. After three months, the early, external signs of pregnancy were for St. Joseph an incredible surprise, an impenetrable mystery overwhelming the soul of this upright and pious Israelite, this "just" man, as the same Evangelist Matthew defines him (v. 19). Not knowing of the virginal conception of the Word, which occurred on the day of the Annunciation in the womb of Mary, St. Joseph found himself overcome by deep anxiety as he sought an explanation for this "fact," a fact rendered still more mysterious by Mary's inexplicable silence and by the genuine candor he saw reflected more than ever in her face.

St. Joseph's greatest anguish was caused by the fact that, as a consequence of Mary's pregnancy, he had to make a decision in regard to Mary and the child she carried in her womb. But upon what grounds would he make his decision?

The Evangelist Matthew, in a few verses (18–25), permits us to grasp intuitively and accurately St. Joseph's profound interior suffering, and, at the same time, how he resolved every problem with the message of the angel, who

1 For knowledge of this event, also, St. Matthew had to draw "directly or indirectly on the secrets of Joseph and Mary" (Leonardi, *L'Infanzia di Gesù*, p. 51; see also p. 54).

restored to Mary's spouse an even deeper peace and serenity of heart.[2]

Now the birth of Jesus Christ was in this wise (v. 18a).

Having established the Davidic lineage of Jesus (vv. 1–17), St. Matthew goes on to describe Jesus' generation and birth, adopting here as well the very term *"genesis"*[3] used at the beginning of the ancient genealogy (1:1). Coupling here the associations linked to these two "geneses" takes on particular significance for the unfolding of God's general plan. "If the initial usage of Matthew in his text," writes Koehler,

> elaborates on the thought of the first account of creation showing how all the divine preparations terminate in Jesus, the subsequent usage (1:18) elaborates on the second account of Genesis directly centering on the formation of man animated by the divine breath: 'Then the Lord God formed man out of the dust of the earth and breathed into his nostrils a breath of life, and man became a living person' (Gen 2:7). Similarly, Matthew explains the origin of Jesus, the new Adam, making a direct reference to the action of the Holy Spirit.[4]

---

2 In verses 18–25, Ceuppens outlines three carefully linked passages: "1) The anxiety of Joseph, vv. 18–19. 2) The explanation of the mystery by the angel, vv. 20–23. 3) The calming of Joseph, vv. 24–25" (*De Mariologia Biblica,* p. 118).

3 The term "*genêsis*" is better translated "generation," rather than "birth" (found only in a few codices), according to Ceuppens (ibid., p. 119). Laurentin, on the other hand, points out that "each of the two pericopes begin with the title 'The Genesis of Jesus Christ' (1:1; 1:8). The use of this word is striking placed at the beginning of a genealogy. Thus the Vulgate has translated it as: '*The Book of the Generation*.' 'Generation,' however, would have been expressed by the word *genêsis* (with two 'n's'). Yet it is clearly *genêsis* which Matthew repeats at the beginning of both pericopes" (*Truth of Christmas*, p. 251; see the interesting n. 1, p. 509, regarding the various translations of the term genesis). See also T. Stramare, O.S.J., *Figlio di Giuseppe di Nazaret* (Rovigo, 1972), pp. 40–41.

4 T. Koehier, S.M., *Maria nella Sacra Scrittura*, p. 56. Cf. also Leonardi, *L'Infanzia di Gesù*, p. 54: the double connotation of the term *genesis* "evidently refers to the genesis of creation and of the first man." Laurentin, in turn, writes: "The use of this word signifies that the Gospel is a new 'beginning,' a book of genesis, like the first book of the Bible known under this name… Jesus the Messiah realizes the new creation promised by the

When Mary, his mother, had been betrothed to Joseph, before they came together, she was found to be with child by the Holy Spirit (v. 18b).

The primary affirmation here regards the virginal conception of Jesus, brought about *"by the work of the Holy Spirit,"* a unique and most original event, not recorded in the apocrypha or in the midrashin of the epoch, although various other details of the Gospel are also recorded by them.[5]

We already know that the expression "espoused" means much more than "fiancée" (*emnêsteumenê*), and in fact connotes a marriage already contracted, to be followed by the cohabitation of the spouses. On this subject, some, with good reason, would speak in terms of a *matrimonium ratum*,[6] normally "consummated" during "cohabitation." Once this occurs, obviously, the term *emnêsteumenê* is no longer an appropriate choice to describe the relation.[7] Yet it seems clear enough that, not only for the sake of legal precision, but out of a certain sensitive delicacy, St. Luke continued to use the term *emnêsteumenê* even after Mary and Joseph had "cohabited," and in reference to Mary's childbirth. For, in fact, the *matrimonium ratum* between the two spouses never became a *matrimonium consummatum* with cohabitation or ever afterward.

The translation, *"before they came together"* (in the Latin of the Vulgate, *antequam convenirent*), intends to exclude here, as a matter of fact, cohabitation of the two spouses

prophets for the eschatological times" (*Truth of Christmas*, pp. 251–252; see also p. 446). Cf. T. Stramare, *La parola di Dio vivente nella Chiesa* (Naples and Rome, 1970), pp. 69–87.

5 Cf. Leonardi, *L'Infanzia di Gesù*, pp. 52–53.

6 Cf. Landucci, *Maria SS. nel Vangelo*, p. 100.

7 Regarding the term. emnêsteumenê, used by St. Luke on the occasion of Mary's giving birth, as well as after the definite "cohabitation" of thespouses, see the solution of Laurentin, *Truth of Christmas*, p. 11.

Mary and Joseph. It does not seem quite so certain, however, that the expression *convenirent* (in Greek, *synelthein*) must be understood here only in the sense of "cohabitation" between the two, and not in the sense of "consummation" of the marriage.[8]

Those who argue for a prior cohabitation between Joseph and Mary do so in order to remove every shadow of dishonor from the Holy Family. For, although the possibility of conjugal relations while the marriage was only *ratum* (or an "espousal") was allowed, these were nevertheless considered "unbecoming and inordinate."[9]

It appears evident, in any case, that the central fact here is Jesus' virginal conception in the womb of Mary by the work of the Holy Spirit. But St. Joseph was ignorant of everything concerning this extraordinary event, begun on the day of the Annunciation. Except by artificially forcing the text and opposing tradition, it must be admitted that St. Matthew excludes the possibility of Joseph being informed by Mary (or by others). But then the question naturally comes to mind: Why did Mary remain silent?

The first, most convincing reply seems that based on Mary's abandonment to God, confident that as God began the work, so He would bring it to completion.[10] Another

---

8 Cf. Ceuppens, *De Mariologia Biblica*, p. 118; A. Paul, *Il vangelo dell'infanzia secondo Matteo* (Rome 1986), p. 60. According to Ceuppens and other authors, the translation of the term *synelthein* would be: "before having intimate relations" or "without having had intimate relations." But see also Leonardi, *L'Infanzia di Gesù*, p. 55.

9 Cf. Stramare, *Figlio di Giuseppe*, pp. 60–63, with a specific bibliography for notes 61–67.

10 J. Knabenbauer had already opted for this view in his day, *Evangelium secundum Matthaeum*, vol. 1 (Paris, 1892), pp. 107ff. See also C. M. Perrella,"B.ma Virgo Maria, cum caelestem excepit nuntium, S. Joseph sponsalibus solis non vero nuptiis iuncta erat," *Divus Thomas* 35 (1932): 398; Garofalo, *La Madonna della Bibbia*, p. 52; Pietrafesa, *La Madonna nella Rivelazione*, p. 209; *The Navarre Bible. St. Matthew's Gospel*, p. 29; T. Stramare, *Vangelo dei misteri de la vita nascosta di Gesù*, Bornato in Franciacorta 1998, p. 101.

possible consideration concerns Mary's virginal modesty, a factor prompting her to be extremely tactful in speaking about this matter.[11]

It is certain that the interior suffering, consequent upon Mary's silence, made "the spouse of Mary," comments A. Lancellotti, "the most authoritative witness of the virginal conception of the Messiah,"[12] and therefore of the physical virginity *ante partum* of Mary. On the subject of Mary's physical virginity, A. Ory writes:

> If, according to a rationalistic exegesis, it is not a question of physical virginity, but spiritual, and Joseph is the father of Mary's child, how can his doubt be justified? Why did Joseph want to break secretly all bonds with Mary? Occasionally a young man no longer wishes to have anything to do with the young girl who bears his child. But how could such a thing be imagined of Joseph, the just man? According to classical exegesis, the virginity of Mary is physical. And in accord with this line of thought, Joseph is not the biological father of Jesus. If he were not the father of the child that Mary carries in her womb, his doubt would not only be motivated, but inevitable. That Joseph might break the engagement merely because Mary was open to God and did the will of the heavenly Father is not plausible. For Joseph is pious. If Mary is the Mother of his child and prays as

---

[11] Cf. J. M. Bover, *El Evangelio de San Mateo* (Barcelona, 1946), p. 44; Pietrafesa, *La Madonna nella Rivelazione*, p. 209. F. Ceuppens synthesizes the two reasons, writing that Mary kept silent "either by reason of virginal chastity, or because she wished to leave to God alone the revelation of a work accomplished by Him in her; God himself had begun it, God also would successfully bring the entire affair to conclusion" (*De Mariologia Biblica*, p. 118).

[12] A. Lancellotti, O.F.M., *Matteo*, p. 42. Who was the first to notice the signs of Mary's pregnancy? In his day St. Jerome responded that it was St. Joseph (PL 26:24). Lagrange, on the other hand, holds that it was first of all Mary's mother, St. Anne (*Evangile selon S. Matthieu* [Paris, 1923], p. 10). Lastly, according to L. Richard, Mary would have confided the event of the Annunciation to her mother, St. Anne, and the latter, after having accompanied Mary to Ain-Karim and having verified the "sign" of St. Elizabeth's pregnancy, upon returning, revealed to St. Joseph the prodigy of Mary's virginal conception (*Dieu est Amour: Marie et l'Evangile de l'Enfance* [Le Puy and Lyon, 1961], pp. 25–42); see also Gaechter, *Maria im Erdenleben*, pp. 155ff.

> he does, Joseph has a double motive for taking her into his home. Instead, in the gospel narrative it is said that he considered breaking the engagement. That is justifiable only if Joseph is not the father of the child that Mary carries in her womb, only on the assumption of physical virginity and not merely spiritual.[13]

This indeed is the concrete testimony lived by St. Joseph and left by him to us.

Joseph her husband, being a just man and not wishing to expose her to reproach, was minded to put her away privately (v. 19).

Understanding of this verse varies according to the different connotations put on the "tribulation" suffered by St. Joseph from the moment he came to learn of Mary's pregnancy.

Suspicion of Infidelity

Some Fathers of the Church and modern authors ground this position on the evident fact that there is no explanation of Mary's pregnancy from a natural point of view except in terms of infidelity. This first, spontaneous assessment, called by Stramare "hypothesis of suspicion,"[14] was bound to throw St. Joseph into a state of profound anguish from the moment he related this information to

---

13 Ory, *Riscoprire la verità*, p. 98. To support this argumentation, the author constructs two "tests of reasonableness," as he calls them (pp. 99–114). Still on the subject of Mary's virginity, moreover, the author refers to and critically examines the opinion of those who reduce it, in substance, to "an 'availability' toward God. Whoever prays and follows the will of God is at God's disposition and can be called a 'virgin.'

"This interpretation of Mary's virginity not only excludes anything even apparently miraculous, but is full of absurdities: a woman can be partially a 'virgin' and even a 'virgin-mother.' In this view, all women who are mothers and who pray from time to time are 'virgin-mothers.' Why then should we call Mary 'virgin-mother'?" (ibid., p. 97).

14 Stramare, *op. cit.*, p. 136.

what he knew of Mary's splendid, uncontaminated purity and her proposal to remain a virgin.[15]

This interpretation, however, is not consistent with that sense of "justice" that on St. Joseph's part would have entailed an accusation of Mary in the true and proper sense of the word, bringing ultimately a condemnation to lapidation.[16] Furthermore, in such a case, at least before taking so grave a step, St. Joseph would have had to speak and clarify matters directly with Mary.

Fear and Humility Before the Mystery of the Virginal Conception

Some contemporary authors, and some ancient ones, hold that St. Joseph, having learned from Mary (or from St. Anne) of the miraculous conception of Jesus by the work of the Holy Spirit, was overwhelmed by a holy fear of interfering in the mystery whose only actors were the Holy Spirit and Mary and that he felt totally unworthy of remaining near the Mother of the Son of God. Seemingly an intruder, he thought for this reason that it would be just to leave Mary, who was called to enter into this divine circle, free of obligation to him. And so, he decided to avail himself of the writ of divorce in order to break the espousals.

Much, however, remains obscure in this opinion, which Stramare calls "hypothesis of fear,"[17] because it does not explain, nor resolve

15 For the opinion of the Fathers of the Church, cf. F. Sottocornola, "Tradition and the Doubt of St. Joseph concerning Mary's Virginity," *Marianum* 19 (1957):127–141.

16 The defenders of such an opinion are forced to translate the term "just" (*dikaios*), referred to St. Joseph, as "meek," "good": such "meekness" would have moved St. Joseph to opt for a repudiation in secret, rather than publicly (cf., for example, J. Schmid, *L'Evangelo secondo Matteo* [Brescia, 1962], p. 62).

17 Stramare, *op. cit.*, p. 136.

> the embarrassment of Joseph and his resolve to repudiate his spouse in a moment when she was particularly in need of his help. He knew of the mystery, was certain of the innocence of his spouse, and yet, out of humility [!] he wanted to repudiate her, thus exposing an innocent woman to danger in a grave situation. To us it seems neither logical nor in accord with elementary charity and justice to act thus![18]

Perplexity Over an "Inexplicable" Fact.

This view of St. Jerome[19] and of St. Peter Chrysologus,[20] supported by a majority of exegetes,[21] is surely the one most in accord with the Gospel account, and is outlined by Garofalo as follows:

> The spouse of Mary was a 'just man,' that is, a perfect observer of the spirit and of the letter of the Law that God had given to his people.... The love Joseph had for his betrothed spouse and the love of the law—a basic characteristic of Hebrew spirituality—at the moment recounted by the Gospel entailed within him a conflict.

After a three-month absence from Nazareth spent in Elizabeth's house, Mary had returned to the village just when those signs that make a spouse leap for joy were visible. But Joseph, unaware of Gabriel's message and of the expressions of joy uttered by Mary at Ain–Karim, suddenly found himself confronting an unexpected and

---

18 Pietrafesa, *La Madonna nella Rivelazione*, p. 207. For an extensive analysis and refutation of this interpretation (with its variant forms and nuances in Frangipane, Rahner, Léon-Dufour), see the study of P. Barbagli, O.C.D., "Joseph, noli timere accipere Mariam conjugem Warn," in *Maria in Sacra Scriptura*, vol. 4, pp. 445–463. Laurentin also defends this interpretation (*Truth of Christmas*, pp. 267–68), but does not offer any new arguments of weight. Much more sophisticated is the textual analysis of I. de La Potterie in support of this interpretation (*Mary in the Mystery*, pp. 37–65).

19 PL 26:25.

20 PL 52:588, 657.

21 To cite only a few names, we mention here Knabenbauer, Lagrange, Buzy, Ricciotti, Ceuppens, Perrella, Bover, Merk, Garofalo, Barbagli, Ory, Testa, Nolli, and the biblicists of *The Navarre Bible*.

inexplicable fact. He had, therefore, to do violence to his heart and consider the frightening implications of the case. He knew he was not responsible for the pregnancy; otherwise he would have been able to celebrate the nuptials without dishonor, because his contemporaries would hardly have thought evil of him. If Joseph had been sure of Mary's guilt, his "justice" would have obliged him to denounce her... The fact that Joseph decisively rejected this course of action—"he did not want" to expose Mary publicly to disrepute—demonstrates that he, in spite of the circumstantial evidence, still believed in the virtue of his bride, which up to that moment he never had reason to doubt. On the other hand, Joseph could not acknowledge a paternity not his own—"justice" was the reason—and so "he was minded" to dissolve the betrothal with Mary secretly, in a way capable of safeguarding her honor.[22]

But while he thought on these things, behold an angel of the Lord appeared to him in a dream, saying: "Do not be afraid, Joseph, son of David, to take to thee Mary thy wife, for that which is begotten in her is of the Holy Spirit. And she shall bring forth a son, and thou shalt call his name Jesus; for he shall save his people from their sins" (vv. 20–21).

How long did St. Joseph's interior anxieties perdure? It is impossible to say. Some exegetes speculate a few[23] and others, several days.[24] In any case, some time had to elapse, during which, on the one hand, St. Joseph, on reflection,

---

22 Garofalo, *La Madonna della Bibbia*, pp. 49–50; see also the same author's Le parole di Maria, pp. 181–184. On the term "*iustus*" see Stramare, *op. cit.*, pp. 139–144.

23 Cf. Garofalo, *La Madonna della Bibbia*, p. 1.

24 Cf. A. Merk, S.J., "La figura di Maria nel Nuovo Testamento," in P. Sträter, *Mariologia*, Rome 1952, p. 58.

decisively rejected[25] public repudiation as a solution, because he was still convinced of Mary's unsullied purity, while, on the other hand, he contemplated a way of *"secretly dismissing her"* so as to avoid claiming a paternity not his.

At this moment, *"the angel of the Lord appeared to him in a dream."* The appropriateness of communicating the mystery of the Incarnation to St. Joseph through an angel has been explained by Barbagli thus:

> We may next note that God directly intervened to reveal the mystery of the Incarnation to all the principal persons concerned: the birth of the Precursor was announced to Zechariah by an angel; to Mary it was the same Archangel Gabriel who brought the message on God's behalf; Elizabeth was enlightened by the Holy Spirit in regard to the 'great things' accomplished by the Lord in her holy relative; the shepherds were invited by angels to visit the crib of Jesus; Simeon and Anna recognized the Messiah in the Child through a revelation of the Holy Spirit. Given the ordinary 'economy'of God, it was natural to expect that Joseph also, so intimately involved in the mystery of the Incarnation, would be directly enlightened by the Lord.[26]

The message of the angel was addressed to Joseph *"son of David."* This is an explicit reference to St. Joseph's Davidic descent, required for that of the Son of Mary, that is, of the Messiah. But the heart of the angelic message is to be found in the words *"do not be afraid to take to thee Mary, thy wife, for that which is begotten in her is of the Holy Spirit."*

---

25 The Greek expression *mè télo*, writes Stramare, quoting P. Joüon, "means 'a repugnance for, a refusal,' instinctively and without pondering" (*Figlio di Giuseppe*, p. 81, n. 114). Garofalo also points out that in regard to St. Joseph's decision "*not to accuse*" Mary, but to "*dismiss her secretly*," "the Greek text of the Gospel clearly shows that, first, instinctively, Joseph 'did not want,' and, only after, 'he pondered.' While 'he considered this plan' an angel appeared to him" (*Le parole di Maria*, p. 182 n. 50). Cf. Merk, "La figura di Maria," p. 58.

26 Barbagli, "Joseph, noli timere," p. 462. Regarding the "dream" of St. Joseph, see the brief chapter "*Le apparizioni in sogno*" (with abundant bibliography) by Stramare, *Figlio di Giuseppe*, pp. 50–56.

These words left St. Joseph at peace. This enlightenment about the divine origin of Mary's maternity not only put to flight all darkness and anxiety, but also filled St. Joseph with ineffable light and joy.

Exegetes who defend St. Joseph's foreknowledge of the virginal conception by work of the Holy Spirit must translate differently the words of the angel, excluding from the Greek particles *"gar... de"* any causal value (in the sense of *because*) and giving them instead the sense of opposition, which would have the angel say, according to Leon Dufour: "Without fear take to yourself Mary your spouse; *in fact,* what has been conceived in her is *certainly* the work of the Holy Spirit, *but* she will bring forth a son."[27] The procedure is forced; it makes the reading and the quite obvious sense of the pericope difficult.

It is to be noted that the expression "angel of the Lord," in Hebrew *malak Jahwèh,* without a precise name is "sometimes interchangeable with Yahweh himself," affirms Laurentin.[28] According to Leonardi, on the basis of the apparitions in the Old Testament (Gen 16:7–14; 17:15–22; Ex 3:2; Judg 6:12; 13:3), one may hold "on solid grounds that 'the angel of the Lord,' who intervened five times in Matthew's infancy gospel, is not for Matthew an angel– creature, distinct from God, but God Himself,

---

27 Quoted by Barbagli, "Joseph, noli timere," p. 452. These are "good philological arguments," Barbaghi points out, "but, in our case, very far from convincing"; and he adds: "It is evident that the value of the particles *gar* and *de* in each proposition is determined by the context in which the phrase is found. Now, the possibility of translating the text of Mt 1:20 in the sense proposed by the author does not depend on the context, but on the 'supposition' that Joseph already knew of the miraculous maternity of Mary. It is to be noted, then, that the causal significance of *gar*, even when it is in opposition to *de*, is much more common" (ibid., p. 453).

28 Laurentin, *Truth of Christmas*, p. 440. The expression "is sometimes little more than a literary device used out of respect for God's transcendence" (pp. 284–285).

who in the dream revealed Himself to Joseph in a humanly perceptible form."[29]

The angel adopted the expression *"take to thee Mary thy wife."* The Greek verb *paralambano* is a generic verb that does not express per se the action of "marrying" or of "cohabitating," but that of welcoming, of receiving, of providing hospitality with oneself.[30] This is a significant nuance, suggesting that St. Joseph is invited to take Mary as his *spouse/ sister,* accepting, that is, "the vocation of putative husband," writes E. Testa, "and of legal father of the Baby, keeping the mystery secret and taking Mary into 'his home' as his wife/sister (Mt 1:24b)."[31]

The virginal conception "*by the work of the Holy Spirit*" already affirmed a little before (1:18), is reconfirmed here as the "main assertion of the episode."[32] Jesus' human origin is *"by the Holy Spirit from the Virgin Mary,"* as stated in the Creed. The action of the Holy Spirit, however, is not such as to render him "Father" of Jesus. The same term "Spirit" is feminine in Hebrew, neuter in Greek: "This significant datum," as Laurentin points out, "which radically excludes every theogamic model, has often gone unobserved."[33] As in the creation of the universe and of man described in Genesis, all the more here the action of the Holy Spirit

29 Leonardi, *L'Infanzia di Gesù*, p. 51. The author cites in support of this studies by Lorenzo da Fara, "Gli Angeli nella Bibbia," *Parola vivente* 13 (1968): 281–293; F. M. Sole, "L'Angelo di Jahweh," *Renovatio* 6 (1971): 531–538.

30 Stramare notes that the verb *paralambano* is a "verb certainly less adapted for indicating the moment specific to nuptials (*to take her into his house*) since its meaning is merely generic: *to take to oneself, to receive, to accept*" (*Figlio di Giuseppe*, pp. 69–70); E. Testa also notes that "the verb *paralambano* in the Septuagint does not refer to matrimony, but to taking someone with oneself, with the same liberty with which one takes a 'brother,' without provoking malicious gossip" (*Maria terra vergine*, vol. 1, p. 301, n. 65).

31 Testa, *Maria terra virgine*, vol. 1, p. 301, n. 65.

32 Leonardi, *L'Infanzia di Gesù*, p. 58.

33 Laurentin, *Truth of Christmas*, p. 404. Cf. also Testa, *Maria terra virgine*, p. 65.

is creative action. In the womb of the Virgin Mary, the action of the Holy Spirit "brought to creation," comments A. Paul, "the full complement that it awaited and for the sake of which it existed. A new creation was required and the action of the Holy Spirit was required, since man alone was unable to bring to fruition this undertaking, or even to initiate it."[34]

Surely this unity of operation, or better interaction, between the Holy Spirit and Mary in the virginal conception of Christ, was and will be the inexhaustible object of theological study whose goal is to unravel this hidden mystery of divine spousal love so ineffable and fecund. But to this it should be added that the unity between the *Panhaghion* and *Panhaghia* has its roots in the Immaculate Conception of the Virgin, and it is a feature of her entire life, being perfected at the Annunciation, Pentecost, and her glorious Assumption.[35]

Meanwhile, to this very extraordinary Child whom Mary would bring forth,[36] it will be St. Joseph who is to impose the name (*kalesei*) already revealed by the angel Gabriel in the announcement to Mary: the name of Jesus.[37] The imposition of the name by St. Joseph effected the legal bond of Davidic descent between St. Joseph, "son

34 Paul, *Secondo San Matteo*, p. 87 (see also pp. 82–89).

35 See the studies of G. Roschini, *Il Tuttosanto e la Tuttasanta*, parts 1–11 (Rome, 1976–1977); D. Bertetto, "L'azione propria dello Spinto Santo," *Marianum* 41 (1979): 400–444; *idem*, "La sinergia dello Spirito Santo con Maria," in *Maria e lo Spirito Santo* (Rome, 1984), pp. 291–302; (and, also, the other studies in *Maria e lo Spirito Santo*) - A special, in-depth study regarding the ineffable relations between the Holy Spirit and the Immaculate is the chapter written by St. Maximilian M. Kolbe: cf. H. M. Manteau-Bonamy, O.P., *Immaculate Conception and the Holy Spirit, The Marian Teachings of Father Kolbe* (Libertyville, IL, 1977).

36 It is important to note: the angel did not say to St. Joseph: "She will bring forth to you a son," but only: "She will bring forth a son."

37 How is it to be explained that the angel Gabriel had already told Mary to give the child the name of Jesus? "It is probable," responds Ceuppens, "that in these circumstances imposition of the name was carried out by common accord of the parents" (*De Mariologia Biblica*, p. 121).

of David," and the Messiah, "descendant of David." The message of the angel of the Lord reveals here the specific sense of St. Joseph's mission in regard to the Messiah: to be the legal father of Jesus in order to assure the royal descent from the Davidic line. Therefore, St. Joseph "will act as father by bestowing the name on the child," writes Laurentin.[38]

The name Jesus (in Hebrew, *Jeôshûa*: "Yahweh is salvation") was explained by the same angel of the Lord with a brief phrase illustrative of the redemptive mission of the Messiah: *"for he shall save his people from their sins."* This rapid presentation of the mission of the Messiah is of great importance. Let us not forget that the Jewish people awaited a socio-political Messiah Savior. The Evangelist here sweeps aside every kind of false expectation. The Messiah will effect salvation, not by restructuring the socio-political realm, but by acting at the very root of all evil, that is, by dealing with sin. He will save *"his people,"* that is, the people of Israel (according to Lagrange), all humanity, or the faithful of the Church (according to Knabenbauer), the new people of God (according to Lohmeyer and Grundmann).[39]

---

38 Laurentin, *Truth of Christmas*, p. 266. Regarding the meaning of the name "Jesus," see p. 314, n. 2; p. 527, n. 31 (where the author states: "Savior, the title of God himself, [is] transferred to Jesus"). It is evident that in verses 20–21, St. Joseph received the mission of adopting Jesus in order to guarantee the Davidic descent of the Messiah, according to I. M. Germano, "Privilegium nominis messianici a S. Joseph imponendi," *Verbum Domini* 47 (1969): 151–62. Regarding the paternity of St. Joseph, which is not merely legal, adoptive, or putative, but also and above all virginal, messianic, "eminent," analogous to that of the eternal Father, see D. J. Lallement, *Mystère de la paternité de Saint Joseph* (Paris, 1986).

39 Cf. L. Sabourin, *Il Vangelo di Matteo* (Rome, 1976), pp. 212–213. Leonardi points out that the angel "is careful immediately to underscore that Jesus would not be merely a political-social savior or terrestrial conqueror, but one who would go to the root of all evils and who would save his people from their sins; from those sins which are odious to God and to one's neighbor and the source of all other evils, even of political-social exploitation and oppression" (*L'Infanzia di Gesù*, p. 54).

Now all this came to pass that what was spoken by the Lord through the prophet might be fulfilled: "Behold, the virgin shall be with child, and shall bring forth a son; and they shall call his name Emmanuel"; which is, interpreted, "God with us" (vv. 22–23).

At this point, the Evangelist Matthew concludes the message of the angel of the Lord to St. Joseph and refers to the celebrated prophecy of Isaiah 7:14, to prove the virginal conception of the Messiah already accomplished in the womb of Mary *"Virgin,"* as well as the Davidic descent of the Messiah through St. Joseph, *"son of David"* and putative father of Jesus.[40]

The text of Isaiah speaks of a "sign" that comes from God and not from men, a portent, therefore, or miraculous sign. What sign? Recently, in full accord with the great exegetical tradition, Schelkle has responded quite decisively: "This, therefore, is the sign: that the Virgin will bring forth the Messiah."[41] And against that "party of modern exegetes" who want to see in the *almâh* the wife of King Ahaz, and in the child Hezekiah, the king's son, Schelkle raises this question: "How could this be the great sign 'that God himself gives'? How can Isaiah say that that child will be the Messiah, God with us?"[42] The Evangelist Matthew, then, clearly demonstrates in the Virgin Mary and in her Son the perfect fulfillment of the prophecy of Isaiah who "announced in his days," continues Schelkle, "the birth of the Messiah from the Virgin; in him the house of David

---

40 Concerning this famous text of Isaiah, see what has been written above in the chapter "The Virgin Mother" (pp. 34–43). "Regarding this prophecy," writes del Paramo, "it is enough for our purposes to know that, according to the authentic interpretation given it by the Evangelist, the virgin to whom Isaiah refers is without doubt Mary, the Mother of Jesus" (*Vangelo secondo Matteo*, p. 54).

41 K. H. Schelkle, *La Madre del Salvatore* (Rome, 1985), p. 39.

42 Ibid.

will last forever. The virgin birth is, in that case, the 'sign' of salvation, not so much as a stupendous prodigy of nature, but for the content signified by such a miracle. The virgin birth signifies that only God brings about salvation."[43]

The prophet Isaiah calls the Messiah, *"Emmanuel, which is interpreted God with us."* Taken strictly, this expression already indicates the divinity of Christ, that is to say, that Jesus is the Son of God conceived in the womb of a virgin, without the cooperation of man. In such wise, Jesus is at the same time Son of God and son of Adam.

Furthermore, to translate the verb *kalesei* (will be called) in the singular does not do justice to the sense of the original in St. Matthew, where the plural form *kalesousin* (*"they will call him"*) is used. The subject "they" of this plural verb who call Him Jesus is all men drawn to the "God with us," and so is a sign of the universality of salvation wrought by Christ. "In this designation of Christ as 'God with us,'" writes A. Paul,

> do we not have a vision of all the nations—and not merely Israel—that will recognize Jesus as one of their own ('with us') come in order to bring them the salvation of Yahweh ('Jesus')? In Mt 1:18–25 this title Emmanuel represents the most splendid epiphany of the Incarnation. Hence, one can understand why here the citation from Isaiah 7:14 has the plural *'kalesousin'* and not the singular *'kalesei'*; certainly it seems probable that the citation has been introduced into the narrative first of all in order to lend support to belief in the virginal conception of Jesus; but thanks to its second part thus modified, specifics particularly surprising are given in regard to the identity of Jesus and nature of his future mission.[44]

---

43 Ibid., p. 40.

44 PAUL, *Secondo San Matteo*, pp. 91–92.

So Joseph, arising from sleep, did as the angel of the Lord had commanded him, and took unto him his wife. And he did not know her till she brought forth her firstborn son. And he called his name Jesus (vv. 24–25).

With these verses, the message of the angel and the prophecy of Isaiah are integrated and shown to complement one another harmoniously. The darkness and anxieties dispelled, St. Joseph now had only to respond to the angel's message. And the holy spouse of Mary gave his assent and acted immediately to implement the angel's command.

As soon as he awoke, in fact, St. Joseph began to carry out all that he had learned from the angel during his dream. He took unto himself Mary—with what supernatural joy!— living with her the ineffable experience of a virgin marriage, in continuous adoration of the "God with us" present in the womb of his immaculate spouse, and awaiting the moment when he might contemplate the sublime face of this divine Son, whose name he would give Him in order to insert Him into the royal Davidic line.

Here, St. Joseph's prompt obedience, in perfect harmony with Mary's, must be esteemed and admired. "In Luke's account," writes Galizzi,

> it is emphasized that Mary accepted her mission and became the *'handmaid of the Lord.'* Here it is stated that Joseph *'did that which the angel of the Lord had commanded him'* (1:24). Thus he is revealed as the *'servant of the Lord'* who immediately assumed as his own the mission that was entrusted to him: he took unto himself Mary and gave to Mary's child the name Jesus (1:25). Here lies the greatness of Joseph: by giving the child a name, he made Him his son. According to the Law, Jesus became a true descendant of David, the bearer of the promise. Indeed, the one who

fulfilled it: *'You will call him Jesus, because he will save his people from their sins'* (1:21).[45]

Finally, with the last two clauses—*"and he did not know her"*[46] and *"and he called his name Jesus"*—St. Matthew wishes to confirm yet one more time both the reality of the virginal conception of Jesus, emphasizing the absence of any conjugal relations between Mary and Joseph before and during the time of gestation,[47] and Jesus' belonging to the lineage of David, through His adoptive father Joseph. Under the sign of virginity and the Davidic descent, then, this pericope of Matthew, a necessary bridge between the visitation and the Nativity of Jesus, is brought to a close.

---

45 M. Galizzi, *Oltre ogni frontiera, Vangelo secondo Matteo* (Turin, 1980), pp. 24–25.

46 The more exact rendition of the text says that St. Joseph "*did not know her until she gave birth*." Laurentin comments: "The word 'until' contains no implication as to what happens after that point. In Semitic usage 'until' designates the 'duration' and the 'limits of' the writer's or speaker's 'interest.' Thus when 2 Samuel 6:23 says that Michal had no child 'until the day of her death' it is likewise clear that she did not have any later on" (*Truth of Christmas*, p. 269). See also *The Navarre Bible. St. Matthew's Gospel*, p. 32.

47 Leonardi has written an interesting note on the Perpetual Virginity of our Lady, based on the *untouchableness* of Mary by St. Joseph until death. For, with the pregnancy (by the work of the Holy Spirit)—according to rabbinical law—Mary "was consecrated to God and was His special property; therefore 'it was forbidden him [Joseph] forever'" (*L'Infanzia di Gesù*, p. 61, n. 58).

13
The Birth of Jesus

Lk 2:1–7

It is quite correct to say that the mystery of Jesus' birth constitutes the definitive fulfillment of two famous prophecies: that of Isaiah concerning the virgin mother of the Emmanuel (7:14), and that of Micah about the woman "in travail" at Bethlehem (5:1–2).

St. Luke and St. Matthew offer us many significant and suggestive details touching the birth of Christ, from the census of Caesar Augustus to the visit of the Magi from the Orient, to the flight into Egypt and return to Nazareth. It is St. Luke, however, who describes for us in greater detail the different phases of the Nativity itself, as is his custom, in elegant style and with historical exactitude, even to the least particulars. Hence, our commentary will be organized around his account of that great event.

Now it came to pass in those days, that a decree went forth from Caesar Augustus that a census of the whole world should be taken. This first census took place while Quirinus was governor of Syria. And all were going, each to his own town, to register (vv. 1–3).

The census taken by Quirinus[1] permits us to understand, firstly, how profane history is in the designs of God directed to serve the plan of salvation and its implementation at appointed moments. Indeed, the point

1 On the chronological difficulties regarding the census of Quirinus, see the solution, including precise facts and extensive bibliography, of P. Benoît, "Quirinus," in *Dictionnaire de la Bible. Supplement*, vol. 7 (Paris, 1977), pp. 693–716. Cf. also O. Battaglia, *op. cit.*, pp. 132–134.

of their intersection is the most fitting, and its moment the most exact. A superior hand conducts both. "Like the preceding sequences," writes Laurentin, "the birth of Jesus begins with an earthly program, which then will open upon the unexpected breakthrough of a celestial program where God is manifested."[2] And St. Luke, explaining the relation between the birth of Jesus and the census ordered by the emperor, introduces the advent of the Savior "against the backdrop of human history embracing all ages," notes Ferraro, "thus illustrating how human history serves the salvific plan of God."[3]

Since Mary and Joseph knew of Micah's prophecy of the birth of the Messiah at Bethlehem, on hearing of the order of the governor Quirinus to go and register in one's city of origin they immediately understood how the prophecy was to be fulfilled to the letter. The journey occasioned by the census became, in God's plan, the journey of her who had been spoken of in prophecy as the woman "in travail" at Bethlehem.

And Joseph also went from Galilee out of the town of Nazareth into Judea to the town of David, which is called Bethlehem—because he was of the house and family of David—to register, together with Mary his espoused wife, who was with child (vv. 4–5).

These verses are focused on Joseph. In the Roman empire, men were obliged to register at the census. Women were not so bound. Married women, however—"at least

---

2 LAURENTIN, *Truth of Christmas*, p. 172.

3 FERRARO, *I racconti*, p. 95 (see also p. 98). Ernst also writes: "That instead of Herod, King of Judea (1:5), Augustus, the ruler of the world, is mentioned, has a very precise reason. Luke wants to show how the humble birth in the remote Bethlehem is significant for the whole world" (*Il Vangelo secondo Luca*, vol. 1, p. 135).

according to an Egyptian papyrus"[4]—came to the registry office with their husbands. For Mary, then, apart from the prophecy of Micah, these were additional, particular motives for accompanying Joseph to Bethlehem: if she too was a descendant of David, an only child, and in an advanced state of pregnancy, her journey with Joseph to Bethlehem was more than proper.[5]

Therefore, with perfect docility and promptness the two holy spouses submitted to the emperor's order and undertook the long journey from Nazareth to Bethlehem. All that is especially significant when one takes account of the tensions aroused by Jewish zealots in a country under foreign domination. "We know from historical sources," writes Ferraro,

> that the imperial order decreeing the census later provoked serious disorders within Judaism and contributed not a little to the birth and growth of the anti-Roman movement of the zealots. Joseph, by obeying the Roman decree, is shown a man far removed from politically motivated protest. And this has great importance for the life and personality of Jesus. He did not come from circles involved in political messianism. Therefore, the messianic prophecies could be fulfilled in Him without being confused with merely human goals and temporal, worldly objectives.[6]

---

4 Leonardi, *L'Infanzia di Gesù*, p. 206. See also Ceuppens, *De Mariologia Biblica*, p. 127; A. Stoeger, Vangelo secondo Luca (Rome, 1966), p. 73; Leal, *Vangelo secondo Luca*, p. 135; Ghidelli, *Luca*, p. 88; De Ambrogio, *San Luca*, p. 65.

5 Cf. Pietrafesa, *La Madonna nella Rivelazione*, p. 215. The author refers to the study of U. Holzmeister, "Cur S. Joseph iter bethlemiticum susceperit et Maria eum comitata sit (Lc. 2:4)," *Verbum Domini* 22 (1942): 263–270. Furthermore, according to some authors, St. Joseph perhaps had some property at Bethlehem, while Mary, an only child, was an heiress: cf. Benoît, "Quirinus," p. 700; Leonardi, *L'Infanzia di Gesù*, pp. 205–206; R. Fabris, "Il Vangelo di Luca," in *I Vangeli* (Assisi, 1975), p. 962.

6 Ferraro, *I racconti*, pp. 99–100. Also J. Ernst writes convincingly: "The fact that Joseph submitted to the orders of the occupying foreign authorities and accepted the difficulties of the journey in 'silent obedience,' is perhaps of even greater significance in the light of the historical-temporal situation of that time. For the zealots, whose determined resistance was profoundly rooted in the expectation of the Messiah, such conduct on the part of one

In these two verses, 4 and 5, St. Luke makes even more explicit the fact that Joseph *"was of the house and family of David."* Why so explicit a remark? "In order to underscore," responds Leonardi, "that Jesus is of Davidic descent, not only by reason of His place of birth, but above all because of His Davidic lineage."[7]

Similarly, St. Luke sets in particular relief the clause *"to the town of David, which is called Bethlehem."* Why so precise a reference is made to Bethlehem as "the city of David," rather than to Jerusalem, also and even more rightly known as "the city of David," because it was conquered and made glorious by David, has been explained by Laurentin thus: "He preferred to link Jesus to the humble beginnings of David at Bethlehem rather than to the royal glory of Jerusalem, because he was partial to poverty, to the poverty of Christ at birth, after that of His Mother in 1:48, and to that of the Shepherds who constituted a part of the scene."[8]

In verse 4, it is clear that St. Luke wishes to list every possible basis for Jesus' "Davidic" descent: the *genealogical*

---

belonging to the lineage of David must have appeared pure defiance of them" (*Il Vangelo secondo Luca*, pp. 140–141).

7 Leonardi, *L'Infanzia di Gesù*, p. 206.

8 Laurentin, *Truth of Christmas*, p. 173. Regarding the birth in Bethlehem, the solid objectivity of the historical and geographical fact—contradicting the undemonstrable hypotheses that tend at least to call it into doubt—is evident when one takes into account that on this point St. Matthew, St. Luke, and the apocryphal gospels coincide. Such coincidence between very different authors is rightly held to be a very strong criterion of historicity (cf., for example, J. Danielou, *I vangeli dell'infanzia* [Brescia, 1968]; [Eng. ed.: *The Infancy Narratives* {New York, 1968}, p. 541; C. Perrot, "Les récits d'enfance dans la Haggada antérieure au IIe siècle de notre ère," *Recherches de Science Religeuse* [1967]: 510ff.; G. Danieli, "A proposito delle origini della tradizione sinottica sulla concezione verginale," *Divus Thomas* 72 [1969]: 312–331; F. Zinniker, *Probleme der sogennanten Kindheitsgeschichte bei Matthaus* [Freiburg, 1972], p. 122; E. Galbiati, "Genere letterario in Mt 1–2," *Bibbia e Oriente* 15 [1973]: 9ff.). A. Ory recently wrote to refute those who deny or call into doubt the birth of Jesus in Bethlehem; using "functional" exegesis, he thoroughly undermines their unreal hypotheses, based on false presuppositions and prejudices: cf. *Riscoprire la verità*, pp. 82–89.

(the family of David),[9] the *topographical* (the city of David),[10] and the *social* (the poverty of Bethlehem).[11] Since it is the father who legally guaranteed the child's descent, it is entirely proper for the historian St. Luke to investigate and publish all the "Davidic" facts that through Joseph and the birth at Bethlehem assured Jesus of a genuine Davidic lineage.[12]

Surprisingly, in verse 5, St. Luke again calls Mary *"espoused wife"* (or fiancée) of St. Joseph, as in 1:27, although adding here that already *"she was with child."* It should be noted here how transparently the truth, both biological and theological, indicated by the term "espoused wife" is formulated in reference to Mary. A kind of osmosis operating between the legal and the transcendent (or mystical) planes effects a fruitful interaction among the persons involved here. We already know that on the legal plane St. Joseph effectively was the spouse of Mary and father of Jesus. On the biological plane, on the other hand, St. Joseph had nothing to do with the conception of Jesus, because that was the exclusive work of the Holy Spirit, who made Mary's virginity fecund in a transcendent manner through the power of the Most High (*virtus Altissimi*) (1:35). One is obliged to say, in fact, that, at such a level and for that event, Mary is in reality the Spouse of the Holy Spirit, and not of Joseph. For this reason, St. Luke

---

9 Cf. Leonardi, *L'Infanzia di Gesù*, p. 206.

10 Laurentin writes that St. Luke gives the basis for the title "Son of David," attributed many times to Jesus (Mt 9:27; 12:23; 15:22; 20:30, 31; 21:9, 15; Mk 10:47–48; 11:10; Lk 18:38, 39; cf. Rom 1:2; 2 Tim 2:8), "solely in virtue of the topographical link" (*Truth of Christmas*, Ital. ed.: p. 243).

11 Cf. R. Laurentin, *Truth of Christmas*, Ital. ed.: p. 243.

12 It is clear that the truly "real" fact, even if not juridical, about the Davidic descent of Jesus remains the *biological* one. But this was made known exclusively by Mary, also of Davidic descent, as St. Paul makes clearly understood when he speaks of Jesus born "*from the seed of David according to the flesh*" (Rom 1:3). In this case the seed of David "*according to the flesh*" could be no other but that exclusive to Mary, the Virgin Mother of Jesus.

still calls her with delicate precision, in relation to St. Joseph, "espoused wife" (*emnêsteumenê*), not withstanding cohabitation, which at this point had already begun some time previously.[13]

St. Luke includes nothing about the journey of the two holy spouses. We know that the distance between Nazareth and Bethlehem is about 150 kilometers [about 95 miles]. There is reason to think that St. Joseph and our Lady joined a caravan, walking continuously for four or five days. Foreseeing an obligatory stay in Bethlehem, St. Joseph probably brought with him some tools of his trade, along with some indispensable household goods, while Mary probably brought poor baby linen for her child.[14]

And it came to pass while they were there that the days for her to be delivered were fulfilled. And she brought forth her firstborn son, and wrapped him in swaddling clothes, and laid him in a manger, because there was no room for them in the inn (vv. 6–7).

It seems clear that Mary and Joseph arrived in Bethlehem some time before the actual childbirth. The Evangelist writes that the time of parturition was accomplished "while they were" in Bethlehem.[15] Therefore, on their arrival in Bethlehem, they had to have enough time to look for suitable quarters. They did not, however, succeed in finding anything desirable. The main reasons were

---

13 This is also in harmony with the interpretation of the *ratified*, but not *consummated* marriage between Mary and Joseph. Leonardi explains: "Mary was for Joseph, even after the marriage, as a betrothed spouse, and therefore her parturition was truly virginal" (*L'Infanzia di Gesù*, p. 206). Cf. also Laurentin, *Truth of Christmas*, p. 174; Poppi, *Sinossi*, p. 266.

14 Cf. Pietrafesa, *La Madonna nella Rivelazione*, p. 216; Leal, *Vangelo secondo Luca*, p. 137; Varón Varón, *Sagrada Escritura*, p. 92.

15 The expression "*her days were accomplished that she should be delivered*, means," explains Leal, "that the birth took place according to the normal cycle (it is the physician Luke who is narrating)" (*Vangelo secondo Luca*, p. 136).

perhaps two: first, the large numbers of visitors who had also come to Bethlehem in order to be enrolled; second, Mary's particular condition, which required a private and tranquil place. The second consideration above all enables us to understand better the decision to take shelter in the solitude of a cave also used as a stable, as indicated by the presence of a manger, something not unusual in those times, nor in ours for that matter.[16]

There is reference to an inn, *katalyma,* where *"there was no room for them."* This *katalyma*[17] would seem to designate either a "caravansary"—a public place for passing pilgrims and their mounts—or a "lodging" that a dwelling house might have for relatives or pilgrims, with stable or grotto–cave attached, for use of their animals.[18] In either case, Mary and Joseph, above all for reasons of privacy, preferred the grotto or stable, where the manger could serve as a crib for the newborn child.[19]

16 Cf. LEONARDI, *L'Infanzia di Gesù*, pp. 109–110. It is possible that there is here question of a cave that might have formed part of or that was not, in any case, far from the "inn" (cf. FEUILLET, *Jesus et sa mère*, p. 1 [Eng. ed: *Jesus and His Mother*, p. 38]).

17 See the interesting note by LAURENTIN, *Truth of Christmas*, pp. 180–182, where the author also treats of the grotto, the stable, the ox, and the ass.

18 Unlike St. Luke, the Evangelist Matthew makes use of the term *oikian*, which, according to the stricter etymological meaning of the word, indicates a "*house*," whereas in the broader sense it connotes a "*dwelling place*" in general. Cf. J. GOMA CIVIT, *El Evangelio según San Mateo*, vol. 1 (Madrid, 1966), p. 63; S. ZEDDA, *I Vangeli* (Milan, 1974), p. 191. The author holds that St. Matthew speaks of a grotto-habitation, or a grotto as a lodging, that is, of a grotto adapted to be a "house," something which occurred with a certain frequency in those times. But the difficulty arising from the differences between the two Evangelists appears irrelevant if one considers that St. Matthew refers not to the place of birth, but to the place of the visit of the Magi, which seems to have taken place sometime after the birth (Mt 2:1). If the grotto, in fact, was a temporary refuge for Mary's parturition, it is logical to think that immediately after the birth of Jesus, St. Joseph would have found a permanent "house" for the Holy Family in which to dwell. Cf. G. RICCIOTTI, *Vita di Gesù Cristo* (Vatican City, 1947), p. 281. Moreover, nothing prevents one from intending for "house" (according to Mt 2:11) the rear section, that is, the grotto-stable adjoining the true and proper "house": cf. P. BENOIT, "Non erat eis locus in diversorio (Lk 2:7)," in A. DESCAMPS, *Mélanges B. Rigaux* (Gembloux, 1970), pp. 173–186.

19 It also seems to be confirmed by archeological findings that such a grotto, in any case, was located in the vicinity of the inhabited area of Bethlehem:

In this very place, lowly and hidden, to such a degree that it is difficult to imagine a place more so, the Virgin Mary *"brought forth her firstborn son."* We note firstly with Leal, that while in the preceding verse "the third person masculine plural is employed: 'while they…,' here, instead, the third person feminine singular occurs: '*she* brought forth…' For the Eastern mind, and especially for the ancient Eastern mind, such a pointed omission of any relation to the father can only be explained in terms of a virginal conception."[20]

In verse 7, the word *"firstborn"* (*prototokon*) is particularly noteworthy. This term had above all a juridical–legal meaning, and designated the "firstborn" who was to be offered to God for his ransom (Ex 13:1–6; Num 3:12–13; 8:5–26; 18:15–16), who had the right to his father's first and most important blessing, and who received a double inheritance in comparison to other sons. Therefore, the first son was called *firstborn* "even if there were no other sons after him," writes Leonardi, "and was therefore an only son. That is confirmed by a Jewish tombstone belonging to the same period as Jesus' birth—5 B.C.—discovered in Egypt, where it is said that a certain Arsinoe died 'in the pains of the childbirth of her firstborn son.'"[21]

Besides the juridical–religious sense, however, the term *"firstborn"* used here by St. Luke makes clear a theological truth of primary importance for the history of salvation. The

cf. E. Testa, "Betlemme e la grotta della Natività," *Bibbia e Oriente* I (1959): 78–80; Leonardi, *L'Infanzia di Gesù*, p. 110, nt. 25.

20 Leal, *Vangelo secondo Luca*, p. 137.

21 Leonardi, *L'Infanzia di Gesù*, p. 207. Cf. Laurentin, *Truth of Christmas*, pp. 503–504, n. 64, where the studies of C. C. Edgar, H. Lietzmann, J. B. Frey, W. Michaelis, G. Kittel, and E. Peretto are cited to demonstrate that the term "firstborn" does not imply the birth of other, younger brothers. J. Ernst also writes that "the text does not contain even the slightest intention of alluding to the possibility of other children who would have been born from the marriage with Joseph" (*Il Vangelo secondo Luca*, p. 141).

redemptive plan of God presents here the *"firstborn among many brothers"* (Rom 8:29), that is to say, the beginning of the new people of God, the new creation inaugurating the new times of the messianic era. Indeed, according to Laurentin, the title of *firstborn* "already insinuates that Jesus, Son of God (1:32a), before becoming the Son of Mary (1:32b), is the firstborn of all creatures (Col 1:15.18) as the only Son of God (ibid., and Jn 1:14, 18; 1 Jn 4:9)."[22]

With utmost simplicity and naturalness, St. Luke then goes on to describe what Mary did after Jesus' birth: *"She wrapped him in swaddling clothes and laid him in a manger."*

The parturition was one in which the woman did everything by herself, alone. She took the child, wrapped Him in swaddling clothes, and laid Him in a poor manger. There is no shadow of labor or pain in this scene so gentle and maternal.[23] Tradition has rightly read therein the mystery of the joyful, virginal birth of Him who had come to bring into the world *"superabundant joy"* (Jn 15:11). From this moment, Mary was no longer the "pregnant Virgin," but the "Virgin Mother" who unites and carries in herself the two seals of glory: that of Perpetual Virginity and of Divine Maternity.[24]

---

22 LAURENTIN, *Truth of Christmas*, Ital. ed.: pp. 594–595 (the entire excursus-note).

23 "Without rendering the narration burdensome through details of doubtful taste—as the apocryphal 'gospels' would later do—the Evangelist shows us a Mother who is fully ready to provide by herself initial care for the babe. In fact, faith tells us that the Mother remained a virgin, and for her parturition was only a joy" (GAROFALO, *La Madonna della Bibbia*, p. 62). See also LAURENTIN, *Truth of Christmas*, pp. 175, 178; VARÓN VARÓN, *Sagrada Escritura*, p. 92.

24 In regard to the "virginal birth" (something quite distinct from the "virginal conception" and from the virginity "after birth," which entail the complete absence of conjugal relations between Mary and Joseph), Leonardi would tend almost to suppress its biological dimension ("integrity of the hymen"), maintaining that maternity with "the uterine scars" as its characteristic sign, is a "glory, not a dishonor, for Mary as well as for all mothers!" (*L'Infanzia di Gesù*, p. 208). In fact, if it is true that maternity has as its sign the "scars in the womb," it is likewise true that *virginity* has as its sign the "integrity of the hymen." Now, the mystery of Mary's "virginal birth"

The *birth* also reveals to us the truth of faith which is the *virginitas in partu*. That mystery entails the full preservation of the permanent virginity of Mary Most Holy: integral virginity both physical and spiritual, moral and psychological. Laurentin writes: 'Virginity in child-birth, if not meaningless, signifies full virginity according to *body and soul, such that any dissociation of "biological virginity" and "spiritual virginity" requires an artificial forcing.*'[25]

In this regard it seems certain that a final, definitive confirmation of this truth of faith which is the *virginitas in partu*, both physical and spiritual, has been given by the Supreme Pontiff John Paul II during his discourse at the close of the *International Congress for the 16th centenary of the Council of Capua*, May 24th 1992. There he effectively links the generation of Christ '*ex intacta Virgine*' with Christ's resurrection '*ex intacto sepulcro*.' Thereby he clearly asserted that 'Mary of Nazareth truly conceived Jesus by the Holy Spirit without intervention of man; that she truly and virginally gave birth to her Son. For this reason she remained Virgin after childbirth. According to the Fathers and Councils which have expressly treated the question, she remained virgin even in what concerns the integrity of the body.'[26]

In perfect accord with the words of Pope John Paul II are those of the Archbishop of Capua Luigi Diligenza, President of the Congress, who writes thus in his concluding address: 'the mystery of Mary's virginity, notwithstanding its multiple aspects, is a "single mystery," not to be split up, but to be studied as much as possible in relation to its fontal unity: the divine condition of the Word postulates a virginal conception; the virginal character of the conception is prolonged in the birth: true birth, sacred and sacralizing

means precisely that. Mary, with the birth of Jesus, has both together; that is, she has "the scars in her womb" (sign and glory of maternity) and she has "the integrity of the hymen" (sign and glory of virginity). These are the *two* glories of the Virgin Mother! This is the mystery of faith of Mary's virginity "during childbirth." Cf. *The Navarre Bible. St. Luke's Gospel*, p. 51.

25 R. Laurentin, *La Vergine Maria. Mariologia postconciliare*, Rome 1983, p. 295. Particularly incisive area pages 284–301. [English Version: *A Short Treatise on the Virgin Mary*, Washington NJ 1991].

26 Cf. P. D. M. Fehlner, *Virgin Mother, the Great Sign* (Washington NJ 1993).

birth, in which the integrity of the Mother also becomes sign of the divinity of the Son; from the virginal conception and birth follows the perfect consecration of Mary to God, which made Her His inviolable sanctuary.'[27]

Mary laid Jesus in the "manger." This is the sign of the poverty and extreme humility of Him who *"emptied himself taking the form of a servant"* (Phil 2:7), "who was laid in a manger, a place for animals," writes Laurentin, "a sign of marginalization, of being outside that society where the Messiah was not received (2:7)."[28]

Mary wrapped Him in "swaddling clothes." These "swaddling clothes" are a sign of the maternal care of Mary, while the child in "the swaddling clothes," laid in the "manger," is the prophetic sign of Him who in the tomb awaiting the Resurrection was also to be "wrapped in a similar manner, bound with linen cloths."[29]

Finally, what is to be said in regard to the ox and the ass that popular tradition always places beside the manger of the Divine Infant of Bethlehem? On this there exist two quite precise and suggestive references to Isaiah and of Habakkuk. Isaiah says: *"The ox knows his owner and the ass his master's crib"* (Is 1:3). Habakkuk says: *"You will be known in the midst of two animals"* (Hab 3:2). From Origen and St. Jerome, from the Protoevangelium of James and from the paintings of the catacombs, tradition has developed this idea of the ox and the ass in the cave of Bethlehem, so

---

27 L. Diligenza, *Relazione conclusive*, in Aa. Vv., *XVI Centenario del Concilio di Capua 392–1992, Atti del Convegno Internazionale di studi mariologici*, Rome 1993, p. 632.

28 Laurentin, *Truth of Christmas*, Ital. ed.: p. 255.

29 Ibid., Ital. ed.: p. 247 (read the entire note concerning "the manger and the swaddling clothes," Eng. ed.: pp. 176–177; see also Ital. ed.: p. 255, n. 14). In regard to the "manger," some describe it as a hollow in the rock of the grotto, edged with mud, straw, and rocks; others, on the contrary, describe it as a kind of movable basket or container placed on the ground: cf. G. Dalman, *Orte und Wege Jesu* (Gütersloh, 1924), pp. 42ff.; J. M. Crehan, *The Gospel according to St. Luke* (London, 1966), p. 34.

reinforcing the validity of the reference above all to Isaiah 1:3, which employs the term *platné* ("manger") used by St. Luke.[30]

What were Mary's sentiments at the time of Jesus' birth? And her maternal feelings while beholding her Divine Son? What were the outpourings of her heart? And what ecstasy did she experience in kissing the tiny face of God become man? "In those moments:" says Garofalo, "Mary, too, spoke the delightful irrelevancies of every mother, with her eyes fixed upon those of her son, lost in a sea of love. And she sang a sweet lullaby in order to quiet the grieved Infant or in order to lull Him to sleep. With a lullaby of the premier Mother begins the history of poetry and music on the threshold of the lost paradise, full of nostalgia for a lost innocence."[31]

Pietrafesa writes:

> Under the dim light of a lamp Mary Most Holy contemplated the newborn Infant. In Him she noticed her own features and with trembling tenderness and love she placed on that face the first kiss. Over that Infant who was the Son of God, but also her son, she rejoiced as no other mother in the world ever has for the birth of her child. Enraptured, she must have adored and contemplated, unable to express her sentiments.[32]

---

30 Cf. B. Rinaldi, "La Mangiatoia," *Bibbia e Oriente* 6 (1968): 243–252; Laurentin, *Truth of Christmas*, p. 182; Ital. ed: p. 255, nn. 15, 16, 17 (he also cites R. Brown among those favorable to the idea of the presence of the two animals); Leonardi, *L'Infanzia di Gesù*, pp. 210–211 (among those favorable he cites Winandy); Pietrafesa, *La Madonna nella Rivelazione*, pp. 220–221.

31 Garofalo, *Le parole di Maria*, p. 152.

32 Pietrafesa, *La Madonna nella Rivelazione*, p. 218.

14
The Announcement to the Shepherds

Luke 2:8–21

To many, the announcement to the shepherds seems only an idyllic event, elaborately and movingly described by St. Luke.[1] In reality, it is an event that contains concisely formulated, wide-ranging, profound implications, summarily revealing the meaning and fulfillment of the ancient prophecies about the course of human salvation. The prophecies regarding the Messiah, King, and Savior of Israel, of the lineage of David (2 Sam 7:12–16; Is 9:6), and a native of Bethlehem, are found in this announcement at the exact point of their fulfillment.

More than an announcement, this pericope might better be called a celestial, angelic symphony, a solemn, theophanic liturgy to celebrate an event indicating and recapitulating in itself the past, the present, and the future of mankind and of the cosmos, up to the very eschaton. Born is *"he who recapitulates in himself all things"* (cf. Eph 1:10).

There were in the same country shepherds who watched during the night, keeping guard over their flock. An

---

1 It has been remarked, for example, how "from verse 8 each chiamus involves a delicate alliteration:

v. 8: a. *poimenes* (shepherds) b. *agraulountes* (keeping watch)
c. *phiassontes* (guarding at night) d. *epi ten poimen* (their flocks)

v.9: a. *aggelos Kyriou* (Angel of the Lord) b. *doxa Kyriou* (glory of the Lord)
c. *ephobethesan phobon megan* (feared with great fear)

vv. 9–10: a. *phobon* (fear) b. *megan* (great)
c. *charan* (joy) d. *megalen* (great)

v. 11, a solemn concluding sentence: 'who is Christ the Lord–in the city of David'" (ERNST, *Il Vangelo secondo Luca*, p. 143).

angel of the Lord appeared to them, and the glory of the Lord surrounded them with light. They were taken with great fear, but the angel said to them: "Fear not; for behold I bring you tidings of great joy that will be to all the people; for today is born to you in the city of David, a Savior, who is Christ the Lord. This will be a sign unto you: you will find an infant wrapped in swaddling clothes and laid in a manger." And suddenly there was with the angel a multitude of the heavenly host, praising God and saying: "Glory to God in the highest; and on earth peace to men he loves" (vv. 8–14).

The first announcement of Jesus' birth was made to shepherds, that is, to the "least" among the social classes according to common opinion. Shepherds, in fact, were the most despised and segregated. "In some rabbinic texts," Ernst tells us, "they were put on the same level with brigands and criminals."[2] "It was suspected that they did not observe the seventh commandment," writes Pietrafesa, "and for this reason were excluded from testifying at trials."[3] The Pharisees, in particular "despised them," affirms Leonardi, "because in their nomadic life they were not able to observe all the prescriptions of the Law (such as washing one's hands before eating)."[4]

The shepherds dwelt in a plain to the east of Bethlehem. According to traditional usage, still in vogue today, for the night they gathered several flocks in a sole enclosure and kept guard by turns. They lived under conditions of great want, supporting innumerable hardships and sufferings.[5]

---

2 Ernst, *Il Vangelo secondo Luca*, p. 140.

3 Pietrafesa, *La Madonna nella Rivelazione*, p. 221. Cf. Ghidelli, *Luca*, p. 90.

4 Leonardi, *L'Infanzia di Gesù*, p. 211. Cf. M. Galizzi, *La scelta dei poveri*, p. 64.

5 Cf. Ghidelli, *Luca*, p. 140.

Now, to such shepherds, while at night they watched over their flock, *"an angel of the Lord appeared … and the glory of the Lord surrounded them with light,"* in order to inform them of the birth of the *"Savior," "Christ the Lord,"* giving them a *"sign"* by which to find Him: the sign of the *"swaddling clothes"* and of the *"manger,"* a sign as humble as it is distinctive of the poverty of Him who had come to *"evangelize the poor"* (Lk 4:18).

This apparition was "theophanic," because the *angel of the Lord,* "who did not bear a name," writes Leonardi, "seems to designate, as in the Pentateuch and in Matthew 1–2, Yahweh himself clothed in sensible form.… God himself, then, and not one of His angels, wished to announce to men the central event in the history of mankind, the birth of the Savior."[6]

"I bring you tidings of great joy": is the theme of the "good news," of the "joyful news," the central theme of the new revelation, which St. Luke in particular underscores in his Gospel.[7] The most joyful news, the true news—joy, above all for the poor and oppressed, is that of the birth of Him who finally came to bring liberation and salvation.

Everyone is called to this *"great joy."* Everyone has need of it. To everyone it is offered. Ferraro writes: "No one is excluded from this joy. The great angelic announcement on the night of the Nativity regards 'all people': the people of Israel who then anxiously awaited their salvation, and the innumerable people composed of all those who at that

---

6 Leonardi, *L'Infanzia di Gesù*, pp. 212, 213. Laurentin writes that "the theophany which announces the Christmas scene is analogous to that of the transfiguration (9:29 and 32) in its radiance and manifestation of glory" (*Truth of Christmas*, p. 179).

7 Cf. Ghidelli, *Luca*, pp. 37–38, 90. "*I announce to you*, literally is '*I evangelize to you*,' that is to say, I transmit to you some '*good news*'" (Leal, *Vangelo secondo Luca*, p. 141). "The word 'joy,'" writes Ernst, "runs like a thread throughout the entire work of Luke" (*Il Vangelo secondo Luca*, p. 145).

time and thereafter received or would receive the message and strive to live it."[8]

"Today": this very precise chronological term is noteworthy for indicating something extraordinary. It is a question here of God's "today," which becomes man's "today." "The adverb *sémeron,"* writes Ghidelli, "indicates the beginning of the Messianic era, the close of all of the history of Israel that was a long preparation for the fullness of time, the *eschaton,* or last time decisive for the salvation of men."[9] More concisely, H. Schürmann writes that the word *"today"* in this verse of St. Luke "stops time and inserts into history the eschatological world of God."[10]

"In the city of David": this is a geographical particular, confirming how for St. Luke salvific events bear upon the spatio-temporal reality of mankind's history. They occur in a concrete time (*"today"*) and in a concrete space (*"in the city of David"*). And these are the human aspects of the Incarnation, which is a human-divine reality.

"Today is born to you a Savior": the term *sôtér* can bear a temporal or spiritual, political, or religious meaning.

> Of Jesus it is predicated with a clear religious and spiritual meaning, as derived from the Old Testament literature and faith (the concept of *sôtêria* is always interpreted this way: cf. 1:47, 69; 2:30). As fundamental texts one should refer to: Is 44:6; 45:15, 21; Hab 3:18; Ps 79(78):9. The salvation intended here is of an exclusively spiritual order, because it requires interior dispositions and moral qualities. Jesus himself would find it necessary to combat to the very

---

8 Ferraro, *I racconti*, p. 114.

9 Ghidelli, *Luca*, p. 91. Similarly, Ferraro writes that "this temporal expression is a term typical of Luke whereby the historical aspect of the salvific mysteries is underlined... It reveals how the salvation bestowed by God is present and working in a person and in its beneficial manifestations" (*I racconti*, p. 115).

10 Quoted by Ernst, *Il Vangelo secondo Luca*, p. 145. See the ample treatment of this matter by B. Prete, *L'Opera di Luca* (Turin, 1986), pp. 104–117.

end (cf. Acts 1:5) a political-nationalistic idea of Messianic salvation.[11]

"Christ the Lord": the term *"Christ"* means "anointed," and is applied to the priest, the king, and the prophet. "Christ" united in Himself these three offices, becoming the source of the priestly, regal, and prophetic anointing for the new Israel, the new people of God, a people of priests, kings, and prophets.[12]

The term *"Lord"* has here an extraordinary meaning because it connotes the "divinity" and the salvific power of Christ. In fact, in biblical language, it is referred to God and "always implies," states Leal, "His divinity and His salvific action."[13]

"This will be a sign unto you": there would customarily be expected an extraordinary "sign," certainly not a common one (hence, one like the "sign" of Elizabeth, for example, who had become fecund in old age). The "sign" announced to the shepherds, instead, consists in some *"swaddling clothes"* in which a newborn infant is wrapped and placed in a *"manger."* What is the meaning of such a "sign"? "It is possible that it is meant to express the paradox of the situation: the Savior-Messiah Lord came into the world as a helpless infant. The complete inattention shown the

---

[11] GHIDELLI, *Luca*, p. 91. Cf. also FERRARO, *I racconti*, p. 116. Leal points out that "it is the first time that this term appears, one which is transliterated in Greek as 'Jesus.' In the Old Testament it normally applied only to God, especially in the Psalms and Prophets, where Yahweh appears in the act of saving the people from Pharaoh, from the kings of Assyria and of Babylon, from every sort of heathen, oppressor and wicked person" (*Vangelo secondo Luca*, p. 141). Varón Varón, in turn, notes that "the name Savior, for the Jewish mind, rings more positive than negative, that is to say, rather than being one who frees from evil, he is more the giver of gifts" (*Sagrada Escritura*, p. 98).

[12] Cf LEAL, *Vangelo secondo Luca*, p. 142.

[13] Ibid. See also FERRARO, *I racconti*, p. 116. "It is the title Lord that manifests the divinity of Christ, because it is with this name that God wished to be called by his people in the Old Testament" (*The Navarre Bible. St. Luke's Gospel*, p. 52).

Messianic and salvific expectations of the Hebrew world constituted the true and proper sign, naturally no longer one satisfying from the viewpoint of appearances."[14]

At this point, the message of the angel of the Lord, that is, of God himself, having been concluded, *"suddenly there was with the angel a multitude of the heavenly host"* singing glory to God and peace to men. The presence of this angelic army over Bethlehem would confirm "that God himself was present in the Infant in the manger: with him also the heavenly court came down from heaven to earth," writes Leonardi.[15] Ernst also follows this interpretation: "For the Hebrew mind these were angels belonging to the divine court. They were participants in a heavenly liturgy that celebrated the entrance of the Messiah Jesus into the world" (Heb 1:6).[16]

We find here the most fitting conclusion for a theophany joining the first (angels) and the last (the shepherds) in *"great joy"* at the birth of the Savior, celebrated in song with a hymn of *"glory to God"* and of *"peace to men,"* object of the infinite mercy (*endokias*) of God.[17]

After the angels departed from them into heaven, the shepherds were saying to one another: "Let us go over to Bethlehem and see this thing which has come to pass, which the Lord has made known to us." Therefore they came with haste and found Mary and Joseph and the babe lying in the manger. And after having seen him,

---

14 Ernst, *Il Vangelo secondo Luca*, p. 146. A. Serra speaks of the "*swaddling clothes*" as a sign to be "interpreted," and he infers from it two meanings: that "of a fragile, weak condition progressing toward death," and that "of the care given by Mary and Joseph" (*Maria secondo il Vangelo*, p. 94ff.).

15 Leonardi, *L'Infanzia di Gesù*, p. 214. Cf also Ghidelli, *Luca*, p. 92.

16 Ernst, *Il Vangelo secondo Luca*, p. 147.

17 Cf. Ferraro, *I racconti*, p. 109. For those who deny the reality of the song of the angels heard by the shepherds, see the lively note of Laurentin, *Truth of Christmas*, p. 535, n. 8.

they related what had been told them concerning the child. And all who heard wondered over the things told them by the shepherds. But Mary kept all these things, pondering them in her heart. Then the shepherds returned glorifying God for all the things they had heard and seen, even as it was spoken to them (vv. 15–20).

The joy at the good news and the exultation over the wonderful apparition from heaven moved the shepherds to come *"with haste"* to Bethlehem. They had received from on high the revelation of the Savior's birth, a confirmation that "the knowledge" of salvation, as Galizzi comments, does not come from human research, but from revelation; the announcement of salvation comes from God. It was in this way that the shepherds came to understand: *"Let us go … and see that which the Lord has made known to us"* (2:15).[18]

At Bethlehem the shepherds *"found Mary, Joseph and the babe lying in the manger."*[19] Simply, quickly, St. Luke presents the sequence of scenes. For the shepherds, as for the poor, all was simple and spontaneous. Exhorting one another, setting out, seeking, finding, seeing, and speaking: everything happened, it might be said, with instinctive naturalness.[20]

---

18 GALIZZI, *La scelta dei poveri*, p. 62. Cf. FERRARO, *I racconti*, p. 127: The words of the shepherds express knowledge of the object of the announcement "whose revelation is directly attributed to God." The same author illustrates well the sense of the expression "*rhèma*," which has the meaning of "word-event" and which recurs three times in this narrative: 2:15, 17, 19 (pp. 124–136).

19 The Greek verb *euriskein*: to *find*, has the sense of to *find after search*. The shepherds to be described, therefore, as finding had first to have searched (cf. FERRARO, *I racconti*, p. 129).

20 "The Gospel does not inform us," Pietrafesa points out, "how the shepherds were able to direct themselves to the grotto where Jesus was. It is probable that they were guided by the flickering beams of an oil lamp which shone from the grotto. Just as Palestinian shepherds today compete in bringing to the mother of a newborn infant daily products, eggs and milk, so on that prophetic night they did not fail to bring to our Lady and to the child their poor gifts" (*La Madonna nella Rivelazione*, p. 222).

Ernst points out an important fact in regard to Mary: She is listed first; the narration makes no mention of the miraculous maternity; for this reason, such an order is all the more surprising as it is unusual for the Hebrew mind."[21] Mary was the first "protagonist" in the birth of Jesus.

The shepherds of Bethlehem, the first, spontaneous evangelists in the field, recounted *"what had been told them concerning the child,"* exciting amazement and wonder in whoever listened to them, and causing Mary carefully to keep *"all these things, pondering them in her heart."* This reflection-remembrance of Mary was very important as she was the source of the news for the gospels of the infancy.[22] St. Luke affirms it here (2:19) and reaffirms it shortly afterward (2:51).[23] Mary is the model of the contemplative soul, capable of silent listening and recollected meditation upon words and events of faith that ought always to be more deeply penetrated.[24] In this state of soul, writes Ferraro,

> Mary is here presented in the attitude of witness to an event and of a revelation concerning the event itself, a revelation and an event centered upon her son Jesus to whom the Angel in the annunciation had made known to her His dignity as Son of the Most High, the Holy One, the Son of God, and of whom the shepherds had related the great news

21 Ernst, *Il Vangelo secondo Luca*, p. 150.

22 "Luke discreetly indicates in this way the source from which he drew his news of the mysteries that he has recounted for us in the chapters of the gospels of the infancy": so states Ferraro, *I racconti*, p. 133, as earlier Garofalo observed, *Le parole di Maria*, pp. 14–18.

23 See the ample, analytical study of A. Serra, *Sapienza e contemplazione di Maria secondo Luca 2, 19.51* (Rome, 1982). See also Varón Varón, *Sagrada Escritura*, pp. 99–101.

24 Leonardi notes that "the expression '*to keep the words (or things) in one's heart*' was a technical formula already in use in the apocalyptical text of Daniel (4:28) and in *non-biblical* texts; it served to conclude a vision or a mysterious divine announcement concerning the Messianic future... Here the Evangelist adds the participle '*pondering them*' ('symballusa'); Mary, literally, 'tossed together' these words and things in order to draw from them their profound sense and then communicate this to others" (*L'Infanzia di Gesù*, p. 217).

received from the Angel who had designated Jesus as the Savior, Christ the Lord.[25]

Finally, *"the shepherds returned glorifying and praising God…"* That which the angels had done previously, was now done by the shepherds, who expressed "their thanks giving by the same word, *ainountes,* which describes the praise given by the angels in Luke 2:13."[26]

The angelic symphony and the theophany *"surrounded with light"* these humble shepherds of Bethlehem, making them the first depositories of the *"announcement"* of the Savior, the first, zealous evangelists of the *"great joy,"* the first, spontaneous glorifiers of God *"for all the things they had heard and seen."*

Rich with allusions and enlightening insights is this page of semiotic study by Laurentin on the visit of the shepherds to Bethlehem:

> The shepherds go spontaneously toward the earthly sign of poverty which was indicated to them. There this conjunction with the Messiah occurs: the conjunction heaven-earth, God-men, king-shepherds, is henceforth accomplished in him. The full meaning of the symbolism is revealed here. What follows is diffusion, the earthly consequence: the shepherds make the Messiah known, the Good News of the humble conjunction between heaven and earth extends to other addressees. The shepherds extend the evangelization (2:18) and praise (2:20) of the angels, while Mary, anomalously mentioned between these two functions of the shepherds, contemplates at length the events which will form the basis of the infancy Gospel.
>
> In short, the movement goes from the earthly realm (the census, birth in precarious conditions) to the heavenly, to

25 Ferraro, *I racconti*, p. 132.

26 Laurentin, *Truth of Christmas*, p. 189. We should not forget that "to a shepherd, Abraham, God has entrusted the promise of salvation for all mankind," says *The Navarre Bible. St. Luke's Gospel*, p. 54.

express the conjunction earth-heaven in the Savior-Christ-Lord, who is also the baby laid in the manger. He realizes the conjunction of God with humanity at the level of the poor. This manger (2:7.12.16) was located in Bethlehem (2:4. 15), which means house of bread according to the popular etymology. It is not impossible that such symbolism is meant to say that the Son of God made man had come in order to offer himself as food. Even if not explicit, the consistency and the poetic strength of the text imply it.[27]

And when eight days were fulfilled for his circumcision, his name was called Jesus, the name given him by the angel before he was conceived in the womb (v. 21).

With circumcision,[28] according to Hebrew law, the newborn infant became a member of the Chosen People, thereby participating in the promises made *"to Abraham and to his seed."*

Jesus, the Messiah, had to be a perfect Hebrew, in all things like unto others (*"in all things like unto his brothers"*: Heb 2:17), with the characteristics native to the Davidic family inherited from His Mother *"according to the flesh"* (Rom 1:3), subject to the Hebrew law according to the established rules, the first of which, for a newborn male infant, was in fact that of "circumcision" on the eighth day after birth.[29] In regard to "circumcision," the law was

27 Laurentin, *Truth of Christmas*, p. 190. Regarding the historicity of this episode of the call of the shepherds to the grotto of Bethlehem, it is to be noted that this also has been denied or called into doubt by those who consider such an event, in which angels, lights, hymns, and shepherds supposedly took part, as only an edifying "invention" of the early "creative community." But Laurentin ironically, and justly, comments: "Too much honor is paid the 'community' attributing to it this bold invention. In exegesis the 'creative community' too often reminds one of a magician's hat from which everything is pulled" (Ital. ed.: p. 258).

28 See E. Galbiati, "La Circoncisione di Gesù (Lc. 2, 21)," *Bibbia e Oriente* 28 (1986): 37–45.

29 A characteristic of St. Luke to be noted is the accent he places on the "temporal" (e.g., "*eight days*") in order to insert "regularly the events comprising the mystery of salvation in the course of human history" (Ferraro, *I racconti*, p. 140).

strict. No Hebrew could exempt himself, nor did he want to exempt himself. To be "uncircumcised" meant to be excluded from the people of God. Even if the eighth day fell on the Sabbath, circumcision had to be done all the same.[30]

St. Luke, it is true, appears to be very hasty in describing the circumcision of Jesus. He says nothing about the rite, nor of Mary and Joseph's impression in seeing the first blood shed by the Divine Infant. Rather, Mary and Joseph, although necessarily present, are not even mentioned by St. Luke.[31] And yet the circumcision of Jesus is an important fact, given that in the Letter to the Colossians (2:11ff.), St. Paul considers it "as the beginning of his consecration and sacrifice and the source of blessings for all who would be united to his body through faith and baptism."[32]

It appears, however, that St. Luke was interested in setting in relief one thing: the conferral of the name Jesus on the newborn Infant, as had been revealed by the angel to Mary (Lk 1:31) and to Joseph (Mt 1:21). On the day of the circumcision, in fact, every child received his own name which served to indicate the ontological and

---

30 De Ambrogio writes: "The Law was formal: every newborn male infant had to be circumcised... The obligation was so demanding that the small surgical operation had to be performed even if the eighth day fell on a Sabbath. No Hebrew could exempt himself from it. The Hebrews placed enormous value on this sacred rite. They saw in it the certificate of their belonging to the People of God. Not to be circumcised meant to belong 'not to the children of the Covenant, but to the children of the Destruction.' To call someone uncircumcised was the most cruel offense that one could inflict on another" (*San Luca*, pp. 69–70).

31 Laurentin speaks of the "eclipse of human actuants. Luke does not specify who performs Jesus' circumcision (2:21), whereas he did for John the Baptist (1:59): the neighbors who came and began a dialogue with the parents (1:60–63). He says only that Jesus '*was circumcised*' and '*was called*' by the name Jesus. The passive does not reveal any particular subject. This concealment is all the more unexpected, given the proclaimation of Gabriel (1:31) which was formally addressed to Mary alone: '*You shall call his name Jesus*.' It would have been expected that this role would be recalled. And instead Luke does not do so" (*Truth of Christmas*, p. 194; Ital. ed.: pp. 266–267).

32 Leal, *Vangelo secondo Luca*, p. 145.

dynamic constitution of his personality.[33] Jesus is the proper name of the Word Incarnate, and means *"the Lord is salvation."* It is composed of two constituent elements, one pertaining to His essence (*Lord*) and the other to His mission (*salvation*).[34]

Even if Mary is not expressly mentioned by the Evangelist, she was, nevertheless, certainly present, together with St. Joseph, in order to give the name Jesus to the Child. And she certainly "understood well," comments Pietrafesa, "that this name embraced in full the entire salvific mission of her Son. It was in order to implement the salvific plan of God that Jesus; had come down to this earth, that he had begun the 'via crucis' by a birth in unpleasant conditions in a squalid cave, and by shedding eight days later those first drops of blood wherewith the Redemption could be considered already in act."[35]

---

33 "Last names did not exist among the Hebrews. Rather one said: 'Son of so-and-so (the Hebrew for 'son' is *ben*; the Aramaic, *bar*). For example, John ben Zachary" (De Ambrogio, *San Luca*, p. 70).

34 "A name," writes Ghidelli, "that summarizes well the dignity of the person bearing it, that encloses within itself the object of the Gospel: salvation" (*Luca*, p. 95).

35 Pietrafesa, *La Madonna nella Rivelazione*, p. 224.

15
The Presentation in the Temple

Luke 2:22–40

"The presentation of Jesus in the Temple," writes Laurentin,

> is not a standard biblical scene. It was not at all customary to recount the presentation of a hero. The only precedent is in chapter one of the first book of Samuel, and Samuel's presentation is quite different. It is not tied to a prescription of the law. The timing is different: in 1 Samuel 1:22–24 it takes place after Samuel is weaned, while in Luke it takes place 40 days after Jesus' birth. Samuel remains there forever (1 Sam 1.22), while Jesus returns to Nazareth (2:39). The significance of the act is quite different, for the presentation of Jesus, according to Luke, has an apocalyptic and theophanic character. He who bears the divine names of *Holy, Lord,* and *Son of God,* visits the temple as a poor child, but he is recognized by the witnesses as the *'Salvation'* (*lytrosis,* 2:38) of Israel. The newness shines forth everywhere, and always in the same direction. Across the anecdotal diversity the great themes converge.[1]

This is a concise synthesis of the presentation. To the author who made it we are indebted for two very ample contributions to our understanding of this mystery, the fruit of literary critical research and semiotic study. Herein, he articulates an analysis of the content and meaning of each pericope in itself and in its general context, discovering in the presentation the so-called "complements" of the literary critics and "programs" of semiotics. The "complements" are those of the "prophecies," of the "oracles of Gabriel" (1:31–

---

1 Laurentin, *Truth of Christmas*, p. 101.

35), of the "law," and of the "Spirit."[2] The "programs" are those of the "ordinary and theophanic," of the "law," of the "Holy Spirit," and of "fulfillment and departure."[3]

When, according to the law of Moses, the time had come for their purification, they brought the child to Jerusalem in order to present him to the Lord—as is written in the law of the Lord: Every firstborn male shall be called holy to the Lord—and to offer in sacrifice a pair of turtledoves or two young pigeons, as is prescribed in the law of the Lord (vv. 22–24).

According to the law of Moses, every woman who had brought forth a male infant had need of purification after 40 days, and had to come to the Temple bringing a lamb, or, if she were poor, a pair of turtledoves to offer in sacrifice. Furthermore, every firstborn male had to be offered to the Lord and redeemed with the offering of five shekels of silver.[4]

St. Luke, however, in verses 22 to 24 refers not only to this *"law of the Lord,"* but also to two important prophecies:

Malachi (3:1–3) and Daniel (9:24). The first speaks of the entrance of the Lord into the Temple in order to purify the sons of Levi. The second speaks of the "fulfillment of the days," that is, 70 weeks, in reference to the Lord's advent in Jerusalem to consecrate His Temple.[5]

---

2 Ibid., pp. 62ff.

3 Ibid., pp. 193ff.

4 It is evident that Mary was not, per se, obliged to this rite of purification "since her virginity," writes VARÓN VARÓN, "remains absolutely intact in the conception and birth of her Son" (*Sagrada Escritura*, p. 103).

5 The 70 weeks were calculated by St. Luke "in the time which separates the announcement to Zechariah and Jesus' entrance into the Temple in Jerusalem" (LAURENTIN, *Truth of Christmas*, p. 66; see also p. 65). Cf. GALIZZI, *La scelta dei poveri*, p. 66.

That which appears in itself as purely a program of fidelity on the part of Mary, the poor Mother,[6] to the observance of the ritual norms prescribed by the "law" (cited three times in these three verses), is in reality a "theophanic" program in which the "Lord" (cited four times) is the true principal agent, the true "protagonist" of this event of presentation in the Temple.

Here are fulfilled the prophecies made at the Annunciation to Mary by the angel Gabriel, who had made known the two names of the Word Incarnate: the name *of Jesus* and the name of *Holy One, Son of God.* The first was a human name; the second, a divine, transcendent name. In the presentation in the Temple, Jesus by now had both names. *"You will call him Jesus"* (1:31); *"he will be called Holy One, Son of God"* (1:35)—so spoke the angel Gabriel. With the circumcision and with the presentation in the Temple, the son of Mary, consecrated to God, was now called *Jesus, Holy One,* and *Son of God.*

> With Jesus' entrance into the temple, Luke, in fact, sees realized *the coming of Yahweh himself into his Temple,* scorned and reviled, as foretold by Malachi 3:14, in order to 'purify' the Levites, restore therein his salvific, redemptive presence (cf. v. 32) and *reestablish therein a sacrifice pleasing to God,* as in times past; *it was to be the sacrifice of his very person and life.*[7]

As to the "purification," there exists an evident difficulty in verse 22 (in the original Greek text), which speaks not of the purification of the mother alone (as decreed by the Law in Leviticus 12:4–8—and as many older English

---

6 "The entire event," writes K. Stock, "presents Mary as an Israelite faithful to the Law, as the mother of a child and as a poor woman" ("Maria nel Tempio. Lc. 22–52," in *Parola Spirito e Vita*, vol. 6, p. 115).

7 Leonardi, *L'Infanzia di Gesù*, p. 225. Cf. Ferraro, *I racconti*, pp. 144–145; Galizzi, *La scelta dei poveri*, p. 67. Laurentin writes: "It is the temple that is defined by his coming rather than he by the temple" (*Truth of Christmas*, p. 70).

translations seem to imply), but of *"their"* purification. The plural *"their,"* in place of the feminine singular (referring to the mother), "could be referred jointly to the mother and the son," J. Leal points out,

> but purification concerns only the mother. For the son other expressions are reserved, such as: *'they brought him,' 'in order to present him,' 'he will be consecrated.'* If Luke had wanted to observe strictly the rules of grammar, he would have had to say: 'when the days of her purification and the days for his presentation were accomplished.' It is clear, however, that Luke intended here to simplify and abridge the construction. Some authors surmount this difficulty hypothesizing that the term 'purification' has here a broader sense and indicates both the proper rite of the mother (purification in the strict sense) and the proper rite of the son (presentation and redemption). In fact, Luke does not use here the term that is used in the Septuagint, *katarsis,* but the term *katarismos,* which has a more general sense and could comprise as much the presentation and the redemption of the infant as the purification and the sacrifice of the mother (Knabenbauer, Lagrange, Marchal, Dorado, Schmid, Zerwick, Crehan).[8]

According to Laurentin, however, it is necessary here to know how to read effectively the "transpositions" made by St. Luke, if the full and complete sense of the Lucan expressions is to be grasped. Reflecting more, we see indeed that the Evangelist, as Laurentin says, "avoided association of the Virgin with this purification and sacrificial offering. He turns the rite away from the Mother, by applying it to a plural subject; neither Mary nor the purification are mentioned subsequently: the Law seems to be referred to only in relation to the presentation (2:22) and the

---

8 Leal, *Vangelo secondo Luca*, p. 147. Cf. Ceuppens, *De Mariologia Biblica*, pp. 557–558; Pietrafesa, *La Madonna nella Rivelazione*, p. 228, n. 1; Varón Varón, *Sagrada Escritura*, p. 104; Laurentin, *Truth of Christmas*, p. 71; Ital. ed.: p. 103.

consecration of the child (2:23; cf. 2:27)."[9] And a little further along the same author states that "Mary remains hidden in the following verse (2:22), the one in which purification is mentioned (Lv 12:8), which should concern her alone, according to the 'Law.' This hiddenness is *the counterpart of the curious transfer which would attribute the purification to a plural subject.*"[10]

Therefore, on the basis of literary criticism and of semiotic study, Laurentin makes note of two important "typological transpositions" in Luke's text:

> The *purification* of the mother (purification from sin and expiation for sin, continually repeated in Lv 12:4–8) is not related to the Mother of Jesus (who is carefully eliminated from the context), but is transferred to the people, of whom Jerusalem is the symbol, and who appear for the first time in this verse: 'their purification' (2:22).
>
> The *redemption* of the first-born is not related to Christ, who is the Redeemer, but transferred to Jerusalem. The sequence concerning the Temple ends with the theme of redemption (*lytrosis*) of Jerusalem (2:38).[11]

Laurentin continues by stating that, in turn, "Jerusalem (2:22.25.38) is a representation of Israel, as these isotopic parallels make clear. This is also confirmed by the textual variant of 2:38, where numerous manuscripts replace Jerusalem with Israel but give an identical meaning."[12]

---

9 Laurentin, *Truth of Christmas*, p. 71. Also G. Ferraro points out that "the accent of the entire passage of Luke is placed upon the presentation of Jesus to God in Jerusalem in the Temple" (*I racconti*, p. 144).

10 Laurentin, *Truth of Christmas*, p. 72.

11 Ibid., p. 197, Ital. ed.: p. 274. According to a study by I. de La Potterie, "Les deux noms de Jerusalem dans l'évangile de Luc," *Recherches des Sciences Religieuses* 69 (1981): 57–60, the term *Hierousalêm* is the sacred name, while *Hierosolyma* is the profane name of the city that kills the prophets (cf. 23:27). Laurentin writes: "Luke chooses the form *Hierosolyma* in 2:22 in order to speak of its purification (that of the people and of the temple)" (*Truth of Christmas*, p. 110, no. 59).

12 Laurentin, *Truth of Christmas*, p. 199.

There is a sort of identification, therefore, between Jesus and the Temple, between Jesus and Jerusalem, between Jesus and Israel. St. Luke, that is, speaks of a *mystery* in this presentation in the Temple, which is in itself a rite "extraneous to the Law," "unknown," as Laurentin states.[13] In a carefully designed picture here, Laurentin presents the context of the "mystery" of the presentation:

> The *redemption* of the first-born, devoid of meaning if applied in regard to this Redeemer and Savior, is transferred to Jerusalem in 2:38; the *purification* (2:22), which does not pertain to the Virgin, is equally transferred to the people. Luke sees here the fulfillment of the prophecy of Malachi 3 concerning the eschatological entrance of the Lord into his temple: 'He will purify the Sons of Levi.' The context refers to the purification of all the people.[14]

Therefore, in the final analysis, it can be said that with the presentation in the Temple, Jesus, rather than being redeemed, came to redeem others, with "this mysterious prelude," notes Landucci, "to his bloody offering on the Cross."[15] For this reason, He was recognized as the "Savior" (via the name *Jesus,* from the circumcision) and proclaimed "Holy One" (*hagion klêthêsetai*), that is, identified as God. Arid in such wise, with His entrance and with His offering, He worked the *redemption* and *purification* of the Temple, of Jerusalem, and of all the people of Israel.

---

13 Even if one wants to connect the "presentation" with the rite of "redemption," nevertheless it remains to be noted that "according to the Law this ransom of the first-born did not take place on the fortieth day (that of the purification of the mother, indicated in 2:22) but 'in the month of birth'" (Laurentin, *Truth of Christmas*, p. 74). Cf. also Ceuppens, *De Mariologia Biblica*, p. 157; Ernst, *Il Vangelo secondo Luca*, p. 154. (He cites Ex 13:13–16.)

14 Laurentin, *Truth of Christmas*, p. 75; see also Ghidelli, *Luca*, p. 95.

15 Landucci, *Maria SS. nel Vangelo*, p. 150. "Jesus was not redeemed," writes M. Galizzi. "His very name says that it is He who redeems; He is the Savior (2:11), He is the Holy One, that is totally consecrated to God" (*La scelta dei poveri*, pp. 65–66).

Mary, on her part, fulfilled a role of primary importance in the presentation in the Temple, because it was she, Pietrafesa points out, who

> solemnly and officially offered the Son to the heavenly Father. It is true that from the first moment of the Incarnation Jesus is offered as an innocent and holy victim to his Father, but it was necessary for our Lady to be associated in a solemn way with this offering, since she, as Mother, had all rights over her Son. Joyfully and sorrowfully, the Blessed Virgin offered her Son to the heavenly Father, but at the same time offered herself also as an associated victim. Mary Most Holy by now was entirely one with her Son, in that she lived with Him, for Him, and in Him. The life of our Lady was bound to that of her Son in an intimate, indissoluble way. The intimate union of our Lady with her Son also implies a spiritual maternity in regard to the mystical body, and, therefore, in presenting herself with her Son, she also offered to the Father all the redeemed, already from the annunciation become her children.[16]

Now in Jerusalem there was a man named Simeon, a just and God-fearing man who awaited the consolation of Israel; the Holy Spirit who was upon him had revealed to him that he would not see death before he had seen the Messiah of the Lord. Therefore, by the Holy Spirit he came into the temple. And when the parents brought in the child Jesus in order to fulfill the law, he took him into his arms and blessed God (vv. 25–28).

The appearance of this venerable man in the Temple was a complete surprise for Mary and Joseph. In an event

16 Pietrafesa, *La Madonna nella Rivelazione*, pp. 228–229. Also G. Leonardi writes: "The Evangelist says, furthermore, that the parents '*presented*' Jesus to the Lord. The verb 'to present' (v. 22: 'paristanai') is used in the *Old Testament for the priests and levites* who 'stand before the sanctuary'; furthermore, it is said that the victim was also 'presented' (cf. Rom 12:1); therefore, Jesus is described as a *priest and victim* offered by Mary and Joseph to God" (*L'Infanzia di Gesù*, p. 225); see also Ferraro, *I racconti*, pp. 144–145.

that had to be unfolded entirely under the shadow of the "law," there appeared instead Simeon, this very old man, who made his appearance as one entirely under the shadow of the "Spirit." *"The Holy Spirit was upon him,"* says St. Luke, and he came to the Temple *"by the Spirit."*[17]

It does not seem that Simeon was a priest. However, he was *"just and devout"*: one of those faithful, trustful Israelites who awaited the Messiah Savior.[18] He cultivated a very intense spiritual life, surely at the level of the gifts of the Spirit, in view of the fact that the Holy Spirit himself had promised him that he would not die before having seen the invoked and longed-for Messiah, *"the consolation of Israel."*[19]

On that day, a new interior inspiration of the Holy Spirit had moved Simeon to go to the Temple, where it was revealed to him that the Child in Mary's arms was the very *"Messiah of the Lord."* He then approached Mary, asked her to permit him to hold the Child in his arms, contemplated Him with tender eyes, and then intoned the short canticle of blessing.[20] "The meeting represents a threshold in the

---

17 In fact, with the figures of Simeon and Anna there is indicated, in the manner characteristic of Luke, the passage from the Law to the prophets: cf. P. Figueras, "Siméon et Anne ou le témoignage de la loi et des prophètes," *Novum Testamentum* 20 (1978): 84–89.

18 Some would try to identify him with Simeon son of Hillel: cf. Leonardi, *L'Infanzia di Gesù*, p. 226; Leal, *Vangelo secondo Luca*, p. 149 (in favor of this he cites Zahn and Plummer).

19 A. Poppi observes, "the Evangelist, in v. 25 and in the verses which follow, underlines a good three times the action of the Spirit upon Simeon, making of him almost a prototype of Christian prophets, 'whose task consists in recognizing and announcing the Christ in the Spirit of God' (Schürmann, p. 248)" (*Sinossi*, p. 268). Cf. also Ferraro, *I racconti*, p. 159.

20 One should note with C. de Ambrogio that "the priest in service did not seem to have taken notice of Jesus. Elizabeth, on the other hand, at the mere sight of the Mother of Jesus was startled and had recognized the presence of the Holy One of God. This priest, a prisoner of a formalism no longer animated by the Spirit, touched the man-God without suspecting or feeling anything" (*San Luca*, pp. 72–73).

history of the world," writes P. Hauck, "and the time of old touched and experienced the new."[21]

"Now permit, O Lord, your servant to go in peace according to your word; because my eyes have seen your salvation, which you have prepared before the face of all peoples; a light to illumine the nations and the glory of your people Israel" (vv. 29–32).

The holy, venerable old man could now die *"in peace,"*[22] *after having seen Him who is the "salvation"* prepared by God *"before the face of all peoples,"* the Messiah, *"a light to illumine the nations,"* a light, that is, for all the men of the earth, and the *"glory"* of Israel, the Chosen People.

Important in this short canticle are the concepts of *salvation, light,* and *glory* as applied to the Messiah. The first concept plainly is related to the proper name *Jesus,* which means, in fact, *Savior.* The other two concepts are to be linked, instead, to the transcendent names of *Holy One* and *Son of God,* God himself.[23]

Evident in Christ here is the linking of God and the people—a theandric aspect of the Word Incarnate—for the universal salvation of mankind. To quote Laurentin again: "The meaning is at one and the same time the identification of Jesus with glory, i.e., with God, and his being linked both to the people of Israel and to the nations which he will

---

21 Quoted by Ernst, *Il Vangelo secondo Luca*, p. 157.

22 One should remember that "peace" is the "Messianic gift par excellence," as Galizzi says, *La scelta dei poveri*, p. 69. In this regard, see the extensive and analytical treatment of B. Prete, *L'opera di Luca* (Turin 1986) pp. 167–184.

23 "Salvation carries the same meaning as the human name of Jesus (2:21)," writes Laurentin, "that is, Savior... but in an abstract form with superlative which has absolute value: your salvation.... *Light* is a tide of God, an attribute of the divine. 'Glory' points more specifically to God himself ... It is to God alone that the word 'Glory,' presented so absolutely, appropriately belongs" (*Truth of Christmas*, pp. 77–78).

transfigure with his light."[24] Likewise clear is the *universal* character of the salvation brought by Christ and already announced by Isaiah (19:24; 22:1ff.; 42:6; 49:6.10; 60:3), this with a nuance not to be overlooked: pagans are given first place before the children of Israel.[25]

Finally, the role of Mary is here the role of the new Ark of the Covenant, because she it was who carried Jesus, she in whom God is present. "Mary as the Ark of the Covenant is the sign of God's presence, because Jesus, who is the Son of God, is there. Before, He was hidden in her womb, but now the eye could behold Him; and hence one could then say of Him that He was *the manifestation of God's presence in Israel.*"[26]

The father and mother of Jesus were wondering at those things which were spoken concerning him. And Simeon blessed them and said to Mary his mother: "Behold, this child is set for the fall and for the resurrection of many in Israel, a sign of contradiction that the thoughts of many hearts may be revealed" (vv. 33–35a).

On seeing and hearing these things during their stay in the Temple of Jerusalem the wonder of Mary and of Joseph must have been spontaneous. Poor, unknown, humble, and recollected, they could not but wonder over knowing that they were, in a certain sense, discovered and had become the recipients of words of admiration and praise for the Child on the part of two unknown persons, the venerable old man and the old woman Anna.

What Mary had already known from the angel of the Annunciation, keeping it in her heart, together with the

---

24 Ibid., p. 200.

25 Cf. Leonardi, *L'Infanzia di Gesù*, p. 227.

26 Galizzi, *La scelta dei poveri*, p. 71.

events that gradually came to pass (cf. 2:19), was verified and confirmed from time to time with new details, even surprising ones.

After having blessed Joseph and Mary, the old man Simeon, under the inspiration of the Holy Spirit, then addressed himself to Mary and informed her of two very important facts: one regarding the Child and one regarding herself. The Child will be a *"sign of contradiction"* and *"her soul a sword shall pierce."* These are two fearsome facts, two prophecies of suffering for the Redemption of mankind.[27] The angel Gabriel, in the announcement to Mary, had revealed in an implicit way the sufferings of the "Savior" (Jesus). Simeon, on the other hand, revealed in explicit, moving terms both the suffering of the Redeemer and the suffering of the Mother associated in the sufferings of the Son.[28]

The Messiah is a "sign of contradiction" (*sémeion anti legómenon*), that is, the cause of "the fall" and "the resurrection" of "many." The contradiction stems from the double effect that the Redemption, dependent on their dispositions, provokes in men: the fall of those who reject it; the resurrection of those who accept it. Simeon did not say of which there would be more, those who would perish or those who would be saved. He used the same term—"many"—in referring to both.

How is such a "sign of contradiction" to be explained? The explanation is located in the fact of human liberty. The Redemption brought about by Christ does not work *automatically* without man's free consent. Jesus wants to

---

27 "It is a question of the only note of suffering in all of Luke's account of the infancy," notes Poppi, *Sinossi*, p. 269. See also Ferraro, *I racconti*, p. 165.

28 For the biblical references to Deutero-Isaiah and other books of the Old Testament see the excursus-note of Laurentin, *Truth of Christmas*, pp. 202–203.

save, and does save all those who wish to be saved, those believing in Him, and those accepting Him. Those, on the other hand, who do not want to believe in Him, nor accept Him (here are *"the thoughts of many hearts"*), will perish. For all mankind, then, Jesus is truly the crucial dividing line between eternal ruin and eternal salvation.[29]

"And your own soul a sword shall pierce" (v. 35b).

The "sword" of which St. Luke speaks (*hereb* in Hebrew, *romphaia* in Greek) "was the sword of the Thracians and of other barbarian peoples, much larger than the *makaira,* a small sword or saber."[30] Metaphorically, it could mean *tongue* (Ps 59:8; 64:4), *chastisement* or *ruin* (Ez 5:1–7; 14:17), or the *judgment* of God's word, which is *"more piercing than any two-edged sword"* (Heb 4:12). Which sword is meant in regard to Mary?[31] Whichever it be, we must consider it a weapon that inflicts a fatal wound.[32] The conversation continues immediately with a reference to the soteriological dimension of the redemptive Incarnation of the Word and the coredemptive Maternity of the Virgin Mary. The suffering of the Redeemer Son is described as a "*sign of contradiction,*" involving the direct "conflict" with anyone refusing and rejecting Him, so crushing such a person: the suffering of the Coredemptrix Mother, instead, is described as a "sword" transpiercing her soul. According to some, if Mary represents Israel, the "division" that the

29 "Christ offers salvation to all," writes Pietrafesa, "but does not impose it. The Christian message is not an imposition, but a free choice. Man finds himself with a choice: to believe such a message or to refuse it. The *yes* to Christ is equivalent to salvation, the *no* to perdition" (*La Madonna nella Rivelazione*, p. 232). Cf. also Nicolas, *La Vergine Maria*, p. 272; Ernst, *Il Vangelo secondo Luca*, p. 160.

30 Landucci, *Maria SS. nel Vangelo*, p. 152.

31 An orderly, complete synthesis of the various answers given this question is that by S. Garofalo, "Tuam ipsius animam pertransibit gladius" (Lc. 2:35), in *Maria in Sacra Scriptura*, vol. 4, pp. 175–181.

32 "The sword piercing the soul can directly signify a fatal suffering" (ibid., p. 176).

"sign of contradiction" would bring to pass in Israel, would also pass through the soul of Mary.[33] Better grounded, according to others, is the view that finds it primarily in the affliction that was Jesus' death, an affliction that would pierce Mary's soul, as recorded in the passage of John: *"They shall look on him whom they pierced"* (Jn 19:37).[34] A better balance is found in considering the two explanations as complementary to one another. For as Laurentin says, "it seems conformable to the very nature of the facts and to the tradition of the Fathers that Mary was wounded by the sufferings of Christ and by the divisions of her people."

Furthermore, one must remember that, if we view the salvific plan of God in its entirety, all the sufferings of Mary, from their very inception, have a coredemptive value by virtue of her association with the Redeemer.[35]

> The sufferings of our Lady are not simply an aspect of the drama of Jesus' passion and death, but are inherent in the very mission of Coredemptrix, which officially began at the Annunciation, and continued during the anxieties of her spouse, Joseph, at the birth of Jesus in Bethlehem and throughout her life. Simeon enlightened our Lady about the sorrowful mission as Mother of the Lord contradicted throughout every stage of his earthly existence.[36]

We can consider the suffering that pierced Mary because of the opposition of the scribes and Pharisees, because of

---

33 So states P. Benoît, "Et toi même, un glaive te transpercera l'âme (Lc. 2:35)," *The Catholic Biblical Quarterly* 25 (1963): 251–267, and *Exégèse et théologie*, vol. 3 (Paris, 1968), pp. 216–227.

34 So claims A. Feuillet, "Le jugement messianique et la Vierge Marie dans la prophetic de Siméon (Lc. 2:35)," in *Studia Mediaevalia*, Mélanges C. Balic (Rome, 1971), pp. 423–447; *Jesus and His Mother*, pp. 48–50; 112–114 (in original French ed.: pp. 61–64, 122–124).

35 Laurentin, *Truth of Christmas*, Ital. ed.: p. 281; see also Eng. ed.: pp. 79–80. The same author (p. 291) links the sorrows of the "sword" predicted by Simeon with those of the loss of Jesus (2:48), the latter a prefiguring of the Passion and death on Calvary with Mary at the foot of the Cross (Jn 19:25, 34, 37). Cf. Ernst, *Il Vangelo secondo Luca*, pp. 160–161.

36 Pietrafesa, *La Madonna nella Rivelazione*, p. 234. Cf. *The Navarre Bible. St. Luke's Gospel*, p. 58.

the open rejection of the Savior on the part of many who will thus bring ruin on themselves. This sword, to penetrate ever more deeply, eventually transfixed her soul at the foot of the Cross, when another lance would transfix the very heart of Christ (Jn 19:34).[37]

Truly profound, therefore, is the object of faith in the words addressed by Simeon to Mary. Pope John Paul II rightly wrote in his encyclical *Redemptoris Mater* that

> Simeon's words seem like a *second annunciation to Mary,* since they tell her of the actual historical dimension in which her son is to accomplish his mission, namely, in misunderstanding and sorrow. While this announcement on the one hand confirms her faith in the accomplishment of the divine promises of salvation; on the other hand, it also reveals to her that she will have to live her obedience of faith in suffering at the side of the suffering Savior, and that her Motherhood will be mysterious and sorrowful.[38]

In conclusion, we can say with Nicolas: "This mystery is one of the most sublime of our Faith. It renews the mystery of the Incarnation; it anticipates that of the Redemption; and unites them in a most majestic ceremony."[39]

> The important and delicate problematic of Marian Coredemption is perfectly evident in the prophecy of the holy old man Simeon, in the verse about the *'sword'* piercing the soul of Mary. This prophecy of the *'sword'* has in fact been defined as 'the great prophecy of the Coredemption.'[40] Leal has written that the expression 'A sword will pierce your

37 Not only that, but this "association," Nicolas points out, "is not limited to the life and death of Jesus. Mary... never ceased to be the companion sharing the contradictions of her Son endured from all peoples and in all successive ages. All the heresies which wounded her Son, pierced the Mother. They were never separated, whether when affirmed or when denied, whether when blessed or when blasphemed. This is fact, as certain as the prophecy is precise" (*La Vergine Maria*, pp. 276–277).

38 *Redemptoris Mater*, no. 16.

39 Nicolas, *La Vergine Maria*, p. 258.

40 R. Rabanos, *La Corredención de Maria en la Sagrada Escritura*, in *Estudios Marianos* 2 (1943) 49.

soul,' has 'a great Mariological importance. The suffering here foretold to Mary is not the generic suffering of any mother in the face of opposition to her child, but one particular and proper to Mary. The incorporation of the faith of the Mother with that of the Son appears so stressed in this verse that it cannot be explained except with the theology of the Coredemption and with recourse to the text of Jn 2:4 and 19:25–27.'[41]

According to K. H. Schelkle, precisely by virtue of this '*sword*' Mary is linked to the Redeemer Son 'as Mother and Coredemptrix.'[42] Father Testa, against those who would interpret the '*sword*' as a doubt of faith on Mary's part, writes that to the contrary Mary Most Holy accepted that '*sword*' 'becoming thus Coredemptrix with the Redeemer.'[43] Fr. Pietrafesa, too, has written that the sufferings of Mary Most Holy, symbolized by the '*sword*' 'are intrinsic to the very mission of the Coredemptrix which officially initiated at the Annunciation, continues... throughout the entire course of her life. Simeon enlightens Our Lady concerning her sorrowful mission precisely as Mother of the Contradicted One in every stage of His earthly journey.'[44]

Since the publications of A. Serra,[45] the most recent extensive biblical study of this celebrated birth of Luke 2:35 by Fr. Settimio M. Manelli[46] has appeared in the series *Bibliotheca*

---

41 J. Leal, *Vangelo secondo Luca*, Rome 1972, pp. 152–153.

42 K. H. Schelkle, *La Madre del Salvatore. La figura di Maria nel Nuovo Testamento*, Rome 1985, p. 70 [Original German: *Die Mutter des Erlösers, Ihre biblische Gestalt*, Dusseldorf 1958].

43 E. Testa, *Maria Terra Vergine*, Jerusalem 1985, vol. 1, p. 35.

44 P. Pietrafesa, *La Madonna nella Rivelazione*, Naples 1970, p. 234.

45 A. Serra, "La profezia di Simeone (Lc 2, 34–35) nella tradizione greco-latina dei secoli II-XVI. Contenuti e proposte," *Marianum* 60 (1998) 239–384; "La 'spada': simbolo della Parola di Dio, nell'Antico Testamento biblico-giudaico e nel Nuovo Testamento," *Marianum* 63 (2001) 18–89; "È anche a te una spada trapasserà l'anima.' Lc 2, 35 alla luce dell'antica tradizione giudaico-cristiana," *Marianum* 64 (2002) 51–111; *"E anche a te una spada trafiggerà l'anima: (Lc 2, 35). Scrittura e Tradizione a confronto*, in E. M. Toniolo, *L'ermeneutica contemporanea e i testi biblico-mariologici. Verifica e proposte*, Rome 2003, pp. 233–324.

46 Settimio M. Manelli, *Maria Corredentrice. "E una spada trapasserà anche la tua stessa anima" (Lc 2, 35)*, Frigento 2003. A part of this study appeared in *Mary at the Foot of the Cross* IV (New Bedford, MA 2004): "The Prophecy of Simeon (Lk 2:34–35) and the Cooperation of Mary in the Salvific Work of Jesus," pp. 71–114.

Corredemptionis B.V. Mariae. The conclusions of this study confirm, we would say definitively, the Mariological sense and soteriological content of the Lucan text: 'the "sword" foretold by Simeon to Mary, whereby she would be united to the mission of her "suffering" Son, thus becomes the most expressive symbol of Mary's maternal cooperation in the Redemption.'[47] In a note the author explains that 'such direct and active collaboration of Mary in the work of Redemption is designated by the term *coredemption*,'[48] a remark approved and supported with references to the life of the Church according to the Fathers and ecclesiastical writers, according to the Roman Liturgy and according to the Magisterium of the Church in the 20th century.[49]

There was also a prophetess, Anna, the daughter of Phanuel, of the tribe of Asher. She was far advanced in years and had lived with her husband seven years from the time in which she was a maiden. Then she remained a widow and now she was eighty-four years old. She never departed from the temple, serving God night and day with fasts and prayers. Having come in at the same hour, she also began to praise God and speak of the child to all that looked for the redemption of Israel (vv. Lk 2:36–38).

St. Luke shows himself to be well-informed about this elderly *"prophetess Anna"* and as a careful historian provides interesting facts that describe the figure and the work of this *"widow,"* this quite extraordinary woman.[50] We are presented with another charismatic figure, who is matched with Simeon, the "just and pious" old man. "These two

47 Ibid., p. 176.

48 Ibid., note 342.

49 Ibid., pp. 181–259.

50 "Among the Jews and in the early Church," writes Leonardi, "widows who did not remarry out of fidelity to a deceased husband and in order to give themselves totally to the Lord and to good works, were held in high esteem. Luke, therefore, proposes her as a model for Christian widows" (*L'Infanzia di Gesù*, p. 232).

elderly people," writes Laurentin, "embodied the hope of the 'small remnant' that was long awaiting the consolation of Israel (2:25; cf. 2:38). Like the shepherds, they belonged to the small group of the poor of Yahweh."[51]

The gift of the elderly Anna was prophecy in the sense that she *"spoke of the child to all that looked for the redemption of Israel"* (v. 38). Furthermore, her life was truly edifying, entirely spent in serving God, worshiping in the Temple *"night and day with fasts and prayers,"* awaiting the arrival of the Messiah.

Having been enlightened that day, Anna recognized the Child to be the longed-for Messiah, and she drew close to Mary and Joseph in order to praise and bless God, contemplating the Child and speaking of Him to all, like her, who awaited the coming of the Savior of Israel.[52]

After they had performed all things according to the law of the Lord they returned into Galilee to the town of Nazareth. And the child grew and waxed strong, full of wisdom; and the grace of God was in him (vv. 39–40).

At this point, it might seem that St. Luke should have inserted the events described by St. Matthew: that of the arrival and adoration of the Magi come from the East; that of the flight of the Holy Family into Egypt; and that of the massacre of the Innocents of Bethlehem. It is perfectly plausible, however, that he might have wanted to place

---

51 LAURENTIN, *Truth of Christmas*, Ital. ed.: p. 176. The abundance of biographical details concerning this prophetess Anna clearly proves, notes G. Ferraro, that "Luke did not write as a composer of legends adjusted to pre-existing literary models, but on the basis of factual tradition" (*I racconti*, p. 165). According to Poppi, the figure of the prophetess Anna confirms that "Luke was always attentive to the feminine presence in the course of his Gospel" (*Sinossi*, p. 269).

52 Laurentin remarks that for the prophetess Anna, in Luke's text, "She is not mentioned as having physical conjunction with the child as Simeon did," and that she "is called 'prophetess,' without her prophecy being specified" (*Truth of Christmas*, p. 204).

certain limits on the structure of his Gospel, leaving to St. Matthew the description of these other events.

The conclusion, then, is a literary device, having a final closing verse that recalls the closing verse of the account of the Baptist's birth (1:80).

The termination of this very important event of the presentation in the Temple marks the point when the Holy Family moves from the "city of David" (Bethlehem) to a poor, unknown village of Galilee (Nazareth). "Just as at the birth of Jesus, there was the passage from glory (2:9) to the lowliness of the manger (2:16), so here there is the passage from the temple of Jerusalem to this discredited locality."[53] And here at Nazareth, the child Jesus was to grow under the maternal care of Mary and with the work of St. Joseph; He was to grow as a man in whom *"dwells all the fullness of the Godhead bodily,"* (Col 2:9). "We find ourselves in the presence of the mystery of a real, authentic man who is identified as the Son of Mary and the Son of the Most High, the Son of man and the Holy One of God."[54]

---

53 LAURENTIN, *Truth of Christmas*, Ital. ed.: p. 289.

54 FERRARO, *I racconti*, p. 149.

16
The Magi in Adoration

Matthew 2:1–12

The adoration offered by the "Magi" to the child Jesus is one of the most significant episodes in the history of the mystery of salvation, a salvation that the Incarnation is intended to accomplish on earth. The plain meaning of the episode centers on the universal call of all men to salvation through Christ. Beyond the closed salvific perspective of the Chosen People of old, there now appear clearly delineated the roots of Christian universalism, already given expression by the old man Simeon when he called the Messiah *"light to illumine the nations"* (Lk 2:32).

As with other episodes in this history, so here certain exegetes do not consider this event as a real, historical fact, but only a "theological construction" of St. Matthew, a "fiction" to make the biblical references of the Old Testament, particularly Psalm 71 (72) about kings come from the East to adore the Messiah, offering Him gold and incense, seem realistic[1] Laurentin, however, rebuts this point of view quite effectively:

> *Matthew clearly does not present the wise men as kings,* in the style of such biblical models; and these texts say nothing at all about myrrh. Thus they do not 'create' the narrative. It is the event which suggests the biblical allusion, without extrapolation or exaggeration. Soares Prabhu, a renowned

[1] A. Ory states plainly: "Just like all the other narratives of the infancy, this one also is considered by some exegetes to be legendary. The reason is always the same: a prejudice. In fact, they go so far as to say that the narrative concerning the Magi is legendary, because it is a narrative about Jesus' infancy! The evangelists, not having on hand materials worthy of credibility in speaking of Jesus' infancy, made recourse to their fantasy, with the help of Jewish practice" (*Riscoprire la verità*, p. 91).

> expert in the use of the historical–critical method, who pushed the method to the limit of its possibilities in seeking to explain this text through other texts, considers that this narrative cannot be explained in this way. A factual tradition seems the most probable source to him: a narrative usually stems from an event, from a fact, and not from a fictitious projection.[2]

A. Ory reaches the same conclusion with his "functional exegesis." Characteristic of this method is the so-called "reasonable test,"[3] a way of confirming that the historicity of the episode of the Magi is well-founded, in view of the closed Jewish mentality and rigid nationalism of the Evangelist Matthew:

> The analysis of the content of the narratives of the birth at Bethlehem teaches us that Matthew did not invent anything. In view of his closed nationalism, he would seem even less capable of inventing a narrative concerning Jesus' birth at Bethlehem and the homage offered by the Magi. Only one explanation is possible: his great respect for the truth of the facts. Being faithful to reality clearly prevailed over his closed nationalism.[4]

---

2 Laurentin, *Truth of Christmas*, p. 369; Ital. ed.: p. 487. Stramare states that "the Gospel episode recounted in Mt. 2:1–12 is as well known in the liturgical cycle by reason of the 'mystery' contained in it, celebrated as 'the solemnity of the Epiphany of the Lord,' as it is problematic in regard to its component elements, such as the place of birth of the Child Jesus, the prophetic citation, the identity of place of origin of the Magi, the nature and time of the star": T. Stramare, *Vangelo dei misteri della vita nascosta di Gesù*, Bornato in Franciacorta, 1997, p. 218; on the entire episode see pp. 209–264.

3 Ory, *Riscoprine la verità*, pp. 91–96.

4 Ibid., p. 95. Severiano del Paramo states that the "historicity" of this episode "is sufficiently proved by the accuracy of the circumstances described by the Evangelist and above all by universal Christian tradition, which we find documented, already in the early ages of the Church, in the pictures of the Catacombs, in particular in the famous Greek Chapel of Saint Priscilla" (*Vangelo secondo Matteo*, pp. 55–56). See also M. Varón Varón, *op. cit.*, p. 111. Stramare writes that "what Matthew reports is plausible and that therefore there is no justification for seeking its source in Haggidic models, or in historic parallels, or in prophetic presuppositions of the Old Testament": *op. cit.*, p. 237; in a note the author refers to studies of C. Clemen and G. Vermes.

When Jesus was born in Bethlehem of Judah, in the days of King Herod, behold, there came wise men from the East to Jerusalem, saying: "Where is he that is born King of the Jews? For we have seen his star in the east, and are come to adore him." And King Herod hearing this was troubled, and all Jerusalem with him (vv. 1–3).

From the East (or more precisely from the Levant: *anatolôn*), came some Magi to Jerusalem in search of the *"newborn King of the Jews,"* to adore Him.

Who were these Magi? In a brief note, A. Poppi responds thus:

> The *magi* remain mysterious dignitaries. Their number, profession and place of origin are unknown. In the Medo–Persian world there existed a noble priestly caste that dedicated itself to the study of astrology, divination, and the sacred sciences. Herodotus remembered them as interpreters of dreams. Later magi were considered as similar to magicians and swindling charlatans. Matthew held them in great veneration.[5]

The Magi saw *"the star in the east"* of the new King of the Jews.[6] They followed its trajectory and thus arrived in Jerusalem.[7] However, having come into the city, they no

---

5 Poppi, *Sinossi*, p. 30. Cf. Paul, *Secondo San Matteo*, pp. 117ff. On the place of origin of the *Magi*, cf. T. Stramare, *op. cit.*, pp. 232–234. Poppi writes that "as place of origin Persia has been proposed, by others Babylon, or even Arabia, the Syrian desert or Transjordan. Their place of origin remains uncertain" (*Sinossi*, p. 30).

6 That St. Matthew may have wanted to make a reference to the messianic "star" of which the prophecy of Balaam speaks (Num 24:10), seems uncertain, given that "the contacts (terms and themes) could hardly be more tenuous—consisting solely in the single root *anatellô*, meaning the Orient, the East or the rising of a star": so writes Laurentin, who concludes saying that "it is not necessary that the mention of 'star' had any connection to Balaam" (*Truth of Christmas*, p. 395), though other exegetes think differently: cf. T. Stramare, *op. cit.*, pp. 237–243.

7 For Laurentin (who cites Leon–Dufour) "that some wise men may have come in search of a King, relying on the stars ... is *not absolutely impossible* since, about the year 70, a magus (called Tiridate) came to adore Nero" (*Truth of Christmas*, p. 369). It is instructive to read the realistic comments of the same author on modern-day usage of astrology, particularly

longer knew in which direction to go. They must have been surprised or troubled to find in that place a people that was not celebrating at all the birth of the new *"King of the Jews,"* or perhaps they must have thought that that city was not the birthplace of the newborn sovereign. In any case, they wisely asked for information: *"Where is he that is born king of the Jews?"* And with this question, Leonardi notes, "they unwittingly became for Herod and for Jerusalem sources of information about the salvific plan of God."[8]

This question was addressed or was brought to King Herod, who was entirely unaware of any such happening. For this reason *"he was troubled,"* nor could he have remained undisturbed by the news about the birth of a direct rival. Furthermore, *"all Jerusalem"* as well was perturbed, surely a strange reaction in the light of the millenary expectation of a Messiah in the history of the Chosen People. Still, it is quite plausible that the people of Jerusalem, well aware of Herod's cruelty, upon hearing this news began rather to fear some other possible massacre on the king's part to combat this new rival. The horrible memory of how King Herod had, for dynastic considerations, strangled his two sons, Alexander and Aristobul (and later would put another son, Antipater, to death), was still fresh.[9] Ruotolo writes: "The Gospel expressly says that *Herod was troubled and all Jerusalem with him*; therefore, not trepidation over the announcement of the newborn King, but a great fear of new, oppressive acts by the tyrant and of painful

---

horoscopes (ibid., pp. 394–396, with n. 11; Ital. ed.: pp. 524–526, with notes 10–11).

8 Leonardi, *L'Infanzia di Gesù*, pp. 72–73. On the Magi's knowledge of the prophecy of the Messiah awaited by the Jews, see T. Stramare, *op. cit.*, p. 244.

9 Cf. Ibid., p. 72; Laurentin, *Truth of Christmas*, p. 372; Ital. ed.: pp. 490–491. This last author points out that the "perturbation" of Jerusalem "fits well within the perspective of Matthew, for whom 'Jerusalem kills the prophets' (23:37; cf. Lk 13:34)" (p. 272). Cf. also Lancellotti, *Matteo*, p. 47; Poppi, *Sinossi*, p. 31.

complications from these in this case ranged the people on the side of the perfidious monarch."[10]

And assembling together all the chief priests and scribes of the people, he inquired of them where the Messiah should be born. But they said to him: "In Bethlehem of Judah. For so it is written by the prophet: 'And thou Bethlehem, of the land of Judah, are not the least among the princes of Judah; for out of you shall come forth the captain that shall rule my people of Israel.'"

Then Herod, privately calling the wise men, learned from them the time of the star's appearance, and sending them into Bethlehem, said: "Go and diligently inquire after the child, and when you have found him bring me word again, that I too may come and adore him." Who having heard the king went their way; and behold, the star they had seen in the east went before them until it came and stood over where the child was. And seeing the star they rejoiced with exceeding great joy (vv. 4–10).

Fear moved Herod to assemble *"all the chief priests and scribes of the people"* in order to learn from them the birth place of the Messiah. With this began what Laurentin calls his "antiprogram,"[11] that is, a program in opposition to that of God, who was leading the Magi to the place where they were to offer homage to the Messiah. The "antiprogram" aimed at violent elimination of the newborn *"King of the Jews."* The religious authorities gave Herod the correct

10 D. Ruotolo, *La Sacra Scrittura. Vangelo secondo Matteo* (Naples, 1978), p. 43.

11 Laurentin, *Truth of Christmas*, p. 272. A. Paul speaks of "an antithetical 'dialogue' between Herod and the Magi" (*Secondo San Matteo*, p. 99).

answer regarding the birthplace of the Messiah, citing the text of Micah 5:1: *"In Bethlehem of Judah."*[12]

As regards Bethlehem, land of Jesus' birth, some have raised questions and doubt. Stramare answers these, not with a page of exegesis but one of reflection and evaluation on the basis of that interdisciplinary study which should accompany exegesis itself:

> It is surprising that, notwithstanding the much desired interdisciplinary quality of the various sectors of theology, this quality can hardly be described as operative within the area of exegesis where no aspect of the *'realia'* should be neglected. Such neglect should be rather easy to avoid since geography, topography and archeology are treated in all general introductions to the study of exegesis. From a historical, topographical, archeological standpoint Bethlehem appears as one of the most 'authentic' of Palestine, such that it cannot be considered an object of doubt. It is rather an absolutely certain point of reference, to the great advantage of exegesis of the text. Here we confront both a methodological and scientific paradox. If the axiom: *contra factum non valet ratio*, applies here, it is incomprehensible why preconceptions, simple hypotheses, suppositions, conjectures and ... suggestions, as people like to say today, should be a basis for denying facts.
>
> We know that the experts on the Holy Places are not popularity seekers and that, therefore, they do not arbitrarily classify the numerous Palestinian sanctuaries as 'devotional,' 'apocryphal' and 'authentic.' It suffices to consult specialized literature for documentation.
>
> D. Baldi has collected in an 82 page study the *'Documenta traditionis'* on Bethlehem, beginning with St. Justin Martyr (c. 160). Among these testimonials we cite as representative of all the *Contra Celsum* I, 51 of Origen (c. 248): 'Should

12 In the answer and in the attitude of the priests and scribes, Leonardi notes "the incredulous indifference of people who, considering themselves the authentic, perfect leaders of Israel, did not feel need of a better leader" (*L'Infanzia di Gesù*, p. 79).

anyone not be satisfied with the prophecy of Micah and the history recorded by the disciples of Jesus in the Gospel, and seek further proof to establish the fact that Jesus was born in Bethlehem, he should recall that in Bethlehem can be seen the cave where He was born; and in the cave the cradle, where He was wrapped in swaddling clothes. All this accords with what is written in the Gospel about the beginning of His life. And in that region this is well known, and even among the enemies of the faith it is acknowledged that in this cave was born Him whom the Christians adore and admire, Jesus.'[13]

One might add that the main opponents of this Holy Place as not authentic were not only the 'enemies of the faith,' but Judeo–Christians who made of Bethlehem their place of birth, precisely because the meeting of the Magi with Jesus occurred there.[14]

Having received the answer, Herod *"privately"* called the Magi and enjoined them to speak for two precise reasons: first, in order to obtain more exact information on the time of the star's appearance (on the basis of which he would organize his murderous plan regarding the children born since the star's appearance); and second, in order to encourage them to proceed to Bethlehem and diligently search out the Child, and, after finding Him, to return and inform him so that he too might go and *"adore him."* Deceit and manipulation, hypocrisy and murderous designs advanced the "antiprogram" of Herod. But none of that was perceived by the Magi. Quite the contrary, they departed tranquilly, on the right road to Bethlehem.

---

13 The Latin text of Origen is as follows: *Iam si quis hoc Michaeae vaticinio historiaque in Evangelio a Iesu discipulis scripta minime contentus, ultra quaesierit quidpiam aliud quo persuadeantur Iesum in Bethleem natum esse; is recogitet in Bethleem monstrari spelunca in qua natus est, et in spelunca presepe, ubi est fasciis obvolutus; quae omnia consentanea sunt narratae in Evangelio de ortu eius historiae. Atque hoc in locis illis pervulgatum est atque etiam apud fidei hostes celebratum, in illa spelunca natum esse eum, quem Christiani adorant et admirantur, Iesum.*

14 T. Stramare, *op. cit.*, pp. 220–221.

With the reappearance of the guiding star, however, there was introduced a totally inexplicable factor: the star no longer moved, as it normally would, from east to west, but followed a paradoxical trajectory from north to south. No scientific hypothesis so far advanced in explanation of this phenomenon seems tenable.[15] In fact, the only possible explanation is one along the lines adopted by St. John Chrysostom in his day, that of a *prodigious sign or phenomenon* worked by God.

> We learn from Scripture that this star is in no wise to be categorized as just another of the stars. To my way of thinking, it was not even a star, but rather some invisible *dynamis* (power serving as a sign of God) which took on the appearance of a star. This can be demonstrated considering the route it followed. For we see the sun, the moon, and the other stars travel toward the west, but this star went north to south... It did not have a proper course, but went and stopped where it should as the occasion required, much like the pillar of cloud which appeared to the Jews when they had to move on or set up camp.[16]

And entering into the house, they found the child with Mary his mother. And falling down they adored him. Then, opening their treasures, they offered him gifts: gold, frankincense, and myrrh. And, having received an answer in sleep that they should not return to

---

15 Laurentin writes: "Theories that have multiplied since Kepler, about a super nova or about a conjunction of Jupiter and Saturn are purely gratuitous and speculative" (*Truth of Christmas*, p. 537, n. 13). Paul also adopts as his own the categorical statement of S. Muñoz Iglesias: "One must absolutely reject any identification of this star with any kind of natural phenomenon" (Paul, *Secondo San Matteo*, p. 116). On the fact that the Magi had been guided by the star to the cave of Bethlehem, cf. T. Stramare, *op. cit.*, pp. 244–246 (with references to the study of L. Cignelli–G. C. Bottini, *Le diatesi del verbo nel greco biblico*, Liber Annuus XLIII, Jerusalem 1993).

16 As quoted by Laurentin, *Truth of Christmas*, p. 396.

Herod, they went back another way into their country (vv. 11–12).

Having come to the place where the Holy Family was, the Magi *"round the child with Mary his mother and, falling down, adored him."* It is to be noted, above all, that according to the text the Magi met only the Child and His Mother. There is no mention of St. Joseph. "Knowing the role of the father in antiquity and among the Semitic race, to mention only the mother without the slightest allusion to the father indicates systematic intent to set this woman apart so as to distinguish her from any other."[17]

The meeting itself is particularly significant. Where was Jesus to be found if not in the arms of His Mother? The inseparability of the Mother from the Son in the universal salvific mission is already presented here as something perfectly natural and abiding.

> Joseph does not appear in this picture, just as in 1:16; Mary and Jesus are spoken of and Joseph excluded. The homage of the men come from the East was offered only to Jesus. But next to the King there is the Queen-Mother. The description is beautiful, and early generations of Christians, prior to any division of Christianity, felt its power greatly and immortalized the scene in the frescoes of the catacombs, later in works of sculpture: Mary seated on a throne with the King in her arms. Whoever honors the King makes the Mother happy.[18]

---

17 Gillard, *Che cosa dice*, pp. 88–89. Also Garofalo writes: "It seems that the Evangelist Matthew wanted to put in particular relief the pair Mary–Jesus, by remaining silent about Joseph's presence; he knew that Jesus was born of Mary, but 'without Joseph's having had sexual relations with her'; and perhaps setting apart the Mother and the Child in the narrative serves to accent still more the supernatural character of Mary's maternity" (*La Madonna della Bibbia*, p. 82).

18 M. Galizzi, *Oltre ogni frontiera*, vol. 1, p. 35. Cf. Testa, *Maria terra vergine*, p. 119. Also Varón Varón points out: "It is most significant that the Evangelist, inspired by God, mentioned Mary in this passage about the Magi. Mary, in effect, is inseparable from Jesus in the universal-salvific plan. God has established that all the peoples of the earth who accept the Messianic-salvific call can realize it alone in 'Jesus with Mary, his Mother'"

Ruotolo's insight is a felicitous one: "The Magi, falling down before Jesus, necessarily had to fall down before Mary, and by adoring Him they venerated His most sweet Mother. We can say, without fear of exaggeration, that our bowing down before Jesus includes bowing down before Mary, and, if from her we receive the Redeemer, from her also we receive every grace."[19]

Unlike St. Luke, the Evangelist Matthew did not describe for us the sentiments of the Blessed Virgin at the visit of the Magi; but we can imagine the wonder that must have come over her on that day in the presence of such extraordinary dignitaries come from afar purposely to adore the Child. A fact of this kind immediately and concretely realized the truth of the prophecy of the old man Simeon concerning the Messiah *"light of the nations."* And what must have been Mary's sentiments of wonder at hearing news of the long journey made by the Magi guided by a prodigious star that led them all the way to Bethlehem? Finally, truly great must have been Mary and Joseph's emotion at seeing the Magi prostrate in adoration before the child Jesus. This was the most concrete, exact proof of that universal call to salvation for and of the response by the *pagans* to that call in recognizing, as the Chosen People did not, the Messiah.[20]

(*Sagrada Escritura*, p. 115). Cf. also B. Martelet, *Giuseppe di Nazareth* (Rome, 1980), p. 76.

19 Ruotolo, *Vangelo secondo Matteo*, p. 46. A. Serra finds in 2:11 a hint of the "ecclesial linked with the '*house*' of Bethlehem, a figure of the Church": "Dimensioni ecclesiali della figura di Maria nell'esegesi biblica odierna," in *Maria e la Chiesa oggi* [Rome, 1985], pp. 220–231.

20 Cf. E. Galbiati, "L'adorazione dei Magi (Mt. 2:1–21)," *Bibbia e Oriente* 4 (1962): 20–22. "Led by the star (a sign from God)," writes Laurentin, "they were able to reach the King-Messiah. The foreigners worshipped the Messiah, while Jerusalem, with Herod, is 'disturbed' (Mt 2:3) and did not go to offer him homage" (*Truth of Christmas*, p. 286; Ital. ed.: p. 380). "Since they did not belong to the Jewish nation, they constituted the first fruits of the Gentiles who were to be called to salvation in Christ"; so reads the commentary in *The Navarre Bible. St. Matthew's Gospel*, pp. 36–37.

The offering of gifts is the finishing touch in the scene of the Magi in act of adoration and has the value of an act of royal homage, because the Child, notes Laurentin, "is characterized by the sign of the star, which made him known as King by the Magi."[21] Furthermore, according to tradition, the Magi themselves have been considered and represented as kings. "Is it Matthew's intent to say that this homage," writes Laurentin, "is due to him from earthly kings themselves?... Herod himself acknowledges a duty of adoring the child (2:8)."[22]

The conclusion of this event is linked to a "dream" in which the Magi were warned from on high not to return to Herod in Jerusalem. This "dream" frustrated the clever "antiprogram" of Herod. "His consummate craftiness is confounded.... His great power is thwarted by nocturnal communications from God, and confounded by failure (2:16–17) and death (2:15, 19–20, 22)."[23]

In conclusion, we make our own Leonardi's exhortation to "meditate silently upon the mystery of human response to Jesus, a response from the time of Jesus' infancy more generous among the less gifted than among those who have enjoyed privilege and favor."[24]

21 Laurentin, *Truth of Christmas*, Ital. ed.: p. 376.
22 Ibid.
23 Ibid., p. 284.
24 Leonardi, *L'Infanzia de Gesù*, pp. 79–80.

17

The Flight into Egypt

Matthew 2:13–15

The episodes of the "flight into Egypt" and of the subsequent "slaughter of the Innocents" are closely related to that of the "arrival of the Magi" from the East. These three episodes constitute a historical triptych of events concerning grace and suffering: of light and darkness, of joy and anguish, of love and bloodletting. Already in them is fulfilled, one is permitted to say "to the letter," the prophecy of the venerable old Simeon regarding the Messiah, the "sign of contradiction," the cause of salvation and of ruin for many (Lk 2:34) and of the "sword" that pierces Mary's soul (Lk 2:35).

And after the Magi departed, behold an angel of the Lord appeared in sleep to Joseph, saying: "Arise, take the child and his mother, and fly into Egypt; and remain there until I tell you. For it will come to pass that Herod will seek the child to destroy him."

He arose and took the child and his mother by night and retired into Egypt. And he was there until the death of Herod that it might be fulfilled what the Lord had spoken by the prophet saying: "Out of Egypt have I called my Son" (vv. 13–15).

As soon as the Magi had left, St. Joseph was again advised in a dream by an angel, warning him to flee at once into Egypt with Mary and the little Jesus because *"Herod will seek the child to destroy him."*[1]

Herod is aware he has been tricked by the Magi, without knowing, however, how this had been done. But the deception irks him even more, inflaming in him that bloodthirsty ferocity which drives him to implement a murderous plan directed not only against the Child of Bethlehem, the *"newborn King of the Jews,"* but against all the male children up to two years of age *"in Bethlehem and in all the borders thereof"* (Mt 2:16).

After the arrival of the angel, Joseph and Mary, with the Child, make their way at once on the desert road toward Egypt (a road hundreds of kilometers long, requiring a walk of at least 10 to 12 days to traverse).[2] "This is the fourth time in one year that our Lady is faced with a long journey. The first three (to and from Elizabeth's home and to Bethlehem) the Blessed Virgin undertook joyfully because the events she was living were happy ones. With this one, however, all is dark, sad, uncertain."[3]

---

1 "We learn only now, through a revelation," notes Laurentin, "of Herod's plan. Thus, the opposition between the fervent quest of the wise men and the malevolent quest of Herod is *finally* made clear" (*Truth of Christmas*, p. 275).

2 Roschini, *La vita di Maria*, pp. 207ff.; Severiano del Paramo, *Vangelo secondo Matteo*, pp. 61–62 (he follows U. Holzmeister and A. M. Vitti). "Anyone who has seen those deserts even once," writes Garofalo, "would have no difficulty imagining the fatigue and anxiety of the fugitives of Bethlehem" (*La Madonna della Bibbia*, p. 85).

3 Pietrafesa, *La Madonna nella Rivelazione*, pp. 241–242. In an interesting article, B. Bagatti, O.F.M., has developed in detail this theme of the "flight into Egypt" as a sorrowful trial for the Holy Family: "La fuga in Egitto, prova per la Santa Familia," *Sacra Dottrina* 24 (1979): 531–541. Essentially, as Garofalo remarks, "Mary must believe that the flight ordered by the angel is not the defeat of the Son of God, but rather a new event to keep in her heart and to meditate upon, comparing it with the others in order to clarify the mystery. The sword predicted by Simeon was not long in coming to deal its first blows" (*La Madonna della Bibbia*, pp. 84–85). "Only a few hours earlier," reflects Merk, "Mary was rejoicing, in serene beatitude, over the homage which the heavenly Father had bestowed on his Son by those adorers come from a distant pagan world, and already the life of this Son of God is threatened in the very land of his birth... Is not this to be the first

Egypt was considered a land of refuge because there was found a very flourishing Jewish community that guaranteed a certain degree of security both in the social environment and for work. The exact place, however, that the Holy Family reached and where they made their home is not known.[4] Moreover, it seems almost certain that the Holy Family did not stay in Egypt a very long time. The probable minimum stay was a few days and the maximum a few years, a calculation that must take account of the death of Herod, a short time after the birth of Jesus.[5]

The biblical reference that St. Matthew claims is verified in this so dramatic episode of the flight into Egypt is the prophecy of Hosea 11:1. In itself this prophecy refers to Israel in exile, but the Evangelist transposes it to Jesus who is Himself exiled and also freed from exile. *"Jesus recapitulates the history of Israel,* reliving the experiences of the Exodus," writes Poppi.[6] Still more, Jesus is the new *Israel, Son of God,* in the truest and fullest sense. The transposition made by St. Matthew is important above all for expressly identifying the Messiah as true *Son of God.* In fact, Laurentin writes: "The Messiah has already been described as *God–with–us* (Mt 1:23) and as having no other father than God (Mt 1:16, 18–20). The prophecy of Hosea formally states His

---

step on that road of sorrow which Simeon foretold?" (MERK, "La figura di Maria," p. 66).

4 Leonardi writes that "it may have been just beyond Rhinocolura (the present El Arish), half-way between Gaza and Pelusius, which at that time marked the border between Palestine and Egypt" (*L'Infanzia di Gesù*, p. 81). See also ROSCHINI, La vita di Maria, p. 210; GAROFALO, *La Madonna della Bibbia*, p. 85. But for Laurentin these are only "speculations... unfortunately artificial" (*Truth of Christmas*, p. 376).

5 See also LAURENTIN, *Truth of Christmas*, p. 375; G. DANIELI, *I Vangeli dell'infanzia*, vol. 4 (Turin, 1970), p. 184; ROSCHINI, *La vita di Maria*, p. 211 (see n. 6, rich in bibliography).

6 POPPI, *Sinossi*, p. 31 Ruotolo gives this beautiful reflection: "As the Hebrew people, coming out of the slavery of Egypt, became a nation, thus the divine Exile, returning to the promised land, was to form the exiles of the eternal Fatherland, into the holy nation, the Church" (*Vangelo secondo Matteo*, p. 49). See also *The Navarre Bible. St. Matthew's Gospel*, p. 37.

connection with God in a title that describes Him and will cause His execution" (Mt 22:45; 26:64).[7]

Meanwhile, A. Ory is critical of the exegetes who establish a contrived parallel between Jesus and Moses in Egypt to demonstrate that the Evangelist Matthew would make of Jesus a "new Moses." "According to rationalistic exegesis," writes Ory,

> the Evangelist would have invented for Jesus a stay in Egypt in order to suggest that Jesus was the new Moses. Why, then, did Matthew not draw this detail from the biography of Moses instead of from that of Jacob? The work of rationalistic exegesis shows itself defective here. How can it be claimed that Matthew wanted to suggest a 'new Moses'? Why did he not recount that Jesus fled to the country of Midian where Moses actually did take refuge? Why did he not depict Jesus on Mount Sinai or along the Nile? They would have been efficacious details to suggest that Jesus was the Moses of the new covenant.[8]

Danieli had already written, rightly, that for the Evangelists "prophecy has the function of explaining the facts, of placing them on the plane of God's foresight, never of depriving them of their historical content (anything but!)."[9] More logical, in this case, would seem the suggestion of Lancellotti, who sees in St. Joseph a "new Moses" who leads Jesus (Israel) back from Egypt, safe and sound, to Palestine, his land.[10]

Obviously, all the fanciful data described in the apocrypha regarding the journey of the Holy Family into Egypt have nothing to do with the authentic historicity of

---

7 LAURENTIN, *Truth of Christmas*, p. 275. See also Poppi, *Sinossi*, p. 31; GALIZZI, *Oltre ogni frontiera*, vol. 1, pp. 37–38.

8 ORY, *Riscoprire la verità*, pp. 80–81.

9 DANIELI, *I Vangeli dell'infanzia*, p. 171.

10 LANCELLOTTI, *Matteo*, p. 51.

this episode.[11] How simple and convincing, on the other hand, is the account written by the Evangelist! Meditating on this dramatic episode, it is easy to understand how the Holy Family is the most perfect and most consoling model for refugees and emigrants of all times,[12] especially when one considers the sufferings of Mary who had to

> flee with all possible speed; she who was reserved, a virgin, poor, simple, whose whole life had been spent in privacy behind domestic walls, and who knows nothing of Egypt except the persecutions that her ancestors have suffered there and that seem to threaten her as well.... Doubtless, faith must have covered Mary with its shield; she need not have feared under the protection of the heavenly promises. But this shield was invisible, these promises darkened, or rather, these promises held a *sword of sorrow* always suspended over her head.... These very guarantees of salvation were then so many trials of Mary's faith. They left her with all her fears, with her anxieties, and with her sorrows for Jesus.[13]

---

11 See, for example, the extensive note on the Coptic tradition in Testa, *Maria terra vergine*, vol. 2, p. 53, n. 2.

12 See also Leonardi, *L'Infanzia di Gesù*, pp. 83–84; Galizzi, *Oltre ogni frontiera*, vol. 1, p. 36.

13 Nicolas, *La Vergine Maria*, pp. 293, 299. Of interest, also, are the reflections of Varón Varón, (*Sagrada Escritura*, pp. 115–117) on the happy connection between Mary's stay in Egypt, in the midst of the Arabs, and the particular veneration which the Moslems have from earliest times, bestowed on Mary, in one "of the most beautiful and impressive chapters of the Koran, the sacred book of the Mohammedans" (ibid., p. 116).

18

The Slaughter of the Innocents

Matthew 2:16–18

Herod implemented his plan to slaughter the children of the Bethlehem neighborhood two years old or younger in accord with an "antiprogram" outlined and developed once he realized he had been duped by the Magi. He was quite unable to abstain from securing the solidity of his throne at any cost, however much blood might be shed.[1]

In this one can verify how Jesus, in the historical events and human circumstances of His birth and infancy, really recapitulates the old Israel with its past prophetically projected on the Messiah–Redeemer. St. Matthew, in fact, sets this forth in its full *Christological* sense. In particulars the two dramatic events of the "flight into Egypt" and the "slaughter of the innocents" concretely confirm that "Jesus relives the two most tragic events of the people of Israel; the slavery in Egypt and the deportation into Babylonia. But as God has intervened to free his people, so now he frees his own Son from the plotting of Herod."[2]

Then Herod, perceiving that he had been tricked by the Magi, was exceedingly angry; and he sent and slew all the boys in Bethlehem and all the neighborhood who

---

1 In support of the historicity of this event of the "slaughter of the innocents," see the exemplary study of R. T. France, "Herod and the Children of Bethlehem," *Novum Testamentum* 21 (1979): 98–120; a study (shared and synthesized by Laurentin, *Truth of Christmas*, pp. 370–374) that reproves those who seek to deny the historicity of the "slaughter of the innocents," so reducing sacred Scripture to the status of a "source of legendary constructions" (*theologoumena*) (ibid., p. 371).

2 Poppi, *Sinossi*, p. 32.

were two years old or under, according to the time that he had carefully ascertained from the Magi (v. 16).

Herod was already accurately informed by the Magi regarding the time of the appearance of the "star" (Mt 2:7) and now he calculates with wide margins for error so that this, his latest rival, the *"newborn king of the Jews,"* may not escape death.[3]

How many children were killed? It does not seem likely that the number exceeded thirty, given the smallness of the region of Bethlehem, which counted fewer than two thousand inhabitants.[4]

The fundamental fact, however, is that this phase of Herod's cruel "antiprogram" also fails miserably without achieving its end. Herod is again "tricked by God." A dream occasions the departure of Jesus. The Messiah does not die; it is Herod who dies (Mt 2:15.19.20.22; note the emphasis on this point). Jesus is being saved for a different death, which will be related at the end of the Gospel."[5]

Humanly speaking, it would certainly seem incomprehensible that the newborn Son of God should have to save Himself by this "flight" into a foreign country, carried by two poor, defenseless creatures such as Mary and

3 "The most noted of his killings," Laurentin points out, "*are dated during Herod's final years, precisely around the time of Jesus' birth*, in frantic reaction to a prediction that his dynasty would lose the throne" (*Truth of Christmas*, p. 372). In a brief description, Garafolo has summarized well the frightening sequence of crimes ordered by the ferocious, bloodthirsty Herod (*La Madonna della Bibbia*, pp. 86–87).

4 Leonardi explains the matter in this way: "Bethlehem with its environs may have had around two thousand inhabitants. At that time the annual birthrate was around thirty children of both sexes for every thousand inhabitants; therefore, in two years these would be sixty male children. Half of these died due to the infant mortality rate then; about thirty of them remained" (*L'Infanzia di Gesù*, p. 85). See DEL PARAMO, *Vangelo secondo Matteo*, pp. 63–64 (of interest is n. 22, where the exegetes in favor of this opinion and those of other opinions are cited).

5 LAURENTIN, *Truth of Christmas*, p. 76. Regarding Herod's horrible death, one may read the frightening description of the historian FLAVIUS JOSEPHUS, *Antiquities of the Jews*, XVII, 6:5.

Joseph. Then, what is even more sorrowful is the realization of the innocent blood poured out with the slaughter of the children of Bethlehem for the sake of Christ. The design of God, His salvific plan, has its cost in sorrow and bloodshed. All this cannot be denied, it is true. But it is precisely this that is and will be the most real proof that Jesus is the *"sign of contradiction, the cause of ruin and of salvation for many,"* and that Mary is to be pierced with a *"sword"* of sorrow, in order that *"the thoughts of many hearts"* may come to light. The Word of God guides and governs events by His sovereign control and confirmation.[6]

Then was fulfilled what was spoken through Jeremiah the prophet, saying: "A voice was heard in Ramah, weeping and loud lamentation; Rachel weeping for her children, and she would not be comforted, because they are no more" (vv. 17–18).

For this tragic event as well, St. Matthew refers to a biblical text from the Old Testament. It is a text that resounds mournfully with wailing over the death of the babes of Bethlehem: *"A voice was heard on high of lamentation, of mourning and weeping..."* (Jer 31:15). Why the choice of this biblical passage on the part of St. Matthew? Above all because the description of the mourning of Rachel over the children of Israel (who were deported to Babylon by Nebuchadnezzar after having gathered them at Ramah, a few kilometers from Jerusalem) is an anticipation or figure of the tragedy of the little innocents massacred at Bethlehem. "The doubly prophetic expression is quite

6 "Superficially," writes Pietrafesa, "brute force comes out looking like the winner because the Holy Family is forced to flee from Bethlehem; but the Child Jesus does not fall into the clutches of the crowned tyrant. In reality, it is God who wins, it is He who directs the course of events" (*La Madonna nella Rivelazione*, p. 243). See also Nicolas, *La Vergine Maria*, pp. 280–302 (pages rich in solid apologetic insights).

beautiful," writes Ruotolo, "because it announces a mourning so grave and profound as to provoke the grief of the deceased Rachel and to make her very bones tremble."[7]

In this regard, Leonardi appropriately writes:

> Matthew believes that as Rachel from her tomb once wept over her deported children, so now she weeps over the nearby sons of her spouse Jacob, cruelly massacred because of Christ, and implores of God, by virtue of their sacrifice, salvation for all her strayed Hebrew children. The prediction, apparently gloomy, is, in Jeremiah, part of an oracle of salvation (cf. Jer 30–31) that announces the end of, and the deliverance from the Babylonian slavery. [8]

According to A. Ory, this oracle quoted by St. Matthew serves to guarantee the historical reality of the fact of the slaughter at Bethlehem against those who, on the contrary, want to consider it merely a legend built upon such biblical references. In fact, this oracle of Jeremiah is, in itself;

> neither prophetic nor historical, but symbolic. It does not consider a fact which really occurred, rather it is a kind of historically based allegory. Jeremiah has, in fact, taken as a symbol of the sorrow of mothers who saw the deportation of the Jewish youths to Babylon, the grief of Rachel, the wife of Jacob, who lived a thousand years before. How can one create, from this text, a legend on the massacre of the innocent children? Nothing seems to invite such a procedure here. [9]

---

7 RUOTOLO, *Vangelo secondo Matteo*, p. 49.

8 LEONARDI, *L'Infanzia di Gesù*, p. 88. See also LANCELLOTTI, *Matteo*, pp. 55–52, n. 18. Regarding the content of "hope" or "salvation" that the oracle of Jeremiah brings with it, Galizzi rightly notes: "In the text of Matthew, however, there is no sign of hope. That which took place at Bethlehem is for him a symbol of a much vaster reality. The children of Israel have been killed or dispersed; as a nation they are no longer. Jerusalem has been destroyed" (*Oltre ogni frontiera*, vol. 1, p. 39). Now, Jesus is the new and true "Israel" and together with His Mother and St. Joseph, He begins the new and true "People of God."

9 ORY, *Riscoprire la verità* p. 78.

That which once again appears evident in Matthew's method of citing the Old Testament is the fact that he does not begin with a prophecy in order to arrive at the narrated event, but on the contrary he begins with a historical event in order to arrive at a prophecy that confirms it. "He begins with a fact," Ory continues, "and then seeks to legitimize it with the oracle of a prophet, if not with a prediction, at least with a comment. This is proof in favor of the hypothesis that reflections on a biblical citation regard historical material." [10]

What must not have been the sorrow of Mary, the Mother of the child Jesus, in the face of so tragic a historical event as the cruel slaughter of the babes of Bethlehem? With what violence must not the *"sword"* of Simeon have pierced her soul by means of this horrible carnage of innocent children? "What a trial for her heart this sword was," Nicolas comments emphatically, "or rather, these thousands of swords of Herod raised over her body strike it with as many horrors as there are victims they claim!"[11]

---

[10] Ibid., p. 80. This also explains why biblical citations are not always fully adapted to the historical event. And so, "Jeremiah's citation of Rachel who mourns her children," Ory points out, "regards adults sent into exile to Babylon. This fact does not serve as the basis for constructing a fictional massacre of children, two years and under (Mt 2:16). The other hypothesis is more logical. Matthew, in his narration, begins with the fact that the children under two years have been slaughtered in the region of Bethlehem. He sought, once again, a citation from a prophet to legitimize his candidate, Jesus, in the minds of the Jewish scribes who claimed that he was in disaccord with the prophecies. Successful or not, the attempt was made.... For the massacre of the Innocents in the region of Bethlehem, he found a comment that spoke of weeping, of lamenting and of Ramah which is found precisely in the environs of Bethlehem. He had to accept other particulars as well (adults who were deported to Babylon) because the text cited was not a Messianic prediction, but simply the word of a prophet. It is this that indicates that these evangelical accounts are historical and not legendary" (ibid., p. 81).

[11] Nicolas, *La Vergine Maria*, p. 297.

19

Return to Nazareth

Matthew 2:19–23

Yet another dream of St. Joseph, head and guide of the Holy Family: a dream of guidance.[1] It indicates the route to follow as traced out in the salvific plan the Savior and His Mother are to implement by overcoming obstacles and enduring trials, all useful in the work of universal Redemption. Some students of St. Joseph's dreams have pointed out that their content is intended for the Mother and her Child.[2] St. Joseph is the "channel" for Jesus and Mary to know how to undertake a journey that God himself marks out according to the sense willed by Him. And in practice, our Lady submits herself and her Child in everything to the directives that come from and are transmitted by St. Joseph: those regarding the flight into Egypt (Mt 2:13–15), the return to Israel (Mt 2:20–21), or the decision to settle at Nazareth (Mt 2:22–23).[3]

When Herod was dead, an angel of the Lord appeared in sleep to Joseph in Egypt, saying: "Arise, take the child and his mother, and go into the land of Israel. For they are dead that sought the life of the child." He arose and

1 The dreams of St. Joseph recorded by Matthew "are also a mediation, that safeguards transcendency," writes Laurentin (*Truth of Christmas*, p. 285). And in ascribing the divine communication to dreams, "Matthew presents the supernatural dimension of the infancy of Christ in the most modest way possible, not resorting to the miraculous, remaining on the common ground of dreams, as opposed to anything spectacular that might shock reason" (ibid., p. 398).

2 Cf. D. C. Arichea, "Matthew 2:13–15, 19–23: Some Pronoun Problems," *Bible Translator* 32 (1981): 243–244.

3 Cf. Pietrafesa, *La Madonna nella Rivelazione*, pp. 245–246.

took the child and his mother and entered the land of Israel (vv. 19–21).

Once Herod was dead, therefore, the *"angel of the Lord,"* as he had already indicated at the moment of the "flight" from Bethlehem (2:13), advises Joseph in a dream, telling him to return to the land of Israel with *"the child and his mother."* The clever, cruel "antiprogram" of Herod, having failed miserably to attain its goal of liquidating the *"newborn King of the Jews,"* ceased definitively with the death of the tyrant. The way to return to Judea, therefore, was open, free of those mortal dangers that so sorely tried the hearts of Mary and Joseph while safeguarding the life of the little Jesus.[4] Without delay, then, St. Joseph *"took the child and his mother and entered into the country of Israel"* (2:21). The long return route involved a journey just as wearisome as that during the "flight"; but surely it was much calmer and hope-filled, now, at the reentry into the land of their own fathers.

An important, oft-repeated particular is not to be overlooked. St. Matthew frequently speaks of the *"child and his mother,"* always united, as it were inseparably linked (2:10.13.14.19.21). This unity of *"the child and his mother"* sets in high relief, both the maternity that forges that indestructible bond between mother and son, and—especially in the Gospel—the close association between *"the child and his mother,"* between Jesus and Mary, in fulfilling the mission to redeem all mankind. *Lumen Gentium* may be read as a commentary on St. Matthew's expression when it affirms: "This union of the Mother with the Son in the

4 St. Matthew speaks in the plural ("they are dead"), because "it is not improbable that the Evangelist associates the hostility of the leaders of the Jews with the persecution of Herod against Jesus, and therefore uses the plural" (Poppi, *Sinossi*, p. 33).

work of salvation is made manifest from the time of Christ's virginal conception up to His death" (no. 57).

But hearing that Archelaus reigned in Judea in place of his father Herod, he was afraid to go there. Being warned in a dream, then, he retired into the region of Galilee. And coming he dwelt in a town called Nazareth, that it might be fulfilled what was said by the prophets: "He will be called a Nazarene" (vv. 22–23).

While still traveling toward Judea, however, St. Joseph hears troubling news. Herod "the Great" was dead, of course, but his son Archelaus, not at all unlike his father in cruelty and ferocity, had become ethnarch of Judea.[5] At this report, St. Joseph was fearful that, returning to Bethlehem, the life of the Child could still be endangered because of Archelaus, should he ever come to learn that the child Jesus had escaped the slaughter of Bethlehem. What was he to do now? Where could he go to find dwelling for his family? A subsequent, last dream freed St. Joseph of every perplexity. This time, the angel indicated that he should establish the family residence at Nazareth of Galilee. For the Evangelist St. Matthew that occurred not by chance, but that *"it might be fulfilled what was said by the prophets: 'He will be called a Nazarene'"* (2:23).

St. Matthew reconstructs here a prophecy with a generic reference. To which "prophets," in fact, does he refer? On the basis of the most recent studies, it would seem that the most probable biblical text is that of Judges 13:5, where the term *nazarene* stems from *nazir* meaning "consecrated" or "holy": *"The child [Samson] shall be a 'nazir' of God from his mother's womb, he will begin to save Israel."* Starting

[5] On the division of Herod's kingdom among his descendants, see Leonardi, *L'Infanzia di Gesù*, pp. 93–94.

with St. Jerome and citing various scholars (Loisy, McNeil, Schaeder, Schweitzer, Sanders, Lyonnet, Soares Prabhu, Perrot), Laurentin affirms that

> Matthew is thus taking the name of *Nazarene,* which had been given to Jesus because of this town, and giving it relevance in function of the holiness signified by the term *nazir* in Judges 13:5. The procedure may seem strained. But in reality *nazir* in Judges 13 is simply the equivalent of *consecrated...* This would seem to be the citation required not only by the analogy between the announcement to Joseph and the announcement to the parents of Samson, but also by the attraction exerted by the title given to Jesus in the Gospel: '*You* are the holy one of God' (Mk 1:24; Lk 4:34; Jn 6:69)... Confirmation that Judges 13:5 is indeed the passage being referred to in Mt 2:23 is to be seen in the detail that the consecrated child (Samson) 'will begin to save Israel.' The *salvation,* of which Samson was a 'beginning' and a first prefiguration, is completed in Jesus, whose very name means Savior: 'You shall give Him the name of Jesus, because He will save His people from their sins,' Matthew described in 1:21.[6]

According to the "functional exegesis" of Ory, this difficulty in identifying the reference for the citation of St. Matthew is certainly a demonstration of the "historicity" of the fact that Jesus lived at Nazareth:

> Matthew has attempted to illumine Nazareth with a concrete, prophetic citation, of which it had need, but he did not succeed, because he did not find any precise reference.

6 Laurentin, *Truth of Christmas*, pp. 278–279; Ital. ed.: pp. 370–371. See in addition (ibid., pp. 277ff.) the other opinions and solutions. In particular, the reference to Is 4:2–3 may be of relevance: "Now he who is born of Zion... shall be called 'holy'" (ibid., p. 279). Cf. also Poppi, *Sinossi*, p. 33. Regarding the term "prophets" in the plural, adopted by St. Matthew, Laurentin notes that "it is not an objection: because the writers of Joshua, Judges, Samuel and Kings (which followed the book of the 'law,' the Pentateuch), were called the first prophets, which would explain the current expression 'the law arid the prophets'" (*Truth of Christmas*, p. 370). For Ory, St. Matthew speaks "of an oracle of the prophets, in the plural, as if to say that it refers to the spirit, not to the letter of the prophets" (*Riscoprire la verità* p. 79). See also Paul, *Secondo San Matteo*, pp. 167–169.

> He had to content himself with the 'spirit' of the prophets. Here one is not dealing with an isolated case, but a system, a procedure used by Matthew. He begins with a fact and then seeks to legitimize it with the oracle of a prophet.[7]

This termination of the gospel of the infancy of Matthew (and of Luke) in Nazareth, in the scorned Nazareth, because of the threat of death for the Child, makes us understand that "the lowly [Nazarene] origins of Christ take on, for the Evangelists, a meaning analogous to that of his passion."[8]

In conclusion, the term "Nazarene," taken in its philological and prophetic sense and in its historical–geographical context, indicates three things: the geographical origin of Jesus from the town of Nazareth, His particular "consecration" to God, and by anticipation, His poverty and rejection on Calvary. *The Navarre Bible* states: "The term 'nazarene' refers to Jesus' geographic origin, but his critics used it as a term of abuse when he began his mission (Jn 1:46). Even in the time of St. Paul the Jews tried to humiliate the Christians by calling them 'Nazarenes' (Acts 24:5). The poverty and contempt which the Messiah would suffer was foretold by many prophets (Is 53 :2ff.; Jer 11:19; Ps 21)."[9]

And Mary, God's Mother, is always with her "Child," united to Him, today and tomorrow, from Bethlehem to Calvary, inseparable from Him in sharing completely His joy and suffering, His humiliations and scorn, for the sake of the redemptive mission to save mankind.[10]

---

7 Ory, *Riscoprire la verità*, p. 80. *The Navarre Bible. St. Matthew's Gospel*, p. 40, says: "The words 'he shall be called Nazarene' are not found as such in any prophetic text. Rather, they are, as St. Jerome points out, a summary of the prophets' teaching in a short and expressive phrase."

8 Laurentin, *Truth of Christmas*, p. 279.

9 *The Navarre Bible. St. Matthew's Gospel*, p. 39.

10 At the conclusion of St. Matthew's Gospel of the infancy, it seems helpful to quote here the sensible and realistic assessment of Laurentin in support of the "historicity" of the various Matthean accounts of the early infancy

of Jesus, not rarely called into doubt: "As to the attempts to explain these accounts as fiction, they are divergent and contradictory, because they proceed from *a priori* assumptions. Historians (however exacting they may be) never cultivate doubt to this extent when they are not dealing with the Gospel. After a stage of absolute doubt, which has been very helpful in that all possible false trails have been investigated, it is healthy for exegesis to return to a serious *evaluation* and agree to grant a favorable presumption to the qualified witness (in this instance, Matthew), as long as there is no substantive argument to the contrary... We are less likely to stray from the truth if we simply stick to the data of Matthew, in the sobriety they already possess. Anything else too often amounts to empty speculation. One hundred fifty years of divergent and ephemeral hypotheses should be enough to invite caution. What a pity this too often conceals, for the majority of the public, the considerable and authentic advances of exegesis. The general public suffers a peculiar degree of deception in this matter" (*Truth of Christmas*, pp. 375–376, continued on p. 531, n. 16).

20
The Finding of Jesus in the Temple

Luke 2:41–52

The infancy and childhood, the adolescence and youth of Jesus pass unchronicled by the Evangelists. Only one record, only one episode of Jesus' childhood is recounted by St. Luke. It is that concerning the loss and finding of Jesus in the Temple.[1]

This episode is extraordinarily important, above all because it acquaints us with the first words of Jesus, which, notes Ferraro, "represent the high point of the gospel of the infancy," since "in these first words, placed by the Gospel on the lips of Jesus, is contained the theme of all the great revelation of the New Testament: Jesus is the only begotten Son of God."[2]

His parents went every year to Jerusalem at the solemn day of the Passover. When he was twelve years old, they went up to Jerusalem as was their custom. And having

1 Fundamental, for the study of this episode, is the work of R. Laurentin, *Jésus au temple. Mystère de Pâsques et foi de Marie en Luc 2, 48–50* (Paris, 1966). Against the *Formgeschichte* school, which considers this episode, too, a "legend," even if of some value as an "edifying account" (according to R. Bultmann), lauding the eminent piety of Jesus, which during His stay in the Temple would be revealed as superior to the piety of His parents (according to M. Dibelius). Laurentin subtly notes how "that is artificial classification. The episode does not highlight the piety of Jesus at all. Not a word is said about his praying, and the story of his eluding his parents does not have the character of good example for children. It is, rather, a paradoxical scene, which acquires its meaning in the same way as the preceding scenes, as prophecy, an apocalypse (manifestation) and theophany" (*Truth of Christmas*, p. 101).

2 Ferraro, *I racconti*, pp. 172, 182. Ghidelli affirms that in this episode St. Luke "concentrates a marvelous synthesis of his Christology" (*Luca*, p. 105). G. Leonardi notes that this episode "contains very complex historical, sociological, and religious data, confirmed by scientific analysis. Luke, therefore, shows himself notwithstanding his Antiochene origin, well informed about Hebrew custom" (*L'Infanzia di Gesù*, pp. 236–237).

fulfilled the days, when they returned, the child Jesus remained in Jerusalem. And his parents did not know it. And thinking that he was in the company, they came a day's journey and sought him among their relatives and acquaintances. And not finding him, they returned to Jerusalem in search of him (vv. 41–45).

Jesus was twelve years old and was taken to the Temple of Jerusalem for the feast of the Passover. St. Joseph and our Lady went every year to celebrate the Passover at Jerusalem, motivated, as Leonardi defines it,[3] only by their "deep piety." They were not in fact obliged by the law, given the long distance from Nazareth. True, the law obliged one to go to Jerusalem three times a year for the solemnities of the Passover, of Pentecost, and of Tabernacles (Ex 23:14–17; 34:23–24; Dt 16:16–17; 1 Sam 1:7; 2:19), but it obliged only those who, not impeded by any major obstacle, lived within a range of about 30 kilometers (about 18 miles) from Jerusalem (one day's journey). Nazareth, however, was at least a three days' journey from Jerusalem.[4] Mary was not bound, because women were exempted from the obligation. Yet, nonetheless, Mary always accompanied St. Joseph, motivated by piety as well as affection for him.[5] Jesus was not bound, before thirteen years of age, when He became *bar Mitzvah,* that is, "son of precept."[6] "But true piety does not allow itself to be smothered by distinctions defining the exact demarcation between obligation and

3 Leonardi, *L'Infanzia di Gesù*, p. 238.

4 Cf. Garofalo, *Le parole di Maria*, p. 110; Laurentin, *Truth of Christmas*, p. 529, n. 5 (where are also cited the studies of I. H. Marshall and J. A. Fitzmyer).

5 "Either out of piety, or out of love for her husband," says Ceuppens, *De Mariologia Biblica*, p. 169.

6 Cf. E. Testa, O.F.M., *Usi e riti Ebrei Ortodossi* (Jerusalem, 1973), pp. 16–17. See also F. Manns, "Luc 2, 41–50, témoin de la Mitsva de Jesus," *Marianum* 40 (1978): 344–349; P. W. Van Der Horst, "Notes on the Aramaic Background of Luke 2, 41–52," *Journal for the Study of the New Testament* 7 (1980): 61–66.

dispensation, the licit and the illicit. Over and above neat categorizations the Holy Spirit 'breathes where He wills': not contrary to the law, but beyond the law."[7]

Every year, then, Joseph and Mary went to Jerusalem for the Passover, and when Jesus was twelve years old there occurred the episode of the loss, an utterly unexpected surprise for this family so united and harmonious.[8]

During the return from Jerusalem, in fact, after *"a day's journey,"* Mary and Joseph noticed that Jesus was not in the caravan. During the journey, they did not notice His absence because boys could travel as they wished either with their parents or with other relatives and acquaintances (it was otherwise for girls who could travel only in the company of their parents).[9] At the stop for night, they called and searched for Jesus *"among relatives and acquaintances."* He was not there. No one had seen Him. There remained nothing to do but to return to Jerusalem, then, and look for Him there. Mary and Joseph set out to return in anguish of spirit. What had happened to their child? Where could they find Him? "It is impossible to form an idea of the suffering of Mary and Joseph upon the loss of Jesus; one would have to be able to measure the love they had for him."[10]

At Jerusalem, the search was anything but easy, due to the presence of so many pilgrims; and that intensified

---

7 Garofalo, *Le parole di Maria*, p. 110.

8 It is reasonable to believe that Jesus was taken to the Temple even before the age of twelve years, because "it can hardly be supposed," notes Ceuppens, "that Mary and Joseph would leave their only, beloved Son to the care of relatives and acquaintances" (*De Mariologia Biblica*, p. 170). Furthermore, it was advisable to strengthen sons in the observance of the law even before the age of precept: cf. Ferraro, *I racconti*, p. 175.

9 Cf. Garofalo, *Le parole di Maria*, p. 118. "That explains why the absence of Jesus passed unobserved until the end of the first day of the journey, when the families reunited to make camp" (*The Navarre Bible. St. Luke's Gospel*, p. 60).

10 Ruotolo, *Vangelo secondo Luca*, p. 91.

even more the suffering in the hearts of Mary and Joseph. "The crowd made the search more arduous, and the delay unsupportable."[11]

After three days, they found him in the temple, sitting in the midst of the doctors, listening to them and asking them questions. And all that heard him were astonished at his wisdom and answers. Seeing him, they wondered. And his mother said to him: "Son, why have you done so to us? Behold, your father and I have sought you sorrowing" (vv. 46–48).

In the atrium of the Temple, meanwhile, Jesus was in the midst of the doctors of the law who every Saturday and on the major solemnities met with disciples, men, women, and even boys, to expound sacred Scripture according to the question-and-answer method.[12]

This time the doctors found themselves in dialogue with a child from Galilee. He was scarcely twelve, it is true, but He uttered a wisdom so advanced as to amaze the elders themselves, the masters of Israel. Highlighting the superiority of the twelve-year-old Jesus over the very doctors of the Temple would suffice to demonstrate and confirm that Jesus was *Wisdom* incarnate, the *Wisdom of the Father,* capable of initiating immediately and successfully, if so willed by the Father, His messianic work.[13]

---

11 Garofalo, *Le parole di Maria*, p. 120. "The sorrowful hours lived by Mary," comments de Ambrogio, "must have made her think of the sword of which Simeon had spoken" (*San Luca*, p. 76). J. Ernst also writes that "the prophecy of the elderly Simeon: 'and your soul also a sword shall pierce' (v. 35), finds a precise confirmation" (*Il Vangelo secondo Luca*, p. 167).

12 Cf. Leal: "The question and answer format was characteristic of the rabbinic methods" (*Vangelo secondo Luca*, p. 157); Spadafora, *Maria Santissima nella Sacra Scrittura* (Rome, 1963), p. 44; Ferraro, *I racconti*, p. 176.

13 "This first public appearance of Jesus," notes Ceuppens, "revealed His exceptional intelligence and wisdom; His later activities confirmed this revelation, and the crowds of Galilee, on hearing Him, exclaimed: 'Never has a man spoken as this man' (Jn 7:46)" (*De Mariologia Biblica*, p. 172).

Precisely while one of these sessions was in progress in the atrium of the Temple, Mary and Joseph arrived sorrowing on the third day. Imagine Mary's heart relaxing and St. Joseph's sigh of relief on seeing Jesus again! The Evangelist notes that they too *"were astonished"*; and indeed some scholars remark that the "amazement" of the relatives connoted by the Greek verb *explesso* was greater than that of the doctors expressed with the Greek verb *existemi.*[14]

Jesus was there, "sitting in the midst of the doctors listening to them and asking them questions."[15] *On seeing him, Mary's first maternal impulse made her say immediately: "Son." It was the first word spoken with the anxiety and love she had in her heart. With what emotion must she have said it?*[16]

"Why have you done so to us?" continues the Mother, beginning the conversation with her Son, the first known to us. "It is in the name of her Motherhood, in virtue of the authority deriving from it, that Mary asks: *'Why have you done so to us?'*"[17] *Mary's words seem to be words of reproach, or at least of bitter disappointment. And instead, as Laurentin*

Cf. also DE AMBROGIO, *San Luca*, p. 76; LEONARDI, *L'Infanzia di Gesù*, p. 239; ERNST, *Il Vangelo secondo Luca*, p. 168.

14 CEUPPENS, *De Mariologia Biblica*, p. 172.

15 Laurentin notes that "the whole scene has a sapiential quality," and he sets in proper relief the profound connection between Jesus' "Wisdom of the Father" and the "Temple," which is the place where wisdom is preserved (Sir 24:10–12) and taught. Jesus, in fact, during His public life "taught every day in the temple" (Lk 19:47) (LAURENTIN, *Truth of Christmas*, pp. 101, 493, n. 145). See also GHIDELLI, *Luca*, p. 107.

16 Let us not forget, as Garofalo says, that "thanks to her particular gifts of light and grace, Mary loved the God become her Son as no other creature ever could claim to have loved Him. If all the love of all men of all times for Christ could be added together, that love which slowly or rapidly consumed the holocaust of the life of the perfect, it would still not equal the love of Mary for Jesus, a love which spills over in the passionate cry: 'Son!'" (GAROFALO, *Le parole di Maria*, pp. 122–123). Cf. ROSCHINI, *La vita di Maria*, p. 231.

17 GAROFALO, *Le parole di Maria*, p. 123. "That the Mother would question the Son," notes J. Leal, "and also do this in the name of the father, is in part explained by the greater affectivity of women, but also by the central personality of Mary and her very vocation, which is more important than that of St. Joseph" (*Vangelo secondo Luca*, p. 157).

explains well, "Mary's question is asked with authority: the word child (teknon, from *titkô,* to give birth), which here replaces *pais* (2:43), indicates a dependent relationship of a child on the one who gave him birth. Mary, nevertheless, does not utter a formal reproach. She questions Jesus on the cause of his surprising conduct. She simply expresses the fact of this search and this sorrow."[18]

Mary's question to her Son is explained thus in *The Navarre Bible*:

> Ever since the Annunciation our Lady had known that the Child Jesus was God. This faith continuously generated an attitude of generous fidelity throughout the course of her entire life, but there was no reason why it should include detailed knowledge of all the sacrifices that God would have asked of her, nor how Christ would go about His redemptive mission. She would have learned this gradually, contemplating the life of her Son.[19]

"Behold your father and I have sought you sorrowing." Here is the last known reference to St. Joseph, called here by Mary herself "father" of Jesus. And in regard to St. Joseph, it is the most important reference. We already know that his virginal and legal paternity has assured the juridical lineage of Jesus, the Messiah, as "son of David." And in this case also, as in the flight into Egypt, St. Joseph is associated with Mary in suffering for Jesus, bearing the burden of primary responsibility as head of the family. "Thus united he shares

---

18 LAURENTIN, *Truth of Christmas*, p. 212. Garofalo comments that "it would be necessary to have listened to these words from the very lips of Mary to be able to perceive their real value as spoken. The cry of a mother's heart cannot be subject to cold analysis. There vibrates in these few words, not the bitterness of an accusation or the harshness of a reprimand, but a loving lament, a sorrowful wonder" (*Le parole di Maria*, p. 123). See also NICOLAS, *La Vergine Maria*, p. 321; PIETRAFESA, *La Madonna nella Rivelazione*, p. 258; LEAL, *Vangelo secondo Luca*, p. 157.

19 *The Navarre Bible. St. Luke's Gospel*, p. 61.

the mystery of suffering," writes Ferraro.[20] *"Your father and I sorrowing"*: emblematic for us is this sharing of anxiety in the search for Jesus on the part of him who is the virginal spouse of Mary and the legal father of Jesus. His "anxiety" is united to that of Mary—to be linked with the "sword" prophesied by Simeon—and so it too attains coredemptive value in the plan of universal salvation.[21]

In a beautiful synthesis, Ruotolo comments thus on the sorrow of Mary and her words to Jesus:

> All her sorrow was expressed in a few words: she called Him 'son,' and with this she said in effect that she had searched for Him as Mother, and as God's Mother; she asked Him why He had done that, and with this she manifested all the anxieties of her heart and of St. Joseph's; she expressed her immense pain in searching for Him, and with this she expressed the love that had made her maternal anguish and St. Joseph's an agony.[22]

And he said to them: "How is it that you sought me? Did you not know that I must be about my Father's business?" (v. 49)

It is sufficiently clear that Mary's question did not regard the reason for the stay of Jesus in the Temple of Jerusalem, but the reason for His deciding to stay *"without his parents knowing it."* Knowing Jesus' perfect docility, His spirit of complete submission to and conformity with the will of His parents, such a gesture appeared truly inexplicable to

20 Ferraro, *I racconti*, p. 180. The term "sorrowful" (*odynomenoi*, in Greek) signifies "a suffering, and even a torture. The word is used to indicate the torture of the rich man in the flames of Hell (16:24–25)" (Laurentin, *Truth of Christmas*, p. 212). See also Pietrafesa, *La Madonna nella Rivelazione*, p. 258, n. 2.

21 An interesting reflection of B. Gillard shows that Mary and Joseph do not imagine themselves to be still that attached to Jesus "and that they already participate, with that distressing search, in the passion, so permitting Him to enlighten the doctors and not to be enlightened by them" (*Che cosa dice*, p. 59).

22 Ruotolo, *Vangelo secondo Luca*, p. 92.

Mary and to Joseph. This is the explanation the Mother sought of the Son.

The response of the Son, however, is a response laden with "mystery," a response engaging the faith of Mary and of Joseph in prophetic perspective.[23] Jesus, in effect, gives a "theophanic" response, knowingly revealing Himself to be the Son of God the Father, "manifesting his own awareness of his divine sonship."[24]

Almost in opposition to the legal father, called by Mary *"your father,"* the twelve-year-old Jesus speaks instead of another Father—*"my Father"*—of whom He considers Himself to be the Son, thus revealing an exact reference to what the angel Gabriel had said of Him to Mary at the Annunciation, calling Him "Son of the Most High," "Son of God." Leal's insight on this point is basic: "With these words, Jesus shows that He possessed, from the beginning, an awareness of His divine sonship and His divine mission. With these words He also proclaims for the first time that His divine sonship will be an occasion of clear division between fathers and sons (cf. Mk 3:31–35)."[25]

---

23 One should note, with Garofalo, that in the words of Jesus "'You must have known...': an intonation unworthy of a devoted son is not possible; rather it is to be supposed that the voice tone of Jesus had its source in an excess of pained kindliness: 'There was no need to worry.... Why? Did you not know?'" (*Le parole di Maria*, p. 124).

24 Testa, *Maria terra vergine*, vol. 1, p. 18. "No other biblical personage," remarks Leal, "dares to invoke God as '*his* Father' in as emphatic a way" (*Vangelo secondo Luca*, p. 157). See also Nicolas, *La Vergine Maria*, p. 323; Spadafora, *Maria Santissima*, p. 45. Laurentin writes appropriately: "Jesus manifests his consciousness of his divine filiation, declared in the message of the annunciation (1:32 and 35). This constitutes, in the infancy Gospel, a final theophany, for which Christ, having become the subject, is himself the single and distinct actuant. It involves the first words of Christ and his first self-confession on earth. It is no longer the angel nor the Spirit who pronounces the oracle, but Jesus himself" (*Truth of Christmas*, pp. 214–215).

25 Leal, *Vangelo secondo Luca*, p. 157. *The Navarre Bible. St. Luke's Gospel*, p. 61, comments: "His words—his first words to be recorded in the Gospel—clearly show his divine Sonship; and they show his determination to fulfill the will of his Eternal Father."

Consequently, the response of Jesus affirms the prior demands of obedience to *"the Father"* before any other authority, in this as in other situations (cf. Mt 10:28–30). "Jesus vindicates an absolute independence when there is question of fulfilling the will of the Father, who has commanded Him to redeem the world."[26] And Ferraro adds that "here for the first time is revealed and affirmed by Jesus himself that His divine sonship transcends natural ties with His human family."[27]

Finally, the response of Jesus manifests the "prophetic" character of His conduct, since He is called to live in *"his Father's house,"* and not in the house of Joseph, who is only His putative father.[28] In that sense, "He has not, therefore, left that paternal house except apparently, and in reality He is within the house of His Father, in the temple which is His Father's house."[29]

That point does not have its logical sequel then, however, because immediately after, He leaves the Temple and returns with Mary and Joseph to Nazareth. This signifies that His words and His stay at Jerusalem are prophetic, projected into the future, in the sense that He will go to live in *"the house of the Father"*—of which the material Temple is only

26 Garofalo, *Le parole di Maria*, p. 125. Cf. also Leonardi, *L'Infanzia di Gesù*, pp. 240–241; Pietrafesa, *La Madonna nella Rivelazione*, pp. 259–260. This last author also speaks of a probable, "symbolic" value of the episode for our Lady, "inasmuch as Jesus wanted to instruct her about a future separation in his public life."

27 Ferraro, *I racconti*, p. 177. Cf. Ernst, *Il Vangelo secondo Luca*, p. 168.

28 Laurentin sustains that "lexicographical and grammatical analysis, according to hundreds of examples taken from biblical, popular (the *Koinê* spoken at the time of Christ) and classical Greek, proves that it is necessary to translate thus: I must be (or it is necessary that I be) 'in the house' of my Father" (*Truth of Christmas*, p. 81; Ital. ed.: p. 117). J. Leal also notes, rightly, that "he was always 'about his Father's business,' whether at Nazareth or at Jerusalem, whether in the company of his parents or in their absence. The temple is assumed here as a personification or symbol of the Father" (*Vangelo secondo Luca*, p. 158).

29 Ferraro, *I racconti*, p. 177.

a figure—by enduring at the end of His earthly sojourn the three days of His redemptive Passion and death.

But they did not understand his words (v. 50).

What did Mary and Joseph not understand of the words of Jesus?[30]

Certainly they understood the *theophanic* value of Jesus' words, because they already knew of His divinity revealed by the angel Gabriel in the announcement to Mary. It could not be a question, therefore, of failure to comprehend the "divine sonship of Jesus, already grasped at the annunciation," writes Leonardi.[31] "Mary's incomprehension cannot contradict the angelic announcement regarding the divinity of the Son," adds Pietrafesa.[32] Of the divine sonship of Jesus, Mary already "had received an explicit revelation concerning this, according to Lk 1:32 and 35," confirms Laurentin.[33] And Garofalo states that Mary was already "perfectly aware of the divine origin of her Son."[34]

They also understood the prior demands of obedience to God over and above obedience to parents and to every other authority who might wish to oppose it.

---

30 On this brief gospel pericope—the stimulus for a remarkable series of interpretations, widely divergent—see the important and thorough studies of R. Laurentin, *Jesus au Temple*; *idem*, "Non intellexerunt verbum quod locutus est ad eos," in *Maria in Sacra Scriptura*, vol. 4 (Rome, 1967), pp. 299–314; A. Martinelli, O.F.M., *Essi non compresero (Lc. 2, 50)* (Rome, 1967); F. Spadafora, "Et ipsi non intellexerunt verbum," *Divinitas* II (1967): 55–70.

31 Leonardi, *L'Infanzia di Gesù*, p. 244.

32 Pietrafesa, *La Madonna nella Rivelazione*, p. 264.

33 Laurentin, *Truth of Christmas*, p. 81.

34 Garofalo, *Le parole di Maria*, p. 127. Other authors can also be cited: see Nicolas, *La Vergine Maria*, p. 326; Roschini, *La vita di Maria*, pp. 232- 233 (where he cites Cornelius à Lapide, Martini, Lesêtre); Merk, "La figura di Maria," p. 70; Leal, *Il vangelo secondo Luca*, pp. 159–160. According to the profound reflection of Pope John Paul II, "she to whom had been revealed most completely the mystery of His divine sonship, His Mother, lived in intimacy with this mystery only through faith!" (*Redemptoris Mater*, no. 17).

"They did not understand," on the other hand, the "profundity" of the words of Jesus, says Ceuppens.[35] That is, they did not understand the "prophetic" value of the words (and of the comportment) of Jesus who spoke, in effect, of His return to the house of the Father to live, and of which the Temple was a figure: a return to be completed, writes Leonardi,[36] "over the sorrowful way of the passion, that is, during the three days of the passion and death, foretold and prefigured by the three days of the finding in the Temple."[37]

Mary and Joseph *"did not understand"* this *ante factum* (before it had been accomplished)—as Laurentin phrases it[38]—but they accepted it in faith, so as to fathom and discover it little by little in time. Laurentin, however, dates the incomprehension of Mary and Joseph as beginning with the contrast between the two expressions *"your father"* (spoken by Mary) and *"my Father"* (spoken by Jesus), each with a different sense: "The way in which Jesus

35 Ceuppens, *De Mariologia Biblica*, p. 174. One should observe, with J. Leal, that "verbs having the basic meaning of 'to know,' as here 'to comprehend,' always take on, in the New Testament, a progressive sense, always express in other terms an awareness that grows and is perfected. The parents of Jesus comprehended something of the response, not all" (*Vangelo secondo Luca*, p. 159). See also *The Navarre Bible. St. Luke's Gospel*, p. 61.

36 Leonardi, *L'Infanzia di Gesù*, p. 244.

37 There is a "paschal" motive in this finding, which occurs precisely during the feast of the Passover. "As the prophecy of Simeon was an announcement of suffering (2:34)," writes M. Galizzi, "so to be found in the house of the Father after three days is an announcement of resurrection and for the disciple an invitation to search for Jesus where he really is" (*Oltre ogni frontiera*, p. 80). Ghidelli also writes: "It can be said, therefore, that Luke narrates the episode of the loss and the finding in the Temple of the twelve-year-old Jesus in the light of the total mystery of Christ and as an anticipation of his paschal destiny" (*Luca*, p. 105).

38 Laurentin, *Truth of Christmas*, p. 86. Ghidelli also notes that the theme of incomprehension "when it occurs in other Lucan passages (cf. 9:45; 18:34; 24:25; etc.) is always found in relation with the passion of Jesus" (*Luca*, p. 109). "Jesus in the answer given His parents," writes Ceuppens, "alludes to His Messianic work, to the work of Redemption to be accomplished by Him; the parents of Jesus, however, who were not thinking of the work of Redemption, did not understand the depth of this answer" (*De Mariologia Biblica*, p. 174).

refers us from the earthly father to the heavenly Father," says Laurentin, "… is the most immediate reason for the parents' misunderstanding."[39]

Moreover, since Jesus had responded that He must be "in the House of the Father," that is, in the Temple, and not at Nazareth, He should not have had to return again to the house of Joseph. But instead, He returns immediately to Nazareth. "This apparently contradictory return," to quote Laurentin once more, "shows that the momentary gesture of Jesus has not an immediate meaning, but a *prophetic* one. His word concerns the future. His meaning could only be grasped with the passage of time."[40]

Finally, most important and significant of all is the typological prefiguration of the Passion, which requires still more time for "comprehension" by Mary and Joseph. This prefiguration, in fact, identifies for us the place of the Passion (Jerusalem), its time (the Passover), its mode in the verbal form "must," which "on the lips of Christ signifies His passion *'in reference to the Scripture'* which announces it."[41] Moreover, we have here the disappearance of Jesus for three days, "which prefigure the 'three days' of His death";[42] the recollection of the sorrow associated with the sword foretold by Simeon "and its first realization by the anguish which Mary expresses in her use of the climactic word *odynômenoi* in Luke 2:48"[43] and many other references,

39 Laurentin, *Truth of Christmas*, p. 84.

40 Ibid., p. 85.

41 Ibid., pp. 86–87; a little before (p. 86), the author wrote that "the narrative of the 'finding' is woven with key words and themes, which Luke (22–24) will later use to describe the passion."

42 Ibid., p. 87.

43 Ibid., p. 87. On the basis of semiotic analysis, Laurentin also writes that "the episode of the finding is likewise programmed by the prophecy of Simeon in 2:35. The piercing of Mary indicated for a distant future, finds a first realization in this sorrowful loss of the child. The words of Mary in 2:48 are more than ever suited to indicate a piercing" (ibid., p. 214; Ital. ed.: p. 294).

among which most expressive and impressive are the last words of Jesus on the Cross: *"Father, into your hands I commend my spirit"* (Lk 23:46), words that proclaim precisely His return and His definitive preeminence *"in the House of the Father,"* at the completion of His redemptive mission. "The first words of Jesus (2:49)," says Laurentin, in summary, "join with his last (23:46). It is this proleptic openness that is intended by the enigmatic word of Lk 2:50: *'They did not understand.'*"[44]

For Mary and Joseph, it is clear, such "incomprehension" was an experience of faith suffered, whose best explanation, as Garofalo affirms with regard to Mary in particular, is grounded objectively in the coredemptive mission to be accomplished for the salvation of mankind:

> In the loss of Jesus in the Temple, the Virgin tasted the first sorrow that collaboration in the salvation of the world would cost her. Sorrow over the poverty of Bethlehem and the ferocious persecution of Herod was primarily the sorrow of a Mother who cannot offer every comfort to her child in need of all, who makes of her body a shield in danger. The sorrow over the loss in the Temple, this too exquisitely maternal, becomes, after the response of Jesus, the first sorrow of the Coredemptrix; it is the first wound that the 'sword,' about which twelve years earlier, in the same Temple, the inspired Simeon had spoken, opens in her soul: the beginning of her career as the Sorrowful Mother to culminate beneath the Cross. The Virgin did not reply to the answer of Jesus. The test of obscurity would increase her faith, her love, her merits.[45]

---

44 Ibid. p. 215. Cf. also Varón Varón, *Sagrada Escritura*, pp. 124–125: interesting are the author's reflections on Mary's journey "ascending" in ever more profound comprehension of the supernatural plan of God for the salvation of humanity.

45 Garofalo, *Le parole di Maria*, p. 128. See also Pietrafesa, *La Madonna nella Rivelazione*, p. 207.

And he went down with them and returned to Nazareth and was subject to them; and his mother kept all these things carefully in her heart. And Jesus advanced in age and grace before God and men (vv. 51–52).

Jesus returned to Nazareth, humble and docile as before, reentering the hidden life for long years of work beside Joseph and Mary, always *"subject to them,"*[46] awaiting the appointed time for inaugurating His public mission.

Near Him, Mary, meanwhile, dedicated herself constantly and solicitously to her daily work, but not ceasing to meditate on the events that had transpired and on those that occurred one after another, those comprehensible and those "incomprehensible."[47] She is the model of the perfect contemplative in action, true disciple of Wisdom, at the service of others, to become the "source" for the gospels of the infancy.[48]

Reflecting on the attitude of Mary described by St. Luke in verses 19 and 51 of the second chapter, Ferraro appropriately defines it as "contemplative, sapiential, theological," and continuing, he writes that "to preserve the memory of events she had experienced, to compare them one with another, begets profound understanding, clear insight, and satisfying wisdom. Thus, Mary is at once

46 "The periphrastic Greek," notes Leonardi, "marks the continuity of such obedience" (*L'Infanzia di Gesù*, p. 244). Cf. also LEAL, *Vangelo secondo Luca*, p. 160.

47 "Mary accepts in her heart that which is obscure and incomprehensible," writes K. STOCK, "and conserves it that it may mature and become clear. She does not permit in any way that such should separate her from her Son, but she remains in intimate and faithful communion with him" ("Maria nel Tempio," p. 123).

48 It does not seem that there can be any doubts in this regard: cf., for example, CEUPPENS, *De Mariologia Biblica*, p. 175; ROSCHINI, *La vita di Maria*, p. 234; GAROFALO, *Le parole di Maria*, pp. 14–16; LEAL, *Vangelo secondo Luca*, p. 267; GALIZZI, *Oltre ogni frontiera*, vol. "p. 79.

an example for contemplatives and for those who dedicate themselves to scholarship and theological wisdom."[49]

Jesus, meanwhile, grew as man, advancing in age, in acquired and experimental knowledge, and in the splendor of the divine grace that gradually and thoroughly permeated Him within and without, in body and soul, in thoughts and actions, *"before God and men."*

All this occurred under the motherly eyes of Mary and with the vigilant assistance of St. Joseph, in that small house of Nazareth, dwelling place, one might say, of the earthly Trinity. Thus, in prayer and work the great public mission of the Son of Mary was readied. Contemporaneously, St. Joseph, silent and industrious as always, was about to exit the scene, for he is not mentioned again in the gospel, except when St. Luke, at the beginning of the public life, would note that Jesus *"was about thirty years of age, being as was supposed, the son of Joseph"* (Lk 3:23).

---

49 Read in this regard, the interesting reflections of Ceuppens, *De Mariologia Biblica*, p. 175; Nicolas, *La Vergine Maria*, pp. 313–317; Leal, *Vangelo secondo Luca*, p. 267; De Ambrogio, *San Luca*, pp. 76–77; *The Navarre Bible. St. Luke's Gospel*, pp. 55, 62 (a commentary rich in content).

21
The Marriage Feast at Cana

John 2:1–11

The wedding of Cana is a chapter of "glory," blooming with a stupendous miracle that first kindles the faith of the disciples of Jesus. It is the "preamble" to the public life of Jesus.

Cana was a small village, perhaps the present Kefr–Kenna, not more than a few miles from Nazareth.[1] It is a village abounding in flowers, giving it a pleasant, rural beauty.

In this village, a wedding feast was being celebrated, that is, the feast when the bride is introduced into the house of the groom, to begin cohabitation and their conjugal life together.[2] The feast was carefully prepared and required much work because it was to last a week, and sometimes even two (cf. Tob 8:19), with a large crowd of guests who shared the common joy, and who brought the preferred gifts of wine and oil.

1 Cf. B. Bagatti, O.F.M., "Le antichità di Kh. Qana e di Kefr Kenna in Galilea," *Studii Biblici Franciscani Liber Annuus*, 15 (1964–1965): 252–263; Testa, *Maria terra vergine*, vol. 2, pp. 59–68.

2 In the usage and customs of the Jewish people, matrimony was celebrated in two very distinct phases. 1) There was the *quiddushin* (which literally means sanctification) consisting in the agreement or contract of marriage. 2) There was the *nishuin* that occurred with the transferring of the bride into the house of the groom to begin the cohabitation and conjugal living together. It is not difficult to see in these two phases an equivalence or at least analogy with the so-called marriage *ratum* (the *quiddushin*) and the marriage *consummatum* (the *nishuin*).

And the third day, there was a marriage in Cana of Galilee and the mother of Jesus was there. Jesus also was invited with his disciples to the marriage (vv. 1–2).

Mary is present at this marriage with her Son, Jesus, who was about to begin His public life.[3] He brings with Him His first disciples: Andrew, John, Peter, Philip, and Nathaniel.[4] The presence of Mary with Jesus is important because "the mystery of Mary is only understood in strictest relation to the mystery of Christ," writes I. de La Potterie, and "the mariological significance of the account of Cana is closely bound up with its christological significance."[5] It is precisely one of the eyewitnesses, John, who reports for us this episode of the marriage of Cana, "following the dazzling account that chants the majesty of the Word in the bosom of the Father and his coming into the world."[6]

At the marriage of Cana, Mary is introduced with a title of grace and honor without equal: she is called the *"Mother of Jesus."* Nowhere in his Gospel does St. John the Evangelist call her by the name of Mary, but always and only *"Mother of Jesus"* (cf. 2:1.3.5, 6:42; 19:25). Why? I. de La Potterie gives an excellent reason: "All the Evangelist's attention is concentrated on her role in relation to Jesus. He wants to accent first of all the fact that she is the *'Mother'*

---

3 On the various interpretations of this account of the marriage of Cana (allegorical, historical, historico-critical, symbolic, theological, messianic, Christological, sacramental, Mariological), see the brief but dense analysis of I. de La Potterie, *Mary in the Mystery*, pp. 161–163. For the Mariological interpretation of the marriage of Cana, see the studies of Braun, Garofalo, Gaechter, Ruotolo, Charlier, Ceroke, Thurian, McHugh, Feuillet, de Ambrogio, Serra, and many others. A more recent study is that of G. Ferraro, *Gesù e la Madre alle nozze di Cana, Studio esegetico di Gv 2, 1–11*, in *Theotokos* 7 (1999) 9–143, with updated bibliography.

4 Cf. Garofalo, *La Madonna della Bibbia*, p. 131. Pietrafesa is of the opinion that "Jesus was invited, perhaps, for motives of kinship, on account of His Mother, or of the disciple Nathaniel, who was of Cana" (*La Madonna nella Rivelazione*, p. 274).

5 de La Potterie, *Mary in the Mystery*, p. 158.

6 Garofalo, *Le parole di Maria*, p. 133.

of *'Him'* who is the Son of God Himself, the Mother of the Word Incarnate.... That which interests John is the role played in the history of salvation by this woman who was the Mother of Jesus and who would become the mother of the disciples."[7] Mary was now older and with motherly affection would have contributed in the preparation of everything touching the greater joy of the spouses and their guests.[8]

The wine failing, the mother of Jesus said to him: "They have no wine" (v. 3).

Mary's finest motherly care was revealed at the moment when she noticed the wine would not suffice for the duration of the wedding feast. Wine was the heart of any banquet. Lack of wine would have meant humiliation beyond measure for the two young spouses and ruin of the feast, which would end in great bitterness. The vigilant eyes of the Mother of Jesus did not fail to assess that situation, whereas the spouses, quite unaware of what is about to transpire, together with their guests, continue to enjoy the festive, tumultuous atmosphere of the banquet, stimulated precisely by good wine.

Before the irreparable might occur, Mary's maternal solicitude became immediately operative. She knew well

7 De La Potterie, *Mary in the Mystery*, pp 69–70. On the other hand, in the East, notes B. Prete, "it is a title of honor for a woman to be designated as the mother of a son ('the mother of Jesus'), because in such a way she appears as a fortunate woman, having begotten a man" (*Il messaggio della salvezza*, vol. 8 [Turin, 1978], p. 172). J. M. Goiocoechea specifies that for St. John to call Mary "the mother of Jesus, was as if to give her proper name, her distinction of honor, the name the early Church gave her" ("Maria, la madre de Jesus, en las bodas de Cana," in *Maria in Sacra Scriptura*, vol. 5 [Rome, 1967], p. 28).

8 Pietrafesa points out that "the manner of expressing the facts—the Virgin is placed in the foreground—gives great probability to the thought that the source of the account, for certain details, is the Mother of Jesus herself... who alone could refer to John her words and those addressed to her by Jesus" (*La Madonna nella Rivelazione*, p. 274).

to whom she might turn. Nor would any other solution have been available to her, if one considers how the long duration of the feast and the notable affluence of guests demanded a respectable quantity of wine. Where else could she find a very large quantity of wine then and there?[9]

Mary would be the only one present who could realize who Jesus is: the very Son of God the Father, Almighty God himself, for whom nothing then is impossible. With the most disarming simplicity, therefore, and with the most natural spontaneity she turns to Him, and says: *"They have no wine,"* asking, in effect, a miraculous intervention, as the great exegetical tradition maintains.[10]

"They have no wine" are the few words necessary to state what is needed and ask for it. The Mother informs the Son of those children's need. These words are emblematic of the mission of Mary before God: she is always the one who presents our needs before God. And she does this with a minimum of words, without adding anything superfluous. This is the essence of mediation. This is direct intercession—one may say "calculated"—for a precise end.

---

9 Rather untenable seem the opinions of some exegetes who in the intervention and in the words of Mary read only the request for a provision in the "ordinary" manner, with the acquisition of other wine in the village: such as M. E. Boismard, *Du Baptême à Cana* (Pans, 1956), pp. 154–158; H. Van Den Bussche, *L'Evangile du verbe (Jean 1–4)* (Brussels, 1959), pp. 4–43; A. Kerrigan, "Spiritualis Mariae Sanctissimae maternitas," in *De Mariologia et Oecumenismo* (Rome, 1962), p. 72. It is enough to say that, in such a case, a much more obvious course would have been to turn to the relatives of the spouses, rather than to Jesus, who could not have been very familiar with the village (cf. Pietrafesa, *La Madonna nella Rivelazione*, pp. 275–276). "If Mary goes to Jesus for help," comments M. Varón Varón, "it is because she has considered that the only solution is to remedy that situation with a miracle" (*Sagrada Escritura*, pp. 133–134).

10 Lapidary in his brevity is St. Augustine: "The miracle, therefore, required the mother" (*In Joannis Evangelium*, PL 35:1455). Cf. R. Schnackenburg, *Il Vangelo di Giovanni*, vol. 1 (Brescia, 1974), p. 460 (Eng. ed.: *The Gospel according to St. John*, vol. 1 [New York, 1968]), where he says expressly that so "hold many Fathers and modern exegetes."

There are exegetes, it is true, who would prefer to interpret Mary's words not as a request for a miracle, but only as an invitation, a nudge to do something. If, however, the entire context is considered, the mark of sureness in Mary's words, before and after Jesus' response (*"They have no wine," "Do whatever he tells you"*), plainly indicates a request for a miraculous intervention, as indeed the majority of the Fathers and exegetes have understood them.[11] As Fr. Vanni clearly explains: "The fact that Mary turns to Jesus signaling the lack of wine, supposes on her part awareness of resolving the problem, that he is able and willing to do so. Her profound and attentive meditation on the events and words of Jesus, her dialogue with Him, as in their documented conversation when he was a twelve year old, a conversation certainly continued and developed, surely made Mary an expert on Jesus."[12]

And Jesus replied: "Woman, what is that to me and to you?" (v. 4a).

At first, Jesus' response appears disconcerting and in some way harsh, almost as if it were from an annoyed

---

11 See the accurate study of C. Spicq, "Il primo miracolo di Gesù dovuto a sua Madre (Gv. 2, 1–11)," *Sacra Doctrina* 18 (1973): 125–144 (with bibliography). Some scholars would maintain that the Mother could not ask the Son for a miracle because up to that time He had not yet worked any (cf. De La Potterie, *Mary in the Mystery*, pp. 183–84; Prete, *Il messaggio*, p. 173). The argument is based solely on the silence of the Gospels, which do not recount anything of the life of Jesus at Nazareth. First of all, the argument "from silence" is not a proof; moreover, one cannot contradict logic and common sense: how can it "apodictically" be denied that Jesus, during *30* years lived at Nazareth, would have been able to work some miracle to provide the necessities for His poor family, this apart from any admission of the typical accounts of the apocrypha? The security and ease with which Mary turned first to Jesus ("They have no more wine") are certainly in favor of Mary's awareness of the miraculous power of her divine Son. What D. Ruotolo writes, then, should not appear so improbable: "Within the tranquil walls of the little house of Nazareth [Mary] assisted at many hidden prodigies of providence worked by Jesus" (*Vangelo secondo San Giovanni* [Naples, 1976], p. 62).

12 U. Vanni, *Maria e l'incarnazione nell' esperanza della chiesa giovannea*, in *Theotokos* 3 (1995/2) 312.

person. On reflection, instead, it becomes evident that the meaning of the words is quite other, even if to grasp their sense, it is necessary to appreciate the characteristic features of a Semitic language, and to make allowance for the vocal into nation of Jesus when speaking such words. "The gospel account of the dialogue between Jesus and His Mother," says *The Navarre Bible,* "does not reveal to us all the gestures and vocal inflections which gave to the words a precise tone."[13]

What should be said at once, then, is that the phrase of Jesus: *"Woman, what is that to me and to you,"* is idiomatic, occurring frequently in the Bible, both in the Old and in the New Testaments, as also in Greco–Roman literature.[14] The intended sense of this phrase is not to be determined from its grammatical structure, but from the particular turn of thought embedded in every idiomatic expression. Garofalo writes that "the best interpretation would seem to be: 'Why do you ask me that,' since the words, used in accord with the genius of the language spoken by Jesus, express rather embarrassment or disappointment at an

---

13 *The Navarre Bible. St. John's Gospel* (Dublin, 1987), p. 62. "Without doubt," writes Garofalo, "the true sense of these words was completely in the intonation of the voice, in the look, perhaps in the gesture" (*Le parole di Maria*, p. 141), and "perhaps Jesus made it understood, from the tone of voice, that behind his severity there was an invitation to confidence" (ibid., p. 144). "Probably from the tone of his voice," F. Ceuppens also says, "or merely from the look of Jesus, she understood Jesus was disposed to hear her; she expected Jesus' intervention" (*De Mariologia Biblica*, p. 181). D. Squillaci adds that such an idiomatic phrase "is still in use among the Jews, and takes its meaning from the tone of voice, facial expression, and the circumstances; for which it could have a negative, prohibitive, teasing, or even affirmative sense of full accord" ("Maria nella 'Donna' del Vangelo," *Miles Immaculatae* [1969]: 44).

14 See the studies cited by de La Potterie, *Mary in the Mystery*, p. 184, n. 74. As regards the term "Woman," it cannot be repeated enough that this "is an honorific title, equivalent, in antiquity, to that of 'lady'; it is a high and solemn way of expressing oneself. On the Cross, Jesus will use the same word with great affection and veneration" (*The Navarre Bible. St. John's Gospel*, p. 62). On the relation between the term "Woman" here and in the chapters of Genesis (1–3) and of Revelation, see M. Navarro Puerto, *La Mujer en Cana. Un relato de los origines*, in *Ephemerides Mariologicae* 43 (1993) 313–338; G. Feraaro, *op. cit.*, pp. 36–39.

unusual request."[15] In substance, a majority of exegetes proposes this interpretation, even if variously nuanced.[16]

More enlightening than any other is still the exposition of M. J. Lagrange: "the interpreter must not alter the natural sense of the words nor study them apart from the context and, I must add, from their circumstances. Palestinian Arabs still made frequent use of *malech, quid tibi?* It is a phrase whose meaning depends entirely on the accents given it. At times it means: 'mind your own business,' and at other times, smilingly: 'okay, let's do it.' Now from the entire account it is evident that the second meaning is the one intended at Cana, with greater dignity in the tone, but without doubt greater affection as well."[17]

The attentive and insightful explanation of Lagrange also sets in belief the higher level of mutual comprehension between Mother and Son, between the souls of Mary and Jesus. One word, the tone of voice, a glance or a smile, and their souls grasped not so much the literal sense of their words, as the higher significance of the love of a Mother of God who asks and of a divine Son who listens. Depth of language, sublimity of meaning, grace prevail in all things: if in the relations between mother and son all appears here in a most delicate human key, nonetheless it is impossible not to unfold connaturally on the transcendent level of

15 Garofalo, *La parole di Maria*, p. 141.

16 Some exegetes, on the other hand, wish to understand the phrase only in the positive sense, almost as if to say, on the part of Jesus: "What difference is there between me and you, O woman?... — What I can do, you can do," e.g., E. Zolli, "Quid mihi et tibi, mulier?," *Marianum* 8 (1946): 3–15; E. Testa, "La mediazione di Maria a Cana," *Liban* (1955): 539–590. According to others, even the second phrase of Jesus is a positive-interrogative:"has my hour not yet come (perhaps)?": e.g., de La Potterie, *Mary in the Mystery*, p. 203 (a reference to Delebecque). But such positive interpretations do not appear tenable, exegetically and critically (cf. 2 Sam 16:10; Jos 22:24; Judg 11:12; 1 Kings 17:18; 2 Kings 3:13; 2 Chron 25:19; Mt 8:29; Mk 1:24, 4:34, 5:7, 8:28).

17 M. J. Lagrange, *Evangile selon saint Jean*, Paris 1925, p. 56.

hypostatic union for Jesus, and for Mary on that level of belonging to the order of the hypostatic union.

After 30 entire years of intimate communion, the most intimate and private, and so most high and sublime, it is not possible to conceive Mary Most Holy except in theological terms of mystical divinization. On this point Vanni has correctly written, even if in a note and with restrained tone: "The reductive image of a Mary of Nazareth as a housemaid who is merely awestruck by her Son and looks on Him only in astonishment without comprehending Him or ever understanding Him from within is biblically untenable. The source for our knowledge of Jesus of Nazareth and so for the relationship between Jesus and Mary in that little town, Luke 1–2, tends to set in relief the theological aspects of this relationship. This is a Mary, we might say, already theologized, indeed a Mary constantly presented thus."[18]

"My hour has not yet come" (v. 4b).

The phrase that follows: *"My hour has not yet come,"* expresses therefore the reason for the disappointment of Jesus in the face of His Mother's request: a disappointment "for the better" as far as Mary is concerned. For, in fact, she can immediately tell the servants to put themselves at Jesus' disposition to do whatever He orders.

According to some exegetes, the "disappointment" of Jesus can be explained by the fact that Mary asked for the miracle primarily as *"Mother,"* relying to a certain extent on rights deriving from consanguinity, whereas Jesus was thinking only in terms of the messianic economy to be inaugurated, that is, of an order superior to and distinct from the domestic one. An analogous case would be that of

---

18 U. Vanni, *Maria e l'incarnazione nell' esperanza della chiesa giovannea*, in *Theotokos* 3 (1995/2) 312, note 22.

the woman who praises Mary as the "physical" Mother of Jesus, while Jesus transfers the praise to the spiritual plane (Lk 11:27–28).[19]

According to other exegetes, on the other hand, Mary was speaking of the material wine necessary to the spouses, while Jesus was speaking of the spiritual wine of His gospel of salvation for mankind.[20]

Of which "hour" did Jesus speak? There hardly seems any difficulty in understanding that He spoke here of the "hour" appointed for initiating His activity as Messiah–miracle worker, so revealing His glory in the redemptive mission, to culminate in the "hour" of Calvary. Even the time periods decreed by God also have rhythms and deadlines in accord with appointed "hours." This was not the hour to begin the working of miracles that would have revealed His omnipotence and His glory as Messiah Son of God.[21] Perhaps the "hour of prodigies," as Garofalo thinks, "had to strike at Jerusalem, in the heart of the holy nation, in the house of the Father, just as in the house of the Father twenty years earlier the first word of the twelve-year-old disciple–master was heard."[22]

There are other exegetical interpretations, however, that view this "hour" of Jesus from different perspectives. According to some, the *"hour"* of which Jesus speaks is the

---

19 Cf. Varón Varón, *Sagrada Escritura*, p. 138.

20 A. Serra, O.S.M., "Salvezza nelle parole e nelle cose," in *La Madre di Dio* (Brescia, 1975), pp. 154–155. For the various interpretations of the words: "What has that to do with me," see S. A. Panimolle, *Lettura pastorale del Vangelo di Giovanni*, vol. 1 (Bologna, 1978), pp. 206ff.

21 "According to the majority of exegetes," writes de La Potterie, "the significance of the pericope of Cana incontestably is that it presents to us the revelation of the Messianic mission of Jesus" (*Mary in the Mystery*, p. 192).

22 Garofalo, *Le parole di Maria*, pp. 141–142. According to Spicq, the appointed "hour" of the Father had to be that of the purification of the Temple, a dramatic episode, that immediately follows the marriage of Cana (Jn 2:13–22). The purification of the Temple, in fact, would have been a very expressive opening messianic action ("Il primo miracolo," p. 530).

"hour" of Calvary, the *"hour"* of supreme sacrifice preceded by the eucharistic–messianic banquet, where wine would be changed into blood, prefigured now by the water changed into wine.[23] For others, instead, the *"hour"* does not concern Calvary directly, because in that *"hour"* Jesus will no longer be able to work. Rather, it refers to the realization of the global salvific plan of Christ, culminating on Calvary, with the birth of the Church. For Mary, it directly concerns a miraculous assistance to be offered two newlyweds. Jesus consents to the miracle requested by His Mother, because it is a prophetic sign of the universal salvific plan, indicated by the superabundance of wine.[24]

There are still other views not mentioned here.[25] But these kinds of interpretations rest primarily on the so-called "stratifications" in the Gospel of St. John, and inevitably lead to one or more forced readings of the gospel text, or entail suppositions and hypotheses difficult to infer from the text and reconcile with the context.[26]

Hence, as regards the entire episode of Cana, a *literal* interpretation of the miracle and a *spiritual* interpretation of the marriage are to be preferred as more faithful to the text and exegetical tradition. The miracle anticipated by Jesus solely because of Mary's motherly care for two young

---

23 J. P. Charlier, E. Boismard, R. Schnackenburg, M. de Goedt, J. P. Michaud, Ortensio da Spinetoli (cf. Pietrafesa, *La Madonna nella Rivelazione*, p. 524, n. 17).

24 Cf. A. Feuillet, "La signification fondamentale du premier miracle de Cana (Jn 2:1–2) et le simbolisme joannique," *Revue Thomiste* 65 (1965): 517–535; *idem*, "L'Heure de Jesus et le signe de Cana," in *Etudes Johanniques* (Bruges, 1962), p. 26 (Eng. ed.: *Johannine Studies* [New York, 1965], pp. 57–37), where the author writes that "one cannot doubt the exact significance of this reference of Jesus to His hour: it concerns the Cross and the definitive foundation of the Church which administers the sacraments and provides the Messianic wine."

25 Cf. Pietrafesa, *La Madonna nella Rivelazione*, pp. 281–283, with quotations from various authors.

26 See the critical notations of Pietrafesa, *La Madonna nella Rivelazione*, pp. 281–290.

spouses is to be understood *literally.* The marriage, however, is to be interpreted *spiritually,* as symbolizing the espousals between the Word and humanity in Mary and through Mary, espousals shown as approved by God via the *sign* of water changed into wine through the mediative action of Mary, who motivates the creative action of Christ.

Without doubt, at the wedding of Cana the love of Jesus for His Mother, His benevolence and power, and the manifestation of His glory together with the faith of the first disciples (v. 11), appear directly linked to the *mediative* action of Mary, an action set in obvious relief by the Evangelist within the context of the entire episode.[27]

> Just as in the first work of grace by the Word Incarnate revealed in the sanctification of John, here also Mary has the role of Mediatrix. Jesus' first miracle, so efficacious in regard to His disciples, is carried out at her prayer. However the details are interpreted, it seems beyond doubt that the miracle would not have been worked without the mediative intervention of Mary, whereby she truly shares in it.[28]

---

27 The "sign" of Cana, says T. Koehler (*Maria nella Sacra Scrittura*) "passes by way of the efficacious mediation of the Mother of Jesus" (p. 95) and Mary is "Mediatrix for the faith of the first disciples" (p. 98). J. P. Michaud in his study "Le signe de Cana et sa portée mariologique," in *Maria in Sacra Scriptura*, vol. 5 (Rome, 1967), p. 92, affirms that "the more commonly held Marian teaching based on the account of John touches the role of Mary as Mediatrix.... The miracle of Cana well illustrates the mediatory role of Mary." And the author goes well beyond in his analysis, quoting Pope Pius XII and *Lumen Gentium*: "For Mary, in every way, is at the source of the miracle of Cana; it is at her intercession that Jesus begins these works, and it is on her that St. John makes the sign of Cana depend. We may go further: if one reflects that Cana is not an ordinary wonder, but that it is the *beginning of signs*, a sign archetype whose import embraces that of all the other signs, that it is, as it were, a prelude to the entire Gospel considered in its entirety as a narrative of signs, that one must understand it is of the entire life of Jesus about which this exercise of maternal mediation deals, about which Pius XII speaks" (ibid., pp. 93–94).

28 Merk, "La figura di Maria," pp. 72–73. "In the dawn of Cana," writes Danesi, "as in the full light of Calvary (19:25ff.), Mary predominates in the position of Mediatrix, near Him who is the central figure. Her action consists in presenting to Him the needs of men and in presenting Him to men: if Jesus is the light and the life (14:6), Mary is the Mediatrix to all humanity" (*Saggi di esegesi*, p. 453).

There are some who also find in the words of Jesus a most explicit annunciation of the salvific mission of Mary precisely as *Coredemptrix*. Gillard, for example, writes that in the reply of Jesus at Cana one can discover as well the announcement to Mary "of her role as New Eve, as Coredemptrix, as helpmate of the New Adam."[29] coredemptive and dispensative mediation here imply each other in a synthesis dense with meaning.

Through the *mediative* action of Mary, in fact, so rich with faith in her Son, in love for the newlyweds, in example to the disciples, there is effected at Cana for the spouses the miracle of the wine, for Jesus, the manifestation of His glory, and for the first disciples, faith.[30] Plainly, all that is highly significant and important for the beginnings of the public life of Jesus. "She enjoys a deciding role at the beginning of Jesus' public life," Garofalo rightly points out.[31] Pietrafesa aptly observes that "our Lady not only has the mission of giving Christ to the world through her maternity, but also to reveal Him and to present Him to mankind, then as always, for all times. For such an office she is constituted Mediatrix of grace."[32]

---

29 B. Gillard, *Maria, che cosa dice di te la Scrittura?*, Turin 1983, p. 66.

30 Cf. Goiocoechea, "Bodas de Cana," p. 34, where he writes, in conclusion: "Mary, with her words to Jesus: 'They have no more wine,' releases that whole process channeled into the miraculous sign of changing water into abundant wine, the manifestation of Jesus' glory and the faith of the disciples in Jesus."

31 Garofalo, *Le parole di Maria*, p. 147.

32 Pietrafesa, *La Madonna nella Rivelazione*, pp. 287–288. A little further on, the author, discussing the first disciples, sets even more in relief that the "sublime faith" of Mary "is at the origin of the faith of the Church, because the first disciples form a first outline of the Church" (p. 289). Cf. also S. A. Panimolle, "La Madre alle nozze di Cana (Gv. 2, 1–12)," in *Parola Spirito e Vita*, vol. 6, pp. 130–135; C. de Ambrogio, *Il Vangelo di San Giovanni* (Turin, 1975), p. 39.

His mother said to the servants: "Do whatever he tells you" (v. 5).

The fact is, however, that here it is His Mother who asks; and confronted by the request of His Mother, Jesus' disappointment turns into consent, as the words Mary addresses immediately to the servants demonstrate: *"Do whatever he tells you."* Incisive and rich in content is the comment of *The Navarre Bible*:

> The response of the Lord seems to indicate that, although the divine plan had not originally intended that Jesus intervene to relieve an embarrassment occurring at a wedding, merely the request of Mary Most Holy persuaded Christ to provide for the need. It is also possible to surmise, however, that the divine plan envisioned that Jesus would work this miracle through the intercession of His Mother. In any event, it was the will of God that the Revelation of the New Testament include this fundamental teaching: the intercession of the most holy Virgin is so powerful that God will attend to all petitions which reach Him through the mediation of Mary. For just such a reason Christian piety, with theological exactitude, has given our Lady the title of 'Omnipotence at prayer.'[33]

Once again it is she, it is Mary who determines a key step in the course of the salvific plan of God. Just as with her fiat at the Annunciation she opened the door to the Incarnation of the Word, so by her intervention with her Son at Cana, she anticipated the hour of messianic revelation of Jesus. "As she [Mary] was the door through which the Son of God passed from heaven to earth, she now introduces Him among men."[34]

---

33 *The Navarre Bible. St. John's Gospel*, p. 62. "From what happens it is clear that He, for love of her, granted an exception in reward of her humility and trust. It is an exception more expressive than an anticipation, because it is all and only for her" (Garofalo, *Le parole di Maria*, p. 142).

34 L. Bouyer, *Il quarto Vangelo* (Turin, 1964), p. 86. The reflection of G. Danesi is also good: "For the synoptics she has a primary place in the Incarnation; for John she has one, instead, in the manifestation of the Messianic work of

Again a few essential words of Mary say all that needs saying. This time the words are addressed to the servants, that is, to men and are the only recorded words of Mary addressed to men. They are words capable of one meaning only, that of urgent attachment to Christ. In substance, Mary says one thing only, and that truly fundamental: it is necessary to listen to and to do all that her Son Jesus says.

In our view, these words of Mary immediately following Jesus' reply would simply be inexplicable in terms of a merely grammatical exegesis of the text. Mary's understanding of that reply, however, had to be such that she felt certain of the miracle and could plainly say to the servants: *"Do whatever he tells you."*[35] This is the explanation of M. J. Lagrange: "The strange thing is that Mary seems to count on the miracle. We are dealing here with a Mother who knows the heart of her Son. More attentive perhaps to the tone of voice, to the glance, to the accent on the words rather than to their material sense, she is convinced that duty and desire to please them can be reconciled."[36] It is quite true that "the idiomatic phrases as reported here lack their lively color as spoken, surely the factor that must have clarified for Mary anything ambiguous in them."[37]

Jesus" ("Saggi di esegesi," in *Introduzione alla Bibbia*, vol. 4 [Turin, 1973], p. 453).

35 "The realization of the miracle," Varón Varón rightly says, "supposes that Mary interpreted Christ's response in a perfect manner" (*Sagrada Escritura*, p. 140).

36 M. J. Lagrange, *op. cit.*, p. 57.

37 Danesi, "Saggi di esegesi," p. 452. Mary "has no doubt that Jesus will do something to ease the anxiety of the spouses and their relatives. This is why she so specifically commands the servants to do whatever Jesus tells them" (*The Navarre Bible. St. John's Gospel*, p. 63). On the other hand, the idea that there is contained a "reproof" or "opposition" in Jesus' reply is refuted "from the context," writes L. Bouyer, "as also by the true significance of this idiomatic phrase, still current in modern Greek" (*Il quarto Vangelo*, p. 85, n. 14).

These words of Mary radiate everlasting truth, are a norm of life, and a code of Christian conduct, guaranteeing fruitfulness in grace and virtue (and even in miracles).

There are those who have sought to discover in these words of Mary both the attitude of the Jewish people in accepting the Covenant with God, when they said: *"All that the Lord has spoken, we will do"* (Ex 19:8), and that of Mary herself in speaking her *fiat* (Lk 1:38), which set in motion the new covenant of salvation.[38]

Now there were six water jars of stone set there, according to the manner of purifying of the Jews, containing two or three measures apiece. Jesus said to them: "Fill the water jars with water." And they filled them up to the brim. And Jesus said to them: "Draw out now and carry to the chief steward of the feast." And they carried it (vv. 6–8).

It is as curious as it is interesting to observe here how the servants immediately prepare themselves to obey Jesus, making no difficulty and offering no resistance, in carrying six or seven quintals of water to fill the six "water jars," each with a capacity of 80 to 120 liters (or 21 to 32 gallons) of water. Did not Mary's words perhaps arouse in those servants sentiments of complete docility toward Jesus' orders? "Such perfect execution of the words of Jesus was effected at the intervention of Mary. Her task consisted in being 'mediatrix' between Jesus and the servants."[39]

38 Cf. A. Serra, *Contributi dell'antica letteratura giudaica per l'esegesi de Gv. 2, 1–12 e 19, 25–27* (Rome, 1977), pp. 139–228; *idem*, *Maria a Cana e presso la Croce. Saggio di mariologia giovannea* (Rome, 1978), pp. 30–37; De La Potterie, *Mary in the Mystery*, pp. 593–596.

39 De La Potterie, *Mary in the Mystery*, p. 190. The same author notes that here one does not speak strictly of "servants," but of "deacons" or "attendants," elsewhere called "disciples" (ibid.), who constitute the primitive outline of the Church, of which Mary precisely is the Mother.

This particular should not be overlooked, for it exemplifies how the action of Mary is effective with the effectiveness of grace in all her children. "In reality," writes S. A. Panimolle,

> as the Israelites declared to Moses that they would do all that the Lord had said (Ex 19:8) and follow all the commandments given by the Lord (Ex 24:3), so Mary disposes the servants to obey the word of her Son, who is the Son of God (Jn 2:5). In this way the Virgin shows herself to be Mother of the faithful, that is, she is to facilitate the acceptance of the revelation of the Word of God.[40]

This is a consoling truth that John the Evangelist has transmitted to us in recounting the wedding of Cana. It is for us, now, to experience and live it. Fittingly, in this regard, Garofalo puts this brief reflection in the form of a greeting card: "Happy is he who is as ready as the servants of Cana. He will see the miracles of God."[41]

Symbolically, the water represents the law, the wine represents the good news, the gospel. The jars represent the "purification" of the Jews.[42] "These jars were therefore filled with the water of the Law of Moses; they represent Jewish legalism. Jesus transforms this water into the wine of the new law, manifesting Himself."[43] The *nuptial* context, then, makes us understand that the New Covenant is symbolized precisely by the messianic nuptials between God and mankind.[44] "The Word moved by love came down from

---

40 Panimolle, "Nozze di Cana," p. 132.

41 Garofalo, *Le parole di Maria*, p. 146.

42 On this symbolism, see the important research of Serra, "Salvezza nelle parole," pp. 202–230.

43 De La Potterie, *Mary in the Mystery*, pp. 194–195. Just beyond (pp. 195–196), the author cites and quotes some splendid passages taken from the work of H. de Lubac, *Exégèse Médiévale. Les Quatre sens de l'Ecriture*, 4 vols. (Paris, 1959–1964).

44 "Cana is a sign, a symbol of the New Covenant," so summarizes A. Feuillet in his fundamental study "L'Heure de Jesus" (Eng. ed.: in *Johannine Studies*, pp. 17–37).

heaven to celebrate His nuptials with humanity. Those nuptials cannot be completed without Mary Most Holy, Mother of Grace and Queen of mercy."[45] Cana presents here, in symbolic form, the celebration of the true *salvific nuptials,* wherein the protagonists are not two young spouses, but Jesus and His Mother Mary.

This fundamental fact of "transposition" in the meaning of "spouses," who no longer are the two young persons of Cana, but Jesus and Mary, the unique workers of the transformation of the water into new wine, that is, of the passage from the Old to the New Testament, from the Old to the New Covenant, must be noted with special care. In effect, one may "say that the Mother of Jesus 'functions' here as the spouse," states I. de La Potterie.[46] This is a most important point. If Jesus, in fact, is the divine "Spouse" of the new people of God, represented in the small group of early disciples, how is Mary's role and position to be interpreted? It is certainly a role of mediation, as has already been said. But there is something more and different. Here Mary is also both Spouse and Mother. She is Spouse of the Word Incarnate, Mother of the Church. These are assertions that at first blush seem, to depart from the sober lines of the narrative. And yet they express its most essential meaning and its most profound content.

The term *Woman* adopted by Jesus in place of *Mother* is intended to indicate something new. The manifestation of the messiahship of Jesus and of the New Covenant, which

---

45 Ruotolo, *San Giovanni*, p. 65. On this very important theme developed from tradition and neglected, unfortunately, by modern exegetes, see the accurate and documented analysis carried out by de La Potterie, *Mary in the Mystery*, pp. 196–207 (even if some assertions of the author are open to question). For a briefer summary see Varón Varón, *Sagrada Escritura*, pp. 153–155.

46 De La Potterie, *Mary in the Mystery*, p. 215: the author cites P. Geoltrain, "Les noces a Cana. Jean 2, 1–12. Analyse des structures narratives," *Foi et Vie* 73 (1974): 83–90.

this establishes, makes it plain that Mary is no longer only the *"Mother of Jesus"*; she is the *Mediatrix* between Jesus and men. She is also, now, the *Woman* associated with the Messiah, she is the *Woman* of the New Covenant.[47]

To say *Woman* in this sense means to recall Eve, the *Woman* who *"was mother of all the living"* (Gen 3:20); and in the great tradition of the Church the theme of "Mary, new Eve" has occupied a prominent place from the earliest times. Consequently, as the first Eve was the spouse of the first Adam, so the "new Eve," Mary, is the spouse of the "new Adam," Christ (cf. Rom 5; 1 Cor 15:21–26; 54–57), in the messianic work of salvation, begun at Cana (with the presence of the *Woman*), to have its fulfillment on Calvary (and there, too, will be the *Woman*: Jn 19:25) and its consummation in Revelation 12, with the *Woman* in battle against the dragon, recalling directly the *Woman* in battle against the serpent (Gen 3:15).[48]

The theme of Mary–Eve is also met and delineated in that of Mary–Daughter of Zion. The Daughter of Zion is also depicted as *"Woman."* The "whole expectation of salvation on the part of Israel is projected upon the symbolic figure of this Messianic 'Daughter of Zion.'"

---

47 Cf. *The Navarre Bible. St. John's Gospel*, pp. 38–40, 62. There are those who, strangely, in Jesus' response and in the use of the term "woman," would see a certain separation from His "Mother" on Jesus' part, a distancing from her, as an autonomous and independent Messiah, as it were, no longer linked to her in the redemptive mission to be accomplished. An exegesis of this kind seems incomprehensible, let alone tenable. It clearly contradicts the text and the context of the episode, in which Jesus and Mary are united and act as "protagonists" in revealing the New Covenant, evidently with a subordination of the Mother to the Son, but with an enrichment equally evident of Mary's role here, both as the *spouse* of the Messiah and the *Mother* of the new Chosen People (the Church).

48 Cf. M. A. Poulin, "Origine de l'appellation 'Femme' dans Jean 2, 4," in *Maria in Sacra Scriptura*, vol. V (Rome, 1967), pp. 139–149. Cf., in this regard, the suggestive reflections of J. P. Charlier, quoted by de La Potterie, *Mary in the Mystery*, pp. 205–206. Cf. also Michaud, "Le signe de Cana," pp. 46–59. On the connection between the "Woman" of Cana and that of Genesis 3:15, see, for example, Goiocoechea, Danesi, Segalla, Varón Varón, Squillaci.

This symbolic figure, described by the prophets, now is suddenly concretized in a daughter of Israel, Mary, who thus becomes the personification of the Messianic people in eschatological times."[49] Such personification signifies, in reality, the Church, the new people of God, not considered in the abstract, but in the concrete, exemplified, that is, in a person, in a *Woman,* Mary, the true spouse of the Word Incarnate, the Christ Messiah.[50]

If, in fact, it is asserted concretely

> that Jesus is the Spouse, who then is the bride in this symbolic marriage? At times it has been replied, Israel. But Jesus is not simply the spouse of Israel, as JHWH in the Old Testament. He is an historical, concrete person, a concrete Spouse. One cannot marry an abstraction, a collectivity. The partners must be situated either both at the historical level or both at the symbolic level. If here the Spouse is a concrete man, Jesus, then it is necessary, for a balanced and coherent theme that a concrete woman intervene at Cana as Bride. In the view of John, it is Mary.[51]

"In this way, at Cana of Galilee, Jesus worked His first miracle and so manifested His glory and His disciples believed in Him" (v. 11).

If it is true that at Cana "the matrimonial theme constitutes the backdrop of the scene," as Ferraro asserts,[52] it is also true that the most obvious consequence of the

---

49 De La Potterie, *Mary in the Mystery*, p. 220.

50 The title of *Sponsa Christi* or *Sponsa Verbi* referred to Mary, is based on Song 4:7–8 and Is. 61:10. On the importance and the extensive use of this title in the writings of the holy Fathers and ecclesiastical writers (up to Scheeben), see the rich summary of A. Piolanti, *Maria e il Corpo Mistico* (Rome, 1957), pp. 168–186.

51 De La Potterie, *Mary in the Mystery*, p. 205. The liturgy has sung well for centuries: "Today the Church is united to the heavenly Spouse because Christ has washed her sins in the Jordan; the Magi hasten to the royal wedding carrying gifts, and the guests rejoice with the water transformed unto wine" (Benedictus Antiphon at Lauds for the solemnity of Epiphany).

52 G. Ferraro, *op. cit.*, p. 14.

event is the revelation of Jesus as Messiah via the glory of his first public miracle. That miracle aroused the faith of the first disciples and revealed Mary as *New Eve*, spouse of the *New Adam*, Mediatrix and Mother of all the redeemed.

It is easy to see how in fact the "Woman" of Cana, the bride of Christ, recalling Eve, bride of the first Adam, is presented also Mother of the new messianic people. The *new Eve,* in fact, is Mother of the *new living.* The *Daughter of Zion* is also called *Mother Zion* (Ps 86:5). Mary, then, realizes in herself not only the physical maternity of Jesus, but also spiritual maternity in regard to the new people of God, that is, the Church. That Church is already being born in first outline in the little group of Jesus' few disciples present at Cana. They represent the "dispersed children of God" (Jn 11:52) symbolized on Calvary by the "seamless tunic" (Jn 19:24).[53] They are precisely those transformed into "believers" before the "glory" of Christ, that is, before His divinity,[54] manifested with the first of the "signs" worked by Him through the intervention of Mary, the solicitous collaboratrix, Mother always fruitful in begetting men of faith.[55]

Panimolle writes: "Mary, in this episode of the wedding at Cana, cooperates at the birth of faith in the heart of men (Jn 2:5–11), therefore she is presented really as the Mother of the Church" and again: "In the passage about the wedding feast at Cana, the Virgin is presented in the role of Mediatrix in relation to the Son and to the faithful. In effect, Mary, with her solicitous intervention in favor of the spouses in difficulty, urges the Son to reveal His glory.

53 Cf. C. de Ambrogio, *La Madonna nei Vangeli*, Turin 1969, p. 120.

54 "The glory that the miracle reveals is the divinity of Jesus, the presence of the Father in Him, the glory, in short, that belongs to Him 'as the only Son' (Jn 1:14)" (Danesi, "Saggi di esegesi," p. 452). In this sense, Spicq writes very well that "Cana is a Christophany" ("Il primo miracolo," p. 126).

55 Panimolle, "Nozze di Cana," pp. 132–133, 134–135.

The faith of the disciples, then, is favored by the mediative work of the Virgin, that faith being the consequence of the extraordinary sign at which they had assisted (Jn 2:11). Mary, therefore, is really the Mediatrix of the revelation of Jesus and of the faith of the disciples."

Ferraro in turn tells us: "The Mother of Jesus by her intervention enters into the revelation of Jesus, which constitutes the essential point of this page."[56] Thus she begets the faith of the first believers around her. Mary's request, in fact, opens the door to the "sign," or miracle worked by Jesus, and initiates the manifestation of His glory. This arouses the faith of the first disciples, who constitute the original nucleus of the '*dispersed children of God*' (Jn 11:52), gathered about Him (cf. Jn 12:32) and close to Him." D. Marzotto states: "It is the Mother who opens the way, who initiates that movement terminating at the manifestation of His glory, at belief in Jesus, and at the converging of believers on Him."[57]

Aptly synthesizing letter and spirit of the Johannine text, Ruotolo writes:

> Jesus changed water into wine at Cana of Galilee of the Gentiles, in order as it were that the brilliance of His power might shine even among the peoples, and to sow also among them the first seed of those spiritual nuptials of love which He wanted to celebrate with all mankind, redeeming it and unifying it in His Church. Mary is present, and through Mary the miracle is accomplished because she is the Mother of all peoples and all call her blessed. The nuptials of the Divine Lamb will be consummated in heaven, where He

56 G. Ferraro, *op. cit.*, p. 37.

57 D. Marzotto, *La Madre di Gesù e il raduno dei dispersi*, in *Theotokos* 7 (1999/2) 616.

will change the water of our sorrows into the fragrant wine of love, inebriating us with eternal happiness.[58]

At this point, making our voice one with that of the living Magisterium of the Church, salutary and authoritative for all, we receive there from the highest confirmation of the truths taught us by the account of the marriage feast at Cana, just as it has been expounded in these pages, especially in regard to Mary's "mediation." In his Marian encyclical *Redemptoris Mater*, number 21, Pope John Paul II expressly writes that

> Mary is present at Cana of Galilee as the *Mother of Jesus*, and in a significant way she contributes to that beginning of the signs which reveal the Messianic power of her Son.... Even though Jesus' reply to his Mother sounds like a refusal (especially if, rather than the request, we consider the blunt statement 'My hour has not yet come'), Mary nonetheless turns to the servants and says to them: 'Do whatever he tells you' (Jn 2:5)... What deep mutual understanding existed between Jesus and his Mother? How can we probe the mystery of their intimate spiritual union? But the fact speaks for itself. It is certain that the event already outlines quite clearly *the new dimension, the new meaning of Mary's Motherhood*.... The description of the Cana event outlines what is actually manifested as a new kind of Motherhood according to the spirit and not just according to the flesh, that is to say, *Mary's solicitude for human beings*, her supplying the wide variety of their wants and needs: At Cana of Galilee there is shown only one concrete aspect of human need, apparently a small one of little importance ('They have no wine'). But it has a symbolic value: this meeting of human need means, at the same time, bringing those needs within the radius of Christ's Messianic mission and salvific power.

58 Ruotolo, *San Giovanni*, p. 67. The reading of the "sacramental" symbolism expressed by the wedding at Cana could also be added. It has been pointed out by several scholars that three sacraments are symbolized and represented in this episode: baptism, the Eucharist, and matrimony. See, in this regard, what has been written by Varón Varón, *Sagrada Escritura*, pp. 155–157.

Thus, there is a mediation: Mary places herself between her Son and mankind at the level of their real wants, needs and sufferings. *She puts herself 'in the middle,' that is, she acts as a mediatrix, not as an outsider, but in her position as Mother.* She knows that as such she can point out to her Son the needs of mankind, and in fact, 'she has the right' to do so. And that is not all. As a Mother she also *wishes the Messianic, power of her Son to be manifested,* that salvific power of His which is intended to help man in his misfortunes, to free him from the evil which in various forms and degrees weighs heavily upon his life.

22

Mary in the Public Life of Jesus

Matthew 12:46–50, 13:55–56; Mark 3:31–35; 6:3; Luke 8:19–21; 11:27; John 2:12

After the episode of Cana (Jn 2:1–11) and before the scene on Calvary (Jn 19:25–27), the presence of Mary recorded in the Gospels during the public life of Jesus appears very limited. It consists, in effect, of references of John the Evangelist (2:12), St. Matthew (13:55–56), and St. Mark (6:3); a brief appearance in an episode described by the three synoptic Evangelists, St. Matthew (12:46–50), St. Mark (3:31–35), St. Luke (8:19–21); and finally, another indirect reference by St. Luke (11:27–28).

Though admittedly only references, they are significant references, of which four accent primarily the interior dimension and spiritual heights of Mary Most Holy, proclaimed by Jesus himself (Mt 12:46–50; Mk 3:31–35; Lk 8:19–21; 11:27–28). The remaining references instead are rather marginal, one linked to the transfer of Jesus with His Mother and with His disciples from Cana to Capernaum (Jn 2:12) and the other an assessment by the people of Nazareth of Jesus and His kin (Mt 13:55–56; Mk 6:3).

I

After this, He went down to Capernaum, he and his mother, his brethren, and his disciples, and they remained not many days (Jn 2:12).

From the village of Cana, after the feast during which occurred the miracle of water changed into wine, Jesus' party *"with his mother, his brethren, and his disciples,"* went to Capernaum, about 40 kilometers [25 miles] distant, where Jesus had fixed, one might say, a more permanent residence at the beginning of His public life.

Apart from the subject of "the brethren" of Jesus—to be treated in detail shortly—one may infer that the presence of Mary at Jesus' side during His public life is a presence not continual, but rather frequent, at times even habitual. It is hardly conceivable, in fact, that the Mother would not have followed the Son with some frequency, together with the other pious women who usually accompanied Jesus, caring for Him and the disciples.[1] Mary's mission of full "association" in the very mission of her Son, with whom in fact she will be found on Calvary to crown the work of Redemption, would seem to require this.

On the other hand, however, it is difficult to think that Mary would have followed Jesus day by day, uninterruptedly, as if, like the others, she had to know and to listen to Jesus, she who had already lived for thirty years in the most profound intimacy with Him. The Evangelists do not even allude to the other pious women. "The Gospels speak of pious women of Galilee who assiduously followed Jesus while He preached and assisted Him out of their possessions, but they remain silent about a habitual presence of His Mother in following Him. This does not

[1] Cf. Roschini, *La vita di Maria*, p. 267.

exclude it, of course, but by the same token allows us to entertain considerations of fitness or conjecture."[2]

It is also legitimate to hold, with Pietrafesa, that "the place of the Blessed Virgin, privileged creature of exceptional perfection of soul, was not in the hubbub of apostolic life, among vulgar people craving miracles and sensations, but in being Jesus' cooperatrix, assiduous in prayer, hidden, living humbly, industriously and simply."[3]

II

Is not this the carpenter's son? Is not his mother called Mary, and his brothers James and Joseph and Simon and Jude? And his sisters, are they not all with us? From where, then, does he have all these things? (Mt 13:55–56).

Is not this the carpenter, the son of Mary, the brother of James and Joseph and Jude and Simon? Are not also his sisters here with us? (Mk 6:3).

The New Testament refers several times to the so-called *"brothers"* and *"sisters"* of Jesus.[4] The fundamental explanation of traditional exegesis is based on three convincing facts.[5]

---

2 Garofalo, *La Madonna della Bibbia*, p. 118. On the other hand, Merk is more certain when he writes: "Mary has no part in that group of women whom we later find among the followers of Jesus; none of the evangelists mentions her name in reference to this. Indeed, it would seem that during the public life of Jesus she might have had some other duty" ("La figura di Maria," p. 73).

3 Pietrafesa, *La Madonna nella Rivelazione*, pp. 298–299.

4 We cite the following passages: Mt 12:46–47, 13:55–56; Mk 3:31–35, 6:3; Lk 8:19–20; Jn 2:12, 7:3.5.10; Acts 1:14; 1 Cor 9:5; Gal 1:19.

5 On this important and delicate subject, the best in-depth, thorough, and documented study is that of J. Blinzler, *I fratelli e le sorelle di Gesù* (Brescia, 1975), p. 186. The brief, incisive summary of Laurentin, *Truth of Christmas*, pp. 319 and 320, where the author also cites the studies of J. McHugh and H. Cazelles, is also useful.

1. None of the so-called "brothers" and "sisters" of Jesus is ever called "son of Mary"; on the other hand, Mary is called only *"Mother of Jesus."* On Mary's part, then, there is no factor or any indication suggesting that Mary had any other children besides Jesus.

2. The Semitic language (Hebrew and Aramaic) does not have specific terms for cousin (male and female). Therefore, in the current parlance, the word "brother" and the word "sister" connote cousin as well,[6] and even other degrees of relationship, as can be readily verified in many Old Testament texts[7] and from the usage of the New Testament in reference to "Sons of brothers (or sisters) or more distant cousins," writes Blinzler,[8] and finally even to other types of relation.[9] For, it must be remembered, the title of *"brothers of the Lord"* had quickly become "a kind of honorific title."[10]

3. In the particular case of the "brothers of Jesus," "James, Joseph, Simon, and Jude," of whom St. Matthew expressly speaks (13:55–56—and St.

6 "Given that in Hebrew and Aramaic there did not exist an appropriate term to express the idea of cousin (male or female), it was not rare to use the word brother (Heb.: 'ah; Aram: 'aha) or sister (Heb.: 'ahôt; Aram.: 'ahata) to avoid complicated circumlocutions" (Blinzler, *I fratelli*, p. 49).

7 See the series of texts adduced by Blinzler, ibid., pp. 1–52.

8 Ibid., p. 54.

9 "It is recognized that the terms in the Bible can mean blood brothers as well as stepbrothers, disciples as well as fellow religious, distant relatives as well as simple co-citizens" (Testa, *Maria terra vergine*, vol. 1, p. 168). In his day, St. Jerome already spoke of references not to "bonds" of blood, but moral, religious bonds (PL 23:206–209).

10 Blinzler, *I fratelli*, p. 54. "Several times in the New Testament," A. Lancelotti also notes, "mention is made of a small group of persons designated with appellative 'brothers of the Lord' who seem to enjoy a certain prestige in the early Church (cf. 1 Cor 9:5)" (*Matteo*, p. 183).

Mark 6:3),[11] Blinzler correctly concludes his extensive and systematic study on the subject thus:

> The so-called brothers and sisters of Jesus were his cousins. Simon and Jude were related to Jesus through their father Cleophas, who was the brother of St. Joseph, and, as the former, was a descendant of David. Their mother's name is unknown. The mother of the brothers of the Lord, James and Joseph, was a Mary different from the 'Mother of the Lord'; she (or her husband) was related to the family of Jesus, but it cannot be ascertained precisely how. There exists some indication that the father of James (and of Joseph) might have been of priestly or levitical origin and that he might have been a brother of Mary.
>
> As can be inferred from the silence of the Gospels regarding Joseph after the second chapter of St. Luke's Gospel, the putative father of Jesus died shortly after the events related there. After his death, the Blessed Virgin and her Son would have joined the family of their nearest relative(s). The children of this family (these families), having grown up together with Jesus, were called by the people his brothers and sisters, because there did not exist in Aramaic any other concise term with which to refer to them.
>
> The early Church adopted this term, and has retained it even in the Greek, so as to honor the relatives of the Lord, who in the meantime became prominent members of the Church. And because it was an excellent way of clearly and

11 In Mark 6:3 the expression "the son of Mary," interestingly, is referred to Jesus without any reference to the father, Joseph (as we read instead in Matthew 13:55). A truly unusual case in a Semitic language, it would make one think that Jesus was born of an unknown father, or that St. Joseph had already died (as if to say, in such a case, that Jesus was the son of the "widow" Mary: cf. BLINZLER, *I fratelli*, pp. 85–86), or, more probably, of the "virginal birth of Jesus." This is something "also quite plausible," says DE LA POTTERIE, "La Mère de Jesus," pp. 46–47; *idem*, *Mary in the Mystery*, pp. 7576; B. RIGAUX, O.F.M., states the same thing in "Sens et portée de Mc 3:31–35 dans la mariologie contemporaine," in *Maria in Sacra Scriptura*, vol. 4 (Rome, 1967), p. 531; and KOEHLER, *Maria in Sacra Scrittura*, p. 50. "Perhaps in the designation 'the son of Mary' there may be an allusion here to the virginal conception and birth": so claims *The Navarre Bible. St. Mark's Gospel*, pp. 105–106.

conveniently distinguishing them from many other people of the same name in the early Church.[12]

On the other hand, as Pietrafesa well notes, if Jesus had a large kin, it is a sign that "even in this he wanted to be a son of His people, a true semite with numerous relatives, since for the Hebrews a numerous offspring was a sign of divine blessing and prosperity. But it is equally certain that Jesus did not have any blood brothers or sisters.[13]

III

As he was yet speaking to the multitude, behold his mother and his brothers stood without, seeking to speak to him. And someone said to him: "Behold, your mother and your brothers stand without, seeking you." But he answering him who told him, said: "Who is my mother and who are my brothers?" And stretching forth his hand toward his disciples, he said: "Behold my mother and my brothers. For whosoever shall do the will of my Father who is in heaven, he is my brother, and sister, and mother" (Mt 12:46–50).

His mother and his brothers came and, standing without, sent to him, calling him. And the multitude sat about him. And they said to him: "Behold your mother and your brothers without seek for you." And answering them, he said: "Who is my mother and who are my brothers?" And looking round about on them who sat around him, he said: "Behold my mother and

12 Blinzler, *I fratelli*, pp. 173–174.

13 Pietrafesa, *La Madonna nella Rivelazione*, p. 296. See also Varón Varón, *Sagrada Escritura*, pp. 159–161; *The Navarre Bible. St. Matthew's Gospel*, pp. 120–121 *The Navarre Bible. St. Mark's Gospel*, pp. 105–106: the authors point out that the absence of "brothers and sisters" of Jesus plays a role in the dogma of Mary's "Perpetual Virginity."

my brothers. For whosoever shall do the will of God, he is my brother and my sister and my mother" (Mk 3:31–35).

And his mother and brothers came to him, but they could not approach him because of the crowd. And it was told him: "Your mother and your brothers stand without, desiring to see you." He answered them saying: "My mother and my brothers are they who hear the word of God and do it" (Lk 8:19–21).

Except for differences and variations in some of the expressions, the content of these three texts of the synoptic Gospels is substantially identical as regards the teaching Jesus wishes to transmit. As before in the Temple (Lk 2:49), He reaffirms here the primacy of the supernatural over the natural, that is, the primacy of the spirit over the flesh, of the divine will over the human will. Natural motherhood and blood brotherhood alone can be described as of secondary importance or, as Ernst says,[14] are in God's plan "relativized" in the presence of supernatural motherhood and of the brotherhood of divine grace, which are obtained only by doing the will of God.

> Jesus does not deny human realities, but to these in them He denies a determinative role in respect to the divine goods of the kingdom of God. No one could have known better than Jesus just how intimate were His spiritual bonds with His Mother, 'full of grace' and 'handmaid of God.' Jesus' strong words were not addressed to Mary, but to those who needed to understand what Mary already knew.[15]

Clearly, these three pericopes of the Synoptics describe for us two different planes: the "natural" plane of the "relatives" who claim to belong to Jesus only because

---

14 Ernst, *Il Vangelo secondo Luca*, p. 373.

15 Garofalo, *La Madonna della Bibbia*, p. 122.

they are His blood relatives; and the "supernatural" plane of Jesus, which, from another perspective, proclaims the existence of a kinship far above that of the flesh, that is, a kinship rooted in faith and divine grace and so assisting one to fulfill the will of God. Schürmann states very concisely: "Doing the will of God, which is manifested by the word of Jesus, establishes 'kinship,' 'communion' with Jesus."[16] It is for just this reason that Jesus' response contains the highest and most direct praise, even if veiled, of Mary's Motherhood. Her Motherhood, in fact, was not only physical, but also and above all spiritual. Indeed, it was first spiritual and then physical, because she conceived Jesus first in her heart and then in her body, hearing and doing the word of God transmitted to her by the angel Gabriel.

In particular, in regard to Mark 3:33–35, the most problematic text, where the "relatives" seem to make common cause with Jesus' adversaries (cf. Mk 3:20–21), Ruotolo comments thus on Mary's presence among the "relatives":

> Jesus Christ did not have an ordinary mother, but a Virgin Mother who had begotten Him by virtue of the Holy Spirit. Therefore, He did not wish to receive her in a manner the same as that in which the relatives had announced her to Him, because so doing He would have lessened her dignity. Without revealing the mystery of her Divine Motherhood, so as not to expose it to the ridicule of those who would not have understood it, He said in a veiled way that Mary was

16 Quoted in Ernst, *Il Vangelo secondo Luca*, p. 373. Garofalo notes: "Jesus evidently cannot exclude His Mother and 'brothers'—among these two, James and Jude, who would be placed among the twelve Apostles—from relationships of spiritual kinship; He simply insists on giving greater prominence to spiritual links" (*La Madonna della Bibbia*, pp. 121–122). J. A. Diaz points out how, in particular, obedience to God would have one sacrifice fleshly relationships "in the case of a vocation to follow Jesus" (*Vangelo secondo Marco* [Rome, 1970] p. 90).

> His Mother, by stating that whoever did the will of God was His mother.
>
> It was, in fact, precisely in an act of the fullest union with the divine will that she was fruitful by the Holy Spirit; when she spoke her 'fiat' to the Angel, she placed herself entirely at the disposition of the Lord, and at the same instant the Holy Spirit overshadowed her and the Word was made flesh in her virginal womb.[17]

Without the slightest quibble, the exegesis of the great ancient and modern commentators[18] can be said to have always grasped in these three pericopes of the Synoptics the genuine content of Jesus' loftiest teaching. It is a teaching aimed at lifting one to the supernatural plane, to the service of the Kingdom of God to be established in this world, to union with Him through bonds of faith and grace, after the example of Mary, Mother of Jesus, of her who was *"full of grace"* (Lk 1:28), *"blessed"* because she believed (Lk 1:45), hearing and doing the word of God.[19]

And may not those last, unique words spoken by Mary at Cana: *"Do whatever he tells you"* (Jn 2:5), as it were a Mother's sublime testament left to all her children, be considered the most limpid, harmonious echo of Jesus' words reported by the Synoptics? They are a delicate outline of her Son's teaching, words resonating with the very voice

---

[17] D. Ruotolo, *La Sacra Scrittura. Vangelo secondo Marco* (Naples, 1980), p. 57.

[18] We cite only a few exegetes: J. Schmid, *L'Evangelo secondo Luca* (Brescia, 1965); Merk, "La figura di Maria," p. 74; F. Uricchio and G. Stano, *La Sacra Bibbia. Vangelo secondo S. Marco* (Rome, 1974), pp. 264–266; Del Paramo, *Vangelo secondo Matteo*, p. 210; Leal, *Vangelo secondo Luca*, pp. 232–233; Pietrafesa, *La Madonna nella Rivelazione*, pp. 300–302; Lancellotti, *Matteo*, p. 184; Ghidelli, *Luca*; Ernst, *Il Vangelo secondo Luca*, p. 373; Galizzi, *Oltre ogni frontiera*, vol. 1, p. 227; Poppi, *Sinossi*, p. 568; *The Navarre Bible, St. Matthew's Gospel*, pp. 120–121, *St. Mark's Gospel*, pp. 90–91, and *St. Luke's Gospel*, p. 113.

[19] In a magnificent passage of the encyclical *Redemptoris Mater*, Pope John Paul II expressly speaks of the "shift into the sphere of spiritual values" that clearly appears in Jesus' words regarding aspects of motherhood and of brotherhood (cf. no. 20). See also *Lumen Gentium*, no. 58.

of Jesus, above all, words first heard and practiced by her in fullness of faith and love, in total obedience and sacrifice: such is the most important value of Mary's words.

Another text of St. Mark (3:20–21) must be considered briefly here. The word "they" found in it may connote "the relatives" of Jesus (according to the more common opinion), among whom the Mother should not and could not have been absent.[20] The passage is the occasion of difficulty primarily in understanding what is said of the relatives who, having seen Jesus pressured by the crowd and *"gone mad,"* wanted to free Him (whether in the *"positive"* sense out of affection and care, or in the *"negative"* sense because they did not believe in Him, is not clear); and then in relation to a possible link between verses 20–21 and 31–35, which some exegetes (not many) believe refer directly to each other. In any case, even in the hypothesis of a connection between the two pericopes (20–21 and 31–35), the presence of Mary in the group designated by *"they"* who went *"to take Jesus"* because they considered him *"mad"* cannot be understood except in the positive sense: she "came to Capernaum," comments the *Sacra Bibbia* of Vaccari to see her Jesus, to be informed about events and to comfort him with her motherly presence."[21]

20 For a philological analysis and synthesis of the interpretations of v. 21, see Uricchio and Stano, *Secondo S. Marco*, pp. 255–256.

21 *La Sacra Bibbia*, ed. Vaccari, vol. 8, p. 146. On the subject of Mk 3:20–21 and 31–35, see the well-documented studies: G. Castellino, S.D.B., "Beata Virgo Maria in evangelo Marci (Mc 3, 31–35)," in *Maria in Sacra Scriptura*, vol. 4 (Rome, 1967), pp. 529–549; Rigaux, "Sens et portée," pp. 528–529; G. Danieli, "Maria e i fratelli di Gesù nel Vangelo di Marco," *Marianum* 40 (1978): 91–109. If this has been the more common exegesis of the pericopes of St. Mark, one must not underestimate the exegesis of those (not just a few) who in the term "they" do not read "relatives," but "the disciples"; who do not judge Jesus to be "mad," but rather the crowd shouting and rioting at the door of the house in order to enter to see and hear Jesus: cf. the documented study—including the philological dimension—of Spadafora, "L'Evangelo dell'infanzia," pp. 56–63. The author states that "from a biblical and theological perspective, both interpretations ('disciples' or 'relatives') are admissible" (p. 63).

IV

While he spoke these things, a certain woman from the crowd, lifting up her voice, said to him: "Blessed is the womb that bore you and the breasts that gave you suck." But he said: "Yea rather, blessed are they who hear the word of God and keep it" (Lk 11:27–28).

A wonderful passage of the encyclical *Redemptoris Mater* of Pope John Paul II can serve as the best exegetical and theological comment on this delicate episode about Mary's physical and spiritual Motherhood.

> The Gospel of St. Luke records the moment when *'a woman in the crowd raised her voice and said to him: "Blessed is the womb that bore you, and the breasts that gave you suck!"'* (Lk 11:27). These words were an expression of praise of Mary as Jesus' Mother according to the flesh. Probably the Mother of Jesus was not personally known to this woman; in fact, when Jesus began his messianic activity, Mary did not accompany him but continued to reside at Nazareth. One might say that in a way the words of that unknown woman brought Mary out of her obscurity. Through these words, there flashed in the midst of the crowd, at least for an instant, the gospel of Jesus' infancy. This is the gospel in which Mary is present as the Mother who conceives Jesus in her womb, gives him birth and nurses him: the nursing mother referred to by the woman in the crowd. *Thanks to this Motherhood, Jesus,* the Son of the Most High (cf. Lk 1:32), is the *true son of man.* He is 'flesh,' like every other man: he is 'the Word [who] became flesh' (cf. Jn 1:14). He is of the flesh and blood of Mary!
>
> But to the blessing uttered by that woman upon her who was his Mother according to the flesh, Jesus replies in a significant way: *'Blessed rather are those who hear the word of God and keep it'* (Lk 11:28). He wishes to divert attention from motherhood understood only as a fleshly bond, in order to direct it toward those mysterious bonds of the spirit that arise from hearing and keeping God's word.

> … Is Jesus thereby distancing himself from his Mother according to the flesh? Does he perhaps wish to leave her in the hidden obscurity that she herself has chosen? If this seems to be the case from the tone of those words, one must nevertheless note that the new and different motherhood Jesus speaks of to his disciples refers precisely to Mary in a very special way. Is not Mary the first of *'those who hear the word of God and do it'*? And therefore does not the blessing uttered by Jesus in response to the woman in the crowd refer primarily to her? Without any doubt, Mary is worthy of blessing by the very fact that she became the Mother of Jesus according to the flesh ('Blessed is the womb that bore you, and the breasts that gave you suck'), but also and especially because already at the Annunciation she accepted the word of God, because she believed it, *because she was obedient to God,* and because she 'kept' the word and 'pondered it in her heart' (cf. Lk 1:38.45; 2:19.51) and by means of her whole life accomplished it. Thus we can say that the blessing proclaimed by Jesus is not in opposition, despite appearances, to the blessing uttered by the unknown woman, but rather coincides with that blessing in the person of this Virgin Mother, who called herself only 'the handmaid of the Lord' (Lk 1:38). If it is true that 'all generations will call her blessed' (cf. Lk 1:48), then it can be said that the unnamed woman was the first to confirm unwittingly the prophetic phrase of Mary's Magnificat and to begin the Magnificat of the ages.[22]

Many indeed are the exegetes who have written penetrating and evocative pages on this brief but significant episode,[23] noting the sense and the very different levels of Mary's beatitude as the *physical* Mother of Jesus, proclaimed by the woman in the crowd, and as the *spiritual* Mother of Jesus, proclaimed by Jesus himself. The wealth of content

22 Pope John Paul II, *Redemptoris Mater*, no. 20. Cf. also *Lumen Gentium*, no. 58.

23 Among the recent exegetes see, for example: Nicolas, *La Vergine Maria*, pp. 365–377; Garofalo, *La Madonna della Bibbia*, pp. 122–124; Ruotolo, *Vangelo secondo Luca* (Naples, 1979), pp. 314–315; Pietrafesa, *La Madonna nella Rivelazione*, pp. 302–304; Varón Varón, *Sagrada Escritura*, pp. 163–167.

in this Lucan account is illustrated, then, in the many exegetical insights found in various commentators, often presented from quite different perspectives. Thus, there are those who, in addition to the affirmation of the primacy of spiritual motherhood over that of the flesh, have read in this gospel passage of St. Luke the first fulfillment of the prophecies of St. Elizabeth (1:42–45) and of Mary herself (1:48).[24]

Others have noted that the expression of the woman in the crowd is typical in the East, and especially of the Hebrews for whom children are the true glory of the woman; and that the phrase of Jesus: "hear the word," does not mean only hearing, but also includes accepting and adhering to that word.[25]

Still others have remarked on the connection between this passage of St. Luke and the other Lucan passage, 8:19–21, which speaks of the "relatives" of Jesus, with this difference, however, that "in the passage of chapter eight the concept of kinship is minimized, while in this one it is not. The phraseology here does not sound a note of contempt or condescension toward the Mother of Jesus, but only articulates the condition on the basis of which she too merits to be proclaimed blessed."[26] Nor should one overlook the "delicacy of expression" wherewith Jesus explains the highest beatitude of Mary, how this is linked to a state of mind constant and faithful in hearing every command of God.[27] Further, it is necessary to ponder the

---

24 Cf. Ghidelli, *Luca*, pp. 268–269.

25 Cf. Leal, *Vangelo secondo Luca*, p. 287.

26 Schmid, *L'Evangelo secondo Luca*, p. 263. Galizzi notes that the adversative "rather" is not fully exact, because the Greek participle "does not have adversative shadings" and is better translated "even more," that is: "even more blessed are they who hear" (M. Galizzi, *La lunga marcia. Vangelo secondo Luca*, vol. 2 (Turin, 1979), p. 48.

27 Cf. Merk, "La figura di Maria," p. 74. "The apparent antithesis," notes Ernst, "between those who hear the word and the Mother of Jesus, is resolved

notable diversity of "accent" between this Lucan verse and the other (8:19–21): that is, the *Christological* accent in chapter eleven and the *ecclesiological* in chapter eight.[28]

In conclusion, we would observe that if in the enthusiastic cry of praise addressed by that woman in the crowd to the Mother of Jesus, many exegetes would see the beginning of the praise of Mary prophesied in the Magnificat (1:48), to us it seems, even more, that the beginning of the truest and highest praise of Mary would come not from that woman in the crowd (who knew nothing of the Divine Maternity of Mary), but from Jesus himself, from Jesus in person, from the Son who inaugurates the interminable praise of her who is Mother of the Word, the spiritual and physical Mother, because she heard and did the word of God.

only when she is recognized as the obedient servant who is full of faith" (*Il Vangelo secondo Luca*, pp. 533–534).

28 Cf. Poppi, *Sinossi*, p. 312. Ernst also discovers a "Christological" note in the cry of the woman who magnifies the Mother for the sake of the Son (*Il Vangelo secondo Luca*, p. 533).

23
"BEHOLD YOUR MOTHER...BEHOLD YOUR SON"

John 19:25–27

In two pages of the Marian encyclical *Redemptoris Mater,* Pope John Paul II offers us a dense and lucid synthesis of the exegesis of this celebrated text of St. John's Gospel. The Holy Father writes:

> If John's description of the event at Cana presents Mary's caring motherhood at the beginning of Christ's messianic activity, another passage from the same Gospel confirms this motherhood in the salvific economy of grace at its crowning moment, namely, when Christ's sacrifice on the Cross, his paschal mystery, is accomplished.
>
> Undoubtedly, we find here an expression of the Son's particular solicitude for his Mother, whom he is leaving in such great sorrow. And yet the 'testament of Christ's Cross' says more. Jesus highlights a new relationship between Mother and Son, the whole truth and reality of which he solemnly confirms. One can say that if Mary's Motherhood of the human race had already been outlined, now it is clearly stated and established. It *emerges* from the definitive accomplishment of the *Redeemer's Paschal Mystery.* The Mother of Christ, who stands at the very center of this mystery—a mystery that embraces each individual and all humanity—is given as Mother to every single individual and to all mankind. The man at the foot of the Cross is John, 'the disciple whom he loved.' But it is not he alone. Following tradition, the Council does not hesitate to call Mary *'the Mother of Christ and the Mother of mankind':* since she 'belongs to the offspring of Adam she is one with all human beings... Indeed she is "clearly the Mother of the members of Christ ... since she cooperated out of love so that there might be born in the Church the faithful."'

And so this 'new Motherhood of Mary,' generated by faith, is *the fruit of the 'new' love,* which came to definitive maturity in her at the foot of the Cross, through her sharing in the redemptive love of her Son.

Thus we find ourselves at the very center of the fulfillment of the promise contained in the *Protoevangelium:* the 'seed of the woman... will crush the head of the serpent' (cf. Gen 3:15). By his redemptive death, Jesus Christ conquers the evil of sin and death at its very roots. It is significant that, as he speaks to his Mother from the Cross, he calls her 'woman' and says to her:

'Woman, behold your son!' Moreover, he had addressed her by the same term at Cana, too (cf. Jn 2:4). How can one doubt that especially now, on Golgotha, this expression goes to the very heart of the mystery of Mary, and indicates the unique *place* she occupies *in the whole economy of salvation?*

The words uttered by Jesus from the Cross signify that *the Motherhood* of her who bore Christ finds a 'new' continuation *in the Church and through the Church,* symbolized and represented by John. In this way, she who as the one 'full of grace' was brought into the mystery of Christ in order to be his mother and thus *the Holy Mother of God,* through the Church remains in that mystery as *'the woman'* spoken of in the Book of Genesis (3:15) at the beginning and in Revelation (12:1) at the end of the history of salvation. In accordance with the eternal plan of Providence, Mary's divine Motherhood is to be poured out upon the Church, as indicated by statements of tradition, according to which Mary's 'Motherhood' of the Church is the reflection and extension of her Motherhood of the Son of God (nos. 23, 24).

Now there stood by the cross of Jesus, his mother and his mother's sister, Mary of Cleophas, and Mary Magdalene. When Jesus therefore had seen his mother

and the disciple standing by whom he loved, he said to his mother: "Woman, behold your son!" (vv. 25–26).

The essential content of this passage in John's Gospel is the *spiritual, universal Motherhood of Mary.* On Calvary, at the foot of the Cross, Mary's divine Motherhood, with the "pangs" of a most painful childbirth, is shown to extend to all the redeemed, brothers of Christ *"the firstborn"* (Rom 8:29).[1] A. Feuillet says that "the greater number of Catholic exegetes see in Jn 19:25–27 at least an insinuation of the Spiritual Maternity of Mary."[2]

The highly dramatic scene portrayed finds its meaning as part of the last testament of Jesus, the supreme and final act of love that brings to fulfillment the salvific plan for all humanity, with the Mother of God close to Him and united to Him at the foot of the Cross.[3] This sense of final accomplishment is also conveyed by the more immediate context of the verses. After the words spoken by Jesus to Mary and John, in fact, there follows immediately the pericope in which the Evangelist says that for Jesus *"all things were now accomplished."* Entrusting us to Mary and

---

1 The presence of the "women" on Calvary is attested both by John and by synoptic tradition (cf. Mt 27:55; Mk 15:40; Lk 23:49). There is only one difference: for John they are "*near the Cross*," while for the Synoptics they are "*afar off*" (it would seem, however, that the Mother, with John, could have approached the Cross). In particular, on the presence of Mary, cf. R. S. Hakel, "Quae sola perfecte stetit," in *Maria in Sacra Scriptura*, vol. 5, pp. 225–233.

2 A. Feuillet, *Maria: Madre del Messia, Madre della Chiesa*, Milan 2004, p. 42, and a little further on affirms that "The commentators should no longer hesitate, as in the past, to recognize Jn 19:25–27 as ascribing to Mary of a true and proper Motherhood in messianic order... And I also add that the Spiritual Maternity of the Mother of Christ is not to be confused with the spiritual maternity of the Church. This text gives rather the impression that the Spiritual Maternity of Mary precedes and prepares that of the Church. St. John suggests exactly this" (p. 44).

3 Serra observes that the pleonasm "by the *Cross of Jesus*" is intentional and serves "to set in relief the communion of Mary, of the pious women and of the disciple more with the *Crucified* than with the Cross": A. Serra, *Maria a Cana e presso la Croce*, Rome 1991, p. 94, note 25.

giving Mary to us, then, Jesus brings to fulfillment the salvific work of mankind.[4]

Mary's presence in this scene clarifies God's plan of salvation in terms of motherly love, revealing, as it were, the *maternal* aspect of the Redemption.[5] The heart of Christ pierced by a *"lance"* (v. 34) and the heart of Mary pierced by a *"sword"* (Lk 2:35) make us realize quite well the totality of the sorrowful love of Christ and Mary who have redeemed a mankind so much in need of salvation.

> It is on Calvary that the mission of coredemptive Motherhood of Mary Most Holy was fulfilled and consummated in a final, total co-immolation in the immolation of the crucified Redeemer Son. As the biblicist, Fr. Allegra, writes, the Mother of God present on Calvary 'united herself intimately with her dying Son on the Cross as our Coredemptrix.'[6] And M. Laconi, another biblicist, confirms this: 'The mission of Mary, although entirely framed in a supernatural context, has one constant coefficient: sorrow, which consecrates her Coredemptrix at the side of Jesus.'[7]
>
> The fundamental biblical text, Genesis 3:15, prophesied the victory of the 'Woman' with her 'posterity' over the seducer serpent of Eve. In fact, writes Fr. Pietrafesa, 'Mary's appointment under the Cross is the culminating point of her mission, already foretold in the earthly paradise (Gen

---

4 The significant philological research done by the English exegete G. Bampfylde on verse 28 leads to the conclusion that the words: "*that the Scriptures might be fulfilled*," are to be placed before the verb "*said*," and are to be linked with the preceding words: "Afterward, Jesus, knowing that all things were now accomplished, *that the Scriptures might be fulfilled*, said in this way, the conclusive terminal sense of this act of Jesus which brings the Scriptures to perfect fulfillment is rendered more evident (cf. "John XIX, 28. A Case for a Different Translation," *Novum Testamentum* II (1969): 247–260. "Without doubt, the office of spiritual motherhood, which Jesus entrusted to His Mother, also pertains to the work of 'consummation'" (Mercado, "De verbis Jesu ad matrem et Joannem," in *Maria in Sacra Scriptura*, vol. 5, p. 135).

5 "On Calvary Christ actuates in Mary the maternal aspect of the Redemption" (Varón Varón, *Sagrada Escritura*, p. 169).

6 G. M. Allegra, *Il Cuore Immacolato di Maria*, Acireale 1991, p. 132.

7 M. Laconi, *Maria nel Nuovo Testamento*, in *Enciclopedia Maria "Theotokos,"* Genoa-Milan 1959, p. 37.

3:15) to the first parents of the human race. Under the Cross Mary would be proclaimed Coredemptrix of the human race, the New Eve, the conqueress of the infernal serpent. As for Jesus, the apparent defeat under the Cross would in reality signal His triumph and the success of His redemptive mission, so for Mary her presence and her unfathomable sorrow at the foot of the Cross would constitute the triumph of her coredemptive mission.'[8]

The biblicist, G. Aranda Perez, states that in the final analysis all 'tradition sees in Mary at the foot of the Cross the New Eve, thus setting in relief the cooperation of Mary in the work of Redemption,'[9] co-immolating herself to pay 'the hard price whereby she won the title Coredemptrix,' as Laconi writes.[10] Mary Most Holy, in fact, as Pope John Paul II stresses 'participated in wondrous manner in the sufferings of her divine Son to be Coredemptrix of mankind,'[11] and had wished 'to suffer with her dying Son on the Cross... to restore supernatural life to souls,' as Vatican II teaches, thus becoming 'our Mother in the order of grace' (*Lumen Gentium,* no. 61).[12]

On Calvary, then, at the foot of the Cross, the most intimate relation between Spiritual Maternity and Coredemption in

---

8 P. Pietrafesa, *La Madonna nella Rivelazione*, Naples 1970, pp. 308–309.

9 G. Aranda Perez, *La collaboracion de Maria a la salvacion en la Biblia*, in *Estudios Marianos*, 1985, p. 47.

10 *Art. cit.*, p. 41.

11 *Insegnamenti di Giovanni Paolo II*, V/3, 1982, Vatican City, p. 404.

12 Recent bibliography on the coredemptive Motherhood of Mary Most Holy according to Jn 19:25–27 is particularly rich. See, e.g., S. M. Manelli, *Maria Corredentrice nella Sacra Scrittura*, in Aa. Vv., *Maria Corredentrice. Storia e Teologia*, Frigento 1998, vol. 1 pp. 91–101 [Eng. Version: *Mary Coredemptrix in Sacred Scripture*, in *Mary Coredemptrix, Mediatrix, Advocate. Theological Foundations 2*, Santa Barbara CA 1997, p. 59–103. The Italian is a slightly longer revision of the English.]; T. M. Sennott, *Mary Coredemptrix*, in *Mary at the Foot of the Cross* 2, New Bedford MA, 2002, pp. 61–62; A. Olivera, *Asemelhança de Maria*, Sao Paulo 1990, p. 20; M. Miravalle, *Mary Coredemptrix, Mediatrix, Advocate: Foundational Presence in Divine Revelation*, in *Mary, Coredemptrix, Mediatrix Advocate. Theological Foundations*, Santa Barbara CA 1995, pp. 256–269 (this study covers Tradition as well as the Pontifical Magisterium); G. Cottier, *La Mariologia dal Concillo Vaticano II ad oggi*, in *L'Osservatore Romano*, 3-4 June 2002, p. 8; S. M. Manelli, "Maria, a titolo unico, è Corredentrice," in *Immaculata Mediatrix* 2 (2002) 247–264 (commentary on the article of Cottier); B. Gherardini, *La Corredentrice nel mistero di Cristo e della Chiesa*, Rome 1998, pp. 217–220.

> Mary Most Holy is brought to life. For this reason it may be said that Jesus Crucified from the heights of the Cross, in giving us His Mother, gave us also the Coredemptrix, or the 'New Eve Coredemptrix,' as the biblicist, Fr. Allegra,[13] appropriately calls her, the true *'Mother of the Living'* (Gen 3:20).[14]
>
> On Calvary, at the foot of the Cross, the Spiritual Maternity and Coredemption are shown to be in reciprocal. In virtue of this, Mary Most Holy is really our Mother because Coredemptrix, and Coredemptrix because our Mother, as Garcia Garces explains so well. He writes: 'in the order of final causality Mary Most Holy is Coredemptrix because our Mother, while in the order of efficient causality Mary is our Mother because Coredemptrix.'[15]

For a long time, the so-called "personal–private" interpretation of verses 25 to 27 predominated in exegetical commentaries. This interpretation understood the scene only as a gesture of Jesus' filial love, concerned to entrust His Mother to John, that she might not be alone after His death.

As many exegetes observe, however, it can hardly be denied that such an exposition of the text ill accords with elementary common sense, the kind postulated by such concern on the Son's part to provide for the future domestic arrangements of a mother: adequately, in good time, without waiting until the final minutes of His life.[16]

---

13 *Op. cit.*, p. 76.

14 See also: G. M. ALLEGRA, *Madre mia, fiducia mia*, Catania 1958, p. 37; *Vaticini mariani dell'Antico Testamento e dell'Apocalisse*, Castelpetroso 1996, pp. 5–9; *I sette dolori di Maria*, Castelpetroso 1998, pp. 28–29.

15 N. GARCIA GARCES, "Dalla Maternità spirituale alla Corredenzione," *Marianum* 3 (1941) 372–396.

16 Cf. M. PEINADOR, "Maria Mater Jesu in Scriptis Johanneis," *Ephemerides Mariologicae* 2 (1952): 100–101; *idem*, "Maria asociada a la obra redentora," *Estudios Marianos* 19 (1958): 25–26; J. LEAL, *La Sagrada Escritura N. T. Evangelios* (Madrid, 1965), pp. 1095–1096. D. RUOTOLO notes that if Jesus had wanted to concern Himself with arrangements for His Mother, He would have addressed John first in order to entrust His Mother to him, and not first His Mother in order to entrust John to her (*San Giovanni*, p. 465). It might also be added that in such a hypothesis it would have been enough

In fact, for some time now, personal–private interpretations, too restrictive of the meaning of the celebrated pericope, have been supplanted, or better, integrated with "personal–communal" and "representative–communal" interpretations. According to these, on Calvary, Mary was proclaimed Mother of the redeemed, represented by St. John. The truth is she cooperated in the universal Redemption both as an *individual person* and as the *personification* of the "daughter of Zion," figure of the Church that generates the new people of God.[17]

Exegetical research, since the beginning of this century, has concluded that an exposition of the literal sense of verses 25 to 27 in terms of the spiritual Motherhood of Mary is supported both by the reference to the wedding feast of Cana (Jn 2:1–11) and by other texts of the Old and New Testaments, and by the very context of the scene on Calvary, as we shall see immediately.

A necessary preliminary observation, however, concerns the structure of the verses 26 and 27a. As a unit, they fall into a literary pattern known as a "revelation genre," a style characteristic of St. John. This consists in articulating three concatenated moments of *seeing,* of *saying,* and of the verb *behold,* followed by a *title* or a word of "revelation."[18] On

---

to address Himself only to John. G. Segalla also points out that "Jesus addresses himself first to Mary as if the principal task were hers" (*Giovanni* [Rome, 1976], p. 454). R. Laurentin supports this, writing that "it is first of all John who is entrusted to Mary: 'Behold your son.' He and we are the beneficiaries of that 'transfer'" (*Un anno di grazia con Maria* [Brescia, 1987], p. 73). Cf. also Squillaci, "Maria nella 'Donna,'" pp. 45–46; Mercado, "De verbis Jesu," p. 130; Varón Varón, *Sagrada Escritura*, p. 170.

[17] Cf. Pietrafesa, *La Madonna nella Rivelazione*, p. 310; *The Navarre Bible. St. John's Gospel*, p. 228. "It is important to keep the personal and ecclesiological implications of Mary's motherhood united. Becoming the Mother of all the disciples of Jesus, Mary becomes Mother of the whole Church" (de La Potterie, *Mary in the Mystery*, p. 223).

[18] Cf. M. de Goedt, "Un scheme de révélation dans le quatrième Evangile," *New Testament Studies* 8 (1961–1962): 142–159. An example is Jn 1:19:"The next day, John *saw* Jesus coming to him, and he *said*: 'Behold the Lamb of God....'"

the basis of this "revelation–genre," applied to verses 26 and 27a, it appears, concretely, that

> Jesus, dying on the cross, reveals that his Mother, as the 'Woman,' with all the biblical resonance of this word, will now also be the Mother of the 'disciple,' because this latter, as the representative of all the 'disciples' of Jesus, will now be the son of his Mother. In other words, He reveals a new dimension of Mary's Motherhood, a spiritual dimension, and a new role of the Mother of Jesus in the economy of salvation; but in a correlative way He reveals at the same time that the first task of the disciples will consist in being 'Sons of the Mother of Jesus.'[19]

The reference to the wedding at Cana (2:1–11) is especially linked to the use of the word *"woman."* This term "woman," addressed to Mary by Jesus, makes of her the "new Eve," the "woman" of the New Covenant, the "woman" of the messianic marriage, the "woman" who is the "Mother Zion" of the new Israel, which is the Church.[20]

The "hour" of Jesus is another reminder of the wedding at Cana, projected there as well as on Calvary, at least as the final and decisive "hour" for the total manifestation of the Redemption, the "hour" in which Jesus would also have proclaimed the spiritual and universal Motherhood of Mary, the new Eve, *"mother of all the living"* (Gen 3:20).[21]

Another significant Johannine text is 11:52 regarding the prophecy of Caiaphas in proposing the death of Jesus

---

19 De La Potterie, *Mary in the Mystery*, p. 218.

20 Regarding the term "*woman*" as applied to Eve and to Mary, see Poulin, "Origine de l'appellation," pp. 139–149; among other things, the author writes that "a convergence of remote and proximate contexts of the word 'Woman' invites us to see in that usage of this term by St. John a clear intention of presenting Mary as the new Eve" (p. 140).

21 One should not overlook the suggestive linkage between Mary's words to the servants at Cana: "*Do whatever he tells you*" (2:5) and the words quoted by the Evangelist at the close of the scene on Calvary: "*They will look upon him whom they have pierced*" (19:37): in both cases the Mother orients her children toward Jesus (cf. de La Potterie, *Mary in the Mystery*, pp. 233–234).

"to gather in one the children of God that were dispersed." By projection, this text also is linked with Calvary, where Mary incarnates "Mother Zion," who recalls her children from exile and gathers them at the foot of the Cross to form the new people of God in unity and stability.[22]

The immediate context of John 19:25–27, moreover, presents first the theme of the unity of the Church, symbolized by the "seamless" tunic, a sign of the reconstituted unity of the people of God, prefigured by Mary, the Mother, and by John, the son. In verse 24, as I. de La Potterie notes, the Evangelist seems to announce "that which in the following scene is about to be positively realized: the new Messianic community is constituted in its *unity* beneath the Cross. Mary and the disciple are the prefiguration."[23]

In verse 34, we read that from the pierced side of Jesus *"blood and water came forth."* With a reflection dense in content, Origen commented thus: "The flesh of Christ, in the spasms of the Cross, begot the Church, when from that flesh blood and water came forth."[24] The fruit of the Passion and death of Jesus is the birth of the new people of God, of the new Israel, which is the Church. "But in this birth of the Church it is Mary who has the role of Mother," de La

22 Cf. A. Serra, "'Donna-Madre' del Popolo di Dio," in *Parola Spirito e Vita*, vol. 6, pp. 139–144.

23 De La Potterie, *Mary in the Mystery*, p. 215. See also Mercado, "De verbis Jesu," p. 127. De Ambrogio observes that "the episode of the seamless garment is a symbol of the unity of the Church. St. John never mentions anything without a purpose": C. de Ambrogio, *La Madonna nei Vangeli*, Turin 1969, p. 120. It is certainly not difficult to discover in this episode that the Coredemption and unity of the Church are reciprocally related, when Mary is proclaimed Mother by Jesus Crucified "precisely in the act of begetting children through the maternal suffering of the Coredemption at the foot of the Cross": S. M. Manelli, *Maria, Corredentrice nella Sacra Scrittura*, p. 101, note 143.

24 PG 87:1741–1742c.

Potterie points out,[25] because it is her divine Motherhood that is extended to the whole Church.

According to many scholars, other Old Testament references related to John 19:25–27 are the following:

GENESIS 3:15 on the "woman" of the *Protoevangelium,* united with her Son in the battle against the serpent, whose head is to be crushed, an event actually occurring on Calvary,[26] where mankind was redeemed by the new Adam (Christ) and by the new Eve (Mary).[27] As Battaglia writes, in Genesis 3:15 "the Creator saw in this new and mysterious human couple made up of Mother and Son [Mary and Jesus] the instrument of reparation for the sin defiling the world. Now this couple, after so many centuries, appears on Golgotha to crush the head of the Evil One."[28]

ZECHARIAH 9:9 (quoted directly by John 12:15) on the "gathering of the dispersed" of Israel in Jerusalem, which is the city of the whole people, the mother–city, the prefiguration, one may say, of Mary, the universal Mother.[29]

SONG OF SONGS 8:3, a verse rich in symbolism: the tree of the Cross, from which sprang the Church personified by Mary and John; the double name "Sinai–Zion"; the

---

25 DE LA POTTERIE, *Mary in the Mystery*, p. 234.

26 On the subject of Mary's sufferings on Calvary, Garofalo writes, briefly yet convincingly, that, at the foot of the Cross, "the sword predicted by Simeon forty days after the birth of Jesus devastated the heart of Mary without missing a single fiber" (*La Madonna della Bibbia*, p. 129).

27 Cf. BRAUN, *La Mere des fidèles*, pp. 77ff. (Eng. ed.: *Mother of God's People*, pp. 75ff.); GAECHTER, *Maria im Erdenleben*, pp. 224ff.; P. KEARNEY, "Gen. 3:15 and Johannine Theology," *Marian Studies* 27 (1976): 99–109; GAROFALO, *La Madonna della Bibbia*, pp. 132–133; VARÓN VARÓN, *Sagrada Escritura*, p. 171; PIETRAFESA, *La Madonna nella Rivelazione*, p. 312.

28 O. BATTAGLIA, *op. cit.*, 329.

29 Here is the text: "Rejoice greatly, O daughter of Zion, shout for joy, O daughter of Jerusalem: Behold your king will come to you, the just and savior. He is poor and riding upon an ass and upon a colt, the foal of an ass." Cf. SERRA, "Donna–Madre," pp. 144–149.

"garden" of Eden and of the canticle with the idyll of the Bride (the daughter of Zion) and Groom (God).[30]

Now, the net impression of these passages from the Gospel of St. John, from his Revelation, and from the Old Testament, taken as a whole, is a richly textured vision of theological insights that harmonize with one another in portraying the ineffable reality of the universal Motherhood of Mary, vividly inserted in the mystery of Christ and of the Church.[31]

If at this point a respectable number of facts touching the figure and maternal mission of Mary in John 19:25–27 has been harvested, it remains true that some of these considerations appear mutually exclusive. The impression, however, is only that. For rightly situated, on different planes or at different angles, the meaning of each of these facts will harmonize with the others and will also lead to further analysis and discovery. In this we follow the path traced out by de La Potterie.

For example, we can see in Mary at the foot of the Cross, with St. John beside her, the "woman" who is at once *Virgin, Spouse,* and *Mother,* this including a direct and suggestive reference to the "Daughter of Zion," considered in prophetic tradition as virgin, spouse, and mother.[32] But how can Mary be at the same time Spouse and Mother

30 Here is the text: "Who is this that comes up from the desert, flowing with delights, leaning upon her beloved? Under the apple tree I raised you up: there your mother was corrupted: there she who bore you was deflowered." Cf. SERRA, "Dimensioni ecclesiali della figura di Maria nell'esegesi biblica odierna," in *Maria e la Chiesa oggi*, Rome 1985, pp. 277–343.

31 It appears even more evident, at this point, how Mariology, Christology, and ecclesiology constitute a sort of "trinity" in which taking the Word as head, and hence the Father and Holy Spirit as well, one implies a relation to the other, requires and implies the other, is found in the other, nor could exist or stand autonomously.

32 Cf. Jer 31:14; Is 62:4–5; Ps 86.

of the Word Incarnate? I. de La Potterie responds well, writing that

> from the biblical point of view the fundamental significance of the mystery of Mary is found, then, in her spousal and maternal role. She is the Mother of Jesus and the Mother of the disciples; but in her relationship with Christ another aspect is added, her role of spouse. She, the 'Woman,' the 'Daughter of Sion,' is the spouse of Christ. It is surprising that many theologians still hesitate to affirm it. How can Mary, we are asked, be at once the Mother of Jesus and His Spouse? This, evidently, is possible only on two different planes. As an individual person, she is the Mother of Jesus. But because of the role she receives in Jesus' mission and because of her symbolic and representative function as 'Daughter of Sion,' she becomes his Spouse in the work of salvation. We must not doubt this truth, because it is clearly contained in Scripture.[33]

Likewise we see that Mary, at the foot of the Cross, represents the Church. Is this doubling of roles possible when they seem mutually exclusive? I. de La Potterie again gives an excellent reply:

> There is no contradiction in saying that Mary is at the same time *image* of the Church and *Mother* of the Church. As an individual person she is the Mother of Jesus, and becomes the Mother of all of us, the Mother of the Church. But her corporeal Motherhood in relation to Jesus is prolonged in a spiritual Motherhood toward believers and toward the Church. And this spiritual Motherhood of Mary becomes the image and the form of the Motherhood of the Church.[34]

---

33 De La Potterie, *Mary in the Mystery*, pp. 232–233.

34 Ibid., p. 223. "Mary's spiritual Motherhood is based on the fact that she is the Mother of Christ," writes A. Feuillet, and he carefully notes that the Church, on the other hand, "is not simply the Mother of Christ, but can only be called our Mother in virtue of a power to beget and sanctify Christians received from Jesus Christ" ("De muliere parturiente et de maternitate spirituali Mariae secundum Evangeium sancti Johannis," in *Maria in Sacra Scriptura*, vol. 5, p. 120); see also the other differences between Mary's Motherhood and that of the Church listed there.

Then he said to the disciple*: *"Behold your mother!" (v. 27a).

Clearly in this verse together with Mary at the foot of the Cross, St. John the Evangelist also fulfills a representative role, both personal and communal. As the Mother of Jesus, Mary is a *single* and *unique* person; as the Spouse of Christ, she also enjoys a moral or *communal* personality, and as such she is the Church. For St. John it is the same: he is a single person as the beloved disciple of Jesus. But he also represents all the disciples of Jesus, and therefore represents the Church, as is generally admitted by the majority of exegetes.

In regard to "representation," it is interesting to observe how "John has the constant tendency to make persons in his Gospel function also as personifications of a group, and in this sense to function as symbols and as 'types.' He does not do this to make them disappear in a void or to turn them into myths, but to make them legitimate representatives of a group."[35]

If Mary and John represent both the Church and her members, there is nevertheless a difference between the two, as de La Potterie notes: "Together they both personify the Church, but in different ways. The disciple whom Jesus loved symbolizes the 'disciples' of Jesus as such, that is, all believers, and in this sense all of the Church. Mary, the Mother of Jesus, symbolizes the Church itself, in its motherly function."[36]

---

35 De La Potterie, *Mary in the Mystery*, p. 218.

36 Ibid., p. 242. Interesting and opportune are the references of the same author to the modern theologians C. Journet, H. U. von Balthasar, and J. Ratzinger on the *Marian*, *feminine*, and *maternal* faces of the Church, quite different from the institutional and masculine face that looms so prominently in the global vision of the Church, especially in the West (cf. ibid., pp. 246–247). Segalla, to the contrary, writes that "in disagreement with I. de La Potterie I would not also see in the Mother of Jesus the figure of the Church. Mary stands as 'Mother' in relation to Jesus, and with Jesus

Maternal function and *filial* role, then. This is to say that the Church is *mother* in Mary, and is *daughter* in John. Mary is the Mother of God and of the Church (represented by John). John is a child of God and of Mary (who personifies the Church). "To become children of God," de La Potterie explains well, "we must become children of Mary and children of the Church. Jesus is her only Son, but we become conformed to Him if we become children of God and children of Mary."[37]

Another element to be analyzed is found in the implications of Jesus' words: *"Behold your son."* On reflection, this phrase not only indicates the maternal mission entrusted to Mary, but is intended to establish a new *condition* or *state of life* for Mary. They are words that are not only *indicative,* but also *constitutive,* and there are those who speak of them as words that are almost "sacramental" or "creative."[38]

The same is true of Jesus' words to John: *"Behold your mother."* These also have a *constitutive–creative* value and place John in a new condition or state of life: the state of *filiation* in relation to Mary, with the relations appropriate to a son with respect to his mother. These are vital relations because they make John a real brother of Jesus who is *"the firstborn among many brothers"* (Rom 8:29). Gillard also has written that on Calvary "the Lord presents His Mother to the beloved disciples as New Eve, namely, as Mother

over against the Church. For the Fourth Gospel Mary stands simply as 'Mother.'"

[37] Ibid., pp. 223–224. Referring to Feuillet, de La Potterie also notes (p. 225) that while St. Luke emphasizes Mary's *divine* Motherhood, St. John "is more concerned to show her as the prototype of the Church," as A. Feuillet expressly writes in "Les adieux du Christ a sa mere (Jn. 19, 25–27) et la maternité spirituelle de Marie," *Nouvelle Revue Théologique* 86 (1964): 487–489.

[38] Cf. Braun, *La Mere des fidèles*, pp. 87ff. (Eng. ed.: *Mother of God's People*, pp. 109ff.); Varón Varón, *Sagrada Escritura*, p. 174; Ruotolo, *San Giovanni*, p. 465; Serra, "Dimensioni ecclesiali," pp. 320–321.

of divine life. Hence, it is precisely Mary who must beget children in the condition of sonship."[39]

Therefore, considering the gravity and the importance of the moment in which Jesus speaks from the Cross, one can not underestimate the fact that He gives John the mission of receiving Mary as Mother, making him her son. John "receives here," notes de La Potterie,

> the unique mission of having Mary for his Mother. His primary task is not to go and preach the gospel; but to become the son of Mary. For him and for all the others it is more important to be believers than apostles. The apostolic mission would be entrusted to him later, after the resurrection (Jn 20:21; 21:20–23). To be a child of Mary and of Mother Church is the first and most essential aspect of the life of a Christian.[40]

At this point it is necessary to underscore two extremely significant aspects of the Maternity of Mary Most Holy in so far as it is coredemptive.

The first aspect is linked directly to the spiritual *Maternity* of Mary, and deals with the generation of all her redeemed children. If Mary is Mother of all the redeemed, this means that She, as true and real Mother, though spiritually and not physically, has begotten each of her redeemed children in the Passion and Death of Christ. But precisely that generation was not accomplished unconsciously, generically or *en masse*. Any mother begets her children one by one, quite consciously and suffering during each, single gestation. This means that Mary Most Holy on Calvary, at the foot of the Cross, Coredemptrix as it were con-crucified with her Redeemer Son, begot each of the Redeemed, knowing each singly and suffering for each singly.

39 B. Gillard, *Maria, che cosa dice di te la Scrittura*, Turin 1983, p. 82.
40 De La Potterie, *Mary in the Mystery*, pp. 230–231.

How could this have been accomplished? Bertrand de Margerie responds to just this question when he affirms[41] that Mary Most Holy, especially at the foot of the Cross received an infused knowledge of the sins of all those for whose salvation she had cooperated in a singular and generous manner as Coredemptrix of mankind, suffering and interceding for each human person. In his study de Margerie cites Saints and Doctors of the Church, such as St. Ambrose, St. Thomas Aquinas, St. Bonaventure, St. Peter Canisius, St. Francis de Sales, Bl. Dominic of the Mother of God. He cites Pope Pius XII and outstanding theologians of the caliber of Suarez, Cardinal Newman, Cardinal Lépicier, Bossuet. Finally he concludes his argumentation affirming that Mary Most Holy is the only Coredemptrix, enjoying therefore the unique and extraordinary privilege of infused knowledge of what she was doing at the foot of the Cross, that is, completing her mission as Mother Coredemptrix for each of her children to be begotten.[42]

The second aspect regards our filiation to Mary Most Holy. If one must hold that the words of Jesus *'Behold Thy Son… Behold Thy Mother'* have a *constitutive–creative* force, that means that being a *child* of Mary, and having Mary as *Mother*, entails a vital reality so true and consistent, that every redeemed person is potentially, we might say, another *Christ–child of Mary*. A particularly significant and genuine verification of this is recorded by St. John. After the proclamation from the heights of the Cross: *Behold Thy Son… Behold Thy Mother*, the Risen Jesus appearing to the Magdalene spoke of His disciples expressly as '*My brethren*' (Jn 20:17). If before the Passion and Death, in fact, He

41 B. de Margerie, *The Knowledge of Mary and the Sacrifice of Jesus*, in *Mary at the Foot of the Cross* I, New Bedford, MA 2001, pp. 31–40. On pp. 31–32 he writes, "She received from her Son and His Spirit, at the foot of the Cross especially, an infused knowledge of the sins of those in whose salvation she collaborated in a unique way, 'singulariter prae aliis generosa socia, singulari modo cooperata est' (*Lumen Gentium* 61). She receives from that Son all the knowledge required to be a worthy coredemptrix of the human family, as she was suffering and interceding for each human person."

42 B. de Margerie, *op. cit.*, p. 40: "She is the only Coredemptrix, and she was endowed with a unique privilege of infused knowledge OF WHAT SHE WAS DOING AT THE FOOT OF THE CROSS."

called His Apostles *'servants,' 'disciples,' 'friends,'* after the Resurrection instead He called them *'brethren.'* Thus when appearing to Mary Magdalene He said: *'Go to my brethren and say to them: I am ascending to My Father and your Father, My God and your God'* (Jn 20:17). The affirmation of St. Paul presenting Christ as *'First born of many brethren'* (Rom 8:29), thus finds the strongest of guarantees.[43] And Manns, too, in his exegetical study of this Johannine pericope, states that 'in Jn 20:17 one of the consequences of the death of Christ is that all man can be called "brethren" of Christ.'[44]

And from that hour the disciple took her into his home (v. 27b).

At this point the sense of the second part of verse 27 can be understood much better. The translation *"into his home"* appears rather prosaic and not very expressive. It would make one think of Mary changing residences, something that is instead secondary. The Greek expression *eis tà 'idia,* highly nuanced, would be better rendered here with a translation making clear the idea of possession of a most precious good. John received Mary as his most precious and intimate good, becoming, in turn, it can be said, the "property" or "possession" of Mary. This is analogous to verse 11 of the Prologue, where the same expression—*eis tà 'idia*—refers to the Word when He came among those to whom He belonged, that is, among *"his own."*[45]

---

43 It has in fact been correctly written that "there is a progressive deepening of Jesus' relationship with His disciples. From servants they come to be called friends: 'No one has a greater love than to give his life for his friends... I do not call you servants but I have called you friends...' (Jn. 15:13–15). And finally, after having entrusted them to His Mother from the heights of the Cross He calls them brethren": A. Carfagna, *Lectio divina di Gv 19,25–27*, in *Theotokos* 7 (1999/2) 515, note 4.

44 F. Manns, *Esegesi di Gv 19, 25–27*, in *Theotokos* 7 (1999/2) 337.

45 On this whole delicate analysis, see de La Potterie, *Mary in the Mystery*, pp. 242–245 (with a bibliography of works, for and against, in nn. 31–33). This was already an intuition of St. Bonaventure, who read in some manuscripts of the Vulgate the version *in suam*, rather than *in sua*, commenting that John immediately received Mary "as his," that is, as "his Mother": *Commentarius in Evangelium Joannis: Opera Omnia*, tome 6 (Ad Claras Aquas, 1893), pp. 498ff.

In this way, John's sonship in relation to Mary, the "Mother," is emblematic for all the disciples of Jesus, that is to say, for all Christians.[46] The primary lesson derived from this for each one of us appears evident: to receive Mary as our Mother, and, therefore, as our most precious and intimate good, in order to become, in turn, her *children* in the totality of dedication and of filial confidence in her, the Mother. And that is the basis of a Marian *devotion* capable of becoming a Marian *life,* dynamic, progressively rendering us ever more "children" of Mary, in perfect "conformity" to her Son Jesus (Rom 8:29).

At the conclusion of this entire discussion of John 19:25–27, in view of synthesizing clearly the theological implications of an exegetical analysis directing us ever more deeply into the mystery of Mary's spiritual Motherhood, we may recapitulate via the following rapid excursus. The basis of Mary's spiritual Motherhood is her Divine Maternity. Radically, Mary becomes the universal Mother at the moment of her *fiat* at the Annunciation (Lk 1:38). Next, when she showed Jesus to the shepherds (Lk 2:16) and to the Magi (Mt 2:11), when she was concerned about the lack of wine at Cana and told the servants to *"do whatever he tells you"* (Jn 2:5): on these occasions, she allowed only certain features of her universal Motherhood to appear. On Calvary, on the other hand, at the foot of the Cross, Jesus made a public, as it were, official proclamation of Mary's spiritual and universal Motherhood, which, with

46 Many ask why St. John was chosen as representative of all the redeemed, and not St. Peter, who was first among the Apostles. Varón Varón answers that "Peter, as chief of the Apostles, was not designated son of Mary, because filiation is not to be defined primarily by reference to the hierarchical order, but is located on the plane of, in the condition of intimacy with and love for Jesus" (*Sagrada Escritura*, p. 175). See the reflections on the significance of the choice of St. John made by Jesus with respect to "virgins" (P. Gutierrez Osorio, S.J., "'Ecce Mater tua' in luce exegeseos Patrum," in *Maria in Sacra Scriptura*, vol. 5, p. 156).

her second fiat, co-immolating herself with her Son for our salvation, completed the *fiat* of the Annunciation,[47] in order to "restore supernatural life to souls" (*Lumen Gentium,* no. 61).

Mary's universal Motherhood is neither metaphorical nor merely juridical; it is neither physical nor merely moral, but *spiritual.* Mary did not beget us in the *physical* order but in the order of *grace.* This is the synthetic, complete formula adopted by Vatican II: Mary is for us "mother in the order of grace" (*Lumen Gentium,* no. 61). It means that as she begot *Jesus* in the physical order, so she has begotten *us* in the order of grace. In other words, in begetting in the physical order Him who is *"the firstborn among many brothers"* (Rom 8:29), she has begotten in the order of grace those who form the Mystical Body of Christ the Head.

On the Cross, nevertheless, the Church "is born as a body distinct from the Head," writes Bertetto. And Jesus, "who, at the wedding of Cana, had once sought the intervention of His Mother to attract to Himself by faith His first disciples, members of the Church in the process of formation, also associates Mary, the new Eve, with Himself in the redemptive sacrifice, whereby with His blood, giving Himself up to death for the Church, He won her."[48]

In this way, Mary's Motherhood became a *coredemptive* or sacrificial motherhood, because at the foot of the Cross she stood "enduring with her only begotten Son His intense suffering, associating herself with His sacrifice in her Mother's Heart, and lovingly consenting to the

47 Cf. J. Leal, *N. T. Evangelios*, pp. 1095ff.; Pietrafesa, *La Madonna nella Rivelazione*, p. 314. Regarding the "sufferings" of Mary Most Holy in the redemptive work of Christ, it may be noted that these are present, directly or indirectly, in several parallel texts, connected with Jn 19:25–27, for instance, Gen 3:15; Jn 11:52, 16:21–22; Rev 12:1–8.

48 D. Bertetto, *Maria la Serva del Signore* (Naples, 1988), p. 501.

immolation of this victim which had been born of her" (*Lumen Gentium,* no. 58). Such a coredemptive motherhood embraces not only the so-called subjective redemption, viz., the implementation of the redemptive order once established, but extends "by virtue of the divine will itself to the accomplishment of the objective or acquisitive redemption, and therefore to the very constitution of the Church, the fruit of the redemptive sufferings of Jesus and of the coredemptive suffering of Mary."[49]

In substance, this doctrine is to be found, as we have seen, in John 19:25–27, the basic text closely concatenated in a series of Old and New Testament texts: the Protoevangelium (Gen 3:15–20), "Mother–Zion" (Ps 86), the passages of Zechariah 9:9 and Song of Songs 8:5, the wedding at Cana (Jn 2:1–11), the prophecy of Caiaphas (Jn 11:52), the "woman in labor" (Jn 16:21–22), the "seamless" tunic (Jn 19:24), the "blood and water" that flowed out of the pierced side of Jesus (Jn 19:34), the "woman" of Revelation (12:1–8) who gives birth in the midst of suffering.

This is the exegetical evidence supporting the spiritual and universal Motherhood of Mary, the Motherhood which, in joy and suffering, in combat and in victory, introduces and concludes the history of salvation with the "woman" of the Protoevangelium and the "woman" of Revelation. Passing from start to finish via the central axis of the Cross on Calvary, there the "woman," Mary, present and suffering, is proclaimed by Jesus himself "Mother" of redeemed humanity, and "we Christians, represented in St. John, are all children of Mary."[50]

---

49 Ibid., p. 502.

50 *The Navarre Bible. St. John's Gospel*, p. 228.

24
"With Mary the Mother of Jesus"

Acts 1:14

Mary on Calvary, at the foot of the Cross: this is the last scene portrayed by St. John the Evangelist in which she is present.

From Calvary to the Cenacle, from the crucifixion and death of Jesus to the descent of the Holy Spirit on Pentecost, events of the greatest importance took place in which, however, Mary seems to many to be absent, because she is never mentioned by the Evangelists. The burial of Jesus, His Resurrection, the appearances during the forty days, the Ascension into heaven: these are all events of the greatest importance that concerned the apostles and disciples after the bloody Passion and death of Jesus.

Mary never appears in the accounts of these events. It is not known whether she assisted in taking Jesus down from the Cross and in burying Him, as paintings and sculptures usually represent her. There is reason to believe, however, that she was present, present with a grieving heart pierced by sorrow.

Neither is it known whether she was favored with even one private apparition of the Risen Jesus. It would seem more than plausible that she was. And it must be admitted that those supporting this view are more than a few. In fact, first among the Fathers, from the time of Tatian, St. Ephrem, and St. Ambrose, then from the time of St. Albert the Great and of Suarez, the pious conviction "has gained ground," writes F. Uricchio, "with the passing of centuries, at every level in the Latin Church and among those in the East."[1]

After a careful analysis of the pertinent Gospel texts, this same exegete, F. Uricchio,[2] concludes that

> Mark and the other Evangelists leave the door open to a belief in the apparition of the Risen Jesus to His Mother, preceding all other apparitions. But neither the second Evangelist nor the other three affirm it, *even implicitly,* because it seems to lie outside their objectives and concerns in writing, just as it also falls outside the scope of the tradition preached and then crystallized in the four Gospels.[3]

Neither does the presence of Mary on the Mount of Olives at the Ascension of Jesus seem entirely certain. Nevertheless, in the first chapter of Acts (vv. 12–14) there is assumed and depicted a certain continuity of movement on the part of a group proceeding from the Mount of Olives to Jerusalem (almost certainly to the Cenacle), *"where [they] abode"* (v. 13). Among the names of those included in that group is found that of *"Mary, the Mother of Jesus"* (v. 14). This should be sufficient to persuade anyone of the

---

1 Highly recommended is the entire exposition of the biblicist F. Uricchio, O.F.M. Conv., in the column "Domande. Risposte," *Miles Immaculatae* 6 (1970): 2–4: he concludes his remarks claiming that an appearance of the Risen Jesus to His Mother before anyone else enjoys "a very solid probability" (p. 4).

2 F. Uricchio, "Apparizioni di Cristo a Maria secondo la Bibbia," *Miles Immaculatae* 6 (1970): 272–279.

3 Ibid., pp. 278–279. More strongly in favor of the apparitions is the biblical scholar Pietrafesa, *La Madonna nella Rivelazione*, p. 334, where he writes that "the first apparition of Jesus Christ was to His Mother, although the Gospel is silent on this point. It was necessary that she should participate in the triumph of the Son, hence be joined with Him in sorrow, in battle, and in triumph." Also de Ambrogio writes: "It is difficult to think that Jesus would not have appeared to His Mother. The silence of the Gospel is a silence of reserve" (*Il Vangelo di San Giovanni*, p. 297). The earliest description of the apparition of the Risen Jesus to His Mother would seem to be the one contained in the apocryphal *Gospel of Gamaliel*: see Testa, *Maria terra vergine*, vol. 1, p. 31.

presence of Mary on the Mount of Olives at the Ascension of Jesus to assist in the last *adieu* of her Risen Son.[4]

All these were persevering with one mind in prayer, with the women and Mary, the mother of Jesus, and with his brethren (v. 14).

After the Ascension of Jesus the group of eleven apostles, some women, and the relatives of Jesus are found gathered together *"with Mary"* in the upper room of the Cenacle, *"persevering with one mind in prayer,"* in expectation of the coming of the Holy Spirit (Acts 1:1–14). It is certain that this group was the primitive nucleus of the Church being born, which was united with Mary and about Mary, the Mother of Jesus, awaiting in prayer to be clothed in the grace of the Holy Spirit.[5]

Here, in the Acts of the Apostles (1:14), the name of Mary appears for the last time in the New Testament. The scene is highly significant. Here is the Church in birth awaiting the seal of the Spirit promised by Jesus (Acts 1:8). And Mary is present at the very center of the Church, she who is *"the Mother of Jesus"* and of all the disciples of Jesus represented by John at the foot of the Cross: *"Woman, behold your son"* (Jn 19:26).

Mary Most Holy in prayer at the very center of the Church at her birth: this is the final image of Mary that St.

---

4 See Pietrafesa, *La Madonna nella Rivelazione*, p. 334. Laurentin holds it as "certain that she (Mary) was present" at the Ascension of Jesus (*Un anno di grazia*, p. 74).

5 On Acts 1:14, see G. Schneider, *Gli Atti degli Apostoli*, I. Brescia 1985 [German Original *Die Apostelgeschichte*, 2 vols. Freiberg 1980–1982; R. Fabris, "La presenza della Vergine al Cenacolo (At 1, 14)," *Marianum* 50 (1988) 397–407; and above all the extensive study of A. Valentini, *In preghiera con Maria, la Madre di Gesù* (At 1, 14), in *Theotokos* 8 (2000) 787–819, where on p. 790 it is stated that we may hold "that the group described in vs. 12–14 are the original and basic nucleus of the primitive community, to which other disciples are added. That nucleus in the Church at its origins occupies a special place."

Luke has left us in a mosaic recalling the many figurations of Mary depicted on various pages of his Gospel. In the Acts of the Apostles, St. Luke offers us, as it were, this last scene, one emblematic of the *spiritual maternity* and *praying maternity* of Mary, lived during her life on earth and continued in the Kingdom of heaven "until the eternal fulfillment of all the elect," to quote *Lumen Gentium* (no. 62). From Acts 1:14, in fact, two dimensions of Mary stand out immediately: Mother of the *infant Church* and the Virgin Mother *"at prayer,"* in active expectation of the Holy Spirit, light and warmth (the *"tongues of fire"*–2:3) of the first ecclesial community.

It is significant, in the first place, that Acts 1:14, in singling out Mary from the women disciples and relatives of Jesus by naming her alone, highlights her presence. "Luke, by mentioning the name of Mary in the summary of Acts 1:14, besides placing the Mother of Jesus in the foreground, attributes to her in the primitive community a position apart. This position apart clearly distinguishes her from the other personages recorded only as a part of the group."[6] Not only this, but the Blessed Virgin is designated with her highest title, the *Mother of Jesus.* This is because "it is from her that Jesus takes his historical origin; it is with her that the mystical Christ has its beginning. No community can be born and develop without Mary."[7]

The infant Church is, in fact, about to be clothed with the Holy Spirit, and Mary is present there, at work with her ineffable prayers, she who is the "Spouse of the Holy

---

6 PRETE, *L'Opera di Luca*, p. 488. A. VALENTINI also writes: "Within that community at its origin the figure of the Mother of Jesus occupies a unique place... Mary is presented, in the suggestive medieval conception, as the *consummatio Synagogae* (consummation of the Synagogue), point of arrival and complement of the faith and spirituality of Israel": *op. cit.*, p. 815.

7 B. MARCONCINI, *Atti degli apostoli*, vol. 1 (Turin, 1983), p. 33.

Spirit," as by inspiration St. Francis of Assisi called her.[8] The Holy Spirit, Mary, the Church: attentive reflection on these mysteries will make it clear that they constitute, together, a kind of trilogy or trinity within a fruitful communion of grace in the Mystical Body of Christ.[9]

"Collaboratrix of the Spirit at Nazareth in the birth of Christ, she collaborates with Him again in the Cenacle at the birth of the mystical Christ. Her presence, then, is not by chance, as it was not by chance at the Annunciation nor at the other crucial moments in the life of Jesus."[10] For

---

8 See O. Van Asseldonk, O.F.M. Cap., "Maria Sposa dello Spirito Santo, in S. Francesco d'Assisi," *Laurentianum* 23 (1982): 414–423. The "spousal communion" between the Holy Spirit and the Immaculate was a favorite subject for profound speculative and mystical study on the part of St. Maximilian M. Kolbe: see Manteau-Bonamy, *Immaculate Conception and the Holy Spirit*; M. D. Philippe, OP., "Il mistero dello Spirito Santo e di Maria secondo il P. Kolbe," *Miles Immaculatae* 18 (1982): 37–59, and above all P. D. M. Fehlner, *St. Maximilian M. Kolbe, Martyr of Charity, Pneumatologist*, New Bedford, MA 2004.

9 On this "trilogy" cf. the important study of L. Diez Merino, *María en Pentecostés: Madre de la Iglesia*, in *Estudios Marianos* 65 (1999) 27–71. On the theme of Mary and the Holy Spirit see the entire volume of *Estudios Marianos*, with the subtitle *El Espiritu Santo y Maria*, Granada 1999.

10 da Spinetoli, *Maria nella Bibbia*, p. 187. The author gives an interesting and suggestive description of the maternal role carried out by Mary in the heart of the first community by her example and words: "In their daily meetings, the Apostles found once again, in her features, the image of their absent Lord, but above all they listened once again to His words. Episodes, sayings, details from the life of Jesus, hitherto unknown, are now revealed to them in the school of Mary. The figure and teaching of the Master presented by His Mother become more penetrating and luminous in their minds. Perhaps in those days as never before, they understood the Christ and His message. This intimate catechesis prepares for and anticipates that which the Spirit must impart to them from on high... Queen of Apostles, acting with them, but with the dignity and veneration which are her due because of her unique relationship with the Savior. She is not a part of the hierarchy, but the hierarchy cannot do without her. There is no activity, there is no movement within the Church, neither on the heights nor at the base, there is no movement in its history that does not for this reason involve Mary as well. She did not choose the twelve, but they do not exercise their mission without her being concerned in the matter.... She had given them the Christ, now she prepares them to receive the Spirit, the soul of their future activity, and she intercedes in their favor" (pp. 186–187). Oddly, there are some who regard statements such as those of da Spinetoli as "exaggerated and theologically anachronistic" (see Prete, *L'Opera di Luca*, p. 484, n. 93). But it is difficult to discover any sign of a theological "anachronism" in the plausible and persuasive presentation of da Spinetoli.

this reason Valentini can write: "Surely it is not an accident that Luke speaks of Mary in the accounts of the infancy and at the beginning of the Acts. The first chapter of both works of Luke can be considered respectively as Gospel of the infancy of Christ and of the Church."[11] If the Holy Spirit chose the Virgin for his immaculate spouse in the virginal conception of Jesus, it was fitting that on the day of Pentecost, at the act of public and official birth of the Church, she should be present as the spiritual Mother of the entire Mystical Body.[12] And the intention of St. Luke in presenting Mary at the beginning of *Acts* seems to be, writes Valentini, that of "making evident the continuity between the historic Jesus, born of the Holy Spirit with the collaboration of Mary, and the birth of the Church through the same Spirit with the presence of Mary as Mother of Jesus, 'firstborn of many brethren' (Rom 8:29)."[13]

In reality, it is not difficult to understand why, in the atmosphere of fear still surrounding the insecure and timid apostles, notwithstanding the Resurrection of Christ, there was need of her, who with her exalted faith and a mother's burning love would take them under her care, encouraging them in their weakness. Cardinal Bea explains:

> The infant Church had need of a Mother, of a Mediatrix with the Lord now ascended into heaven and seated at the right hand of the Father. For Mary that little community in the Cenacle, that creature weak and frail, represented the precious inheritance that was left to her by her Son when He said to her *'Behold your son,'* directly indicating St. John,

---

11 A. Valentini, *op. cit.*, pp. 812–813, and Feuillet confirms this stating that "more than once the resemblance between the beginning of the Third Gospel and the Acts of the Apostles has been underscored": A. Feuillet, *Maria, Madre del Messia, Madre della Chiesa*, Milan 2004, p. 32.

12 See X. Pikaza, "Maria y el Espiritu Santo (Hech 1, 14): Apuntes para una mariologia pneumatológica," *Estudios Trinitarios* 15 (1981): 32–35; Serra, "Aspetti mariologici della Pneumatologia di Lc. 1, 35a," pp. 196–99; Varón Varón, *Sagrada Escritura*, pp. 183–188.

13 A. Valentini, *op. cit.*, p. 814.

but in him, as Origen has observed, all those in whom Christ lives (*Comm. In John* 1, 3, 23; PG 14, 32). To that community she turned all her maternal love.[14]

* * *

The other aspect of Mary, presented by St. Luke in verse 14, is that of the *Mother at prayer.* St. Luke is not speaking of the solitary or private prayer of Mary, but rather of her prayers in common with the apostles, the women, and the relatives of Jesus.[15]

An initial reflection easily reveals that St. Luke intends to sketch an inspiring image of the first apostolic community formed precisely as a praying community. "Prayer is the first act of the apostolic Church from its very foundation and beginnings; prayer for Luke represents the principal duty and concern of the primitive believing community."[16]

Now, precisely there, at the very center of this community, is the Mother of Jesus. Together with the community, she, by her ardent prayer, prepares the apostles for the advent of the Holy Spirit on Pentecost. According to the tradition of the Fathers and Doctors of the Church, it is above all through the prayers of Mary that will occur the descent of the Holy Spirit "who will manifest himself openly in the formation of the mystical body of Jesus; whereas at the annunciation he manifested himself in secret, forming the

14 A. Bea, S.J., "Erant perseverantes... cum Maria Matre... in fractione panis," in *Alma Socia Christi*, vol. 6, fasc. 1 (Rome, 1952), pp. 34–35. And Valentini adds that Mary Most Holy "occupies a singular position at the beginnings of the Church, when the spirit who earlier had overshadowed her descended at Pentecost, in the same way, on the Apostles, enabling them to bring Christ to the world (cf. Acts 1:8)": *op. cit.*, p. 816.

15 In his writing, St. Luke often recommends community prayer, insisting on this a good twenty-five times. An exhaustive study of this particular theme is that of L. Monloubou, *La prière selon Saint Luc. Recherches d'une structure* (Paris, 1976).

16 Prete, *L'Opera di Luca*, p. 464. On the other hand it is true that "prayer, in the broadest sense, is a *leitmotif* of Luke's works," A. Valentini, *op. cit.*, p. 793.

physical body of Jesus."[17] And with the pouring out of the Holy Spirit on the community in prayer the entire apostolic work and mission of the Church for the Kingdom of God begins. Valentini notes that "the prayer of the Church at its origin must be seen in relation to Luke 3:21 where a significant Christological reference is given. As Jesus at His Baptism, while in prayer, received the Spirit and so undertook His ministry (Lk 3:23), so the first nucleus of the New Testament was first in prayer to receive the Spirit enabling it to undertake its mission of witness."[18]

Here again Mary is the "woman" who opens the doors to the entrance of the Spirit, deciding the course of events, advancing the implementation of the redemptive plan of Christ. Her prayer at Cana of Galilee obtained an anticipation of the "hour" for the signs of her Son's messianic manifestation. Now her prayer in the Cenacle obtains the coming of the promised Holy Spirit upon the infant Church, upon the Mystical Body of Christ, to animate and vivify all mankind during its salvific course, to the very *eschaton* itself.[19]

Lumen Gentium (no. 59), too, comments that in Acts 1:14, Mary Most Holy is "by her prayers imploring the gift of the Spirit, who had already overshadowed her in the Annunciation." And the conciliar decree *Ad Gentes* (no. 4)

---

17 Pietrafesa, *La Madonna nella Rivelazione*, p. 335. J. P. Charlier gives a good explanation of the significant parallel existing between the beginning of the Gospel of St. Luke and the beginning of the Acts of the Apostles in the small volume *L'Evangile de l'infance de l'Eglise. Commentaires des Actes 1–2* (Brussels and Paris, 1966). On the parallel between Mary's presence at the beginning of the life of Jesus and at that of the life of the Church, see the studies of R. Schnackenburg, *La Chiesa nel Nuovo Testamento* (Brescia, 1966), pp. 14–15; Prete, *L'Opera di Luca*, p. 489; A. Feuillet, "L'Esprit Saint et la Mere du Christ," *Etudes Mariales* 25 (1968): 52–54.

18 A. Valentini, *op. cit.*, p. 797.

19 "With Mary the Church is born," writes Ortensio da Spinetoli, "with her it shall live along its long and troubled path. She will be, perpetually, the invisible bond between the Son and the redeemed. Invisible, but not for this less active" (*Maria nella Bibbia*, p. 107).

underscores still more the relation between Pentecost and the Incarnation: "The 'ACTS OF THE APOSTLES' began with 'Pentecost,' just as by the work of the Holy Spirit Christ was conceived in the Virgin Mary."

> The characteristics of prayer in Acts 1:14 are two: perseverance (they were '*steadfast*') and unanimity (they were '*in accord*'). It is well known, in effect, that insistence and perseverance in prayer constitute, one might say, a *continuum* in the writings of St. Luke. A. Valentini, citing Lk 6:12; 18:1; 22:44; Acts 12:5, states: 'the Lucan *topos* of insistent and continuous prayer is well known';[20] and perseverance in prayer is well expressed by the Greek word '*proscartereo*,' meaning etymologically 'to keep at some task with determination,' in the sense that 'one is constant, persevering.'[21]
>
> Interestingly, it is noteworthy that this verb '*proscartereo*' can denote a 'creation' in the New Testament, as Valentini also informs us. He cites C. Spicq according to whom its frequent use 'reveals not only a state of fact in the primitive Church, but also an apostolic requirement… in application of an apostolic communication of the Master' on insistence and continuity in prayer to be carried out '*at all times*': Lk 21:36.[22]
>
> As regards *unanimity* in prayer, or the union of minds and hearts in the community of the Cenacle praying with Mary, the Mother of Jesus, it must be said with Valentini that 'this element stands out with particular clarity in Acts 1:14.' Further, community prayer in effect 'constitutes a novelty of Acts in comparison with the Gospel of Luke.' He explains that 'the secret of this change vis-à-vis the Gospel: the stressing of community prayer, depends on the fact that believers were now experiencing what it means to be

20 A. VALENTINI, *op. cit.*, p. 801.

21 Ibid., pp. 801–802; see also note 57 with its references to the studies of E. HAENCHEN and BLASS–BEBRUNNER.

22 C. SPICQ, *Note di lessicografia neotestamentaria*, II, Brescia 1994, p. 472.

"church": a community assembled by the Spirit and united with the Apostles in the name of the Lord Jesus.'[23]

The Greek term for expressing *unanimity* is the adverb *omotumadon*, familiar in the vocabulary of St. Luke, a word rich in 'mutual acceptance, strong and intensely religious,' as B. Prete writes.[24] This term, in fact, is encountered in Acts 2:46; 4:24; 4:32; 5:12. It recalls both the exhortation of St. Paul to oneness of mind among believers (cf. Rom 15:6) and the will of Christ in regard to the unity of the sheepfold under a sole shepherd (cf. Jn 17:22).

Finally, the exegetical discussion of Acts 1:14 is fittingly concluded by an authoritative citation from *Redemptoris Mater,* a concise and balanced synthesis linking the Annunciation and Pentecost:

> In the redemptive economy of grace, brought about through the action of the Holy Spirit, there is a unique correspondence between the moment of the Incarnation of the Word and the moment of the birth of the Church. The person who links these two moments is Mary: *Mary at Nazareth* and *Mary in the upper room at Jerusalem.* In both cases her discreet yet essential presence indicates the path of 'birth from the Holy Spirit.' Thus she who is present in the mystery of Christ as Mother becomes—by the will of the Son and the power of the Holy Spirit—present in the mystery of the Church. In the Church, too, she continues to be a *maternal presence,* as is shown by the words spoken from the Cross: 'Woman, behold your son!'; 'Behold your Mother' (no. 24).

23 A. Valentini, *op. cit.*, pp. 798–799.

24 B. Prete, *Il sommario di At 1, 13–14 e suo apporto per la conoscenza della Chiesa delle origini*, in *Sacra Doctrina* 18 (1973) 71.

25
THE WOMAN CLOTHED WITH THE SUN

Revelation 12:1–18

According to one scholar, "no two exegetes are in perfect agreement about the twelfth chapter of Revelation."[1] The interpretation of this splendid, dramatic page of the Book of Revelation, in fact, has been and remains difficult because of the complexity of elements composing it, because of the variety of its literary genres (prophetical, Apocalyptical, Johannine), and because of the multiple references to the Old and to the New Testament. Here is the text:

And a great sign appeared in heaven: a woman clothed with the sun, and the moon was under her feet, and upon her head a crown of twelve stars. And being with child, she cried out in her travail and was in the anguish of delivery. And another sign was seen in heaven, and behold, a great red dragon having seven heads and ten horns, and upon his heads

---

[1] J. SICKENBERGER, "Die Messiasmutter im 12ten Kapitel der Apokalypse," *Theologische Quartalshrift* 126 (1946): 388. But much earlier, St. Augustine, with a bit of subtle humor, wrote that "in this book, called *Apocalypse*, many are the statements sharply testing the reader's acumen, and few are the clear ones helpful in understanding the more obscure" (*The City of God*, XX, c. 17). Some of the more recent, exegetical studies on Revelation 12 are: P. PRIGENT, *L'Apocalisse di S. Giovanni*, Rome 1985; U. VANNI, *L'Apocalisse. Ermeneutica, esegesi, teologica*, Bologna 1988; BIBBIA DI NAVARRA, *Nuovo Testamento*, 1988, vol. III, pp. 788–789; F. CONTRERAS MOLINA, *La mujer en Apocalipsis, in Ephemerides Mariologicae*, 43 (1993) 367–391; G. M. ALLEGRA, *Vaticini mariani dell'Antico Testamento*, Castelpetroso 1996, pp. 21–39; A. VALENTINI, "Il 'grande segno' di Apocalisse 12. Una Chiesa ad immagine della Madre di Gesù," *Marianum* 59 (1997) 31–63; P. FARKAS, *La "Donna" di Apocalisse 12. Storia, bilancio, nuove prospettive*, Rome 1997; S. M. MANELLI, *Maria Corredentrice nella Sacra Scrittura*, in AA.VV., *Maria Corredentrice. Storia e Teologia*, Frigento 1998, vol I, pp. 37–114 (on Rev. 12, pp. 103–111) [Eng. Version: *Mary Coredemptrix in Sacred Scripture*, cit.]; G. BIGUZZI, *La Donna, il Drago e il Messia in Ap 12*, in *Theotokos* 8 (2000) 17–66; L. SEBASTIANI, *Una pagina di luminosa oscurità*, in *Theotokos* 8 (2000) 129–164; M. MASINI, "Una rassegna di interpretazioni di Apocalisse 12," *Marianum* 62 (2000) 263–269.

seven diadems. And his tail was dragging along the third part of the stars of heaven, and it dashed them to the earth; and the dragon stood before the woman who was about to bring forth, that when she had brought forth he might devour her son. And she brought forth a male child, who is to rule all nations with a rod of iron; and her child was caught up to God and to his throne. And the woman fled into the wilderness, where she has a place prepared by God, that there they may nourish her a thousand, two hundred and sixty days.

And there was a battle in heaven; Michael and his angels battled with the dragon, and the dragon fought and his angels. And they did not prevail, neither was their place found any more in heaven. And that great dragon was cast down, the ancient serpent, he who is called the devil and Satan, who leads astray the whole world; and he was cast down to the earth, and with him his angels were cast down. And I heard a loud voice in the heavens saying:

> *Now has come the salvation, and the power and the kingdom of our God, and the authority of his Christ; for the accuser of our brethren has been cast down, he who accused them before our God day and night. And they overcame him through the blood of the Lamb and through the word of their testimony, for they did not love their lives, even in the face of death. Therefore, rejoice, O heavens, and you who dwell therein. Woe to the earth and to the sea, because the devil has gone down to you in great wrath, knowing that he has but a short time.*

And when the dragon saw that he was cast down to the earth, he pursued the woman who had brought forth the male child. And there were given to the woman the two wings of the great eagle, that she might fly into the wilderness unto her time, and times and a half time, away from the serpent. And the serpent spewed out of his mouth after the woman water like a river, that he might cause her to be carried away by the river. And the earth helped the woman, and the earth opened her mouth and swallowed up the river that the dragon had cast out of his mouth.

And the dragon was angered at the woman, and went away to wage war with the rest of her offspring, who keep the commandments of God, and hold fast the testimony of Jesus.

And he stood upon the sand of the sea. (12:1–18).

* * *

An outline–overview of the contents of this chapter of the Book of Revelation should include three events or three phases of a drama developed according to the Semitic method of "concentric circles," as Le Frois remarks,[2] namely:

> ***First circle:*** the pregnant 'Woman'; the dragon ready to devour the child that is to be born; the male child delivered and taken up to heaven; the woman taking refuge in the desert (vv. 1–6).
>
> ***Second circle:*** the victorious combat of Michael and his angels against the dragon; the dragon hurled down to the earth; the hymn of victory (vv. 7–12).
>
> ***Third circle:*** the dragon moves against the woman; the woman is taken to a safe place; the anger of the dragon vented upon the 'offspring' of the woman (vv. 13–18).

The more prominent Old Testament references, in the plot of Revelation 12, are certainly the Protoevangelium (Gen 3:15), Isaiah (7:14), and Daniel (7:7; 10:13) as well as numerous other minor texts. The Protoevangelium reminds us of the "woman" with her Son in victorious combat against the "serpent." Isaiah recalls to us the marvelous "sign" of the Virgin who conceives and gives birth to a son, the Emmanuel. Daniel recalls the figure

---

2 J. Le Frois, *The Woman Clothed with the Sun, Individual or Collective? An Exegetical Study* (Rome, 1954), pp. 189–206.

of the dragon (7:7) and of the war of the angel Michael against Lucifer (10:13).

To these must also be added the passage of the Song of Songs (6:9) for the description of the "woman" (*"Who is she that cometh forth as the morning rising, fair as the moon, bright as the sun, terrible as an army set in array?"*), and the passage of the prophet Micah, which reminds us of the woman "bringing forth" and of the "remnant" of Israel (5:2).

The more important New Testament references are the "wedding at Cana," where the "woman" is present together with her Son who works the first "sign" (Jn 2:1–11), and Calvary, where again the "woman" is together with her Son (Jesus), and the "rest of her offspring," represented by John (Jn 19:25–27). Not to be forgotten is the *"Woman"* of whom St. Paul speaks (Gal 4:4), who is at the human origin of the Incarnate Word, and the *"Woman"* of Jn 16:21 who gives birth in pain and so obtains the joy of motherhood.

The Red Dragon and the Son of the Woman

The historical and moral description of the "dragon" and of the "male child" does not, in the general opinion of exegetes, ancient and modern, involve major problems of interpretation.

The *"great dragon"* is identified by St. John himself as the *"ancient serpent, the one whom we call the devil and Satan and the one who seduces the whole world"* (v. 9). There is a facile recollection here of the *serpent* of Genesis 3, seducer of the first parents of mankind (cf. also Is 27:1). His exterior features—*"an enormous red dragon with seven heads and ten horns and over the heads seven diadems"* (v. 3)—and his terrifying destructive power—*"his tail pulled down one third of the stars from the sky, hurling them down upon the earth"* (v. 4)—are described. The "great dragon" is the adversary, the assassin, the beast powerful and exceedingly ferocious against all: against the "male child" of the woman, against "Michael and his angels," against the "woman," against the "rest of her offspring." Finally, however, he will be defeated by all, and his eternal end will be *"the pool of fire and of sulphur"* (20:10).

The *"male child"* of the woman is the Messiah, that is, the one who is destined *"to rule all the nations with a rod of iron,"* according to Psalm 2, verse 9, quoted here and also in chapter 19, verse 15, of the Book of Revelation, where St. John speaks expressly of the "Word of God." He is the primary object of the hatred of the *"red dragon,"* who is awaiting His birth in order to devour Him (v. 4). But the *"son"* does not fall into the jaws of the dragon, for He is *"immediately taken up toward God and toward his throne"* (v. 5), a clear reference to the Ascension of Jesus into heaven, where He is seated at the right hand of the Father.

On the Ascension of Jesus into heaven follows the war in the heavens between the angelic army of Michael and the diabolic army of the "great dragon." One is easily persuaded that the rebel angels intended at that time to attempt a last assault on Paradise; but the confrontation with the angelic army of Michael results in defeat, and they are definitively cast out and hurled down upon the earth, so that there is "no more place for them in heaven" (v. 8).

At this point, cast down upon the earth, the dragon rushes upon the *"woman"* who has given birth to the *"male child"* (v. 13); but the woman, too, is snatched away from his rage, for there are given to her *"the two wings of a great eagle, in order to fly to the desert"* (v. 14), where she is fed, protected from assault of the dragon who in vain tries to have her overthrown by *"a river of water... spewed out from his mouth"* (vv. 15–16).

All the more enraged by this last defeat in the fight against the woman, the dragon now plans the assaults *"against the rest of her offspring"* (v. 17). At least against this *"rest"* of the offspring of the woman, the dragon hopes to be able to unleash his murderous rage and his destructive fury. But even in this, in the end, he suffers the most humiliating defeat, because *"they overcame him through the blood of the Lamb and through the word of their testimony"* (v. 11).

As it is easy to understand even after a single reading, this chapter 12 of Revelation contains facts and events of cosmic, historic and meta-historic import in regard to God, the Son of God Incarnate, the Mother of the Son of God Incarnate, the Messiah and the Church, the offspring of the "Woman," the battle between the Angels led by Michael and the demons of the "great Dragon," the victory of the Angels and defeat of the "great Dragon," the losses of the "great Dragon" in opposing the "Woman," the persecution of the rest of the "offspring" of the "Woman" by the "great Dragon."

By reason of this it is hardly a surprise if not a few scholars and exegetes maintain chapter 12 of Revelation to be of primary importance. It is useful to mention here a few of these assessments, ancient and modern. E.–B. Allo, for example defines chapter 12 as "the culminating point" and the "central chapter" of Revelation.[3] A. Rivera considers it "fundamental";[4] T. Gallus calls it "key to the entire drama."[5] For P. Prigent it is even more "the center and key to the

---

3 E.-B. Allo, *Saint Jean. L'Apocalypse*, Paris 1921, p. 155

4 A. Rivera, *"Inimicitias ponam..." (Gen 3:15) "Signum magnum apparuit..." (Ap 12, 1)*, in *Verbum Domini* 21 (1941) 117.

5 T. Gallus, *Scholion ad "mulierem" Apokalypseos (12, 1)*, in *Verbum Domini* 30 (1952) 336.

entire book," as it is to Fr. G. Allegra who declares it to be "the key to this mysterious book" called Revelation.[6] D. H. Lawrence, in turn, states that "this passage is truly center of Revelation."[7] Valentini considers it "the central point" and "key to understanding."[8] E. Bianchi, finally summarizes the generally accepted evaluation when he affirms that to hold Revelation 12 "as center and key to the entire book" is "an opinion well-nigh generally shared by scholars."[9]

The Sign of the Woman

Who is the *"woman,"* who is the principal protagonist of these events? In answering this question with an astounding variety and diversity of opinion, reflecting ancient and modern trends in hermeneutics, exegetes divide into numerous groups. Listed summarily, the views of biblical scholars on the identity of the *"woman clothed with the sun"* fall into these categories. She could be: *a*) Mary; *b*) Mary and the Church; *c*) Israel, the Chosen People; *d*) the people of the Old and New Testament; *e*) the Church of Christ; *f*) the Church as eschatological community, with her archetype in heaven.[10]

6 G. M. Allegra, *Vaticini mariani...*, p. 39.

7 D. H. Lawrence, *Apocalisse*, Rome 1995, p. 69.

8 Valentini, "Il 'grande segno' di Apocalisse 12. Una Chiesa ad immagine della Madre di Gesù," *Marianum* 59 (1997) 34, 41. For L. Sebastiani, in the midst of the great obscurity characterizing so much of Revelation, this passage "stands apart for the special fascination it holds": *op. cit.*, p. 130. For M. G. Masciarelli it "is one of the most celebrated passages of Revelation": *La Donna di Ap 12 e il futuro ultimo dell'esistenza cristiana*, in *Theotokos* 8 (2000) 165.

9 E. Bianchi, *Lectio divina su Apocalisse 12*, in *Theotokos* 8 (2000) 182. See also G. Biguzzi, *op. cit.*, p. 17, note 2.

10 On the various interpretations of the *"woman,"* see the extensive and systematic exposition by H. Gollinger, *Das "grosse Weibchen" von Apokalypse 12* (Würzburg and Stuttgart, 1971), pp. 25–72, with bibliography to 1972. With bibliography to 1976, see X. Pikaza, "Apocalipsis XII: el nacimiento pascual del Salvador," *Salmanticensis* 23 (1976): 217–256.

A more critical analysis of the theories, however, shows that as in yesteryear, so today there are but two basic interpretations of the "woman" of Revelation 12, namely: *Mary* and the *Church*. Traditionally, there has been "a pendulum movement between the two interpretations," writes I. de La Potterie, "and neither of the two aspects can be totally excluded in the interpretation of this mysterious symbol."[11] We would qualify this assessment somewhat to grasp the precise line of development followed by exegetical thought from patristic to medieval tradition. There occurred, in fact, a slow passage from the ecclesiological interpretation (prevalently patristic) to the Mariological (prevalently medieval).[12] Prescinding from the problems of those who uphold an exclusively ecclesiological or an exclusively Mariological interpretation—"two

---

11 De La Potterie, *Mary in the Mystery*, p. 242. Valentini also admits that the Mariological interpretation of Rev. 12 "is not rare and has found defenders from antiquity to the present... It is shared by a certain number of Fathers and ancient writers..., by some monastic authors of the middle ages and by a widespread liturgical and iconographical tradition." For this reason it must be said that "the mariological sense, from the stand point of exegetical history, appears anything but secondary": *op. cit.*, pp. 32–33.

12 Apropos antiquity, it seems certain that the earliest Mariological interpretation of Revelation 12 dates from the second century, according to the important study of B. Bagatti, O.F.M., "L'interpretazione mariana di Apocalisse 12, nel 11 secolo," *Marianum* 40 (1978): 153–159. It is found in an Arabic text of the *Historia Josephi Fabri Lignarii* (History of Joseph the Carpenter), where the words spoken by the angel to Joseph in a dream are modified with the phrase of Rev 12:5: "Joseph, son of David, do not fear to take Mary your wife because he to whom she will give birth is pure, and you will call him by the name Jesus: it is he who will guide his people with an iron rod." See also the interpretations of the symbolic events, such as the flight of the Holy Family into the desert, the slaughter of the Innocents suggested to Herod by the dragon (Satan), the stay for "three years and a half" in the desert of Egypt, in relation to vv. 1–6. "As far as I know," Bagatti concludes, "this is the oldest text which comments on this chapter of Apocalypse and until now has never been utilized by scholars" (ibid., p. 159). The neglect of so ancient a text by exegetes is simply inexplicable. Valentini remarks: "if the dates are confirmed: a document of the second century within the Johannine tradition, then the interpretation of Rev. 12 would have to be completely rethought" (*op. cit.*, p. 33). That is another way of saying the directly Mariological interpretation could not be given first place over the directly ecclesiological interpretation. Thereby "the mariological sense together with the ecclesial would have to be held as original": *op. cit.*, p. 33.

positions extremely difficult to defend," de La Potterie justly observes[13]—the problem, in substance, consists in harmonizing or properly balancing the two aspects, Mariological and ecclesiological. The Mariological aspect, in effect, always appears consistent with the ecclesiological, and vice-versa. L. Sebastiani says that "the differences regard the weight, the centrality to be attributed to one or the other in the process of interpretation."[14] Which of the two is primary? Is the *"woman"* Mary, also representing the Church? Or does the *"woman"* connote the Church, personified as Mary?

It is our conviction that the *"woman"* is *Mary, also exemplifying the Church,* that is to say, she is Mary as a physical person, the Mother of Jesus, and she is Mary as a mystical figure, Mother of all of the believers, "heavenly model" of the Church (*Lumen Gentium,* no. 65). The *"Woman"* of Revelation recapitulates and expresses the total reality of Mary's divine and ecclesial maternity. The *"Woman"* of Revelation recapitulates and expresses the whole reality of the divine Motherhood and of the ecclesial Motherhood of Mary. She is the Mother of the Messiah, *"the male child"* (v. 5), and she is the Mother of those who believe in Jesus, namely, of the *"rest of her offspring… those who observe the commandments of God and have possession of the testimony of Jesus"* (v. 17).

---

13 De La Potterie, *Mary in the Mystery*, p. 242. Valentini writes: "in our opinion the ecclesial and Mariological senses are not alternatives, as is so often thought, but complementary, indeed reciprocally postulating each other." A. Valentini, *op. cit.*, p. 62

14 L. Sebastiani, *op. cit.*, p. 131. Such is, for example, the comparative evaluation Valentini establishes between the "*Woman*" of Rev. 12 and that of Jn. 19:25–27. The Woman of Rev. 12 "presents an ecclesial significance and only indirectly a Mariological one, whereas that of the Gospel refers directly to Mary, but with ecclesial implications. The Gospel reveals the Marian physiognomy of the Woman-Church of Revelation 12, while Revelation underscores the ecclesial dimension of the Mother of Jesus": A. Valentini, *op. cit.*, p. 62.

There is more than one certain clue to identify the "Woman–Mary" in Revelation 12. Let us examine these clues.

First, the term *"woman"* is expressly linked in the text to Old and New Testament passages where Mary is present and acts as protagonist. Such is the prophetic text of Genesis where the *"woman,"* with her Son, is the triumphant enemy of the *"serpent,"* seducer of our first parents.[15] In Galatians 4:4, the "woman"—Mary—is the human origin of the Word made flesh, thus inserted into human history. At Cana of Galilee, Mary is the *"woman"* who prepares the way for the public manifestation of the Messiah-Savior, persuading Jesus to work the first of His "signs" (Jn 2:1–11) Next, beneath the Cross, at the consummation of the universal salvific mission, Mary is present as the *"woman"* associated with Christ in the work of Redemption and proclaimed by Jesus himself *"Mother"* of redeemed humanity (Jn 19:25–27). In the text of Revelation 12, finally, the same *"woman"* recapitulates and concludes the salvific plan of God already predicted at the dawn of humanity, in Genesis.[16]

At this point, it is easy enough to see how the word *"woman"* functions, as it were, as an *alpha* and *omega* term, appearing initially in Genesis 3:15—the first and crucial

---

15 The points of direct contact and mutual reference between Gen 3:1 and Rev 12 appear evident. F. M. BRAUN believes they are suggested by "1) the manner in which the Woman is set before the Dragon; 2) the identification of the great Dragon with the ancient Serpent (v. 9); 3) the identification of the Dragon's adversary with the offspring of the Woman, represented as sperma or seed; 4) the victory of the Child or the Lamb (v. 11) over the Dragon–Serpent; 5) the powerlessness of the Dragon with regard to the Child (v. 5) and his Mother (vv. 6, 13–16); 6) the cohesion of the group composed of the Woman and her Child (vv. 3–5). Just as in the Protoevangelium, the vision of Apocalypse chap. 12 is dominated by the Savior's Mother, designated simply as the Woman, with the article, indicating a person supposedly known" (*La Mère des fidèles*, pp. 143–144 [Eng. Ed.: *Mother of God's People*, pp. 138–139], quoted by PIETRAFESA, *La Madonna nella Rivelazione*, pp. 344–345.

16 See the important article of L. CERFAUX, "La vision de la femme et du dragon," pp. 21–34.

moment of human history—and running like a thread throughout all written revelation, reappearing at four other decisive moments: in Galatians 4:4, at the human origin of Christ; at Cana of Galilee, at the "hour" of the first messianic and salvific manifestation of Christ; on Calvary, at the hour of the Passion and death for the fulfillment of the Redemption; and finally, in Revelation, at the last act in the manifestation of Christ as Judge and Sovereign of the universe.[17]

Continuing the exegetical analysis of Revelation 12, we clearly see that the *"woman clothed with the sun"* is the Mother of the Messiah. Apropos of this identification, it is fair to describe the consensus among exegetes as unanimous. The Mother of the Messiah is indubitably Mary, and only Mary. Consequently, Mary is the *"woman"* who, together with her Son, unifies all of written revelation from Genesis to Revelation. She is, therefore, the *"woman"* presented with her *"seed"* (the Son) in Genesis 3:15; she is the *"woman"* of whom Jesus *"is born"* (Gal 4:4); she is the *"woman"* who is *"the Mother of Jesus"* at Cana and on Calvary (Jn 2:1–11; 19:25–27); she is the *"woman"* who is *"pregnant"* with the Messiah, the *"male child,"* in Revelation 12.

This *"woman"* and this *"Mother,"* therefore, can only be Mary. For only she conceives and bears the Messiah. This is beyond question. "She is, therefore, the Mother of the Messiah: no one else can be," R. Laurentin firmly states.[18]

Whoever attempts an explanation in terms of a metaphorical motherhood of Israel in relation to the Messiah flies in the face of clearly evident and highly concrete

---

17 Pope John Paul II, in his Marian encyclical *Redemptoris Mater* (no. 24), also speaks of the continuity and identity of "the woman indicated in the book of Genesis (3:15) at the beginning and in Apocalypse (12:1) at the end of the history of salvation."

18 Laurentin, *Tutte legenti*, p. 45.

exegetical data, showing immediately the Mother of the Messiah to be a real and true woman. Nowhere in the Old Testament, J. Salgado points out, can an instance be found where the people of God, Israel, personifies the Mother of the *individual* Messiah. The "Daughter of Zion" is at times called "mother," but not of the individual Messiah. And the Church—the people of the New Covenant—is presented as the "Spouse" of Christ and "Mother of the faithful," but never as the Mother of Christ. The only Mother of the Messiah *"in flesh and blood,"* to borrow the phrase of J. J. Weber, is Mary alone.[19] And if this "woman"—Mary—also exemplifies the "Church," that is by no means a reason to deny that of the two, "ontologically" Mary has the first place.[20] "Guided by the Holy Spirit, St. John saw first in this woman the Virgin Mary herself, then the Church, the whole of Christianity, because the Church would not exist without Mary."[21]

In a summary, compact and incisive, Laurentin writes that in identifying the Apocalyptic *"woman"*

> difficulties arise from a one-way exegesis: from the moment that the woman appears to represent *also* the Church, it

---

19 See the important citations of J. M. Salgado, who quotes M. Tobac, J. Le Frois, F. M. Braun, R. Laurentin, J. J. Weber, as well as numerous biblical references: "Apoc. XII a la lumière des Procédés littéraires de St. Jean," in *Maria in Sacra Scriptura*, vol. 5, p. 331. Taking in substance the same position are A. Romeo, "La donna ravvolta dal sole, Madre di Cristo e dei cristiani nel cielo (Ap. 12)," *Rivista Biblica* (1956): 218–232, 314–329 (the author also quotes in support: J. Lortzing, A. Rivera, J. F. Bonnefoy, J. Weber); P. Grelot, in "Maria è il suo nome. Itinerario storico-teologico," in *Sacra Scrittura* (Rome, 1985), p. 33; G. Roschini, *Dizionario di Mariologia* (Rome, 1957), pp. 13–16; C. de Ambrogio, *L'Apocalisse* (Turin, 1981), pp. 77–79; O'Carroll, *Theotokos*, pp. 375–377.

20 "Ontologically Mary remains in first place," J. M. Salgado writes, "Procédés littéraires," p. 332. "This person is Mary," affirms D. Bertetto, "mother of Christ and of Christians, that is, of the physical Christ and of the mystical Christ. Mary is primarily understood and described in the vision of the woman; however, Mary represents the Church, to which secondarily and appropriately can be applied the things that are predicated of Mary" (*Maria la Serva del Signore*, p. 59).

21 Gillard, *Che cosa dice*, p. 118.

> is claimed, the term cannot connote Mary. But one must not forget that according to the Gospels of Luke and John, Mary, the Mother of the Messiah, is the daughter of Zion in whom the people of Israel is personified. She is, then, at the same time, Mother of the Messiah and Mother of the new people inseparably united to Him.[22]

The point, then, on which the identification of the *"woman"* hangs, is the dual maternity realized indivisibly and only *in Mary*: she is the real, physical Mother of the Messiah; she is the real, mystical Mother of the Church, the new people of God.[23] This is the thread that, without a break in continuity, starts with Genesis and reaches to Revelation, passing through Cana and Calvary. In Genesis 3:15 and in Revelation 12, in fact, we find the *"woman," "the Son,"* and the *"rest of the offspring"* in victorious combat against the serpent. The picture is substantially neat and linear. All other questions or problems will touch only specific details of prophetic symbols not always easily interpreted from the text. That occurs, because in Revelation, "in each word there are hidden many meanings."[24]

The exegetical interpretation of Revelation 12 of the Venerable Fr. G. M. Allegra with clarity and sureness of touch witnesses to the priority of the Mariological sense in respect to the ecclesiological. In fact, in replying to the question concerning the identity of the "Woman" of Revelation 12, Fr. Allegra examines, analyzes and calls into

---

22 Laurentin, *Tutte legenti*, p. 45.

23 "The Woman is therefore, at the same time, Mother of Christ and of believers," writes S. Garofalo, *L'Apocalisse per oggi* (Florence, 1978), p. 167. The relationship is effectively stated by F. M. Braun when he writes: "As Mary on Calvary is both the Mother of Christ and Mother of the disciple as representative of the Christian community, the Woman mentioned in Apoc. 12 appears to us then to possess a twofold posterity, individual and collective, the first signified by the male Child (v. 5), the second by the rest of her offspring (v. 17). Mother of the first, she is also Mother of the others who form one body with Him" (*La Mere des Fidèles*, p. 152; Eng. ed.: *Mother of God's People*, pp. 148–149).

24 St. Jerome, *Epistula LIII ad Paulinum*, no. 8. PL 22:549.

question the opinion according to which the "Church" would be the "Woman" of chapter 12 of Revelation. He shows why from an exegetical point of view this opinion cannot be maintained:

> I answer that primarily and directly such a position [viz., the woman primarily and directly denoting the Church] does not explain chapter 12 correctly, nor take into consideration the complete theology of Revelation.[25] The Church founded by Christ cannot beget Christ. The Church is not the Mother of Christ. The Church is sanctified by the mystical Christ and is the body and fullness of Christ, but not His Mother (Eph 1:23). The Church, finally, in the Johannine theology is the bride of Christ, not Mother.
>
> Who, then, is this woman? A correct exegesis requires that any reply take account of all the elements, above all those apparently contrary to it.
>
> On these premises it seems to us that only the mariological interpretation gives an adequate explanation to the entire chapter, and illustrates it with sufficient clarity.
>
> But here we speak of Mary Most Holy in the full sense, or better we contemplate her in the individual and collective sense as in chapter 2 of Daniel where the golden head of the statue refers to the King Nabuchodonosor, and also to the entire Babylonian Empire, or again in chapter 7 of the same book, where the figure of the Son of man is a symbol of the Messiah and also of the people of God… Thus we hold that in chapter 12 of Revelation 'Woman' denotes a single person, who can only be Mary (vv. 5, 9, 17), because She alone is Mother of the historic Christ and of the disciples of Christ. On the other hand 'woman' also denotes a collective person who is organically one with Mary, namely the Church, born of Mary with Christ, of which Mary is Mother, type and ideal.

25 On the theology of Rev. 12 see the brief chapter by Fr. G. M. Allegra in his *Vaticini mariani…* pp. 35–39.

> The Church is not so much anti-type of Mary, as her prolongation. As the mystical Christ derives from the historic Christ, and is not a duplicate of Him, but His extension, His fullness, so from the historic maternity of Mary a mystical, spiritual maternity of the Church takes its origin.
>
> Mary, Mother, is type of the Church, mother.
>
> Mary is type, the Church anti-type. What Mary accomplished for the historic Christ and for the budding community of Christ, She continues to do for the faithful through the Church, whose work as it were is an extension in time and space of the activity of Mary.
>
> Mary finally, is the ideal of the Church militant and its rock of defense, above all in the epoch at the end of time. This exegesis is confirmed by the parallelism between chapter 12 of Revelation and chapter 3 of Genesis.[26]

"Decifering" Other Passages

The pains of childbirth of the *"woman"* seem to constitute a particular problem, if they are referred to the virginal childbirth of Mary at Bethlehem.[27] If, instead, they are referred to the childbirth of Mary on Calvary, where she is constituted "truly the Mother of the members of [Jesus] Christ," as St. Augustine affirms (quoted by *Lumen Gentium,* no. 53), then we too can understand with other exegetes, among them D. Squillaci, that to our Lady "is to be ascribed a double childbirth: one *natural* and virginal, by which, without pain or injury of any kind, she begot the Son of God, the physical Christ; the other *spiritual,* by means of which on Calvary, uniting her sufferings to those of the Redeemer, she begot the Mystical Body of Christ."[28]

---

26 G. M. Allegra, *op. cit.*, pp. 31–33.

27 The prevailing ecclesiological exegesis in patristic times stems from this difficulty: cf. F. M. Braun, "La Femme vêtue de soleil," *Revue Thomiste* 55 (1955) 640–641; Laurentin, *La Vergine Maria*, p. 51.

28 D. Squillaci, "Maria nella Donna dell'Apocalisse," *Miles Immaculatae* (1969): 51. D. Ruotolo writes that "the virginal birth of the Redeemer did

According to R. Laurentin, the difficulty over the pains of childbirth on the part of the *"woman"* of Revelation can be eliminated by a comparison:

> In Revelation 5:6, Christ appears in heaven in the form of an *immolated lamb* (cf. Jn 19:36). The sufferings of the woman who also appears in heaven in Revelation 12:2, stand in relation to the *immolation* of the celestial Lamb. Thus, in the 12th chapter of Revelation, the reference is not to the childbirth at Bethlehem, but to the words of Christ on the Cross: 'Son, behold your Mother' (Jn 19:25). It is a question of the spiritual Motherhood of Mary and of the compassion with which the Mother of Jesus shares in the sufferings of the immolated Lamb. John 19 and Revelation 12 are, therefore, in strict relation to one another. In each passage Mary's Motherhood *in relation to the disciples* entails a context of suffering (Jn 19:25; Rev 12:2).[29]

On this subject, some speak of superimposed planes or of the "law of two phases" in a single prophetic perspective, one including both the joyful virginal childbirth of Christ, the Head, at Bethlehem and the painful spiritual childbirth of the members—already included in the humanity of Christ (but not born)—on Calvary. For thus God wished to insert into an organic, redemptive plan the sufferings of Mary, associated with her Son in ransoming mankind.[30] If

---

not cause the most holy Virgin any suffering, indeed it was accomplished in the most ineffable joyous ecstasy; but the generation of the Mystical Body of the Lord cost her the unspeakable sufferings of Calvary, because she was the Coredemptrix of mankind. The Church was established in the great sufferings of Jesus and Mary, but in her turn, the Church does not beget the holy people, which is the kingdom of Jesus Christ, without great suffering" (*L'Apocalisse* [Naples, 1974], p. 340).

29 LAURENTIN, *Tutte le genti*, pp. 51–52: the author refers to Cerfaux, Braun, Feuillet (ibid., n. 28). See in particular A. FEUILLET, "Le Messie et sa Mere d'aprés le chapitre XII de l'Apocalypse," *Revue Biblique* 66 (1959): 55–86 (Eng. tr.: *Johannine Studies*, pp. 257–292).

30 J. M. SALGADO, quoting Allo, Le Frois, Dillenschneider, Feuillet, Romeo, writes: "Treated here is simply the projection within a single perspective of the virginal birth of the Messiah and the spiritual birth of the rest of the offspring of the woman (a birth to be continued in time and to be acutely painful); it is this which some exegetes call the 'law of two phases.' Here we encounter the most orthodox teaching of Catholic theology: we know in effect that Mary is the Mother of believers only because she is first

the whole Son of Mary is Jesus, Head and Body, Mary is shown in joy at Bethlehem as the *Mother of the Head,* and on Calvary as the *Mother of the Body* regenerated unto the supernatural life of grace.[31] Koehler succinctly summarizes: Mary "is the Woman who in Jesus (therefore born at Bethlehem and at Calvary) gives to God mankind reborn to divine sonship."[32]

In regard to other elements composing the splendid, dramatic picture of Revelation 12, exegetes primarily part company in their interpretations by reason of the different hermeneutic perspectives they adopt. The rich symbolism proper to the Apocalyptic genre and the superimposed planes characteristic of the prophetic genre make possible multiple senses in the text.[33] The woman clothed with the sun and the moon under her feet and a crown of twelve stars on her head (v. 1); the flight of the woman into the desert where she is nourished for 1,260 days (v. 6); the two wings of an eagle given to the woman to fly into the desert where she is to remain for a time, two times and a half of a time (v. 14); the river of water spewed out by the dragon against the woman and the chasm that swallows the river (vv. 15–16): all are elements of a complex symbolism and

---

the Mother of Christ (in whom we are all included), and because God has willed to insert as factor in the organic whole of the redemptive plan the sufferings of the Mother, associated with his Son in the work of ransoming the human race" ("Procédés littéraires," p. 347). A little before, the author also analyzed the meaning of the verb "basanizo" in the context of the apocalyptic-prophetic genre of Johannine writing.

31 Cf. Varón Varón, *Sagrada Escritura*, p. 9, where he writes: "The whole son of Mary is Jesus, the Head, and Jesus, the members. Now, the mystical members of the Body of Christ, or 'the rest of the offspring,' were made son of the Virgin when we were reborn to the supernatural life of grace."

32 Koehler, *Maria nella Sacra Scrittura*, p. 109. The interpretations more recently proposed by Pikaza, *Apocalipsis XII*, based on the multilayered symbolism of Rev. 12, contains some interesting data. Cf. also E. Corsini, *Apocalisse prima e dopo* (Turin, 1980); De La Potterie, *Mary in the Mystery*, pp. 240–243.

33 Cf. U. Vanni, "La decofidicazione del 'grande segno' in Apocalisse 12, 1–6," *Marianum* 40 (1978) 121–152.

of a prophetic language, referred now to Mary, now to the Church; now to Mary the individual person, now to Mary the mystical person, Mother of believers and image of the Church; now to Mary the Mother, now to the Church the daughter.[34]

Thus, to mention only a few points, the flight of the woman into the desert is referred to Mary the Mother of Christ and of the Church (with an allusion to the Assumption?); "the rest of the offspring" of the woman, on the other hand, is referred to the Church, subjected to the infernal assaults of the dragon who manifests his terrible power with the seven heads and ten horns, and his dominion ("prince of this world": Jn 12:31) with seven diadems.[35]

Of great importance, in particular, is the description of the exterior features of the *"woman,"* rich in a symbolism quitc unusual. *"Clothed with the sun,"* Mary was really flooded by divine grace that consecrated her immaculate from conception and transformed her into the Mother of God.[36] *"The moon under her feet"* signifies that all things

---

34 Cf. de La Potterie, *Mary in the Mystery*, pp. 253–254, where the author quotes a brief text of E.-B. Allo, who uses the same argument in regard to Christ the Lord: "There are certain traits which are suitable both to the personal Christ and to the mystical Christ, while others regard only the personal or only the mystical Christ." For the analytical explanation of a considerable part of the symbolism of Revelation 12 from a Mariological perspective, cf. the study of Romeo, "La donna ravvolta," pp. 239–252.

35 Cf. Spedalieri, *Maria nella Scrittura e nella Tradizione*, p. 123. "St. John in verse 17 clearly distinguishes the woman and her Son who is the physical Christ, from the other children, brothers of Jesus Christ. Therefore, the woman of whom he previously spoke is not the Church militant directly, but Mary.... After Mary withdraws from the serpent, the Church militant is no longer designated with the name of woman, but with the name 'the rest of the descendants of the woman' against whom are directed the snares of the devil (Apoc. 12:17)," so writes Bertetto, *Maria la Serva del Signore*, p. 59.

36 Cf. the important observations of Laurentin, "La Vergine Maria," p. 52, fl. 29, on the allusions, in Rev 12, to the truth of the Immaculate Conception of Mary, according to L. Cerfaux, A. M. Dubarle, and others. Cf. also A. Strobel, "L'Immaculée Conception dans la révélation de l'économie actuelle," in *Virgo Immaculata*, vol. 3, pp. 144–148; Grelot, "Maria è il suo nome," p. 33

created and passing—symbolized by the moon, which appears and disappears—are under the feet of the Queen of the universe. *"On her head a crown of twelve stars"* is the symbol of Mary's reign over the angels (stars), over the Chosen People (the "twelve" tribes), over the Church (the "twelve" apostles).[37]

To these symbolic elements are also connected the truths of Mary's Assumption into heaven and of her universal reign. The liturgy of the Assumption, for example, "recognizes in Revelation 12 the biblical icon of the Assumption," writes Laurentin, even if it is not so easy for exegesis to justify this type of interpretation.[38]

Another element of great value is the Marian interpretation of the combat between the *"woman clothed with the sun"* and *"the great red dragon."* In this battle, Mary becomes the one who guarantees to the redeemed truth and faith, grace and virtues. In fact, "having entered deeply into the history of salvation, Mary, in a way, unites in her person and re-echoes the most important doctrines of faith," says *Lumen Gentium* (no. 65), thus becoming a distinctive sign of a true believer and "banner of unity" for the whole Church.[39]

On this subject, a passage interesting and rich in insight, accurate as it is delicate, has been written by I. de La Potterie:

> A very important insight of modern exegesis has brought to light how the mystery of Mary in some way forms a synthesis of all of the preceding revelation about the people of God, about all that which God, through his salvific action, wishes

---

37 Cf. Varón Varón, *Sagrada Escritura*, pp. 191–192.

38 Laurentin, *Tutte le genti*, p. 52. Cf. also Romeo, "La donna ravvolta," pp. 239ff. Spadafora, *Maria Santissima*, p. 72, where he quotes, in support, M. Jugie, F. M. Braun, P. C. Landucci, A. Romeo, R. J. de Roo.

39 Cf. Paul VI, *Signum Magnum*, no. 25.

> to realize for his people. In Mary are accomplished all of the important aspects of the promises of the Old Testament to the Daughter of Sion, and in her concrete person is anticipated that which will be realized for the new people of God, which is the Church. Now, the history of revelation regarding the theme of the Woman Sion concretized in the person of Mary, and extended to the Church, constitutes a doctrinal bastion, an unshakeable, well-structured ensemble for understanding the history of salvation, from its origins to the last times.[40]

Finally, to complete the theological picture inherent in the Mariological interpretation of Revelation 12, it is important to keep in mind the authoritative guidance of the pontifical Magisterium, especially of the more recent popes, who have clearly confirmed the Mariological sense of this chapter. It is enough to cite here St. Pius X in his encyclical *Ad diem illum,* Pius XII in the dogmatic bull *Munificentissimus Deus,* Paul VI in the Marian exhortation *Signum magnum,* and John Paul II in his encyclical *Redemptoris Mater.*

To all this must be added the testimony of the liturgy—"a theological locus"—which, in the Mass for the solemnity of the Assumption and in the Mass in honor of the Virgin Mary, Help of Christians, applies this passage of Revelation 12 to Mary.[41]

Not to be forgotten is the *sensus fidelium* of the Christian people, who love images and medals of Mary Immaculate shown with a crown of twelve stars on her head and the moon and serpent under her feet: "The iconographic

---

40 De La Potterie, *Mary in the Mystery*, p. 262. Particularly interesting is the discussion of the theological weight to be assigned the Marian antiphon "Rejoice, O Virgin Mary, you alone have destroyed all heresies in the whole world," which, it is hoped, will be restored to liturgical use (ibid., pp. 276–277, nn. 34–35). On the action of Mary against heresies, cf. the impassioned pages of Ruotolo, *L'Apocalisse*, pp. 356–358, 367–372.

41 Cf. *Roman-Franciscan Sacramentary*, p. 671A; *Collection of Masses of the Blessed Virgin Mary*, vol. 2, *Lectionary*, pp. 180–181.

tradition of the Immaculate, represented as the woman of John's vision, is the witness of Christian devotion."[42]

Mother and Queen of heaven and earth, Mother and Teacher of believers, "the exalted figure" of the Church journeying toward the next life: this is, in conclusion, Mary, the *"woman clothed with the sun,"* the Mother of God and of humanity, who so perfectly personifies the Church, as to justify fully the statement of Cardinal Journet: "The whole Church is Marian."[43]

"That great woman," wrote pseudo-Augustine, echoing Epiphanius, Andrew of Caesarea, and Arietas—Eastern Fathers—"represents the Virgin Mary who, intact, begot our Head intact, becoming model for Holy Church."[44]

42 Garofalo, *L'Apocalisse per oggi*, p. 171.

43 C. Journet, *L'Eglise du Verbe incarné*, vol. 2 (Paris, 1962), p. 248.

44 Quoted in Testa, *Maria terra vergine*, vol. 1, p. 444, with quotations in nn. 52–55.

26
Synthesis of Biblical Mariology: The Immaculate

Among many possible choices there are two texts of sacred Scripture that would express most forcefully and symbolize most meaningfully the mystery of Mary: expressing her extraordinarily graced personality; emblematic of her universal salvific mission linked with that of her Son until the end of human history. The first is that of Genesis: *"I will put enmity between you and the woman, and your seed and her seed: she will crush your head, and you will lie in wait for her heel"* (3:15). The second is that of Revelation: *"And a great sign appeared in heaven: a woman clothed with the sun, and the moon under her feet, and on her head a crown of twelve stars"* (12:1).

Prophecy and final (eschatological) fulfillment, Incarnation and Redemption are recapitulated in these two biblical texts intertwined with one another in delineating for us the exalted figure of Mary: at her first appearance in the Old Testament as *"the morning rising"* (Song 6:9), and in the New Testament with the full brightness of midday, *"clothed with the sun"* (Rev 12:1).

In the first text (Gen 3:15), significantly called the Protoevangelium, we are made aware of the figure and mission of Mary that foretell the messianic salvation of mankind. The *"woman"* is the Mother of the Messiah-Redeemer, prefigured and symbolized down the subsequent centuries and millennia on many pages of the ancient revelation that accompanied and illumined the path of the Chosen People in expectation across the millennia. In the second text (and its context: Rev 12:1–18), as it were a summary of the entire biblical "revelation" of the mystery of Mary, we contemplate her image and mission in the splendor of the eternal midday, the superhuman prodigy of maternal queenship over the created universe, over both heaven and earth.

In the first text (Gen 3:15) we preview, antithetically, the reality of Mary's mission: in opposition to the serpent (the *"enmity"*); in union with the Messiah-Redeemer (her *"seed"*) fighting and crushing the head of the serpent; in contrast with Eve, seduced and conquered by the serpent (Gen 3:13; 2 Cor 11:3). The prophetic vision embraces the entire salvific plan. In the words of Genesis "there opens a vision of the whole of Revelation," writes Pope John Paul II, "first as a preparation for the Gospel and then as the Gospel itself."[1] The dramatic scene of Genesis 3:15 speaks of mystery, and in revealing it pinpoints our gaze on this "woman," so heroic and sublime—the antithesis of poor Eve—who goes forth with her Son to reverse the fortunes of fallen man.

In the second text (Rev 12), we contemplate, in metahistorical synthesis, the reality of the person and mission of Mary, the "woman" radiant in grace ("clothed with the sun"), in royal majesty over the angels (the crown of "stars") and over creation ("the moon under her fret"), Mother of God incarnate ("the male child") and Mother of the Church ("the rest of her offspring"), which is the Mystical Body of Christ, begotten and co-redeemed by her on Calvary amidst sufferings ("she cried out in the anguish of delivery"), the powerful adversary, Satan ("the great dragon"), checkmated and rendered impotent by the

1 Apostolic Letter *Mulieris Dignitatem*, no. 11.

mystery of the Immaculate Conception, of the Assumption, and of the Queenship.

The tableau of Revelation 12 is complete with its magnificent scenario, rich in illustrative detail, even if in every instance not easily understood. On this scene converge, marvelously coordinated, every dimension of the redemptive plan traced out in the Old and New Testaments touching the "mystery of that '*woman*' who, from the first chapters of the Book of Genesis up to the Book of Revelation, accompanies the unveiling of God's salvific plan for humanity."[2] In the light of Revelation 12, we can formulate these fundamental conclusions about the "mystery of that 'woman.'"

Mary is the *"woman"* (Rev 12:1), the same *"woman"* of the *Protoevangelium* (Gen 3:15), of whom *"is born"* the Son of God; sent by the Father (Gal 4:4);[3] the *"woman"* present and wholly absorbed in the sufferings of her Son crucified on Calvary (Jn 19:25–26).

Mary is the *"virgin"* who is shown alone with the Son, without husband, in the Protoevangelium (Gen 3:15), then in Isaiah (7:14), and in Micah (5:2); her virginity prefigured by the *"burning bush"* (Ex 3:1–11), by the *"rod of Aaron"* (Num 9:16–24), by the *"fleece of Gideon"* (Judg 6:36–40), by the *"enclosed garden, sealed fountain"* (Song 4:12); finally, described by St. Matthew and by St. Luke in

---

2 *Redemptoris Mater*, no. 47. J. H. NEWMAN wrote with reason that Rev 12 "crowns and canonizes Mary" (quoted by SCHELKLE, *La Madre del Salvatore*, p. 80).

3 John Paul II points out the importance of this Pauline text in connection with that of Genesis (3:15), precisely in the use of the term "woman": "It is significant," he writes, "that the Apostle does not call the Mother of Christ by the proper name of 'Mary,' but identifies her as 'Woman': thus effecting a concordance with the words of the Protoevangelium in the Book of Genesis (cf. 3:15). That same 'woman' is present in the central salvific event, which is decided in the 'fullness of time': this event is realized in her and through her" (*Mulieris Dignitatem*, no. 3).

terms of the most essential biographical and historical facts of her life.

Mary is the *"mother,"* pregnant and giving birth to a son, though remaining a virgin, according to the prophecies of Genesis 3:15, Isaiah 7:14, Micah 5:1–2; and the woman *"Mother of the Lord"* or *"Mother of Jesus,"* as she is called eleven times in the New Testament;[4] she is the *"mother"* of mankind, represented by St. John on Calvary (Jn 19:25–27).

Mary is the *"spouse"*: not only the virginal, legal spouse of St. Joseph (Mt 1:18; Lk 1:27), but the virginal, real spouse of God the *Father* who willed her to be the Mother, according to His human nature, of His only-begotten Son (Gal 4:4); the spouse of God the *Son,* the Redeemer, who intimately associated her with Himself in His redemptive work, as the new Eve beside the "new Adam";[5] the spouse of God the *Holy Spirit,* who, overshadowing her, enabled her to conceive Jesus (Lk 1:35).

Mary is the *woman immaculate*: namely, she is the only human creature unstained by sin, because, together with her Son, she is the unvanquished, victorious adversary of the infernal serpent (Gen 3:15); not only this, but she is the only creature *"full of grace"* (Lk 1:28), true *panaghia* (all holy one), pure *"dawn"* (Song 6:9) of the sun who is Christ, "fashioned by the Holy Spirit and formed as a new creature"[6] in order to become Mother of the Word Incarnate.

Mary is the *Coredemptrix,* associated with her Son in the work of ransoming man from sin (Gen 3:15), strong as

4 Cf. Mt 2:11, 13, 20, 12:46–50; Mk 3:31–35; Lk 1:42–43, 2:33–34, 48–50, 8:19–21; Jn 2:1–3, 5:12, 6:42, 19:25–26; Acts 1:14.

5 Cf. Rom 5:12ff., 1 Cor 15:21–26, 54–57; see also Jn 2:1–11.

6 *Lumen Gentium*, no. 61.

"an army set in array" (Song 6:9), already prefigured by the "strong," courageous women of Israel,[7] present at the foot of the Cross on Calvary (Jn 19:25–27) to crush the head of the serpent with her immaculate foot.

Mary is the *Mediatrix,* who brings Jesus to men and men to Jesus, who cares for things spiritual and temporal (Lk 1:39ff.; Jn 2:1–11) present and active at the birth of the Church on Calvary (Jn 19:25–27) and in the Cenacle (Acts 1:14).

Mary is the *Queen,* who wears on her head the crown of twelve stars (Rev 12:2) signifying the angels (the *"stars"*), the twelve tribes of Israel (the Chosen People) and the twelve apostles (the Church). She is the Queen assumed into heaven, carried on the wings of the *"great eagle"* (Rev 12:14), dashing to the ground the destructive furies of the *"dragon"* (Rev 12:3–4). She is the "exalted daughter of Zion," seated as *"Queen at the right hand"* of the King in the Kingdom of heaven (Ps 44:10).

Mary is the woman *"blessed"* for the faith she placed in the words of the angel Gabriel at the Annunciation (Lk 1:45), for hearing and observing the Word of God (Lk 11:27–28), for her faithful fulfillment of the will of the Father (Mk 3:31–35), as the "poor one of Yahweh" (Ps 9) and *"the handmaid of the Lord"* (Lk 1:38).

From the book of Genesis to the book of Revelation, therefore, we may well underscore how this *"woman,"* according to the design of God the Father, is always one with her Son, always relative to that Son, *"leaning upon her beloved"* (Song 8:5), intimately associated with Him in the same mission of saving man and leading him back to the bosom of the Father.

---

[7] Consider, for example, the figures of Deborah (Judg 4:4–24), Judith, Jahel (Judg 4:17–20, 5:24).

At every crucial point in the history of salvation, from the Protoevangelium, after the fall of our first parents (Gen 3:15), to the announcement of the Incarnation of the Word (Lk 1:26ff.), from the beginning of the public mission of Jesus at Cana (Jn 2:1–11), to His redemptive sacrifice consummated on the Cross (Jn 19:25–27), up to the accomplishment of the very last detail in the universal salvific plan (Rev 12), Mary is the *"woman"* always present with her Son, never alone, to fulfill her role of "generous companion and humble handmaid of the Lord."[8]

And together with the Son there are "children," who are also brothers and *"co-heirs"* of Christ (Rom 8:17), who constitute the Mystical Body, the Church. Thus, in Genesis the "woman" is presented together with her "seed" (which also has an inclusive sense); at Cana (Jn 2:1–11) the "woman" is with the first "disciples" of Jesus; on Calvary (Jn 19:25–27), at the foot of the Cross, the "woman" has beside her John the Evangelist, who represents all the "disciples" of Jesus; in Revelation 12, finally, the "woman" is found again with "the rest of her offspring" (the Church).

To conclude, then, Mary's whole reason for existing is found in the Son (and in the children), according to the salvific plan of God the Father. Without the Son, Mary would not have existed at all. This is a thesis dear to dogmatic theologians, and "soundly based on fact"[9] and especially so to the Franciscan School in the footsteps of Blessed John Duns Scotus.

In this concluding summary, it is necessary to observe how, by prophecy in the Old Testament, by existence in the New, the Maternity and the Coredemption, the

8 *Lumen Gentium*, no. 61.

9 Cf. G. Alastruey, *La SS. Vergine Maria* (Rome, 1952), pp. 78–81 (Eng. ed.: *The Blessed Virgin Mary*, 2 vols. [St. Louis, 1963–1964], vol. 1, pp. 39–40).

Mediation and the Queenship—all rooted in the divine, virginal Maternity—give us the most complete biblical and theological portrait of Mary as the "woman" conceived and willed by God "from the beginning and before the world was created" (Sir 24:14), planned by Him "in one and the same decree" with the Son (bull *Ineffabilis Deus*), "blessed" among all women (1:42), "woman" with all the potential of the so-called "eternal feminine,"[10] "woman" virgin, daughter, spouse, mother, each to the full extent of perfection these terms signify, in living relation with God the Father, of whom Mary is daughter, with God the Son, of whom Mary is Mother, with God the Holy Spirit, of whom Mary is spouse; in living relation with the Church and with mankind, of whom Mary is "Mother in the order of grace."[11]

Thus, Mary realizes in herself the highest synthesis of nature and grace; an ineffable synthesis at its base and at its crown, *alpha* and *omega,* as it were, of the human person associated with the Divine Person of the Word Incarnate—the divine "alpha and omega" (Rev 1:8)—the work of universal salvation, by a unique, absolutely exclusive, distinctive relation: the "relation" of virginal maternity embracing the corporal and the spiritual, the human and the divine.

But a single phrase, encapsulating and articulating the total biblical reality, it seems to us, might be this: Mary is above all the *woman immaculate,* or still more briefly, she is the *Immaculate.*

---

10 Pope John Paul II writes that Mary "takes one back to that 'beginning' where one finds the 'woman' as she was intended in her *creation*, therefore in the eternal mind of God, in the bosom of the Most Holy Trinity," and he speaks of the "discovery of all the richness, of all the resources of femininity, of all the eternal originality of the 'woman' just as God willed her" (*Mulieris Dignitatem*, no. 11). Cf. the interesting study of Gonzalo Girones, "Vocación eterna de lo femenino," *Marianum* 42 (1980): 64–83.

11 *Lumen Gentium*, no. 61.

Today, the title *Immaculate* would express most aptly the rich content of the mystery of Mary, both as predestined to the divine and spiritual maternity of the *"seed"* (Gen 3:15) and of *"her offspring"* (Rev 12:17), "in one and the same decree" with the Word Incarnate (bull *Ineffabilis Deus); and* as *preredeemed,* without stain, opposed to sin, victorious adversary of the *"serpent"* (Gen 3:15) and *"dragon"* (Rev 12:3); and as *"full of grace"* (Lk 1:28) and *"clothed with the sun"* (Rev 12:1), filled within, that is, and invested without, by all the graces of the Holy Spirit she received for herself and for others, so as to be, in the terminology of Greek Orthodox theology the "icon of the Holy Spirit."[12]

The conception without original sin, the Divine Maternity, the Perpetual Virginity, the Mediation and Coredemption, the Assumption into heaven, the universal Queenship, permit us to behold Mary truly *"full of grace"* and *"clothed with the sun"* for herself and for us, the channel of grace in unique relation to the Most Holy Trinity, a relation appropriated to the Holy Spirit who rendered her Mother of the Word, according to the design of the Father.

The title *Immaculate,* today, in itself, is the one term giving precise expression to that singular thread that begins with Genesis and concludes in Revelation,[13] making of the mystery of Mary a kind of intertestamental synthesis, a revelation of the entire creative and redemptive plan of God. It has been written very fittingly that "the Immaculate

---

12 Cf. A. Amato, "Spirito Santo," in *NDM*, p. 1327–1362. This article is important for the summaries (pp. 1338–1358) of the thought of the best qualified authors concerning the relation between pneumatology and Mariology (H. Mühlen, H. M. Manteau-Bonamy, G. Roschini, D. Bertetto, H. U. von Balthasar, L. Boff, X. Pikaza), with an accompanying bibliographical note (p. 1362).

13 It should be pointed out that art and iconography also, in portraying the Immaculate, have joined these two famous biblical texts of Genesis (3:15) and of Revelation (12:1–8), placing the *"serpent"* (3:15) under the feet of Mary crowned with *"twelve stars"* (Rev 12:1). The same lucid insight is part of the *sensus fidelium*.

is that beginning which anticipates in itself its end,"[14] a synthesis of past and future, *alpha* and *omega,* as it were, of the whole mystery of Mary, resting on the mystery of the Trinity, incorporated into the mystery of Christ, prolonged and completed in the mystery of the Church. From her conception, *from her origin,* in fact, the immaculate is the *"woman"* presented and proclaimed by God himself to be without stain, opposed to the serpent (Gen 3:15). She is the *"woman"* ever *"virgin"* (Is 7:14) and *"full of grace"* (Lk 1:28). She is the Mother of the *"Son of the Most High"* (Lk 1:32), the *"Mother of Jesus"* (Jn 2:1.3) and of redeemed humanity (Jn 19:25–27). She is the Queen *"enthroned"* at the right hand of the Son (Ps 44 [45]:10), maternal sovereign of grace in the highest heavens.[15]

In the Immaculate, we truly have the "re-creation" of the original human nature, all grace without shadow of sin, "fullness of innocence and holiness," according to the bull *Ineffabilis Deus*; we have the perfect Redemption, because she was redeemed "in a more perfect way," this bull continues; we have the fulfillment of the Church—"the Virgin made Church," according to the suggestive phrase used by St. Francis of Assisi[16]—which prolongs in time, to the *end of time* (the *eschaton*), the virginal maternity of Mary, modeling itself on hers and realizing itself in her, as Spouse of the Word Incarnate and Mother of the redeemed.

Bright dawn and burning midday, soft beauty of the moon and radiant splendor of the sun, the strength of an army in array (a likeness for grace as opposed to sin), are

---

14 A. Serra, O.S.M, "Immacolata," in *Nuovo Dizionario di Mariologia*, p. 695.

15 She "is the only creature," writes E. Testa, "who would enter the 'circle of fire' which surrounds the throne of the Most Holy Trinity, but without being burned, like the burning bush of Moses, and who would be seated, together with her Son, at the right hand of the Father, in the highest heavens" (Testa, *Maria terra vergine*, vol. 1, p. 453).

16 Cf. P. D. Fehlner, "Maria nella tradizione francescana: 'la Vergine fatta Chiesa,'" *Miles Immaculatae* 17 (1981): 180–198.

the stupendous biblical symbols, first used in the Song of Songs (6:9),[17] and repeated in Revelation (12:1), to express the mystery of Mary, viz., the mystery of "a 'woman,' the measure of the cosmos," Pope John Paul II proclaims, "the measure of the whole work of creation":[18] this "woman"—the new Eve alongside the new Adam—belonging to the old and new dispensations, so human and so transcendent, so much ours and so much God's, it is she whom we name and invoke *Immaculate.*

---

17 Cf. the recently published work on the Song of Songs, explained and commented upon in a Mariological sense by St. Francis Anthony Fasani, a commentary centered on the mystery of the Immaculate Conception: *Mariale. Interpretazione allegorico-spirituale del Cantico dei Cantici* (Padua, 1986).

18 *Mulieris Dignitatem*, no. 30.

INDEX OF BIBLICAL REFERENCES

Old Testament

New Testament

INDEX OF AUTHORS

The Academy of the Immaculate

The Academy of the Immaculate, founded in 1992, is inspired by and based on a project of St. Maximilian M. Kolbe (never realized by the Saint because of his death by martyrdom at the age of 47, August 14, 1941). Among its goals the Academy seeks to promote at every level the study of the Mystery of the Immaculate Conception and the universal maternal mediation of the Virgin Mother of God, and to sponsor publication and dissemination of the fruits of this research in every way possible.

The Academy of the Immaculate is a non-profit religious-charitable organization of the Roman Catholic Church, incorporated under the laws of the Commonwealth of Massachusetts, with its central office at Our Lady's Chapel, POB 3003, New Bedford, MA 02741-3003.

Special rates are available with 25% to 50% discount depending on the number of books, plus postage. For ordering books and further information on rates to book stores, schools and parishes: *Academy of the Immaculate, P.O. Box 3003, New Bedford, MA 02741, Phone/FAX (888)90.MARIA [888.90.62742], E-mail academy@marymediatrix.com.* Quotations on bulk rates by the box, shipped directly from the printery, contact: *Franciscans of the Immaculate, P.O. Box 3003, New Bedford, MA 02741, (508)996-8274, E-mail: ffi@marymediatrix.com. Website: www.marymediatrix.com.*